P9-BEE-614

DIAGNOSIS AND TROUBLESHOOTING OF AUTOMOTIVE ELECTRICAL, ELECTRONIC, AND COMPUTER SYSTEMS

DIAGNOSIS AND TROUBLESHOOTING OF AUTOMOTIVE ELECTRICAL, ELECTRONIC, AND COMPUTER SYSTEMS

Second Edition

James D. Halderman

Sinclair Community College

Prentice Hall

Upper Saddle River, New Jersey   Columbus, Ohio

Library of Congress Cataloging-in-Publication Data
Halderman, James D.
    Diagnosis and troubleshooting of automotive electrical,
electronic, and computer systems / James D. Halderman.—2nd ed.
        p. cm.
    Includes index.
    ISBN 0-13-520578-6
        1. Automobiles—Electric equipment—Maintenance and repair.
    2. Automobiles—Electronic equipment—Maintenance and repair.
    I. Title.
    TL272.H223 1996
    629.25'4—dc20   96-22138
                                                              CIP

Cover Art/Photo: © James D. Halderman
Editor: Ed Francis
Production and Editing Services: Carlisle Publishers Services
Design Coordinator: Jill E. Bonar
Cover Designer: Brian Deep
Production Manager: Deidra M. Schwartz
Marketing Manager: Danny Hoyt

This book was set in Century Book by Carlisle Communications, Ltd., and was printed and bound by Courier/Kendallville, Inc. The cover was printed by Phoenix Color Corp.

© 1997, 1991 by Prentice-Hall, Inc.
Simon & Schuster Company/A Viacom Company
Upper Saddle River, New Jersey 07458

All rights reserved. No part of this book may be reproduced, in any form or by any means, without permission in writing from the publisher.

Printed in the United Sates of America

10   9   8   7   6   5   4   3   2   1

ISBN 0-13-520578-6

Prentice-Hall International (UK) Limited, *London*
Prentice-Hall of Australia Pty. Limited, *Sydney*
Prentice-Hall of Canada, Inc., *Toronto*
Prentice-Hall Hispanoamericana, S. A., *Mexico*
Prentice-Hall of India Private Limited, *New Delhi*
Prentice-Hall of Japan, Inc., *Tokyo*
Simon & Schuster Asia Pte. Ltd., *Singapore*
Editora Prentice-Hall do Brasil, Ltda., *Rio de Janeiro*

CONTENTS

TECH TIPS

PREFACE

This second edition is updated and streamlined to make learning electrical and electronic systems easy. At the request of service technicians and instructors from throughout the United States and Canada, information on computer sensors, high-intensity discharge (HID) headlights, antilock brakes, OBD II, and digital meter usage have been included. A sample, ASE-style test is included in the appendix.

Like the first edition, this book presents automotive electrical and electronic system concepts and operation in a simple, concise format with more detail than is found in most electrical systems books. Also provided is an explanation of the effects that one component or circuit can have on another, with the goal of improving diagnostic and troubleshooting skills.

Incorporated into this edition are the following:

1. Objectives at the beginning of each chapter
2. Clear, concise definitions of terms in the text and glossary
3. Symptoms of defective components and troubleshooting
4. Hundreds of photographs and line drawings
5. Detailed captions that provide a greater understanding of the illustrations
6. Examples of troubleshooting, using actual problems experienced by professionals in the field
7. Explanation of operation, with an emphasis on why they work
8. Examples and practical application in every chapter
9. Diagnostic trouble codes for General Motors, Ford, Chrysler, Honda, Toyota, and OBD II generic
10. Sample ASE certification test in the appendix

To ensure that the needs of the reader are met, every topic has been presented in the following format:

1. Basic operation
2. Parts involved
3. Testing methods and results, using both low-cost equipment and electronic test equipment
4. Symptoms of defective operation (characteristics)
5. Diagnosis and service procedures
6. Troubleshooting examples with solutions
7. Troubleshooting guides included in selected chapters
8. Chapter summaries at the end of each chapter.
9. Multiple-choice ASE-type questions at the end of each chapter
10. Tech tips included throughout

ACKNOWLEDGMENTS

A large number of people and organizations have cooperated in providing the reference material and technical information used in this text. The author wishes to express sincere thanks to the following organizations for their special contributions:

Arrow Automotive

Automotion, Inc.

Automotive Parts Rebuilders Association (APRA)

Automatic Transmission Rebuilders Association (ATRA)

Battery Council International (BCI)

Bear Automotive

British Petroleum (BP)

Champion Spark Plug Company

Chrysler Corporation

Ford Motor Company

Fluke

General Motors Corporation

Society of Automotive Engineers (SAE)

I also wish to thank my colleagues and students at Sinclair Community College in Dayton, Ohio, for their ideas and suggestions. Most of all, I wish to thank my wife, Michelle, for her assistance in all phases of manuscript preparation.

James D. Halderman

Diagnosis and Troubleshooting of Automotive Electrical, Electronic, and Computer Systems

ELECTRICAL SYSTEM PRINCIPLES

OBJECTIVES

After studying chapter 1, the reader will be able to

1. Define electricity.
2. Explain the units of electrical measurement.
3. Discuss the relationship among volts, amperes, and ohms.
4. Explain how magnetism is used in automotive applications.

The electrical system is one of the most important systems on a vehicle today. Every year more and more components and systems use electricity. Those technicians who really know and understand automotive electrical and electronic systems will be in great demand.

ELECTRICITY

The word *electricity* comes from the Greek word *elektron,* meaning amber (a fossil resin). The ancients produced electric charges by rubbing amber with wool. This produced **static electricity,** which was the first known type of electricity. It is called static (motionless) because the charge is at rest and not moving through a wire.

It was detected that there are actually two types of electrical charges. When a rubber rod was rubbed with flannel or fur, a **negative (-) charge** was generated in the rod. When a glass rod was rubbed with silk, the glass rod had a **positive (+) charge**. See figure 1–1.

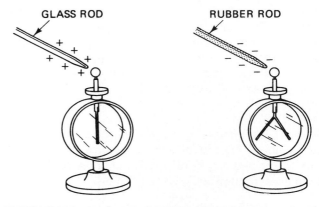

FIGURE 1–1   A test instrument called an electroscope illustrates that positive and negative charges are opposite.

It was also discovered that objects with like charges (both positive or both negative) repelled or moved away from each other. Objects with unlike charges (one positive and one negative) attracted or moved toward each other. The negative charges were determined to be caused by an atom with an extra number of negative-charged electrons. See figure 1–2. Electricity is actually the movement of electrons from one atom to another.

THE ATOM AND ELECTRONS

To begin to explain electricity, one must convey an understanding of the composition of an atom. An atom is the smallest unit of all matter in the universe.

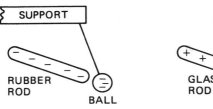

FIGURE 1–2 Two negative (or positive) charges repel, whereas unlike charges attract.

Our universe is composed of matter, which is *anything* that has mass and occupies space. Matter is, therefore, anything *except* the nothingness of space. Matter can be in a solid form such as a table, or in a liquid form such as water or gasoline. It can also be in a gaseous state such as water vapor (steam) or gasoline fumes. All matter is made from slightly over 100 individual components called **elements**.

If an element is cut down or reduced in size, the smallest remaining part that can still be identified as that particular element is called an **atom**. See figure 1–3. The dense center of each atom is called the nucleus. The nucleus contains **protons**, which have a positive charge, and **neutrons**, which are electrically neutral (have no charge). In orbits surrounding the nucleus are the **electrons**, which have a negative charge and weigh only about 1/1800 of the weight of a proton. Each atom contains an equal number of electrons and protons. Because the number of negative-charged electrons is balanced with the same number of positive-charged protons, an atom has a **neutral charge** (no charge).

NOTE: To get a feel for the relative sizes of the parts of an atom, consider that if an atom were magnified so that the nucleus were the size of the period at the end of this sentence, the whole atom would be bigger than a house.

ELECTRON ORBITS

Each element in the universe has its own individual characteristic atom, each having its own number of protons, neutrons, and electrons. An atom has the same number of electrons in orbits around the nucleus as there are protons. These electrons travel in orbits of varying distance from the center of the nucleus, depending on the number of electrons. These different orbits (called shells) are identified by letters: *K, L, M, N, O*, and so on.

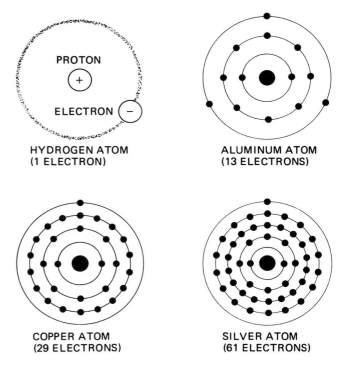

FIGURE 1–3 The hydrogen atom is the simplest atom, with only one proton, one neutron, and one electron. More complex elements contain higher numbers of protons, neutrons, and electrons.

The orbit closest to the nucleus is the K orbit, and it has a limit of two electrons. If an atom has more than two electrons, the additional electrons have to move farther away from the nucleus. See figure 1–4. The second orbit from the nucleus is called the L shell, and it has a maximum capacity of eight electrons. There are many different shells, and each shell has its own limit for the number of electrons that can occupy that shell. The five closest shells, together with the number of electrons needed to fill them, are as follows:

shell K, 2 electrons

shell L, 8 electrons

shell M, 18 electrons

shell N, 32 electrons

shell O, 32 electrons

ENERGY LEVELS

The farther the electrons are from the nucleus of the atom, the higher the energy level of the electrons. Some atoms do not completely fill all of their inner shells with

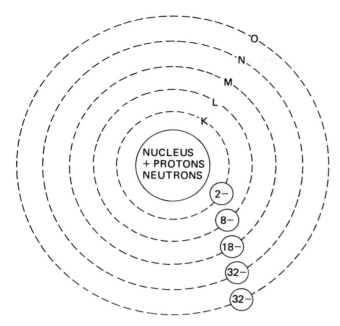

FIGURE 1–4 Electron shells. As a shell (electron orbit) close to the nucleus becomes filled, additional electrons for a particular atom must start to fill electron orbits farther from the nucleus.

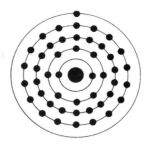

FIGURE 1–5 Silver atom. The element silver has the lowest resistance of any conductor because the one free electron is loosely bound.

electrons; instead, the higher-energy electrons circle the nucleus in more distant shells.

No element has more than eight electrons in its outer orbit.

The element aluminum contains thirteen electrons. These electrons will fill the K shell (two) and the L shell (eight) and start to fill the M shell with its remaining three electrons. Because the M shell has a capacity for eighteen electrons, this leaves the outer orbit relatively empty with its three electrons.

If an element has fewer than four electrons in its outer orbit, the electrons are called **free electrons** because they can be easily "bumped" out of their shell and into the shell of an identical adjacent (next to) atom by an electrical force.

These outer-shell electrons are also called **valance electrons** because they can interact with other electrons to create bonding between elements where they are shared, or they can interact with the electrons of another atom of the same element to form molecules, compounds, or other combinations of atoms.

The farther the free electrons are from the nucleus, the weaker the "pull" of the proton's positive force in the nucleus on the electron's negative pull. See figure 1–5 for an example of an atom with one free electron. The resistance of the free electrons moving from one atom to another is *lower* with elements that have fewer electrons in their outer orbit.

This movement of free electrons explains how static electrical charges are produced. A rubber rod rubbed with flannel or fur actually transfers free electrons from the flannel or fur into the outer orbit of the rubber rod, temporarily creating rubber atoms that have more negative electrons than positive protons. The resulting rubber atoms have a negative charge. If a glass rod is rubbed with silk, the silk *removes* electrons from the glass rod and gives the rod a net positive charge.

CONDUCTORS

Conductors are materials with fewer than four electrons in their atom's outer orbit. Copper is an example of an excellent conductor because it has only one electron in its outer orbit. This orbit is far enough away from the nucleus of the copper atom that the pull or force holding the outermost electron in orbit is relatively weak. (Copper is the most used conductor in vehicles because the price of copper is reasonable compared to the relative cost of other conductors with similar properties.)

All good conductors of electricity are also good conductors of heat and cold. Conductors are also classified as **metals**. Iron, steel, copper, aluminum, silver, and gold are examples of metals (conductors). Metals can be further classified as those containing iron (ferrous metals), such as cast iron or steel, and those metals not containing iron (nonferrous metals). Copper, silver, mercury, gold, and aluminum are examples of nonferrous metals.

HOW CONDUCTOR RESISTANCE INCREASES WITH HEAT

As any conductor, such as copper wire, increases in temperature, its electrical resistance also increases. This increased resistance is due to the countless collisions of

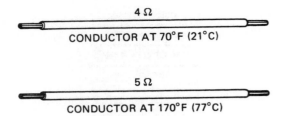

FIGURE 1–6 As the temperature of a conductor increases, its electrical resistance also increases.

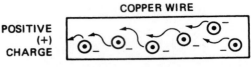

FIGURE 1–7 Current electricity is the movement of electrons through a conductor.

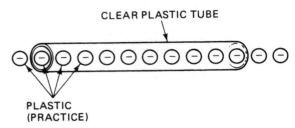

FIGURE 1–8 The movement of electrons through a conductor is similar to the action of golf balls being pushed through a plastic tube.

electrons with the rapidly vibrating conductor atoms. At higher temperatures, the vibrations of the atoms become stronger and the resistance to current flow increases. See figure 1–6.

Because of this, many starter motors have heat shields to prevent engine heat from affecting hot engine starts. If the heat shield were left off, engine heat could cause the copper windings of the starter and solenoid (if equipped) to increase in resistance. The result would be a slowly turning starter motor when the engine was hot, even though the starter would operate normally when the engine was cooler.

INSULATORS

Insulators are materials with more than four electrons in their atom's outer orbit. Because they have more than four electrons in their outer orbit, it becomes easier for these materials to acquire (gain) electrons than to release electrons. Examples of insulators include plastics, wood, glass, rubber, ceramics (spark plugs), and varnish for covering (insulating) copper wires in alternators and starters.

SEMICONDUCTORS

Materials with exactly four electrons in their outer orbit are neither conductors nor insulators and are called semiconductor materials. See chapter 3 for a further explanation and applications.

CURRENT ELECTRICITY

Movement of electrons through a conductor is called **current** (moving) **electricity,** in contrast to static electricity, in which there is no electron movement. In fact, once static electricity is discharged, it becomes current electricity because the electrical charges are then in motion and no longer static.

HOW ELECTRONS MOVE THROUGH A CONDUCTOR

A conductor contains neutral atoms whose electrons are constantly moving at random in the material. The electrons are normally being knocked in all directions by the atoms, which are vibrating at a rate of millions of times per second. If an outside source of power, such as a battery, is connected to the ends of a conductor, a positive charge (lack of electrons) is placed on one end of the conductor and a negative charge is placed on the opposite end of the conductor. The negative charge will repel the free electrons from the atoms of the conductor, whereas the positive charge on the opposite end of the conductor will attract electrons. As a result of this attraction of opposite charges and repulsion of like charges, electrons will flow through the conductor. See figure 1–7. These electrons actually travel a zigzag course from one atom to another. Because each electron bumps other electrons in a chain reaction, the overall effect is the flow of electrons through the conductor traveling near the speed of light. This electron action is similar to the movement seen when one knocks down a row of dominoes or hits a row of pool balls. See figure 1–8.

CONVENTIONAL THEORY VERSUS ELECTRON THEORY

It was once thought that electricity had only one charge and moved from positive to negative. This theory of the flow of electricity through a conductor is called the

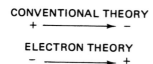

FIGURE 1–9 The conventional theory of electricity states that current flows from positive to negative. The electron theory states that current flows from negative to positive.

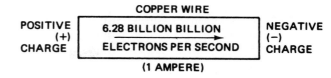

FIGURE 1–10 One ampere is the movement of 1 coulomb (6.28 billion billion electrons) past a point in 1 second.

conventional theory of current flow. See figure 1–9. After the discovery of the electron and its negative charge, came the **electron theory,** which indicates that there is electron flow from negative to positive. Most automotive applications use the conventional theory. This book will use the conventional theory unless stated otherwise.

AMPERES

The **ampere** is the unit used throughout the world as a measure of the amount of current flow. When 6.28 billion billion electrons (the name for this large number of electrons is a **coulomb**) move past a certain point in 1 second, this represents 1 ampere of current. See figure 1–10. The ampere is the electrical unit for the amount of electron flow, just as gallons per minute is the unit that can be used to measure the quantity of water flow. It was named for a French electrician, André Marie Ampère (1775–1836). The usage, conventional abbreviations, and measurement for amperes are summarized as follows:

1. The ampere is the unit of measurement for the amount of current flow.
2. *A* and *amps* are acceptable abbreviations for *amperes.*
3. The capital letter *I*, for *intensity*, is used in mathematical calculations to represent amperes.
4. Amperes are measured by an **ammeter** (not ampmeter).

VOLTS

The **volt** is the unit of measurement for electrical pressure. It is named for Alessandro Volta (1745–1827), an Italian physicist. The comparable unit using water as an example would be pounds per square inch (psi). It is possible to have very high pressures (volts) and low water flow (amperes). It is also possible to have high water flow (amperes) and low pressures (volts). Voltage is also called **electrical potential,** because if there is

voltage present in a conductor, there is a potential (possibility) for current flow. Voltage does *not* flow through conductors, but voltage does cause current (in amperes) to flow through conductors. The usage, conventional abbreviations, and measurement for voltage are as follows:

1. The volt is the unit of measurement for the amount of electrical pressure.
2. **Electromotive force,** abbreviated EMF, is another way of indicating voltage.
3. *V* is the generally accepted abbreviation for *volts.*
4. The symbol used in calculations is *E*, for *electromotive force.*
5. Volts are measured by a **voltmeter.**

OHMS

Resistance to the flow of current through a conductor is measured in units called **ohms,** named after a German physicist, Georg Simon Ohm (1787–1854). The resistance to the flow of free electrons through a conductor results from the countless collisions the electrons cause within the atoms of the conductor. The usage, conventional abbreviations, and measurement for resistance are as follows:

1. The ohm is the unit of measurement for electrical resistance.
2. The symbol for ohms is Ω (Greek capital letter omega), the last letter of the Greek alphabet.
3. The symbol used in calculations is *R*, for *resistance.*
4. Ohms are measured by an **ohmmeter.**

CONDUCTORS AND RESISTANCE

All conductors have some resistance to current flow. Several principles of conductors and their resistance include the following:

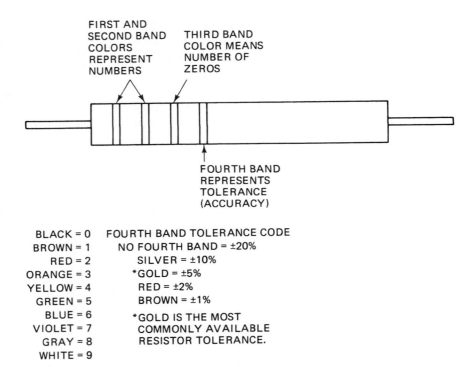

EXAMPLES:

470 Ω

GOLD (IF 5%)

YELLOW, VIOLET, BROWN (1 ZERO)
(4)   (7)

3900 Ω

GOLD (IF 5%)

ORANGE, WHITE, RED (2 ZEROS)
(3)   (9)

BLACK = 0
BROWN = 1
RED = 2
ORANGE = 3
YELLOW = 4
GREEN = 5
BLUE = 6
VIOLET = 7
GRAY = 8
WHITE = 9

FOURTH BAND TOLERANCE CODE
NO FOURTH BAND = ±20%
SILVER = ±10%
*GOLD = ±5%
RED = ±2%
BROWN = ±1%

*GOLD IS THE MOST
COMMONLY AVAILABLE
RESISTOR TOLERANCE.

FIGURE 1–11 Resistor color code interpretation.

1. If the conductor length is doubled, its resistance doubles. This is the reason why battery cables are designed to be as short as possible.

2. If the conductor diameter is increased, its resistance is reduced. This is the reason why starter motor cables are larger in diameter than other wiring in the vehicle. See chapter 5 for further details on wiring sizes.

3. As the temperature increases, the resistance of the conductor also increases. This is the reason for heat shields installed on some starter motors. The heat shield helps to protect the conductors (copper wiring inside the starter) from excessive engine heat to help reduce the resistance of starter circuits. Because a conductor increases in resistance with increased temperature, the conductor is called a **positive temperature coefficient** (PTC) resistor.

NOTE: Most temperature sensors used by vehicle computers use a semiconductor material that actually decreases in resistance as the temperature increases. This is called a **negative temperature coefficient** (NTC) resistor. (It is also called a thermistor because the resistance changes with the thermometer [temperature].) The difference between a PTC and NTC is the direction the resistance changes with increasing temperature. See chapter 3 for additional information on thermistors.

RESISTORS

Resistance is the opposition to current flow. Resistors represent an electrical load, or resistance to current flow. Most electrical and electronic devices use resistors of specific values to limit and control the flow of current. Resistors can be made from carbon or from other materials that restrict the flow of electricity. Resistors are available in various sizes and resistance values. Most resistors have a series of painted color bands around them. These color bands are coded to indicate the resistance of the resistor. See figure 1–11.

The size of the resistor is related to how much current the resistor is designed to control. The size (not the resistance value) is rated in units called **watts** (abbreviated W). A watt is current in amperes multiplied by the voltage in the circuit (Watts = Amperes × Volts). See figure 1–12. A resistor can be measured with an ohmmeter or multimeter set to measure ohms to check its resistance and compare it to what it should be according to its color code. See figure 1–13.

VARIABLE RESISTORS

Two basic types of mechanically operated variable resistors are used in automotive applications. A **potentiometer** is a *three*-terminal variable resistor in which

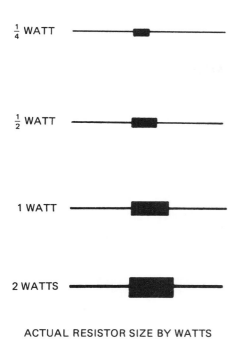

$\frac{1}{4}$ WATT

$\frac{1}{2}$ WATT

1 WATT

2 WATTS

ACTUAL RESISTOR SIZE BY WATTS

FIGURE 1–12 The power-handling (wattage-handling) capabilities of a resistor depend largely on the size of the resistor. (Shown actual size by wattage rating.)

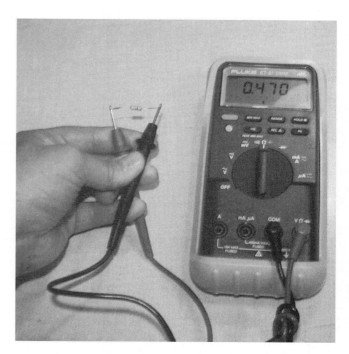

FIGURE 1–13 Testing a resistor using a digital multimeter (DMM). The selector knob is turned to ohms (Ω), and the face of the meter reads 0.470 KΩ, which is exactly 470 Ω, the nominal value of the resistor. The K means 1000 from the preface kilo. (Remember, 0.470 KΩ is less than 1/2 of 1000 ohms.) Polarity of the meter leads does not matter when measuring resistors.

the majority of the current flow travels through the resistance of the unit and a wiper contact returns a variable voltage. See figure 1–14.

Potentiometers are most commonly used as throttle position (TP) sensors on computer-equipped engines. See chapter 16 for general specifications and testing procedures.

Another type of mechanically operated variable resistor is the **rheostat.** A rheostat is a *two*-terminal unit in which all of the current flows through the movable arm. See figure 1–15.

A rheostat is commonly used for a dash light dimmer control. See chapter 3 for information on electronic (semiconductor) types of variable resistors.

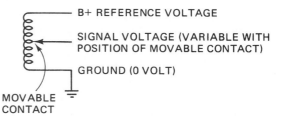

B+ REFERENCE VOLTAGE

SIGNAL VOLTAGE (VARIABLE WITH POSITION OF MOVABLE CONTACT)

GROUND (0 VOLT)

MOVABLE CONTACT

FIGURE 1–14 A three-wire variable resistor is called a potentiometer.

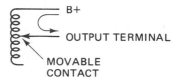

B+

OUTPUT TERMINAL

MOVABLE CONTACT

FIGURE 1–15 A two-wire variable resistor is called a rheostat.

SOURCES OF DIRECT-CURRENT ELECTRICITY

The sources of direct-current electricity are as follows:

1. *Chemical.* A battery is a chemical device that produces a voltage potential between two different metal plates submerged in an acid. Lead dioxide

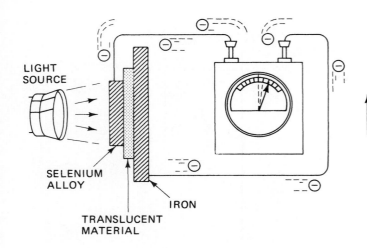

LIGHT
SOURCE

SELENIUM
ALLOY

IRON

TRANSLUCENT
MATERIAL

ELECTRON
FLOW

FIGURE 1–16   Electron flow is produced by light striking a light-sensitive material.

and lead plates in a sulfuric acid electrolyte are commonly used for automotive applications.

2. *Photoelectric.* This source was discovered by Heinrich Rudolf Hertz (1857–94), a German physicist. When light strikes the surface of certain sensitive materials, such as selenium or cesium, electrons are released. See figure 1–16. Such materials are used to construct photoelectric cells that can be used to control headlights and optional automatic day-night mirrors.

3. *Thermoelectric.* Electron movement can be created by heating the connection of two dissimilar metals. If the two metals are connected to a voltage-sensitive gauge, such as a **galvanometer**, an increase in the temperature of the wire junction will increase the voltage reading. See figure 1–17. This type of thermometer is called a thermoelectric **pyrometer.** A pyrometer is often used to measure exhaust temperature on diesel trucks.

4. *Piezoelectric.* Certain crystals, such as Rochelle salt and quartz, become electrically charged when pressure is applied to the crystals. The difference in potential produced increases with increased pressure. See figure 1–18. A phonograph pickup crystal is an example of piezoelectric principles changing the varying grooves of a record into electrical pulses. Piezoelectric units are used in detonation (knock) sensors on computer-operated automotive systems.

5. *Electromagnetic induction.* A current can be created in any conductor that is moved through a magnetic field. The conductor can be stationary, and the magnetic field moved. The voltage induced is increased with the speed of the movement and the number of conductors that are cut. All alternators, starters, and ignition systems work as a result of electromagnetism.

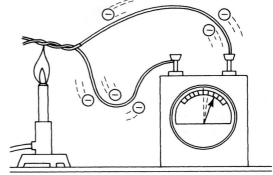

FIGURE 1–17   Electron flow is produced by heating the connection of two different metals.

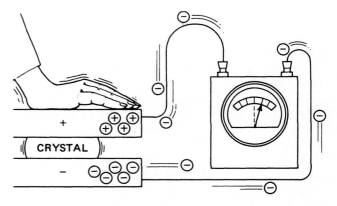

CRYSTAL

FIGURE 1–18   Electron flow is produced by pressure on certain crystals.

CAPACITORS OR CONDENSERS

Capacitors (also called **condensers**) are electrical components that can be used to perform a variety of functions. Electrons can be "stored" on the inside of a

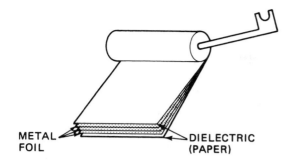

FIGURE 1–19 A foil and paper condenser (capacitor) can store electrons on the surface of the foil.

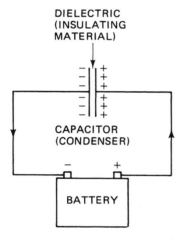

FIGURE 1–20 A condenser (capacitor) is charged when connected to a voltage source such as a battery.

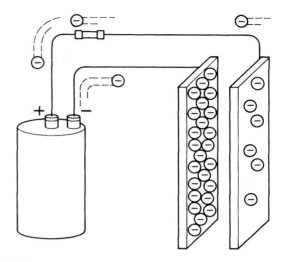

FIGURE 1–21 Simple condenser. Air is the dielectric between two conductor plates. Notice that when the condenser is connected to a battery, the electrons tend to "pile up" on the negative plate of the condenser.

electric between the plates. The charge is stored in the capacitor until the plates are connected to a lower-voltage circuit. This will cause the stored electrons to flow out of the capacitor and into a conductor that has a lower voltage. A capacitor can pass current that is constantly changing its direction of flow (alternating current [AC]) but blocks the flow of direct current (DC).

COMPARISON BETWEEN A CAPACITOR AND A WATER TOWER

A capacitor can store electrons similarly to the way in which a water tower can store water for use at a later time. The comparisons are as follows:

Water Tower	*Capacitor*
1. Water can be pumped into a water tower if the water pressure is high enough to make the water flow into the tower.	1. Electrons can flow into a capacitor if it is connected to a power source such as a battery.
2. As the water level gets higher, the pressure of the water in the tower increases and therefore a greater pressure is required to	2. As the capacitor builds up a charge, the voltage increases in the capacitor and higher and higher voltages are required to maintain

capacitor on two or more conductor plates separated by an insulator called a **dielectric.** The dielectric material in a condenser can be paper, mica (a type of silicate rock in thin layers), or air. See figure 1–19. The greater the dielectric strength of a material, the greater the resistance of the material to voltage penetration.

If a capacitor is connected to a battery or another electrical power source, it is capable of storing the electrons from the power source. See figures 1–20 and 1–21. This storing capacity is called **capacitance** and is measured in the unit called **farad,** named for Michael Faraday (1791–1867), an English physicist. A farad is the capacity to store 1 coulomb of electrons at 1 volt of potential difference between the plates of the capacitor. This is a very large number, so most capacitors for automotive use list values measured in microfarads (one millionth of a farad).

A capacitor will accept electrons when connected to a power source until the capacitor's maximum charge is reached. Electrons do not flow through a capacitor because of the insulating strength of the di-

maintain water flow into the tower.

3. If a valve is opened at the base of a water tower, water will flow quickly out of the tower, but only for a short time because of the limited amount of water stored in the tower.

4. A water tower is used to store water when more water is available than can be used immediately (which could cause flooding), but which could be used later during a dry season.

5. A water tower acts as a "surge tank" that tends to smooth out pulses of a water pump. A large tank can absorb the very high pressures, and slowly and evenly release the water when the pulses of the pump are weak.

current flow *into* the capacitor.

3. If a conductor is connected to both sides of a capacitor, current will flow quickly out of the capacitor, but only for a short time because of the limited amount of stored electrons.

4. A capacitor can temporarily store electrons (electrical energy) when too much energy could damage electrical components. An example is given by the capacitor (condenser in a point-type ignition system) used to protect the ignition points from damage due to arcing by the high voltage induced in the ignition coil when the points open.

5. A capacitor acts as a surge tank for voltages connected to the capacitor, which vary quickly from very high voltage to very low voltage. A capacitor can absorb electrons during the time when the voltage is high and release the electrons when the voltage is low. As a result of this "smoothing out" of the voltage, radio interference that would normally be produced by the rapidly changing voltages is reduced. A capacitor used for this purpose is called a **filter capacitor** and is used on alternators and ignition systems to reduce **radio-frequency interference** (RFI).

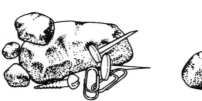
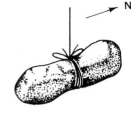

FIGURE 1–22 Lodestone (magnetite) is a variety of natural magnet.

MAGNETISM

Like electricity, magnetism is sometimes difficult to visualize. Although electricity and magnetism cannot be seen, the *effects* can be both seen and felt.

NOTE: Magnetism is extremely important to automotive applications because everything electrical in the automobile, except the lights and the cigarette lighter, work as a result of magnetism.

Magnetism was first observed in the way a natural stone called **lodestone** reacted to metal objects. Lodestone is a variety of magnetite (a type of iron ore) that attracts pieces of iron and will point to the earth's magnetic north pole if a long piece of this ore is suspended from a string. See figure 1–22.

The end of the lodestone that points toward the earth's north pole is called the **north pole** or **N pole**. The opposite end is the **south** or **S pole**. These poles of a magnetic substance act similarly to electrostatic charges: Like poles repel each other, whereas opposite poles are attracted. Because a magnet also shows attraction for metal products such as tacks, nails, and iron filings, it is clear that a force surrounds the magnetic material. Magnetic lines of force are invisible, but when iron filings are placed on a piece of paper held above a magnet, the filings move and then become stationary along a definite pattern formed between and around both the north and south poles. This pattern indicates parallel (side by side and not touching) lines of magnetic force that leave the north pole and enter the south pole. See figure 1–23.

WHAT MAKES A MAGNET MAGNETIC

The most accepted theory (scientific explanation) indicates that the normal random positions of the atoms in a magnetic material become all aligned in one direction

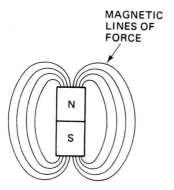

FIGURE 1–23   The magnetic lines of force leave the north pole and enter the south pole.

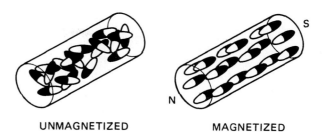

UNMAGNETIZED   MAGNETIZED

FIGURE 1–24   When a material is magnetized, the atoms all align in one direction.

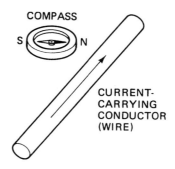

FIGURE 1–25   Surrounding any conductor carrying an electrical current is a magnetic field.

◀ **TECH TIP** ▶

A CRACKED MAGNET BECOMES TWO MAGNETS

Magnets are commonly used in vehicle crankshaft, camshaft, and wheel speed sensors. If a magnet is struck and cracks or breaks, the result is two smaller strength magnets. Because the strength of the magnetic field is reduced, the sensor output voltage is also reduced. A typical problem occurs when a magnetic crankshaft sensor becomes cracked, resulting in a no-start condition. Sometimes the cracked sensor works well enough to start an engine that is cranking at normal speeds, but will not work when the engine is cold.

1. **Permalloy** (permanent alloy), made from nickel and iron
2. **Alnico**, an alloy of aluminum, nickel, and cobalt
3. **Cunife**, an alloy of copper (Cu), nickel (Ni), and iron (Fe)
4. **Magnequench**, made of neodymium, iron, and boron, a powerful alloy developed in the mid-1980s by General Motors for initial use in permanent-magnet starter motors

Permanent magnets can be made into many shapes, including bar and horseshoe shapes.

so that their combined forces generate the magnetizing force. The strength of a magnet varies greatly with the type of material used. See figure 1–24.

CLASSIFICATION OF MAGNETIC MATERIALS

There are natural magnets such as lodestone and many other materials that can be *made* magnetic. If iron, for example, is rubbed by a strong magnet, the magnetic properties will be transferred to the iron. This transfer of magnetic properties is called **magnetic induction.** Magnetic induction creates new **permanent magnets** if the material is of the proper type. The best materials for permanent magnets are hard metals or metal alloys. An alloy is a combination of two or more metals. Common alloys include the following:

ELECTROMAGNETISM

It was not until about 1820 that it was discovered that a wire carrying an electrical current had an effect on a compass. See figure 1–25. Until that time, the only thing known to affect a compass was a magnetic field. Further study revealed that a magnetic field surrounds any conductor (wire) that carries an electrical current. A magnetic field created by current flow is called **electromagnetism.** The characteristics of electromagnetism can be summarized as follows:

1. The direction of the lines of force is determined by the **right-hand rule.** Place your right hand around

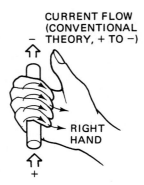

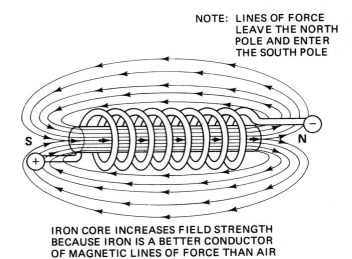

FIGURE 1–26 The right-hand rule for conventional current flow theory.

NOTE: LINES OF FORCE LEAVE THE NORTH POLE AND ENTER THE SOUTH POLE

IRON CORE INCREASES FIELD STRENGTH BECAUSE IRON IS A BETTER CONDUCTOR OF MAGNETIC LINES OF FORCE THAN AIR

FIGURE 1–27 The use of a soft-iron core greatly increases the magnetic field strength of an electromagnet.

the wire with your thumb pointing in the direction of conventional current flow (positive to negative), and your fingers will point in the direction of the magnetic lines of force. See figure 1–26.

2. The magnetic lines of force do *not* move except to progress farther away from the conductor with greater current flow.

3. The density and strength of the magnetic lines of force increase directly with increased current flow (in amperes) through the conductor.

HOW ELECTRICITY AND MAGNETISM ARE RELATED

Whenever there is electricity flowing through a conductor, magnetic lines of force are produced around the conductor.

Whenever there is a conductor near a *moving* magnetic field, electricity is produced (i.e., induced) in the conductor.

MAGNETIC FIELDS IN A COIL OF WIRE

If a wire (conductor) is coiled and current is sent through the wire, the same magnetic fields that would surround straight wires combine to form one larger magnetic field with true north and south poles. The north pole can be determined by the right-hand rule for **coils** (fig. 1–27): Grasp the coil with the fingers pointed in the direction of current flow (conventional current flow, or positive to negative), and the thumb will point toward the north pole of the coil. Current flowing through a coil of wire creates a useful magnetic field and is the principle used in countless electrical components. However, a still more powerful magnetic field

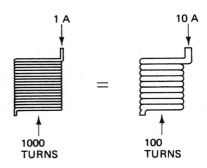

FIGURE 1–28 Ampere-turns is the unit used to measure electromagnetic field strength.

can be generated by placing an iron core in the center of the coil of wire.

The iron in the center of the coil provides an excellent conductor for the magnetic field that travels through the center of the wire coil. The measurement of a material's ability to conduct magnetic lines of force is called **permeability.** The permeability of various materials is rated numerically, with 1 being assigned to air, which is a poor conductor of magnetic lines of force. The permeability of iron is 2000, and that of some alloy steels can be 50,000 or more. The increase in magnetic field strength is the reason that most coils and electromagnets contain an iron core.

MAGNETIC FIELD STRENGTH

The strength of the magnetic field surrounding a coil is increased by one or both of the following factors:

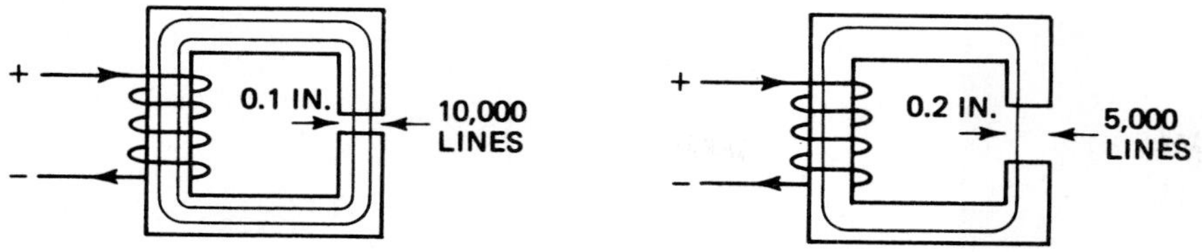

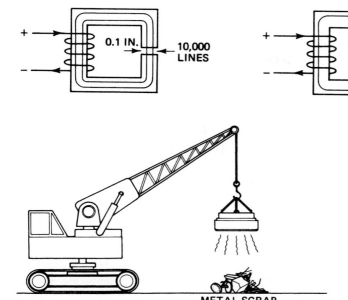

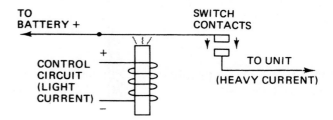

FIGURE 1–29 Increasing the air gap greatly decreases the magnetic field strength. Manufacturers of ignition coils can make slight changes in the air gap to change the operating characteristics of the coil.

FIGURE 1–31 Electromagnetic switch. A light current (low amperes) produces an electromagnet and causes the contact points to close. The contact points then conduct a heavy current (high amperes) to an electrical unit.

FIGURE 1–30 Electromagnetic crane. When electrical current is sent to large electromagnets, the crane can pick up ferrous metal products of any shape.

1. An increased number of turns of wire in a coil
2. An increased amount of current flow through the coil, measured in amperes

The magnetic field strength for automotive use is measured in **ampere-turns** (AT). See figure 1–28. The magnetic field strength is measured by multiplying the current flow through a coil in amperes by the number of complete turns of wire in the coil. For example, a 1000-turn coil with 1 ampere of current would generate 1000 ampere-turns. This 1000-turn coil would have the same field strength as a similar coil of 100 turns times 10 amperes or 1000 ampere-turns. The ampere-turn strength of a coil also depends on the resistance to the magnetic lines of force.

RELUCTANCE

The resistance to the movement of magnetic lines of force is called **reluctance.** Reluctance is reduced by using highly permeable materials for the cores of coils, and it is increased by placing air gaps in the coil cores. (Remember, air is a poor conductor of magnetic lines of force.) See figure 1–29. Therefore, most automotive coils use an iron core, because the magnetic field strength is increased for coils with cores as compared to similar coils without a core.

ELECTROMAGNETIC USES

The relationship between electricity and magnetism is very important because many electrical components on an automobile use electromagnetism. An electromagnet can be made by wrapping an iron bar (core) with a coil of wire connected to a battery or another electrical power source. An example of an electromagnet is a scrap metal crane. See figure 1–30. Whenever current is flowing through the coil of an electromagnet, it is magnetized with a force proportional to the ampere-turns of the magnet.

ELECTROMAGNETIC SWITCHES

Electromagnets are widely used in automotive electrical systems in the form of electromagnetic switches. An electromagnetic switch is one that opens or closes electrical contacts using an electromagnet. See figure 1–31.

A low-current electromagnetic switch is usually used to control (open or close) a high-current circuit. For example, an ignition switch circuit (low current) can control a high-current starter motor circuit by using an electromagnetic switch.

HOW AN ELECTROMAGNETIC SWITCH WORKS

When the electromagnetic wires are connected to a power source, the resulting magnetic pull on the upper movable contact point forces the switch into contact

FIGURE 1–32 Solenoid mounted on top of a starter. Not only does the solenoid conduct the high starter motor current, but the movable core engages the drive pinion into the engine flywheel.

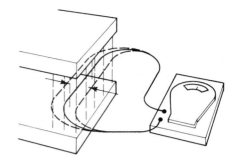

FIGURE 1–33 A wire (conductor) moving through a magnetic field generates a voltage.

with the lower contact point. These contact points complete (close) another circuit. Because the electromagnetic switch controls a higher current than the control current, it is often called a **relay,** because it "relays" heavy current in the circuit.

RELAYS AND SOLENOIDS

If an electromagnetic switch uses a movable arm, it is called a relay. If an electromagnetic switch uses a movable iron core, it is called a **solenoid.** A solenoid, besides operating as a switch, can also use a movable core to perform mechanical work, such as engaging a starter gear. Solenoids are usually constructed to transfer heavier current than a movable arm relay. A solenoid may, therefore, be called a relay when used to transfer heavy current such as that used in diesel engine glow plug circuits. The proper term to use is determined by the individual automobile manufacturer as specified in the service literature. See figure 1–32.

RESIDUAL MAGNETISM

Residual magnetism is the term used to describe the magnetism remaining in the core of an electromagnet *after* the magnetizing electrical current is shut off. The cause of some residual magnetism is the fact that the magnetizing force "lags behind" the applied current. This lag is called **hysteresis,** from the Greek word *hysterein*, which means to be behind, or to lag. To reduce residual magnetism, "soft iron" (a pure iron with little

carbon content) is used as a core because it can be magnetized easily but cannot remain magnetized after the current is removed. If hard iron were used, some magnetizing power would remain. In some cases, residual magnetism is an unwanted side effect of an electromagnet. In other applications, residual magnetism may be useful.

ELECTROMAGNETIC INDUCTION

In 1831, Michael Faraday discovered that electrical energy can be induced from one circuit to another by using magnetic lines of force. When a conductor is moved through a magnetic field, a difference of potential is set up between the ends of the conductor, and a voltage is induced. This action is called **electromagnetic induction.** See figure 1–33. This voltage exists only when the magnetic field *or* the conductor is in motion.

To induce 1 volt, 100,000,000 (100 million) magnetic lines of force must be cut per second. The induced voltage can be increased by increasing the *speed* with which the magnetic lines of force cut the conductor, or by increasing *the number of conductors* that are cut. Electromagnetic induction is the principle behind the operation of all ignition systems, starter motors, generators, alternators, and relays.

A coil is often referred to as an **inductor.** As the current increases through the coil, the magnetic strength eventually reaches a leveling-off point at which an additional increase of the magnetizing force current no longer increases the magnetic field strength. This condition is called **saturation.** The magnetic lines of force represent stored energy. If the applied voltage is removed, the lines of force collapse, returning the energy back into the wire.

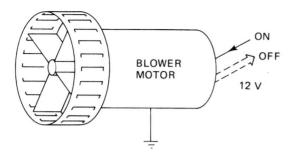

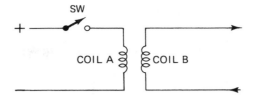

FIGURE 1–35 Mutual induction can create a current in coil B if the current flow through coil A is switched on and off.

FIGURE 1–34 Every electric motor contains magnetic windings. Whenever electrical power is shut off, self-induction produces a voltage of the opposite polarity from the applied current flow.

To reduce or eliminate this high-voltage arc, capacitors (condensers) and/or diodes are commonly connected in the circuit to absorb or direct the high voltage created by the switching on and off of inductive circuits.

SELF-INDUCTION

Self-induction is the generation of an electric current in the wires of the coil itself when a current is *first* connected or disconnected. This induced current is in the *opposite* direction from that of the applied current and tends to reduce the magnetizing force. This is the reason that coils become fully saturated only after a slight delay. Self-induction also tends to maintain the applied voltage when the circuit is opened by a switch, because the energy in the coil becomes a source of voltage. Self-induction was first observed in 1834 by Heinrich Lenz (1804–65), a German physicist. The law of self-induction, called **Lenz's law**, states that an induced current is in such a direction that its magnetic effect opposes the change by which the current is induced. It is the *change* in current, not the current itself, that is opposed by the induced EMF. Self-induction is a generally *undesirable* electrical characteristic. Any coil, called an inductor, stores electrical energy when current is flowing. When the power is removed, the energy stored in the inductor is released. This causes an electrical arc to occur in the switch of any electrical circuit. Self-induction is commonly found in the following:

1. Ignition circuit—ignition coil
2. Air conditioning—electromagnetic clutch coil
3. Blower motors—motor field and armature windings (fig. 1–34)
4. Any other component containing a coil or an electric motor

Self-induction is further undesirable because it can create extremely high voltage surges (7000 volts or more) throughout the entire automotive electrical system. Computer systems are subject to damage if these high-voltage spikes are not controlled or prevented.

◀ TECH TIP ▶

WHAT DOES RMS MEAN?

Root mean square (RMS) is a common method of expressing alternating-current electrical power. Alternating current flows continually, but its voltage changes. The voltage looks like a sine wave if observed on a scope. See figure 1–36. The power (watts) that electrical energy can deliver is expressed as amperes times volts. But because the voltage is constantly changing, a method called RMS gives the *effective* power (watts) of a circuit. The RMS method involves squaring all values (multiplying each by itself), then calculating the mean (average of all values), then taking the square root of the results. This method is used because all negative numbers (all values below the zero line) become positive when squared. To convert RMS values to and from peak-to-peak values, use the following conversions:

Peak × 0.707 = RMS
RMS × 1.414 = Peak

This information may be helpful, for example, in determining the peak power of an amplifier so that the correct speakers can be selected.

100-W RMS amplifier × 1.414 = Peak 141.4 W

Use speakers rated for at least 142 watts.

NOTE: Most amplifiers are rated in RMS, and speakers are usually rated in peak (maximum) watts.

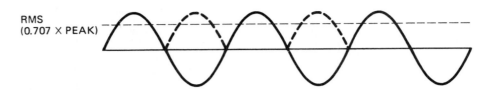

FIGURE 1–36 The root mean square (RMS) is a measure of the effective power of an alternating voltage source.

MUTUAL INDUCTION

Mutual induction is the *desirable* induction of a voltage in a conductor (coil) due to a changing magnetic field of an adjacent coil. Mutual induction is used in ignition coils, where a rapidly changing magnetic field in the primary winding of the coil creates a voltage in the secondary winding of the coil. See figure 1–35. The voltage induced in the secondary windings is basically determined by the number of turns of wire in both windings. The operation of the ignition coil and the ignition circuit is discussed in chapter 12.

SUMMARY

1. Electricity is the movement of electrons from one atom to another.
2. Automotive electricity uses the conventional theory that electricity flows from positive (+) to negative (-).
3. The ampere is the measure of the amount of current flow.
4. Voltage is the unit of electrical pressure.
5. The ohm is the unit of electrical resistance.
6. Capacitors (condensers) are used in numerous automotive applications. Because of their ability to block direct current and pass alternating current, they are used to control radio-frequency interference and are installed in various electronic circuits to protect and control changing current.
7. Most automotive electrical components use magnetism, and the strength of the magnetism depends on both the amount of current (amperes) and the number of turns of wire of each electromagnet.
8. The strength of electromagnets is increased by using a soft-iron core.
9. Voltage can be induced from one circuit to another.

REVIEW QUESTIONS

1. Define electricity.
2. Define ampere, volt, and ohm.
3. List three functions that a capacitor (condenser) can perform.
4. Describe the difference between self-induction and mutual induction.

MULTIPLE-CHOICE QUESTIONS

1. An electrical conductor is an element with _____ electrons in its outer orbit.
   a. Less than two
   b. Less than four
   c. Exactly four
   d. More than four
2. Like charges _____ .
   a. Attract
   b. Repel
   c. Neutralize each other
   d. Add
3. Carbon and silicon are examples of _____ .
   a. Semiconductors
   b. Insulators
   c. Conductors
   d. Photoelectric materials
4. Which unit of electricity does the work in a circuit?
   a. A volt
   b. An ampere
   c. An ohm
   d. A coulomb

5. As temperature increases, _____ .
  a. The resistance of a conductor decreases
  b. The resistance of a conductor increases
  c. The resistance of a conductor remains the same
  d. The voltage of a conductor decreases

6. The _____ is a unit of electrical pressure.
  a. Coulomb
  b. Volt
  c. Ampere
  d. Ohm

7. Piezoelectric crystals can create a voltage whenever _____ .
  a. Pressure is put on the crystals
  b. The crystals are heated
  c. The crystals are cooled
  d. The crystals are exposed to moisture (water)

8. Materials that release electrons when exposed to light are called _____ .
  a. Thermoelectric
  b. Selenium or cesium
  c. Piezoelectric
  d. Chemical-electrical energy sources

9. Magnetic field strength is measured in units called _____ .
  a. Watts
  b. Ampere-turns
  c. Reluctance
  d. Hysteresis

10. Ignition coils use which type of electromagnetic induction?
  a. Mutual induction
  b. Self-induction
  c. Residual induction
  d. Both a and c

◀ Chapter 2 ▶

ELECTRICAL CIRCUITS AND OHM'S LAW

OBJECTIVES

After studying chapter 2, the reader will be able to

1. State Ohm's law.
2. Identify a series and a parallel circuit.
3. Explain voltage drops.
4. Discuss electrical power measured in watts.

A thorough understanding of electrical circuits is important to the technician to enable the diagnosing and troubleshooting of electrical problems.

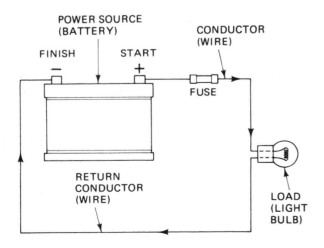

FIGURE 2–1 All complete circuits must have a power source, a power path, protection (fuse), an electrical load (light bulb in this case), and a return path back to the power source.

CIRCUITS

A **circuit** is a path that electrons travel from a power source (such as a battery) through a resistance (such as a light bulb) and back to the power source. It is called a circuit because the current must start and finish at the same place (power source). See figure 2–1.

For *any* electrical circuit to work at all, it must be continuous from the battery (power), through all the wires and components, and back to the battery (ground). A circuit that is continuous throughout is said to have **continuity.**

PARTS OF A COMPLETE CIRCUIT

Every **complete circuit** contains the following parts:

1. A **power source,** such as a vehicle's battery.
2. **Protection** from harmful overloads (excessive current flow). Fuses, circuit breakers, and fusible links are examples of electrical circuit protection devices.
3. A **path** for the current to flow through from the power source to the resistance. This path from a power source to the resistance (a light bulb in this example) is usually an insulated copper wire.
4. The **electrical load** or resistance—that which the electrical current is operating or lighting.
5. A **return path** for the electrical current from the load back to the power source so that there is a

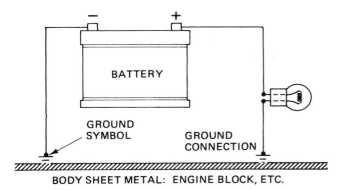

FIGURE 2–2 The return path back to the battery can be any electrical conductor, such as the metal frame or body of the vehicle.

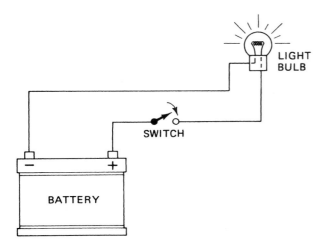

FIGURE 2–3 An electrical switch opens the circuit and no current flows. The switch could also be on the return (ground) path wire.

OPEN CIRCUITS

An **open circuit** is any circuit that is *not* complete, or that lacks continuity. See figure 2–4. *No current at all* will flow through an incomplete circuit. An open circuit may be created by a break in the circuit or by a switch that opens (turns off) the circuit and prevents the flow of current. In any circuit containing a power source, a load, and a ground, an open anywhere in the circuit will cause the circuit not to work. A light switch in a home

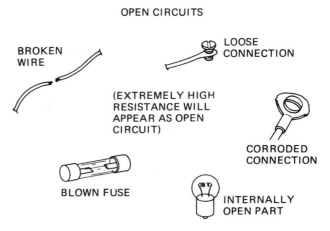

FIGURE 2–4 Examples of common causes of open circuits. Some of these causes are often difficult to find.

◀ **TECH TIP** ▶

OPEN IS A FOUR-LETTER WORD

An open in a circuit breaks the path for current flow. The open can be any break in the power side, load or ground side of a circuit. A switch is often used to close and open a circuit to turn it on and off. Just remember

open = no current flow

closed = current flow

Trying to locate an open circuit in a vehicle is often difficult and may cause the technician to use other four-letter words.

and the headlight switch in a vehicle are examples of devices that open a circuit to control its operation.

SHORT TO VOLTAGE

If a wire (conductor) or component is shorted to voltage, it is commonly called **shorted**. See figure 2–5. A **short circuit**

1. Is a complete circuit in which the current bypasses *some* or *all* of the resistance in the circuit
2. Involves the power side of the circuit
3. Involves a copper-to-copper connection
4. Is also called a **short to voltage**
5. Usually affects more than one circuit

---

complete circuit. This return path is usually the metal body, frame, and engine block of the vehicle. This is called the **ground return path**. See figure 2–2.

6. **Switches and controls** to turn the circuit on and off. See figure 2–3.

6. *May* or *may not* blow a fuse (fig. 2–6)

See diagnostic story for a short-to-voltage example.

SHORT TO GROUND

A **short to ground** is a type of short circuit wherein the current bypasses part of the normal circuit and flows directly to ground. Because the ground return circuit is metal (vehicle frame, engine, or body), this type of circuit is identified as having current flowing from **copper to steel**. A defective component or circuit that is shorted to ground is commonly called **grounded**. For example, if a penny was accidently inserted into a cigarette lighter socket, the current would flow through the penny to ground. Because the penny has little resistance, excessive amount of current flows, which causes the fuse to blow.

EARTH GROUND, CHASSIS GROUND, AND FLOATING GROUND

A ground represents the lowest possible voltage potential in a circuit. There is actually more than one ground. The "earth" is the most "grounded" ground.

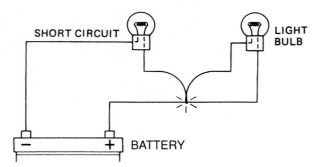

FIGURE 2–5   A short circuit permits electrical current to bypass some or all of the resistance in the circuit.

◀   **TECH TIP**   ▶

"THAT'S NOT IMPORTANT— IT'S ONLY A GROUND"

The statement that ground wires are not important is often heard when beginning technicians are attempting to repair a weird electrical problem. A missing ground strap(s) from the engine block to the body of the vehicle can cause any or all of the following problems:

1. Dim headlights
2. Slower than normal blower motor (heating and air conditioning)
3. Slower than normal or inoperative electric cooling (radiator) fan
4. Slow or inoperative wipers
5. Inoperative rear window defogger
6. Inoperative or sick-sounding horn(s)

The long-term effects of operating a vehicle without proper body-to-engine ground wires include the following:

1. Driveshaft U-joint failure. This is caused by the electrical current for the lights and accessories, which normally grounds through the body-to-engine ground wires, actually flowing through the moisture, dirt, etc., and through the driveshaft, "finding ground" at the engine block.
2. Front wheel drive axle bearing failure.
3. Automatic or manual transmission failure. This type of failure usually involves damaged bearings due to the current arcing across the bearings.

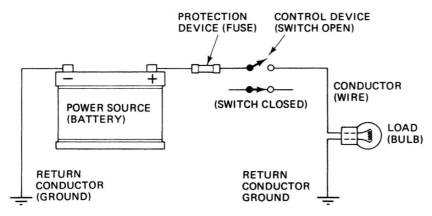

FIGURE 2–6   A fuse or circuit breaker opens the circuit to prevent possible overheating damage in the event of a short circuit.

◀ DIAGNOSTIC STORY ▶

THE SHORT-TO-VOLTAGE STORY

A technician was working on a Chevrolet pickup truck with unusual electrical problems including the following:

1. Whenever the brake pedal was depressed, the dash light and the side marker lights would light.
2. The turn signals caused all lights to blink and the fuel gauge needle to bounce up and down.
3. When the brake lights were on, the front parking lights also came on.

The technician tested all fuses using a conventional test light (not a low-current test light) and found them to be okay. All body–to–engine block ground wires were clean and tight. All bulbs were of the correct trade number as specified in the owner's manual.

NOTE: Using a single-filament bulb (such as a #1156) in the place of a dual-filament bulb (such as a #1157) could cause many of these same problems. (See chapter 6 for further bulb number information.)

Because most of the trouble occurred whenever the brake pedal was depressed, the technician decided to trace all the wires in the brake light circuit. The problem was found near the exhaust system. A small hole in the tail pipe (after the muffler) directed hot exhaust gases to the wiring harness containing all of the wires for circuits at the rear of the truck. The heat had melted the insulation and caused most of the wires to touch. Whenever one circuit was activated (such as when the brake pedal was applied), the current had a complete path to several other circuits. A fuse did not blow because there was enough resistance in the circuits being energized so that the current (in amperes) was too low to blow any fuses. See figures 2–7 and 2–8.

FIGURE 2–7 The wiring for this pickup truck runs parallel and very close to the exhaust system. Even a slight exhaust leak can cause the melting of the insulation and a possible short affecting the various circuits running to the rear of the truck.

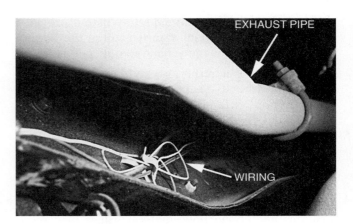

FIGURE 2–8 Another view of the truck shown in figure 2–7. Here the exhaust pipe is seen to be close to the trailer wiring harness on this new truck. The wiring is routed this way at the factory!

ing ground. This ground acts as the return circuit for an electrical component in a vehicle wherein no part of the circuit connects to the chassis. A floating type of ground is commonly used for radio and speaker connections.

Whenever the word *ground* is used in this book, it will mean chassis ground unless stated otherwise.

NOTE: The *Society of Automotive Engineers (SAE) Handbook* specifies that the negative side of the battery should be grounded. Before the early 1960s, some vehicles grounded the positive battery post.

A vehicle with rubber tires is insulated above this ground. The battery and all electrical components are connected to the chassis or frame of the vehicle, and this type of ground is called **chassis ground.** There is another type of ground that is called **float-**

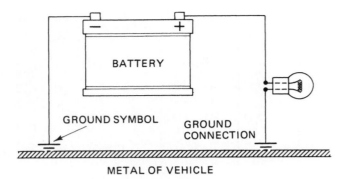

BATTERY

GROUND SYMBOL   GROUND
CONNECTION

METAL OF VEHICLE

FIGURE 2–9 The metal components of the vehicle provide the ground return path for most automotive electrical components.

ONE-WIRE SYSTEMS

A one-wire system is used for most automotive electrical circuits wherein the ground return path is provided by connecting the circuit return path to the battery through the metal of the vehicle's body and/or frame. See figure 2–9.

HOW THE ONE-WIRE SYSTEM CAN CAUSE PROBLEMS

Because, in a one-wire system, *all* of the current has to flow through the vehicle's metal frame and/or body to return to the negative side of the battery, there are many locations and connections that can cause high resistance for the entire circuit.

Most vehicles have ground wires connecting the negative side of the battery to the vehicle's *body*. Remember, all current flowing to any part of the body will ground to the body, and because the negative battery cable connects to the engine, there must be an electrical connection between the engine block and the body. The body is usually electrically insulated from the engine because of the following rubber insulators:

1. The engine is mounted in rubber motor mounts.
2. The exhaust system is insulated from the body with rubber hangers.
3. The drivetrain and suspension are insulated from the body by rubber spring insulators and bushings.

Lights, horns, or other electrical accessories may not operate correctly (or at all) if body ground wires are loose or corroded. Transmission and other drive-line problems can also be caused by loose or missing engine-to-body ground wires. Current normally travels through the body ground wires. If these wires are not properly connected, current can flow through dirt and moisture under the vehicle and then through the transmission as it tries to return to the negative side of the battery. This current (up to 35 amperes), as it flows through the driveshaft and transmission, can arc or spark across the transmission bearings and U-joints. Always check the condition and tightness of all ground wires and do not fail to reconnect the wires attached to the valve covers and other engine and body locations.

DISCONNECTING ONLY THE NEGATIVE BATTERY CABLE

If work is being performed on any automotive electrical component, the negative battery cable should be disconnected. This creates an open circuit and is safe for the following reasons:

1. Removing *either* battery cable from the battery disconnects (opens) the entire vehicle's electrical system.
2. The negative cable is connected to the engine block. Ground wires electrically connect the engine block to the vehicle's body and frame. If the wrench used to remove the battery cable from the battery accidentally touched the vehicle's body or frame, nothing would happen. If, however, the positive cable were being removed and the wrench happened to touch the vehicle body, a spark would occur that could cause a battery explosion. A spark could occur because current could flow through the wrench from the positive post of the battery directly to ground.

Always remember that the negative cable should be *the first cable removed* and the *last cable installed* whenever electrical work is being performed.

SERIES CIRCUITS

A **series circuit** is a complete circuit with two or more resistances connected so that the current has to go through one resistance to go through the next. See figure 2–10. A series circuit can have any number of resistances in the circuit. The resistances can be any of the following:

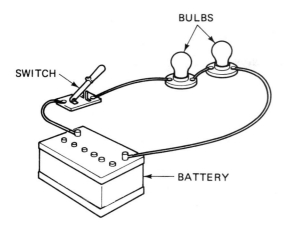

FIGURE 2–10 Series circuit with two resistances. All of the current must flow through both bulbs. Because each bulb offers resistance, the bulbs will be dim as a result of the reduced current flow.

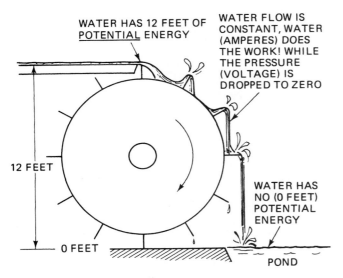

FIGURE 2–11 Electrical flow through a circuit is similar to water flowing over a waterwheel. The more the water (ampere in electricity), the greater the amount of work (water). The amount of water remains constant, yet the pressure (voltage in electricity) drops as the current flows through the circuit.

1. Resistors
2. Light bulbs
3. Horn
4. Electric motors
5. Coils
6. Relays
7. Solenoids
8. Heating elements (cigarette lighter)
9. Connectors or junctions
10. Lengths of wire or conductors

◄ **TECH TIP** ►

THINK OF A WATERWHEEL

A beginning technician cleaned the positive terminal of the battery when the starter was cranking the engine slowly. When questioned by the shop foreman as to why only the positive post had been cleaned, the technician responded that the negative terminal was "only a ground." The foreman reminded the technician that the current, in amperes, is constant throughout a series circuit (such as the cranking motor circuit). If 200 amperes leaves the positive post of the battery, then 200 amperes must return to the battery through the negative post.

The technician just could not understand how electricity can do work (crank an engine), yet return the same amount of current, in amperes, as left the battery. The shop foreman explained that even though the current is constant throughout the circuit, the voltage (electrical pressure or potential) is dropped to zero in the circuit. To explain further, the shop foreman drew a waterwheel. See figure 2–11.

As water drops from a higher level to a lower level, high-potential energy (or voltage) is used to turn the waterwheel and results in low-potential energy (or lower voltage). The same amount of water (or amperes) reaches the pond under the waterwheel as started the fall above the waterwheel. As current (amperes) flows through a conductor, it performs work in the circuit (turns the waterwheel) while its voltage (potential) is dropped.

In a series circuit, the voltage varies across each resistance, but the current flow in amperes is constant throughout the entire circuit.

PARALLEL CIRCUITS

A **parallel circuit** is a type of complete circuit in which the current flows through the circuit by more than one path. The concept is similar to that of traffic going through a city. A driver can travel straight through the city, fighting heavy traffic (high resistance), or go around the city using a long bypass. Since both paths are available to all traffic, each road carries fewer vehicles.

In picture form, a parallel circuit appears as shown in figure 2–12. In a parallel circuit, the voltage in each leg of the circuit is the same, but the current

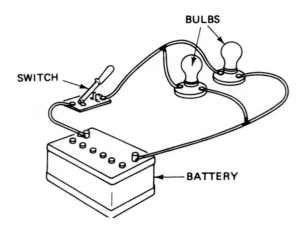

FIGURE 2–12   Parallel circuit with two resistances. Electrical current from the battery can flow through either bulb. Because each bulb has its own power and ground, the bulbs will be bright.

flow in amperes varies according to the resistance in each leg.

HOW TO DETERMINE A PARALLEL CIRCUIT

To test whether a circuit is truly a parallel circuit, pretend to cut one wire to one of the light bulbs. See figure 2–13. If the other bulbs are still connected to both a power source and a ground, the circuit is still complete and current can still flow. The circuit is therefore a parallel circuit.

WHERE PARALLEL CIRCUITS ARE USED IN A VEHICLE

Parallel circuits are used in almost every automotive electrical component. The exterior lights are all controlled by the headlight switch and are wired in parallel. If they were wired in series and one bulb burned out, *all* lights would go out because of the open circuit caused by the one defective bulb. This does not occur with a parallel circuit. If any bulb is defective, current can still flow through the other resistances (bulbs) as if nothing has happened.

SERIES-PARALLEL CIRCUITS

A **series-parallel circuit** is any type of circuit containing resistances in both series and parallel in one circuit. Series-parallel circuits are also called **combination** or

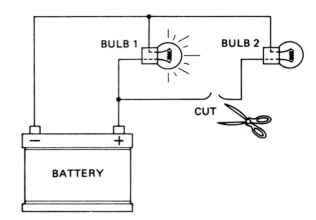

FIGURE 2–13   If the wire going to bulb 2 is cut, the bulb will not light because of the open circuit created. Bulb 1 is still connected to a complete circuit and will operate normally.

compound circuits. A series-parallel circuit is the most commonly used type of automotive circuit.

THE FOUR BASIC AUTOMOTIVE CIRCUITS

All fundamental automotive electrical components use four types of operating circuits, and all of these are series-parallel circuits. These circuits, all of which use the battery, are classified by function. During troubleshooting, a technician must know what components are connected together and their function in each specific circuit. Then, by use of a systematic testing procedure, the defective component can be located. These four circuit types are as follows:

1. *Ignition circuit.* The components in the ignition circuit are designed to generate and deliver a high-voltage spark at the exact time necessary to fire the spark plugs in the correct order. The components include
   a. Battery
   b. Ignition coil
   c. Distributor (including all electrical components)
   d. Spark plugs
   e. Spark plug wires
2. *Cranking circuit.* The cranking circuit includes all of the components needed to crank the engine. The components include
   a. Battery
   b. Starter motor
   c. Starter solenoid or relay
   d. Connecting cables and connections

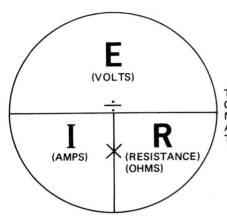

TO SOLVE OHM'S LAW PROBLEMS,
COVER THE UNIT OF ELECTRICITY
NOT KNOWN. IF THE VALUES OF
ANY TWO UNITS ARE KNOWN, THE
THIRD CAN BE CALCULATED.

EXAMPLE: VOLTS – COVER "E" = I × R
AMPERES – COVER "I" = E ÷ R
OHMS – COVER "R" = E ÷ I

FIGURE 2–14   Circle diagram of Ohm's law.

3. *Charging circuit.* The charging circuit includes all components required to keep the battery fully charged. The components include
   a. Battery
   b. Alternator or generator
   c. Voltage regulator
   d. Connecting wires and connections
4. *Lighting and accessory circuits.* The lighting and accessory circuits include all other circuits:
   a. Battery
   b. All lights
   c. All dash instruments
   d. Horn
   e. Windshield wipers washers
   f. Radio
   g. All other safety and convenience items

OHM'S LAW

The German physicist Georg Simon Ohm established that electric pressure (EMF) in volts, electrical resistance in ohms, and the amount of current in amperes flowing through any circuit are all related. See figure 2–14. According to **Ohm's law,** it requires 1 volt to push 1 ampere through 1 ohm of resistance. This means that if the voltage is doubled, the number of amperes of current flowing though a circuit will also double if the resistance of the circuit remains the same.

Ohm's law can also be stated as a simple formula that can be used to calculate one value of an electrical circuit if the other two are known:

$$I = \frac{E}{R}$$

where

I = Current in amperes (A)
E = Electromotive force (EMF) in volts (V)
R = Resistance in ohms (Ω)

1. Ohm's law can determine the *resistance* if the volts and amperes are known: $R = \frac{E}{I}$.
2. Ohm's law can determine the *voltage* if the resistance (ohms) and amperes are known: $E = I \times R$.
3. Ohm's law can determine the *amperes* if the resistance and voltage are known: $I = \frac{E}{R}$.

OHM'S LAW APPLIED TO SIMPLE CIRCUITS

If a battery with 12 volts is connected to a light bulb with a resistance of 4 ohms as shown in figure 2–15, how many amperes will flow through the circuit? Using Ohm's law, we can calculate the number of amperes that will flow through the wires and the bulb. Remember, if two factors are known (volts and ohms in this example), the remaining factor (amperes) can be calculated using Ohm's law.

$$I = \frac{E}{R} = \frac{12V}{4\Omega}$$

The values for the voltage (12) and the resistance (4) were substituted for the letters E and R. I is thus 3 amperes (12/4 = 3).

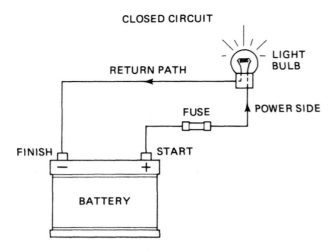

FIGURE 2–15 Closed circuit, including a power source, power-side wire, circuit protection (fuse), resistance (bulb), and return path wire.

If we want to connect a light bulb to a 12-volt battery, we now know that this simple circuit requires 3 amperes to operate. This may help us for two reasons:

1. We can now determine the wire diameter that we will need based on the number of amperes flowing through the circuit.
2. The correct fuse rating can be selected to protect the circuit.

WATTS

The **watt** is the electrical unit for *power*, the capacity to do work. It is named after a Scottish inventor, James Watt (1736–1819). The symbol for power is *P*. Electrical power is calculated as amperes times volts:

$$P \text{ (power)} = I \text{ (amperes)} \times E \text{ (volts)}$$

This can easily be remembered by thinking of what the letters spell: pie. For example, how many watts are used to run an electric motor on 110 volts using 2 amperes?

$$P = I \times E = 2\text{ A} \times 110\text{ V}$$

P is, therefore, 220 watts. This could also be expressed in kilowatts (kW). One thousand watts equals 1 kilowatt; therefore, 220 watts equals 0.22 kilowatts. A watt is also the metric standard for engine power. One horsepower (hp) equals 746 watts. Therefore, an automotive engine with 150 horsepower would be rated at 111,900 watts (150 × 746 = 111,900) or 111.9 kilowatts.

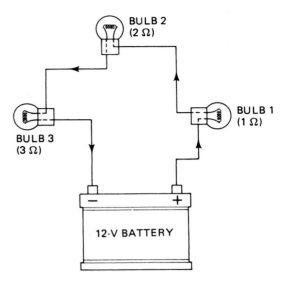

FIGURE 2–16 Series circuit with three bulbs. All of the current flows through all of the resistances (bulbs). The total resistance of the circuit is the sum of the total resistance of the bulbs, and the bulbs will light dimly because of the increased resistance and the reduction of current flow (amperes) through the circuit.

OHM'S LAW AND SERIES CIRCUITS

A series circuit is a circuit containing more than one resistance in which all of the current must flow through all of the resistances in the circuit. Ohm's law can be used to calculate the value of one unknown (voltage, resistance, or amperes), if the other two values are known.

Because *all* of the current flows through *all* of the resistances, the total resistance is the sum (addition) of all of the resistances. See figure 2–16. The total resistance of the circuit shown here is 6 ohms (1 Ω + 2 Ω + 3 Ω). The formula for total resistance (R_T) for a series circuit is

$$R_T = R_1 + R_2 + \ldots$$

Using Ohm's law to find the current flow, we have

$$I = \frac{E}{R} = \frac{12V}{6\Omega} = 2\text{ A}$$

Therefore, with a total resistance of 6 ohms, using a 12-volt battery in the series circuit shown, 2 amperes of current will flow through the entire circuit. If the amount of resistance of a circuit is reduced, more current will flow.

In figure 2–17, one resistance has been eliminated and now the total resistance is 3 ohms (1 Ω + 2 Ω). Using Ohm's law to calculate current flow yields 4 amperes.

$$I = \frac{E}{R} = \frac{12V}{3\Omega} = 4\text{ A}$$

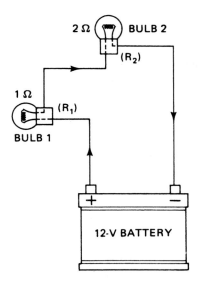

FIGURE 2–17   Series circuit with two bulbs.

Notice that the current flow was doubled (4 amperes instead of 2) when the resistance was cut in half (from 6 ohms to 3).

SERIES CIRCUIT LAWS

Series circuit laws are as follows:

1. The total resistance in a series circuit is the sum total of all of the individual resistances.
2. The current is constant throughout the entire circuit. If 2 amperes of current leaves the battery, 2 amperes of current returns to the battery.
3. Although the current (in amperes) is constant, the voltage drops across each resistance in the circuit. The sum total of all of the individual voltage drops adds up to equal the applied source voltage.

FARSIGHTED QUALITY OF ELECTRICITY

Electricity almost seems to act as if it knows what resistances are ahead on the long trip through a circuit. If the trip through the circuit has many high-resistance components, very few electrons (amperes) will choose to attempt to make the trip. If a circuit has little or no resistance (for example, a short circuit), as many electrons (amperes) as possible attempt to flow through the complete circuit. If the flow exceeds the capacity of the fuse or the circuit breaker, the circuit is opened and all current flow stops.

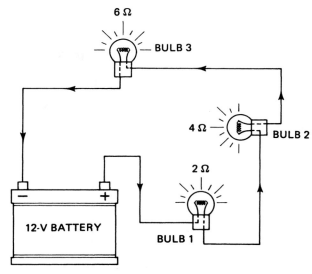

FIGURE 2–18   In a series circuit, the voltage is dropped or lowered by each resistance in the circuit. The higher the resistance, the greater the drop in voltage.

SERIES CIRCUITS AND VOLTAGE DROPS

The voltage that flows through a series circuit drops with each resistor in a manner similar to that in which the strength of an athlete drops each time a strenuous physical feat is performed. The greater the resistance, the greater the drop in voltage.

KIRCHHOFF'S VOLTAGE LAW

A German physicist, Gustav Robert Kirchhoff (1824–87), developed laws about electrical circuits. **Kirchhoff's second law** (called the **voltage law**) concerns voltage drops and states: The voltage around any closed circuit is equal to the sum (total) of the voltage drops across the resistances.

APPLYING KIRCHHOFF'S VOLTAGE LAW

Kirchhoff states in his second law that the voltage will drop in proportion to the resistance and that the total of all voltage drops will equal the applied voltage. Using figure 2–18, the total resistance of the circuit can be determined by adding together the individual resistances ($2\,\Omega + 4\,\Omega + 6\,\Omega = 12\,\Omega$). The current through the circuit is determined by using Ohm's law, $I = \frac{E}{R} = \frac{12V}{12\Omega} = 1\ \text{A}$.

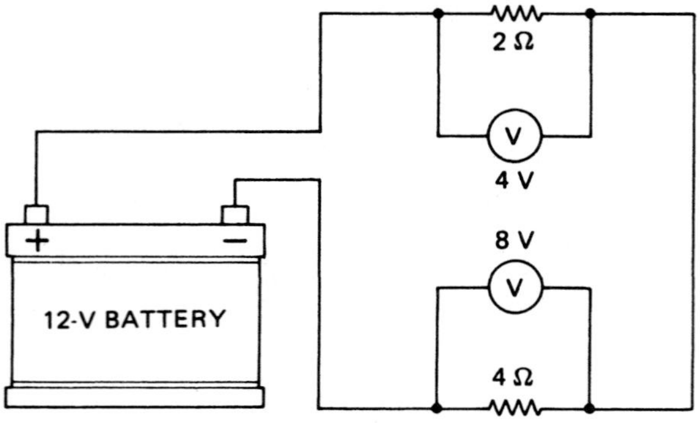

A. I = E/R (TOTAL "R" = 6 Ω)
    = 12/6 = 2 A

B. E = IR (VOLTAGE DROP)
    AT 2 Ω RESISTANCE =
    E = 2 × 2 = 4 V
    AT 4 Ω RESISTANCE =
    E = 2 × 4 = 8 V

C. 4 + 8 = 12 V
    SUM OF VOLTAGE DROP
    EQUALS APPLIED VOLTAGE

FIGURE 2–19

Therefore, in the circuit shown, the following values are known:

Resistance = 12 Ω

Voltage = 12 V

Current = 1 A

Everything is known *except* the voltage drop caused by each resistance. The **voltage drop** can be determined by using Ohm's law and calculating for voltage (E) using the value of each resistance individually:

$$E = I \times R$$

where

E = Voltage

I = Current in the circuit (remember, the current is constant in a series circuit; only the voltage varies)

R = Resistance of only one of the resistances

The voltage drops are as follows. Voltage drop for bulb 1:

$$E = I \times R$$
$$= 1\,A \times 2\,\Omega$$
$$= 2\,V$$

Voltage drop for bulb 2:

$$E = I \times R$$
$$= 1\,A \times 4\,\Omega$$
$$= 4\,V$$

Voltage drop for bulb 3:

$$E = I \times R$$
$$= 1\,A \times 6\,\Omega$$
$$= 6\,V$$

According to Kirchhoff, the sum (addition) of the voltage drops should equal the applied voltage (battery voltage):

$$\text{Total of voltage drops} = 2\,V + 4\,V + 6\,V = 12\,V$$
$$= \text{Battery voltage}$$

This proves Kirchhoff's second (voltage) law. Another example is illustrated in figure 2–19.

THE USE OF VOLTAGE DROPS

The voltage drops due to built-in resistance are used in automotive electrical systems to drop the voltage in the following examples:

1. *Dash lights.* Most vehicles are equipped with a method of dimming the brightness of the dash lights by turning a variable resistor. This type of resistor can be changed and therefore varies the voltage to the dash light bulbs. A high voltage to the bulbs causes them to be bright, and a low voltage results in a dim light.
2. *Blower motor* (heater or air-conditioning fan). Speeds are usually controlled by a fan switch sending current through high-, medium-, or low-resistance wire resistors. The highest resistance will drop the voltage the most, causing the motor to run at the lowest speed. The highest speed of the motor will occur when *no* resistance is in the circuit and full battery voltage is switched to the blower motor.

VOLTAGE DROPS AS A TESTING METHOD

Any resistance in a circuit causes the voltage to drop in proportion to the amount of the resistance. Because a high resistance will drop the voltage more than a lower resistance, we can use a voltmeter to measure resistance. Voltage-drop testing for determining high resistance in wiring or connections is discussed in detail in chapters 10 and 11.

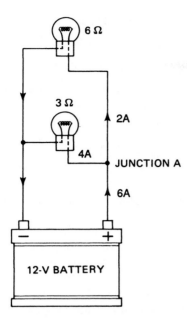

FIGURE 2–20 The amount of current flowing into junction point A equals the total amount of current flowing out of the junction.

CURRENT FLOW THROUGH PARALLEL CIRCUITS

A parallel circuit is a complete circuit wherein the current has more than one path to travel to complete the circuit. A break or open in one leg or section of a parallel circuit does not stop the current flow through the remaining legs of the parallel circuit.

KIRCHHOFF'S CURRENT LAW

Kirchhoff's first law (called the **current law**) states that the current flowing into any junction of an electrical circuit is equal to the current flowing out of that junction.

Kirchhoff's current law can be illustrated using Ohm's law, as seen in figure 2–20. Kirchhoff's law states that the amount of current flowing into junction A will equal the current flowing out of junction A.

Because the 6-ohm leg requires 2 amperes and the 3-ohm resistance leg requires 4 amperes, it is necessary that the wire from the battery to junction A be capable of handling 6 amperes. Also notice that the sum of the current flowing out of a junction (2 + 4 = 6 A) is equal to the current flowing into the junction (6 A), proving Kirchhoff's current law.

PARALLEL CIRCUIT LAWS

Parallel circuit laws are as follows:

1. The total resistance of a parallel circuit is always less than that of the smallest-resistance leg.
2. The voltage is the same for each leg of a parallel circuit.
3. The amount of current flow through a parallel circuit may vary for each leg depending on the resistance of that leg. The current flowing through each leg results in the same voltage drop (from the power side to the ground side) as for every other leg of the circuit.

***

NOTE: A parallel circuit drops the voltage from source voltage to zero (ground) across the resistance in each leg of the circuit.

***

DETERMINING TOTAL RESISTANCE IN A PARALLEL CIRCUIT

There are five methods commonly used to determine total resistance in a parallel circuit.

***

NOTE: Determining the total *resistance* of a parallel circuit is very important in automotive service. Electronic fuel injector and diesel engine glow plug circuits are two of the most commonly tested circuits wherein parallel circuit knowledge is required. Also, when installing extra lighting, the technician must determine the proper gauge wire and protection device.

***

Method #1. The total *current* (in amperes) can be calculated first by treating each leg of the parallel circuit as a simple circuit. See figure 2–21. Each leg has its own power and ground, and therefore, the current through each leg is independent of the current through any other leg.

Current through the 3-Ω resistance =
$$I = \frac{E}{R} = \frac{12V}{3\Omega} = 4 \text{ A.}$$

Current through the 4-Ω resistance =
$$I = \frac{E}{R} = \frac{12V}{4\Omega} = 3 \text{ A.}$$

Current through the 6-Ω resistance =

$$I = \frac{E}{R} = \frac{12V}{6\Omega} = 2 \text{ A}.$$

The total current flowing from the battery is the sum total of the individual currents for each leg. Total current from the battery is, therefore, 9 amperes (4 A + 3 A + 2 A = 9 A).

If **total circuit resistance** (R_T) is needed, Ohm's law can be used to calculate it because voltage (E) and current (I) are now known.

$$R_T = \frac{E}{I} = \frac{12V}{9A} = 1.33\Omega$$

Note that the total resistance (1.33 Ω) is smaller than that of the smallest-resistance leg of the parallel circuit. (The resistance of the smallest-resistance leg in figure 2–20 is 3 ohms.) This is one characteristic of a parallel circuit and is the case because not all of the current flows through all of the resistances as in a series circuit.

Because the current has alternative paths to ground through the various legs of a parallel circuit, as additional resistances (legs) are added to a parallel circuit, the total current from the battery (power source) *increases*. Additional current can flow when resis-

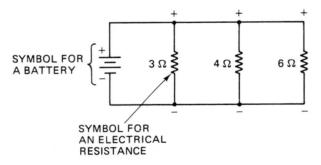

FIGURE 2–21 Typical parallel circuit. Each resistance has power and ground, and each leg operates independently of the other leg of the circuit.

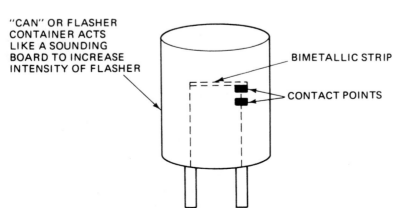

THE TURN SIGNAL STORY

A beginning technician was assigned the job of connecting lights on a rental trailer to a customer's vehicle wiring. Using a test light and crimp-type wiring connectors, the technician connected all of the wiring to the trailer's lights.

The customer returned, complaining that the turn (directional) signals were flashing rapidly. Another technician replaced the turn signal flasher unit with a heavy-duty (HD) constant-rate flasher.

The increased current flow caused by the trailer lights being connected in parallel caused the bimetallic strip inside the department of transportation (DOT) fixed-load type of flasher unit to flash too rapidly. The extra current flow through the bimetallic strip was heated at a faster rate than normal and bent upward with the heat, opening the turn signal circuit (fig. 2–22). Changing to a constant-rate flasher unit (variable-load flasher) restored the proper operation of the turn (directional) signals so that they flashed at the normal rate of about 1 or 2 times per second (60–120 flashes per minute). See chapter 6 for further details on turn (directional) signal and flasher unit operation.

tances are added in parallel because each leg of a parallel circuit has its own power and ground, and the current flowing through each leg is strictly dependent on the resistance of *that* leg.

Method #2. If only two resistors are connected in parallel, the total resistance (R_T) can be found using the formula

$$R_T = \frac{(R_1 \times R_2)}{(R_1 + R_2)}$$

FIGURE 2–22 Typical variable-rate (series-type) flasher unit.

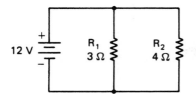

FIGURE 2–23

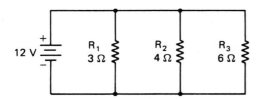

FIGURE 2–24

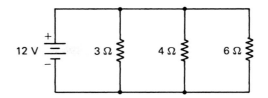

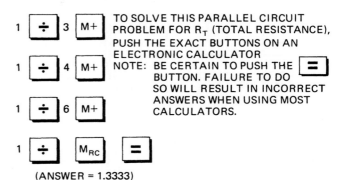

TO SOLVE THIS PARALLEL CIRCUIT PROBLEM FOR R_T (TOTAL RESISTANCE), PUSH THE EXACT BUTTONS ON AN ELECTRONIC CALCULATOR
NOTE: BE CERTAIN TO PUSH THE ▢ BUTTON. FAILURE TO DO SO WILL RESULT IN INCORRECT ANSWERS WHEN USING MOST CALCULATORS.

(ANSWER = 1.3333)

FIGURE 2–25

For example, using the circuit in figure 2–23 and substituting 3 ohms for R_1 and 4 ohms for R_2.

$$R_T = \frac{(3 \times 4)}{(3 + 4)} = \frac{12}{7} = 1.7\Omega$$

Note that the total resistance (1.7 Ω) is smaller than that of the smallest-resistance leg of the circuit.

NOTE: Which resistor is R_1 and which is R_2 is not important. The position in the formula makes no difference in the multiplication and addition of the resistor values.

This formula can be used for more than two resistances in parallel, but only two resistances can be calculated at a time. After solving for R_T for two resistors, use the value of R_T as R_1 and the additional resistance in parallel as R_2 and solve for another R_T. Continue the process for all resistance legs of the parallel circuit. However, note that it might be easier to solve for R_T when there are more than two resistances in parallel by using method #3 or #4.

Method #3. A formula that can be used to find the total resistance for any number of resistances in parallel is

$$\frac{1}{R_T} = \frac{1}{R_1} + \frac{1}{R_2} + \frac{1}{R_3} + \dots$$

To solve for R_T for the three resistance legs in figure 2–24, substitute the values of the resistances for R_1, R_2, and R_3:

$$\frac{1}{R_T} = \frac{1}{3} + \frac{1}{4} + \frac{1}{6}$$

The fractions cannot be added together unless they all have the same denominator. The lowest common de-

nominator in this example is 12. Therefore, 1/3 becomes 4/12, 1/4 becomes 3/12, and 1/6 becomes 2/12.

$$\frac{1}{R_T} = \frac{4}{12} + \frac{3}{12} + \frac{2}{12} = \frac{9}{12}$$

Cross multiplying,

$$R_T = \frac{12}{9} = 1.33\Omega$$

Note that the result (1.33 Ω) is the same regardless of the method used (see method #1). The most difficult part of using this method (besides using fractions) is determining the lowest common denominator, especially for circuits containing a wide range of resistance values for the various legs. For an easier method using a calculator, see method #4.

Method #4. This method uses an electronic calculator, commonly available at very low cost. Instead of determining the lowest common denominator as in method #3, one can use the electronic calculator to convert the fractions to decimal equivalents. The memory buttons on most calculators can be used to keep a running total of the fractional values. Use figure 2–25 and calculate the total resistance (R_T) by pushing the indicated buttons on a calculator. Also see figure 2–26.

NOTE: This method can be used to find the total resistance of *any number* of resistances in parallel.

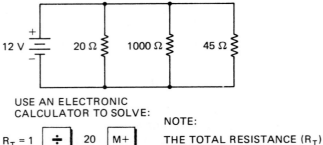

USE AN ELECTRONIC
CALCULATOR TO SOLVE:

$R_T = 1$ [÷] 20 [M+]

1 [÷] 1000 [M+]

1 [÷] 45 [M+]

1 [÷] [M$_{RC}$] [=]

NOTE:

THE TOTAL RESISTANCE (R_T)
MUST BE LESS THAN THE
SMALLEST RESISTANCE
(LESS THAN 20 Ω IN THIS
EXAMPLE).

FIGURE 2–26

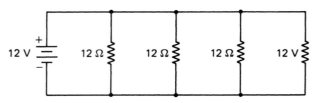

FIGURE 2–27

The memory recall (MRC) and equals (=) buttons invert the answer to give the correct value for total resistance (1.33 Ω). The increase (1/X) button can be used with the sum (SUM) button on scientific calculators without using the memory button.

Method #5. This method can be easily used whenever two or more resistances connected in parallel are of the same value. See figure 2–27.

To calculate the total resistance (R_T) of equal-value resistors, divide the number of equal resistors into the value of the resistance.

$$R_T = \frac{\text{Value of equal resistance}}{\text{Number of equal resistances}} = \frac{12\Omega}{4} = 3\Omega$$

NOTE: Since most automotive and light-truck electrical circuits involve multiple use of the same resistance, this method is the most useful. For example, if six additional 12-ohm lights were added to a vehicle, the additional lights would represent just 2 ohms of resistance (12 Ω/6 lights = 2). Therefore, 6 amperes of additional current would be drawn by the additional lights ($I = E/R = 12\,\text{V}/2\,\Omega = 6\,\text{A}$).

◀ **TECH TIP** ▶

WATTAGE INCREASES BY THE SQUARE OF THE VOLTAGE

The brightness of a light bulb, such as automotive headlights or courtesy light, depends on the number of watts available. The watt is the unit by which electrical power is measured. If the battery voltage drops, even slightly, the light becomes noticeably dimmer. The formula for calculating power (*P*) in watts is

$$P = I \times E$$

This can also be expressed as Watts = Amps × Volts.

According to Ohm's law, $I = E/R$. Therefore, E/R can be substituted for *I* in the previous formula, resulting in

$$P = \frac{E}{R} \times E$$

or

$$P = \frac{E^2}{R}$$

E^2 means *E* multiplied by itself. A small change in the voltage (*E*) has a big effect on the total brightness of the bulb. (Remember, household light bulbs are sold according to their wattage.) Therefore, if the voltage to an automotive bulb is reduced, such as by a poor electrical connection, the brightness of the bulb is *greatly* affected. A poor electrical ground causes a voltage drop, and because the sum of the voltage drops must equal the applied voltage (Kirchhoff's law), the voltage at the bulb is reduced and the bulb's brightness is reduced.

MAGIC CIRCLE

The formulas for calculating any combination of electrical units are shown in figure 2–28.

SUMMARY

1. All complete electrical circuits have a power source (such as a battery), a circuit protection device (such as a fuse), a power-side wire or path, an electrical load, a ground return path, and a switch or a control device.

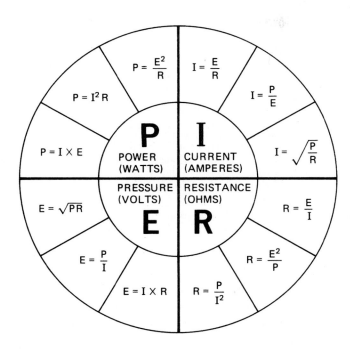

FIGURE 2–28 "Magic circle" of most of the formulas for problems involving Ohm's law. Each quarter of the "pie" has formulas used to solve for a particular unknown value: current (amperes), in the upper right segment; resistance (ohms), in the lower right; voltage (E), in the lower left; and power (watts), in the upper left.

2. A short to voltage involves a copper-to-copper connection and usually affects more than one circuit.

3. A short to ground involves a copper-to-steel connection and usually causes the fuse to blow.

4. An open is a break in the circuit resulting in no current flow at all through the circuit.

5. In a simple series circuit, the current remains constant throughout, but the voltage drops as current flows through the resistances of the circuit.

6. A parallel circuit, such as is used for all automotive lighting, has the same voltage available to each resistance (bulb).

7. The greater the resistance, the greater the voltage drop.

REVIEW QUESTIONS

1. List the parts of a complete electrical circuit.

2. Describe the difference between a short to voltage and a short to ground.

3. Describe the difference between an open and a short.

4. State Ohm's law.

5. Explain what occurs to current flow (amperes) and wattage if the resistance of a circuit is increased because of a corroded connection.

MULTIPLE-CHOICE QUESTIONS

1. If an insulated wire rubbed through a part of the insulation and the wire conductor touched the steel body of a vehicle, the type of failure would be called _____.
   a. A short to voltage
   b. A short to ground
   c. An open
   d. A chassis ground

2. If two insulated wires were to melt together where the copper conductors touched each other, the type of failure would be called _____.
   a. A short to voltage
   b. A short to ground
   c. An open
   d. A floating ground

3. If 12 volts are being applied to a resistance of 3 ohms, _____ amperes will flow.
   a. 12
   b. 3
   c. 4
   d. 36

4. How many watts are consumed by a light bulb if 1.2 amperes are measured when 12 volts are applied?
   a. 14.4 watts
   b. 144 watts
   c. 10 watts
   d. 0.10 watts

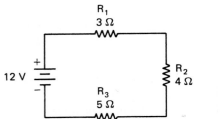

$R_T = 12\ \Omega$

$$I = \frac{E}{R} = \frac{12\ V}{12\ \Omega} = 1A$$

$E_{DROP} = I \times R_1$

FIGURE 2–29

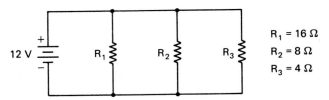

HINT: THE VOLTAGE DROP IS THE SAME FOR
EACH LEG OF A PARALLEL CIRCUIT —
ONLY THE CURRENT (AMPERES) CHANGES,
DEPENDING ON THE RESISTANCE OF EACH
LEG.

FIGURE 2–30

5. What is the voltage drop across R_1 in figure 2–29?
    a. 12.0 volts
    b. 1.0 volts
    c. 4.5 volts
    d. 3.0 volts

6. What is the voltage drop across R_2 in figure 2–30?
    a. 12 volts
    b. 8 volts
    c. 0.41 volts
    d. 3.4 volts

7. Calculate the total resistance and current in the circuit
    in figure 2–30 using any of the methods (calculator sug-
    gested). What are the values?
    a. 19.90 ohms (1.66 amperes)
    b. 13.66 ohms (0.88 amperes)
    c. 6.66 ohms (1.80 amperes)
    d. 15 ohms (0.8 amperes)

8. If an accessory such as an additional light is spliced into
    an existing circuit in parallel, what happens?
    a. The current increases in the circuit.
    b. The current decreases in the circuit.
    c. The voltage drops in the circuit.
    d. The resistance of the circuit increases.

◀ Chapter 3 ▶

ELECTRONIC AND SEMICONDUCTOR FUNDAMENTALS

OBJECTIVES

After studying chapter 3, the reader will be able to

1. Identify semiconductor components.
2. Explain precautions necessary when working around semiconductor circuits.
3. Discuss where various electronic and semiconductor devices are used in vehicles.
4. Describe how to test diodes and transistors.

Electronic components are the heart of computers. Knowing how electronic components work helps take the mystery out of automotive electronics.

SEMICONDUCTORS

Semiconductors are neither conductors nor insulators. The flow of electrical current is caused by the movement of electrons in conductors having *fewer* than four electrons in their atom's outer orbit. Insulators contain *more* than four electrons in their outer orbit and cannot conduct electricity because their atomic structure is stable. **Semiconductors** are materials that contain exactly four electrons in the outer orbit of their atom structure and are, therefore, neither good conductors nor good insulators. Two examples of semiconductor

materials are germanium and silicon, which have no free electrons to provide current flow. However, both of these semiconductor materials can be made to conduct current if another material is added to provide the necessary conditions for electron movement. When another material is added to a semiconductor material in very small amounts, it is called **doping.** The doping elements are called **impurities;** therefore, after their addition, the germanium and silicon are no longer considered **pure elements.** The material added to pure silicon or germanium to make it electrically conductive represents only one atom of impurity for every *100 million* atoms of the pure semiconductor material. The resulting atoms are still electrically neutral because the number of electrons still equals the number of protons of the combined materials. These combined materials are classified into two groups depending on the number of electrons in the bonding between the two materials. They are called N-type or P-type materials.

N-TYPE MATERIAL

N-type material is silicon or germanium that is doped with an element such as phosphorus, arsenic, or antimony, each having five electrons in its outer orbit. These five electrons are combined with the four electrons of the silicon or germanium to total nine electrons. There is room for only eight electrons in the

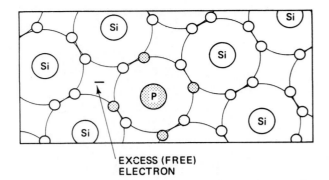

FIGURE 3–1 N-type material. Silicon (Si) doped with a material (such as phosphorus [P]) with five electrons in the outer orbit results in an extra free electron.

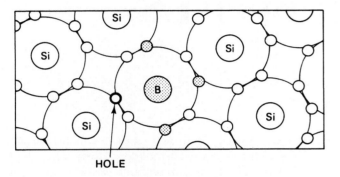

FIGURE 3–2 P-type material. Silicon (Si) doped with a material (such as boron [B]) with three electrons in the outer orbit results in a hole capable of attracting an electron.

bonding between the semiconductor material and the doping material. This leaves extra electrons, and even though the material is still electrically neutral, these extra electrons tend to repel other electrons outside the material. See figure 3–1.

P-TYPE MATERIAL

P-type material is produced by doping silicon or germanium with the element boron or the element indium. These impurities have only three electrons in their outer shell and, when combined with the semiconductor material, result in a material with seven electrons, one electron *less* than is required for atom bonding. This lack of one electron makes the material able to attract electrons, even though the material still has a neutral charge. This material tends to attract electrons to fill the holes for the missing eighth electron in the bonding of the materials. See figure 3–2.

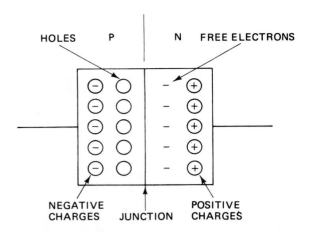

FIGURE 3–3 Unlike charges attract, and the current carriers (electrons and holes) move toward the junctions.

HOW HOLES MOVE

Current flow is expressed as the movement of electrons from one atom to another. In semiconductor and electronic terms, the movement of electrons fills the holes of the P-type material. Therefore, as the holes are filled with electrons, the unfilled holes move opposite to the flow of the electrons. This concept of the movement of the holes is called the **hole theory** of current flow. The holes move in the direction opposite that of electron flow. See figure 3–3.

SUMMARY OF SEMICONDUCTORS

The following is a summary of semiconductor fundamentals:

1. There are two types of semiconductor materials: P-type and N-type. N-type material contains extra electrons, and P-type material contains holes due to missing electrons. The number of excess electrons in an N-type material must remain constant, and the number of holes in the P-type material must also remain constant. Because electrons are interchangeable, movement of electrons in or out of the material is possible to maintain a balanced material.

2. In P-type semiconductors, electrical conduction occurs mainly as a result of holes (absence of electrons). In N-type semiconductors, electrical conduction occurs mainly as a result of electrons (excess of electrons).

3. Hole movement results from the jumping of electrons into new positions.

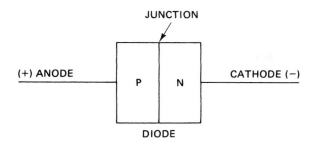

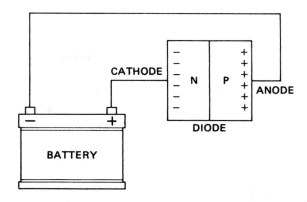

FIGURE 3–4   A diode is a component with P- and N-type material together. The negative electrode is called the cathode and the positive electrode is called the anode.

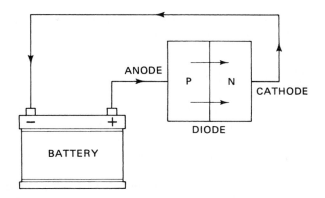

FIGURE 3–6   Diode connected with reversed polarity. No current flows across the junction between the P-type and N-type material. This connection is called reverse bias.

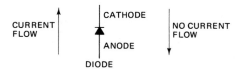

FIGURE 3–7   Diode symbol and electrode names.

FIGURE 3–5   Diode connected to a battery with correct polarity (+ to + and − to −). Current flows through the diode. This condition is called forward bias.

4. Under the effect of a voltage applied to the semiconductor, electrons travel toward the positive terminal and holes move toward the negative terminal. The direction of hole current agrees with the conventional direction of current flow.

DIODES

A **diode** is an electrical one-way check valve made by combining a P-type material and an N-type material. The point where the two types of materials join is called the **junction.** The word *diode* means having two electrodes. Electrodes are electrical connections. The positive electrode is called the **anode.** The negative electrode is called the **cathode.** See figure 3–4.

The N-type material has one extra electron that can flow into the P-type material, which has a need for electrons to fill its holes. If a battery were connected to the diode, positive to P-type material and negative to the N-type material, as illustrated in figure 3–5, the electrons that left the N-type material and flowed into the P-type material to fill the holes would be quickly replaced by

the electron flow from the battery. As a result, current would flow through the diode with low resistance. This condition is called **forward bias.**

If the battery connections were reversed and the positive side of the battery were connected to the N-type material, the electrons would be pulled toward the battery and away from the **junction** of the N- and P-type materials. (Remember, unlike charges attract, whereas like charges repel.) Because electrical conduction requires the flow of electrons through the junction of the N- and P-type materials and because the battery connections are actually reversed, the diode offers very high resistance to current flow. This condition is called **reverse bias.** See figure 3–6.

Therefore, diodes allow current flow only when current of the correct polarity is connected to the circuit. Diodes are used in alternators to control current flow in one direction. Diodes are also used in computer controls, air-conditioning circuits, and many other circuits to prevent possible damage due to reverse current flows that may be generated within the circuit. See figure 3–7.

ZENER DIODES

A **zener diode** is a specially constructed diode designed to operate with a reverse-bias current. Zener diodes were named in 1934 for their inventor, Clarence Melvin Zener, an American professor of physics. A zener diode acts as any diode in that it blocks reverse-bias current, but only up to a certain voltage. Above this certain voltage (called the **breakdown voltage** or **zener region**), a zener diode will conduct current without damage to the diode. A zener diode is heavily doped, and the reverse-bias voltage does not harm the material. The voltage drop across a zener diode remains practically the same before and after the breakdown voltage, and this factor makes a zener diode perfect for voltage regulation. Zener diodes can be constructed for various breakdown voltages and can be used in a variety of automotive and electronic applications, especially for electronic voltage regulators. See figure 3–8.

CLAMPING DIODES

Diodes can be used as a high-voltage clamping device when the power (+) is connected to the cathode (−) of the diode. If a coil is pulsed on and off, a high-voltage spike is produced whenever the coil is turned off. (See chapter 1 for an explanation of self-induction.) To control and direct this possibly damaging high-voltage spike, a diode can be installed across the leads to the coil to redirect the high-voltage spike back through the coil windings to prevent possible damage to the rest of the vehicle's electrical or electronic circuits. See figure 3–9.

Clamping diodes can also be called **despiking** or **suppression diodes**.

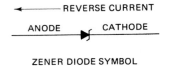

ZENER DIODE SYMBOL

FIGURE 3–8 A zener diode blocks current flow until a certain voltage is reached; then it permits current to flow.

Diodes were first used on AC compressor clutch coils in the early 1970s when electronic voltage regulators were first used. The diode was used to help prevent

◀ **TECH TIP** ▶

BURN IN TO BE SURE

A common term heard in the electronic and computer industry is **burn in.** To burn in means to operate an electronic device, such as a computer, for a period from several hours to several days.

Most electronic devices fail in infancy, or during the first few hours of operation. This early failure occurs if there is a manufacturing defect, especially at the P-N junction of any semiconductor device. The junction will usually fail after only a few operating cycles.

What does all of this information mean to the average person? If purchasing a personal or business computer, have the computer burned in before delivery. This step helps ensure that all of the circuits have survived infancy and that the chances of failure of a chip are greatly reduced. Display model sound or television equipment may be a good value, because during its operation as a display model, it has been burned in. The automotive service technician should be aware that if a replacement electronic device fails shortly after installation, the problem may be a case of early electronic failure.

NOTE: Whenever there is a failure of a replacement part, the technician should always check for excessive voltage or heat to and around the problem component.

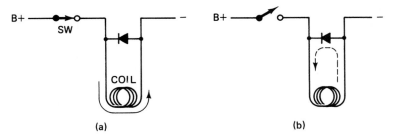

FIGURE 3–9 *(a)* Notice that when the coil is being energized, the diode is reverse biased and the current is blocked from passing through the diode. The current flows through the coil in the normal direction. *(b)* When the switch is opened, the magnetic field surrounding the coil collapses, producing a high-voltage surge in the reverse polarity of the applied voltage. This voltage surge forward biases the diode, and the surge is dissipated harmlessly back through the windings of the coil.

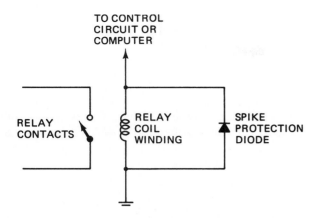

FIGURE 3–10 Spike protection diodes are commonly used in computer-controlled circuits to prevent damaging high-voltage surges that occur anytime current flowing through a coil is stopped.

damage to delicate electronic circuits anywhere in the vehicle's electrical system. See figure 3–10. Because most automotive circuits eventually are electrically connected to each other in parallel, a high-voltage surge anywhere in the vehicle could damage electronic components in other circuits.

NOTE: The circuits most likely to be affected by the high-voltage surge, if the diode fails, are the circuits controlling the operation of the AC compressor clutch and related circuits such as those of the blower motor and climate control units.

ZENER DIODE DESPIKING PROTECTION

Zener diodes can also be used to control high-voltage spikes and keep them from damaging delicate electronic circuits. Zener diodes are most commonly used in electronic fuel-injection circuits that control the firing of the injectors. If clamping diodes were used in parallel with the injection coil, the resulting clamping action would tend to delay the closing of the fuel-injector nozzle. A zener diode is commonly used to clamp only the higher-voltage portion of the resulting voltage spike without affecting the operation of the injector. See figure 3–11.

DESPIKING RESISTORS

All coils must use some protection against high-voltage spikes that occur when the voltage is removed from any coil. Instead of a diode installed in parallel with the coil

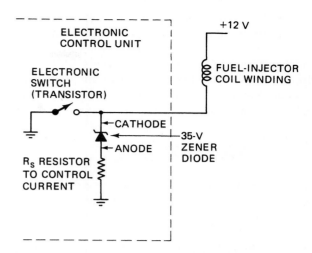

FIGURE 3–11 A zener diode is commonly used inside automotive computers to protect delicate electronic circuits from high-voltage spikes. A 35-volt zener diode will conduct any voltage spike resulting from the discharge of a coil safely to ground through a current-limiting resistor in series with the zener diode.

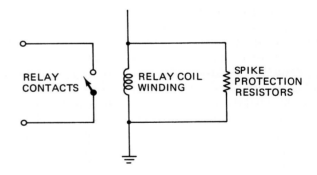

FIGURE 3–12 A despiking resistor is used in many automotive applications to help prevent harmful high-voltage surges from being created when the magnetic field surrounding a coil collapses when the coil circuit is opened.

windings, a resistor can be used. See figure 3–12. Resistors are often preferred for two reasons:

1. Coils will usually fail shorted rather than open. This shorted condition results in greater current flow in the circuit. A diode installed in the reverse-bias direction cannot control this extra current, whereas a resistor in parallel can help reduce potentially damaging current flow if the coil becomes shorted.
2. The protective diode can also fail, and diodes usually fail shorted before they blow open. If a diode becomes shorted, excessive current can flow through the coil circuit, perhaps causing damage. A

resistor usually fails open, and therefore, even in failure, could not in itself cause a problem.

Resistors on coils are often used in climate control circuit solenoids used to control vacuum to the various air management system doors as well as other electronically controlled applications.

DIODE RATINGS

Most diodes are rated according to their maximum current flow in the forward-bias direction and their resistance to high voltage in the reverse-bias direction. This rating of resistance to reverse-bias voltage is called the **peak inverse voltage** (PIV) rating; it is also known as the **peak reverse voltage** (PRV). Typical 1-ampere diodes use a code that indicates the PIV rating. For example:

1N 4001—50 V PIV

1N 4002—100 V PIV

1N 4003—200 V PIV

1N 4004—400 V PIV

1N 4005—600 V PIV

The third rating in the list (1N 4003—200 V PIV) is the one most commonly used for automotive applications.

The "1N" means that the diode has one P-N junction. A higher-rated diode can be used with no problems (except for slightly higher cost, even though the highest-rated diode generally costs less than one U.S. dollar). Never substitute a *lower*-rated diode than is specified.

The voltage drop across a diode is about the same voltage as that required to forward bias the diode. If the diode is made from germanium, the forward voltage is 0.3 to 0.5 volt. If the diode is made from silicon, the forward voltage is 0.5 to 0.7 volt.

LIGHT-EMITTING DIODES

All diodes radiate some energy during normal operation. Most diodes radiate heat because of the junction barrier voltage drop (typically 0.6 volt for silicon diodes). Light-emitting diodes (LEDs) radiate light when current flows through the diode in the forward-bias direction. See figure 3–13. The forward-bias voltage required for an LED ranges between 1.5 and 2.2 volts.

An LED will only light if the voltage at the anode (positive electrode) is at least 1.5 to 2.2 volts higher than the voltage at the cathode (negative electrode).

If an LED were connected across a 12-volt automotive battery, the LED would light brightly, but only for a

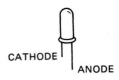

CATHODE ANODE

FIGURE 3–13 Typical LED. The longer of the two electrodes of an LED is the anode. Some LEDs use equal-length electrodes, and the determination of which to connect to which polarity must be made using an ohmmeter or the "diode check" position of a digital meter.

second or two. Excessive current (amperes) that flows across the P-N junction of any electronic device can destroy the junction. A resistor *must* be connected in series with every diode (including LEDs) to control current flow across the P-N junction. This protection should include the following:

1. The value of the resistor should be from 300 to 500 ohms for each P-N junction. Commonly available resistors in this range include 470-, 390-, and 330-ohm resistors.
2. The resistors can be connected to either the anode or the cathode end. (Polarity of the resistor does not matter.) Current flows through the LED in series with the resistor, and the resistor will control the current flow through the LED regardless of position in the circuit.
3. Resistors protecting diodes can be actual resistors or other current-limiting loads such as lamps or coils. Therefore, the symbol usually assigned to P-N junction protection is either R_S or R_L.

    R_S means *r*esistor in *s*eries with the P-N junction;

    R_L means *r*esistive *lo*ad protecting the P-N junction.

With the current-limiting devices to control the current, the average LED will require about 20 to 30 milliamperes (mA), or 0.020 to 0.030 amperes.

PHOTODIODES

All P-N junctions emit energy, and most in the form of heat or light such as with an LED. In fact, if an LED is exposed to bright light, a voltage potential is established between the anode and the cathode.

Photodiodes are specially constructed to respond to various wavelengths of light with a "window" built into the housing. See figure 3–14.

Photodiodes are frequently used in steering wheel controls. If several photodiodes are placed on the steer-

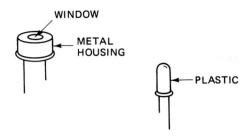

FIGURE 3–14 Typical photodiodes.

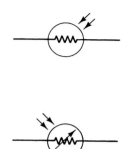

FIGURE 3–16 Either symbol may be used to represent a photoresistor.

FIGURE 3–15 Symbol for a photodiode. The arrows represent light striking the P-N junction of the photodiode.

ing column end and LEDs or photo transistors are placed on the steering wheel side, data can be transmitted between the two moving points without the interference that could be caused by physical-contact types of units.

A photodiode is a diode that is sensitive to light. When light energy strikes the diode, electrons are released and the diode will conduct in the forward-bias direction. (The light energy is used to overcome the barrier voltage.)

The resistance across the photodiode decreases as the intensity of the light increases. This characteristic makes the photodiode a useful electronic device for controlling some automotive lighting systems. The symbol for a photodiode is shown in figure 3–15.

PHOTORESISTORS

A **photoresistor** is a semiconductor material (usually cadmium sulfide) that changes resistance with the presence or absence of light.

DARK = high resistance

LIGHT = low resistance

Because resistance is reduced when the photoresistor is exposed to light, the photoresistor can be used to control headlight dimmer relays, plus many other nonautomotive applications. See figure 3–16 for the symbols for a photoresistor.

VARISTORS

Varistors are resistors whose resistance depends upon the level of voltage applied. A varistor, or metal oxide varistor (MOV), operates similarly to two back-to-back

zener diodes. Varistors offer high resistance at lower voltages yet become highly conductive at higher voltage levels. Varistors are therefore commonly found in computer circuits where they help prevent high-voltage transients from damaging delicate electronic circuits. If a high-voltage surge is applied to a varistor, the varistor becomes conductive, and it can be connected with another standard resistor to conduct the high voltage to ground.

SILICON-CONTROLLED RECTIFIERS

A **silicon-controlled rectifier** (SCR) is commonly used in the electronic circuits of various automotive applications.

An SCR is a semiconductor device that looks like two diodes connected end to end. See figure 3–17. If the anode is connected to a higher-voltage source than is the cathode in a circuit, current will not flow as would occur with a diode. If, however, a positive voltage source is connected to the **gate** of the SCR, then current can flow from anode to cathode with a typical voltage drop of 1.2 volts (double the voltage drop of a typical diode—0.6 volts).

If the voltage source at the gate is shut off, the current will still continue to flow through the SCR until the source current is stopped.

See figure 3–18 for a typical application in which SCRs can be used to construct a circuit for a **center high-mounted stoplight** (CHMSL). If this third stoplight were wired into either the left- or right-side brake light circuit, the CHMSL would also flash whenever the turn signals were used for the side that was connected to the CHMSL. When two SCRs are used, both brake lights must be activated to supply current to the CHMSL. The current to the CHMSL is shut off when both SCRs lose their power source (when the brake pedal is released, which stops the current flow to the brake lights).

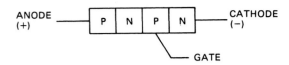

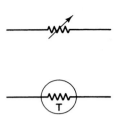

FIGURE 3–17 Symbol and terminal identification of an SCR.

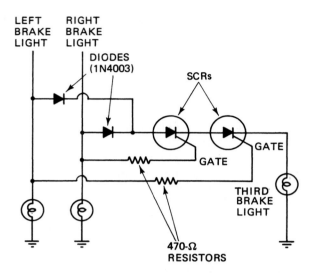

FIGURE 3–18 Wiring diagram for a CHMSL.

THERMISTORS

A **thermistor** is a semiconductor material such as silicon that has been doped to provide a given resistance. When the thermistor is heated, the electrons within the crystal gain energy and electrons are released. This means that a thermistor actually produces a small voltage when heated. If voltage is applied to a thermistor, its resistance decreases because the thermistor itself is acting as a current carrier rather than as a resistor at higher temperatures.

A thermistor is commonly used as a temperature-sensing device for coolant temperature and intake air temperature. Because thermistors operate in a manner opposite to that of a typical conductor, they are called **negative coefficient thermistors** (NCT); their resistance decreases as the temperature increases. Thermistor symbols are shown in figure 3–19.

RECTIFIER BRIDGES

The word *rectify* means to set straight; therefore, a **rectifier** is an electronic device (such as a diode) that is used to change a changing voltage into a straight or con-

FIGURE 3–19 Symbols used to represent a thermistor.

stant voltage. A rectifier bridge is a group of diodes that is used to change alternating current into direct current. A rectifier bridge is used in alternators to rectify the alternating current produced in the stator (stationary windings) of the alternator. These rectifier bridges contain six diodes—one pair of diodes for each of the three stator windings. See chapter 11 for further information and testing procedures.

PASSIVE AND ACTIVE CIRCUITS

Passive components or **circuits** are electrical devices that control or direct electrical signals, voltage, or current without adding power to the circuit. Examples of passive electronic components include resistors, diodes, and inductors (coils). When these components are used in simple circuits, the power output (watts) never exceeds the input power.

Active components or **circuits** are components or circuits that amplify the input power of the circuit. Examples of active components include transistors and other devices that can increase circuit power output such as a power supply.

TRANSISTORS

A **transistor** is a semiconductor device that can perform the following electrical functions:

1. Act as an electrical switch in a circuit
2. Act as an amplifier of current in a circuit
3. Regulate the current in a circuit

The word *transistor*, derived from the words *transfer* and *resistor*, is used to describe the transfer of current across a resistor.

A transistor is made of three alternating sections or layers of P- and N-type material. See figure 3–20. A transistor that has P-type material on each end, with N-type material in the center, is called a **PNP transistor.**

NPN TRANSISTOR   PNP TRANSISTOR

FIGURE 3–20

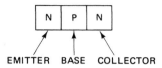

EMITTER BASE COLLECTOR

FIGURE 3–21

Another type, with an arrangement exactly opposite, is an **NPN transistor.**

The center section of a transistor is called the **base,** and it controls current flow through the transistor. See figure 3–21.

The material at one end of a transistor is called the **emitter,** and the material at the other end is called the **collector.** On all symbols for a transistor, there is an arrow indicating the emitter part of the transistor. The arrow points in the direction of current flow (conventional theory).

NOTE: When an arrowhead appears in any semiconductor symbol, it stands for a P-N junction and it points from the P-type material toward the N-type material. The arrow on a transistor is always attached to the emitter side of the transistor. See figure 3–22.

HOW A TRANSISTOR WORKS

A transistor is similar to two diodes back to back that can conduct current in only one way. As in a diode, N-type material can conduct electricity by means of its supply of free electrons, and P-type material conducts by means of its supply of positive holes.

A transistor will allow current flow if the electrical conditions allow it to switch on, in a manner similar to the working of an electromagnetic relay. The electrical conditions are determined, or switched by means of the base B. The base will carry current only when the proper voltage and polarity are applied. The main circuit current flow travels through the other two parts of the transistor: the emitter E and the collector C. See figure 3–23.

If the base current is turned off or on, the current flow from collector to emitter is turned off or on. The current controlling the base is called the **control cur-**

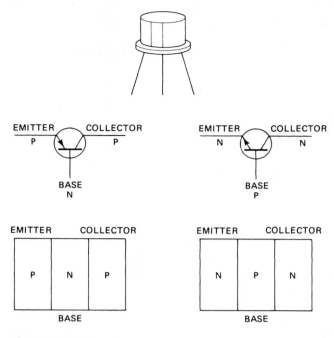

FIGURE 3–22

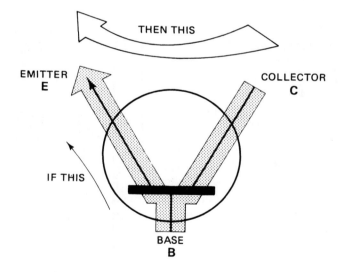

FIGURE 3–23 Basic transistor operation. A small current flowing through the base and emitter of the transistor turns on the transistor and permits a higher-amperage current to flow from the collector and the emitter.

rent. The control current must be high enough to switch the transistor on or off. (This control voltage, called the **threshold voltage,** must be above approximately 0.3 volt for germanium and 0.6 volt for silicon transistors.) This control current can also "throttle" or regulate the main circuit, in a manner similar to the operation of a water faucet.

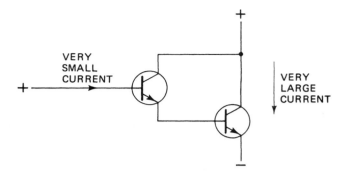

FIGURE 3–24 A Darlington pair consists of two transistors wired together, allowing a very small current to control a large current flow.

HOW A TRANSISTOR AMPLIFIES

A transistor can amplify a signal if the signal is strong enough to trigger the base of a transistor on and off. The resulting on-and-off current flow through the transistor can be connected to a higher-powered electrical circuit. This results in a higher-powered circuit being controlled by a lower-powered circuit. This low-powered circuit's cycling is exactly duplicated in the higher-powered circuit, and therefore any transistor can be used to amplify a signal. However, because some transistors are better than others for amplification, specialized types of transistors are used for each specialized circuit function.

DARLINGTON PAIRS

A **Darlington pair** consists of two transistors wired together. This arrangement permits a very small current flow to control a large current flow. The Darlington pair is named for Sidney Darlington, an American physicist for Bell Laboratories from 1929 to 1971. Darlington amplifier circuits are commonly used in electronic ignition systems, computer engine control circuits, and many other electronic applications. See figure 3–24.

TRANSISTOR GAIN

A transistor can do more than switch on and off when the base is triggered. Most transistors can also amplify. In an NPN transistor, for example, if the base voltage is higher than emitter voltage (by about 0.6 volts or more), current will flow from collector to emitter. However, as the current at the base increases, the current from the collector to the emitter also increases, up to a point called **saturation**. The ratio between base-to-emitter current and collector-to-emitter current is called the **gain** of the transistor and is represented by the capital second letter of the Greek alphabet, beta or β.

$$\text{GAIN } (\beta) = \frac{I_{CE}}{I_{BE}}$$

where

I_{CE} = Collector-emitter current (I)

I_{BE} = Base-emitter current (I)

For example, what is the **gain** of a transistor wherein the base-emitter current is 49 microamperes (μA) and the collector-emitter current is 7.4 milliamperes? The first step that should be done to solve this problem is to convert both amperage readings into decimal fractions of an ampere.

NOTE: This step is required here because the base-emitter current was expressed in microamperes and the collector-emitter current in milliamperes. They both have to be converted to the same unit; for best results, use a standard calculator.

Step #1 is to convert to decimal fractions of whole units:

$$I_{BE} = 49 \ \mu A = 0.000049 \text{ A}$$
$$I_{CE} = 7.4 \text{ mA} = 0.0074 \text{ A}$$

Step #2 is to substitute the whole-ampere figures into the equation for gain factor.

NOTE: Most transistors have a gain of between 100 and 200.

$$\beta = 0.0074/0.000049 = 151$$

In other words, the current flowing through the collector and emitter of a transistor can be 100 to 200 times the amount of current flowing through the base of the transistor.

NOTE: Not all transistors are used for amplifying. Each transistor is manufactured for a specific purpose.

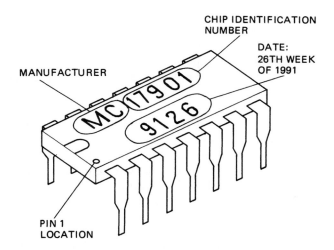

FIGURE 3–25 Typical dual inline package chip with identifying information explained.

SOLID-STATE, INTEGRATED-CIRCUIT, AND DUAL INLINE PACKAGE COMPONENTS

Solid-state is a term used to describe many electronic semiconductor components and/or circuits. They are called solid-state because they contain no movement, just higher or lower voltage levels within the circuit. **Discrete** (individual) **diodes,** transistors, and other semiconductor devices were often used to construct early electronic ignition and electronic voltage regulators. Newer-style electronic devices use the same components, but they are now combined (integrated) into one group of circuits. This is called an **integrated circuit** (IC).

Integrated circuits are usually encased in a plastic housing called a chip with two rows of inline pins called **dual inline pins** (DIP). See figure 3–25.

Therefore, most computer circuits are housed as an integrated circuit in a DIP chip.

HEAT SINK

Heat sink is a term used to describe any area around an electronic component that, because of its shape or design, can conduct damaging heat away from electronic parts. Examples of heat sinks include the following:

1. Ribbed electronic ignition control units
2. Cooling slits and cooling fan attached to an alternator
3. Special heat-conducting grease under the electronic ignition module in all General Motors high-energy ignition (HEI) systems

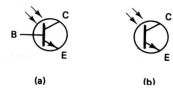

FIGURE 3–26 Symbols for a phototransistor. *(a)* uses the line for the base; *(b)* does not.

Heat sinks are necessary to prevent damage to diodes, transistors, and other electronic components due to heat. Excessive heat can damage the junction between the N- and P-type materials used in diodes and transistors.

WHAT CAUSES A TRANSISTOR OR DIODE TO BLOW

Every automotive diode and transistor is designed to operate within certain voltage and amperage ranges for each individual application. For example, transistors used for switching are designed and constructed differently from transistors used for amplifying signals.

Because each electronic component is designed to operate satisfactorily for its particular application, any severe change in operating current (amperes), voltage, or heat can destroy the junction. This failure can cause either an open circuit (no current flows) or a short (current flows through the component all the time when the component should be blocking the current flow).

PHOTOTRANSISTORS

Similar in operation to a photodiode, a **phototransistor** uses light energy to turn on the base of a transistor. A phototransistor is an NPN transistor that has a large exposed base area to permit light to act as the control for the transistor. Therefore, a phototransistor may or may not have a base lead. Many phototransistors do not have a base lead; they have only a collector and emitter lead. When the phototransistor is connected to a powered circuit, the light intensity is amplified by the gain of the transistor. Phototransistors are frequently used in steering wheel controls. Figure 3–26 shows phototransistor symbols.

SOLAR CELLS

Solar cells are another type of semiconductor device. In a solar cell, light energy is used to produce a small current flow by dislodging electrons within the structure.

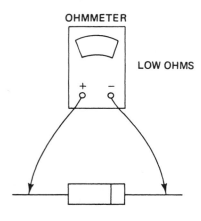

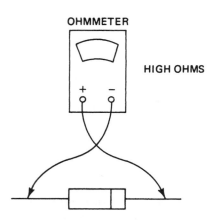

FIGURE 3–27   Checking a diode using an ohmmeter. A good diode should measure four ohms connecting the leads as shown on the top and low ohms when the meter leads are reversed as shown at the bottom.

Solar cells are stacked and/or grouped in large sections to enable them to supply useful amounts of current.

HOW TO TEST DIODES AND TRANSISTORS

Diodes and transistors can be tested with an ohmmeter. The diode or transistor being tested should be disconnected from the circuit for best results. Use an ohmmeter and set it to low ohms, or use the diode-check on a digital multimeter. See figure 3–27.

Diodes. A good diode should give a high-ohm reading with the test leads attached to each lead of the diode in one way, and a low-ohm reading when the leads are reversed.

1. A low-ohm reading with the ohmmeter leads attached both ways across a diode means that the diode is *shorted* and must be replaced.
2. A high-ohm reading with the ohmmeter leads attached both ways across a diode means that the diode is *open* and must be replaced.

Transistors. A good transistor should show continuity between the emitter (E) and the base (B) and between the base (B) and the collector (C) with an ohmmeter connected one way, and high ohms when the ohmmeter test leads are reversed. There should be a high ohmmeter reading (no continuity) in both directions when a transistor is tested between the emitter (E) and the collector (C). See figures 3–28 through 3–30. A transistor tester can also be used if available.

TRANSISTOR GATES

An understanding of the basic operation of electronic gates is key to the understanding of computers. A **gate** is an electronic circuit whose output depends on the location and voltage of two inputs. Whether a transistor is on or off depends on the voltage at the base of the transistor. If the voltage is at least 0.6 volt different from that of the emitter, the transistor is turned on. Most electronic and computer circuits use 5 volts as a power source. If two transistors are wired together, several different outputs can be received depending on how the two transistors are wired. See figure 3–31.

If the voltage at A is higher than that of the emitter, the top transistor is turned on. But the bottom transistor is off unless the voltage at B is also higher. If both transistors are turned on, the output signal voltage will be high. If only one of the two transistors is on, the output will be zero (off or no voltage). Because it requires both A and B to be on to result in a voltage output, this circuit is called an **AND gate.** In other words, both transistors have to be on before the gate opens and allows a voltage output. Other types of gates can be constructed using various connections to the two transistors. For example:

AND gate—requires both transistors to be on to get an output

OR gate—requires either transistor to be on to get an output

NAND (NOT-AND) gate—output is on unless both transistors are on

NOR (NOT-OR) gate—the only time when the output is on is when both transistors are off

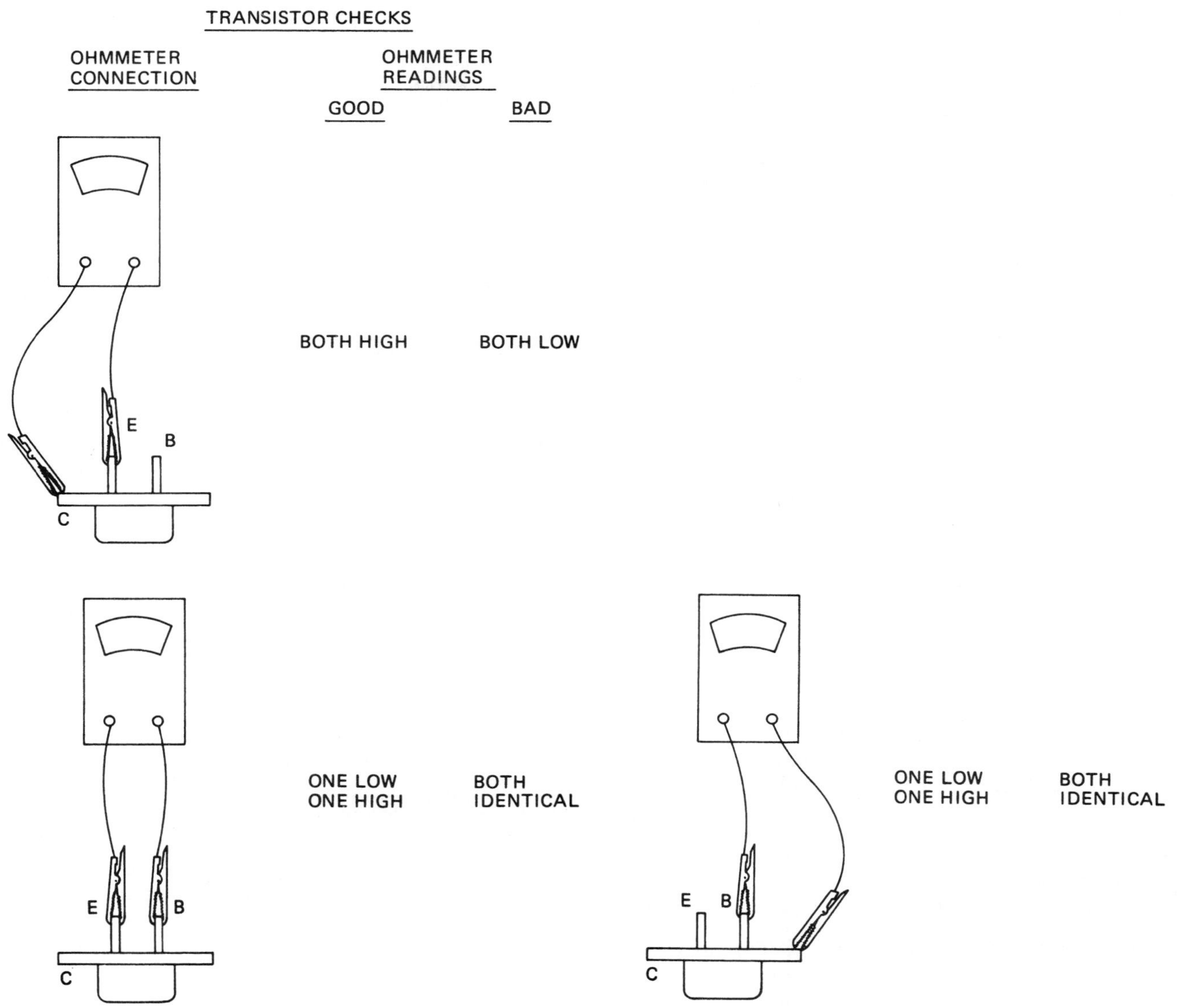

TRANSISTOR CHECKS

OHMMETER CONNECTION	OHMMETER READINGS	
	GOOD	BAD
	BOTH HIGH	BOTH LOW
	ONE LOW ONE HIGH	BOTH IDENTICAL
	ONE LOW ONE HIGH	BOTH IDENTICAL

E   B

C

E   B

C

E   B

C

FIGURE 3–28   Testing a transistor using an ohmmeter.

Gates represent logic circuits that can be constructed so that the output depends on the voltage (on or off; high or low) of the inputs to the bases of transistors. Their inputs can come from sensors or other circuits that monitor sensors, and their outputs can be used to operate an output device if amplified and controlled by other circuits.

PNP   NPN

FIGURE 3–29   PNP and NPN transistor look alike if you are not familiar with small, detailed manufacturers' markings. The best way to determine which type of transistor you have is to test it.

LOGIC HIGHS AND LOWS

All computer circuits and most electronic circuits (such as gates) use various combinations of high and low voltages. High voltages are typically those above 5 volts,

FIGURE 3–30 If the red (positive) lead of the ohmmeter (a multimeter set to diode-check) is touched to the center and the black (negative) lead touched to either end electrode, the meter should forward bias the P-N junction and this should be indicated on the meter as low resistance. If the meter reads high resistance, reverse the meter leads, putting the black on the center lead and the red on either end lead. If the meter indicates low resistance, the transistor is a good PNP type. Check all P-N junctions in the same way.

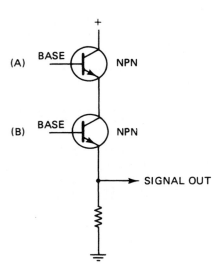

FIGURE 3–31 Typical transistor AND-gate circuit. Notice that both transistors must be turned on before there will be voltage present at the point labeled "signal out."

and low is generally considered zero (ground). However, high voltages do not *have* to begin at 5 volts. **High, or the number 1, to a computer is the presence of voltage above a certain level.** For example, a circuit could be constructed wherein any voltage higher than 3.8 volts would be considered high. **Low, or the number 0, to a computer is the absence of voltage or a voltage lower than a certain value.** For example, a voltage of 0.62 may be considered low. Various associated names and terms can be summarized as follows:

Logic low = low voltage = number zero (0) = reference low

Logic high = higher voltage = number 1 = reference high

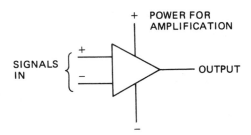

FIGURE 3–32 Symbol for an operational amplifier (op-amp).

TRANSISTOR-TRANSISTOR LOGIC

Transistor-transistor logic (TTL) uses 5 volts as a reference, with high being slightly less than 5 volts and low being slightly above 0 volts. Most automotive (and other) computers use a 5-volt reference because of the original TTL usage. TTL is most often incorporated into a single integrated circuit or chip. TTL chips consume more electrical power, and therefore generate more heat, than newer ICs using **complementary metal oxide semiconductor** (CMOS) technology. CMOS chips consume less current, but they are more sensitive to static electricity, or **electrostatic discharge** (ESD), than are typical TTL circuits.

OPERATIONAL AMPLIFIERS

Operational amplifiers are frequently referred to simply as **op-amps**. Op-amps are used in circuits to control and amplify digital signals. Op-amps are frequently used as motor control for climate control (heating and air conditioning air flow control) door operation. Op-amps can provide the proper voltage polarity and current (amperes) to control the direction of permanent magnetic (PM) motors. The symbol for an op-amp is shown in figure 3–32.

POLARITY

Polarity, in electrical terms, means positive or negative electrical potential of a wire, component, or circuit.

Polarity usually indicates which terminal of a battery (or other power supply) should be connected to which terminal of a component.

For example, resistors do not require a particular polarity to function. Either end of a resistor can be positive or negative. However, diodes, transistors, some types of capacitors, and most other electronic components must have the proper polarity (positive or negative) connected to function correctly.

ELECTRONIC COMPONENT FAILURE CAUSES

Electronic components, such as electronic ignition modules, electronic voltage regulators, on-board computers, and any other electronic circuit, are generally very reliable; however, failure can occur. Some frequent causes of premature failure include the following.

Poor Connections. It has been estimated that most engine computers returned as defective have simply had poor connections at the wiring harness terminal ends. These faults are often intermittent and hard to find.

HINT: When cleaning electronic contacts, use a pencil eraser. This cleans the contacts without harming the thin protective coating used on most electronic terminals.

Heat. The operation and resistance of electronic components and circuits are affected by heat. Electronic components should be kept as cool as possible and never hotter than 260° F (127° C).

Voltage Spikes. A high-voltage spike can literally burn a hole through semiconductor material. The source of these high-voltage spikes is often the discharge of a coil without proper (or with defective) despiking protection.

A poor electrical connection at the battery or other major electrical connection can cause high-voltage spikes to occur because the *entire wiring harness creates its own magnetic field* similar to that formed around a coil. If the connection is loose and momentary loss of contact occurs, a high-voltage surge can occur through the entire electrical system.

To help prevent this type of damage, make certain that all electrical connections, including grounds, are properly clean and tight.

Excessive Current. All electronic circuits are designed to operate within a designated range of current (amperes). If a solenoid or relay is controlled by a computer circuit, the resistance of that solenoid or relay becomes a part of that control circuit. If a coil winding inside the solenoid or relay becomes shorted, the resulting lower resistance will increase the current through the circuit. Even though individual components are used with current-limiting resistors in series, the coil winding resistance is also used as a current control component in the circuit. If a computer fails, always measure the resistance across all computer-controlled relays and solenoids. The resistance should be within specifications (generally *over* 20 ohms) for each component that is computer controlled.

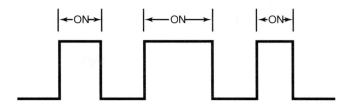

FIGURE 3–33   The length of "on time" is called the pulse width.

NOTE: Some computer-controlled solenoids are pulsed on and off rapidly. This type of solenoid is used in many electronically shifted transmissions. Their resistance is usually about one-half of the resistance of a simple on-off solenoid—usually between 10 and 15 ohms. Because the computer controls the "on time" of the solenoid, the solenoid and its circuit control are called **pulse-width modulated (PWM)**. See figure 3–33.

ELECTROSTATIC DISCHARGE

Static charges can build up on the human body whenever we move. The friction of the clothing and the movement of shoes against carpet or vinyl floors cause a high voltage to build. Then when we touch a conductive material, such as a doorknob, the static charge is rapidly discharged. These charges, although just slightly painful to us, can cause severe damage to delicate electronic components. The following are typical static voltages:

If you can feel it, it is at least 3000 volts.

If you can hear it, it is at least 5000 volts.

If you can see it, it is at least 10,000 volts.

Although these voltages seem high, the current, in amperes, is extremely low. However, sensitive electronic components such as vehicle computers, radios, and instrument panel clusters can be ruined if exposed to as little as 30 volts. This is a problem, because harm can occur to components at voltages lower than we can feel. To help prevent damage to components, follow these easy steps:

1. Keep the replacement electronic component in the protective wrapping until just before installation.
2. Before handling any electronic component, ground yourself to a good conductor to drain away any static charge.
3. Do not touch the terminals of electronic components.

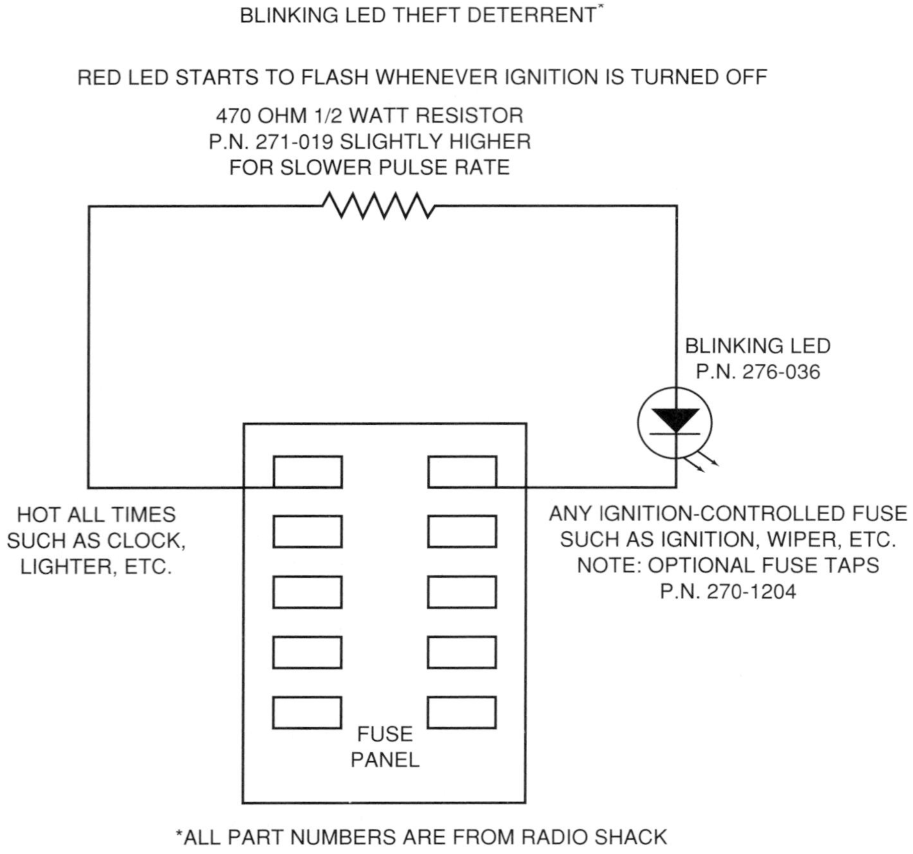

BLINKING LED THEFT DETERRENT*

RED LED STARTS TO FLASH WHENEVER IGNITION IS TURNED OFF

470 OHM 1/2 WATT RESISTOR
P.N. 271-019 SLIGHTLY HIGHER
FOR SLOWER PULSE RATE

BLINKING LED
P.N. 276-036

HOT ALL TIMES
SUCH AS CLOCK,
LIGHTER, ETC.

ANY IGNITION-CONTROLLED FUSE
SUCH AS IGNITION, WIPER, ETC.
NOTE: OPTIONAL FUSE TAPS
P.N. 270-1204

FUSE
PANEL

*ALL PART NUMBERS ARE FROM RADIO SHACK

FIGURE 3–34 Schematic for a blinking LED theft deterrent.

If these precautions are observed, ESD damage can be eliminated or reduced. Remember, just because the component works after being touched does not mean that damage has not occurred. Often, a section of the electronic component may be damaged, yet will not fail until several days or weeks later.

SUMMARY

1. Semiconductors are constructed by doping semiconductor materials such as silicon.
2. N-type and P-type materials can be combined to form diodes, transistors, SCRs, and computer chips.
3. Diodes can be used to direct and control current flow in circuits and to provide despiking protection.
4. Transistors are electronic relays that can also amplify.
5. All semiconductors can be damaged if subjected to excessive voltage, current, or heat.
6. Never touch the terminals of a computer or electronic device; static electricity can damage electronic components.

◀ **TECH TIP** ▶

BLINKING LED THEFT DETERRENT

A blinking (flashing) LED consumes only about 5 milliamperes (5/1000 of one ampere or 0.005 A). Most alarm systems use a blinking red LED to indicate that the system is armed. A fake alarm indicator is easy to make and install.

A 470-ohm, 1/2-watt resistor limits current flow to prevent battery drain. The positive terminal (anode) of the diode is connected to a fuse that is hot at all times, such as the cigarette lighter. The negative terminal (cathode) of the LED is connected to any ignition-controlled fuse. See figure 3–34.

When the ignition is turned off, the power flows through the LED to ground and the LED flashes. To prevent distraction during driving, the LED goes out whenever the ignition is on. Therefore, this fake theft deterrent is "auto setting" and no other action is required to activate it when you leave your vehicle except to turn off the ignition and remove the key as usual.

REVIEW QUESTIONS

1. Explain the difference between P-type material and N-type material.

2. Describe how a diode can be used to suppress high-voltage surges in automotive components or circuits containing a coil.

3. Explain how a transistor works.

4. List the precautions that all service technicians should adhere to in order to avoid damage to electronic and computer circuits.

MULTIPLE-CHOICE QUESTIONS

1. A semiconductor is a material _____ .
   a. With fewer than four electrons in the outer orbit of its atoms
   b. With more than four electrons in the outer orbit of its atoms
   c. With exactly four electrons in the outer orbit of its atoms
   d. Determined by other factors besides the number of electrons

2. The arrow in a symbol for a semiconductor device_____ .
   a. Points toward the negative
   b. Points away from the negative
   c. Is attached to the emitter
   d. Both a and c

3. To forward bias a silicon diode _____ .
   a. The voltage at the anode must exceed the voltage at the cathode by 0.5 to 0.7 volts.
   b. The voltage at the cathode must exceed the voltage at the anode by 0.3 to 0.5 volts.
   c. The voltage at the anode must exceed the voltage at the cathode by 0.3 to 0.5 volts.
   d. The anode must be connected to a resistor (300 to 500 ohms) and 12.0 volts with the cathode also connected to 12.0 volts.

4. A transistor is controlled by the polarity and current at _____ .
   a. The collector
   b. The emitter
   c. The base
   d. Both the collector and the emitter

5. A transistor can _____ .
   a. Switch on and off
   b. Amplify
   c. Throttle
   d. All of the above

6. Clamping diodes _____ .
   a. Are connected into a circuit with the positive voltage source to the cathode and the negative voltage to the anode
   b. Are also called despiking diodes
   c. Can suppress transient voltages
   d. All of the above

7. A zener diode is normally used for voltage regulation. A zener diode, however, can also be used for high-voltage spike protection if connected _____ .
   a. Positive to anode, negative to cathode
   b. Positive to cathode, ground to anode
   c. Negative to anode, cathode to a resistor and then to a lower-voltage terminal
   d. Both a and c

8. The forward-bias voltage required for an LED is _____ .
   a. 0.3 to 0.5 volt
   b. 0.5 to 0.7 volt
   c. 1.5 to 2.2 volts
   d. 4.5 to 5.1 volts

9. A good NPN transistor should test low resistance (low voltage drop) between the _____ and _____ .and high resistance (over-limit voltage drop) between the _____ and _____ .
   a. Base; emitter; emitter; collector
   b. Emitter; collector; gate; trigger
   c. Trigger; base; collector; gate
   d. Collector; base; emitter; base

10. Another name for a computer ground is _____ .
    a. Logic low
    b. Zero
    c. Reference low
    d. All of the above

◀ **Chapter 4** ▶

ELECTRICAL AND ELECTRONIC TEST EQUIPMENT

OBJECTIVES

After studying chapter 4, the reader will be able to

1. Explain how to connect and read a voltmeter, ohmmeter, and ammeter.
2. Describe how to use a test light and logic probe.
3. List the various scales used on digital multimeters.
4. Discuss the need to use high-impedance test equipment with computer circuits.

The proper use and reading of electrical and electronic test equipment is very important to the service technician. Trying to determine exactly what the meter reads is sometimes confusing. This chapter is full of examples to make meter usage easy.

TEST INSTRUMENTS

There are two basic types of test meters: **digital,** which display numbers, and **analog,** which use a needle to indicate readings. Analog or needle meters all basically consist of a d'Arsonval movement, a fine wire-wound coil mounted on bearings within a permanent magnetic field. The basic analog meter construction and operation is shown in figure 4–1. Digital meters are electronic but must be hooked up in the same way as the analog type.

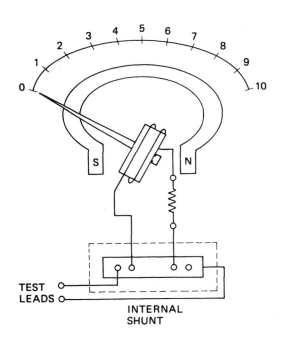

FIGURE 4–1 Basic ammeter.

DMM stands for **digital multimeter** and *DVOM* stands for **digital volt-ohm-milliammeter.** These are abbreviations commonly used for electronic high-impedance test meters. High-impedance meters, required for use on computer circuit measurements, are digital

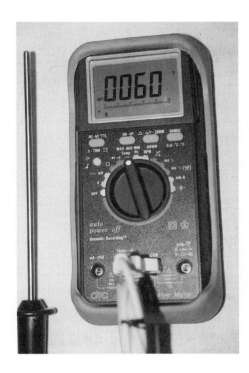

FIGURE 4–2 Typical digital meter with temperature probe. The temperature probe plugs into the meter and the temperature is displayed on the meter face.

meters. However, not all digital meters have the required 10 megohms (MΩ) (10 million ohms) of internal resistance. Analog (needle-type) meters are almost always lower than 10 megohms and should *not* be used to measure any computer circuit. A high-impedance meter can be used to measure any automotive circuit within the ranges of the meter. Therefore, a technician would be wise to purchase a high-impedance meter that can be safely used on all automotive systems rather than save some money and purchase a less expensive analog multi-tester that cannot be used to measure any computer-related circuits. Most digital meters can also measure temperature, using a temperature probe as shown in figure 4–2.

AMMETERS

An **ammeter** measures the flow of current through a complete circuit in units of amperes. The ammeter has to be installed in the circuit (in series) so that it can measure all of the current flow in that circuit, just as a water flow meter would measure the amount of water flow (in cubic feet per minute, for example). An ammeter contains a **shunt,** a device that allows heavy current to flow through the meter without harming the meter.

FIGURE 4–3 A Sun VAT-40 (volt amp tester, model 40) is an example of an analog voltmeter and ammeter.

CAUTION: An ammeter must be installed in the circuit to measure the current flow in the circuit. If a meter set to read amperes is connected in parallel, such as across a battery, the meter or the leads may be destroyed by the current available across the battery.

In an analog (needle-type) meter, the greater the current flow, the stronger the electromagnet on the needle becomes and the more the needle is attracted toward the right side of the meter (higher reading). The north pole of the needle is attracted toward the south pole of the meter. See figure 4–3.

Digital meters require that the meter leads be moved to the ammeter terminals. Most digital meters have an ampere scale that can accommodate a maximum of 10 amperes. See the tech tip Fuse Your Meter Leads.

VOLTMETERS

A **voltmeter** measures the pressure or potential of electricity and measures in units of volts. A voltmeter is connected to a circuit in parallel. All voltmeters have a large built-in resistance so that the current flow through the meter will not affect the circuit being tested or the meter. Most digital meters have an internal resistance of 10 million ohms or more on the voltmeter scale only. This is called the **impedance** of the meter and represents the total internal resistance of the meter circuit due to internal coils, capacitors, and resistors. A typical analog voltmeter has only about 12,000 ohms of internal resistance. Although this may sound like a lot of resistance, it is too low for electronic and computer circuit measurement. When a voltmeter is connected to measure

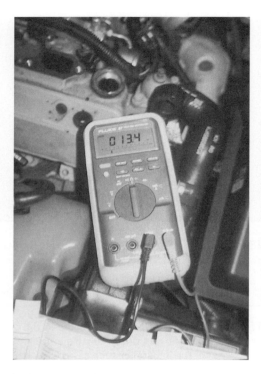

FIGURE 4–4 Typical digital multimeter (DMM) set to read DC volts.

FIGURE 4–5 Student using a digital voltmeter to check voltage at various points at a breakout box (BOB) while testing an antilock brake problem. A breakout box plugs into the wiring harness at the controller for the antilock brake system (ABS). A manual is used to determine what voltage or resistance should occur at which terminal.

voltage, the meter itself becomes a part of the circuit. This is the reason that vehicle manufacturers specify that a high-impedance digital meter be used. The high internal resistance has little effect on the circuit or component being measured. See figures 4–4 and 4–5.

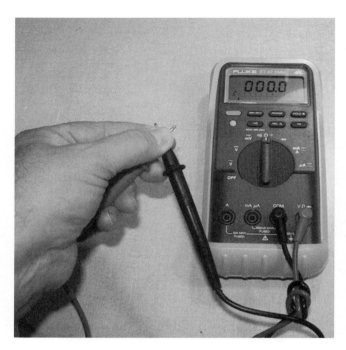

FIGURE 4–6 A digital ohmmeter with both leads shorted. The reading should be zero ohms.

OHMMETERS

An ohmmeter measures the resistance in ohms of a component or circuit section when no current is flowing through the circuit. An ohmmeter contains a battery (or other power source). When the leads are connected to a component, current flows through the test leads and actually measures the difference in voltage (voltage drop) between the leads, which the meter registers as resistance on its scale. Zero ohms means no resistance between the test leads. This indicates that there is continuity or a continuous path for the current to flow in a closed circuit. Infinity means no connection, as in an open circuit.

With a closed circuit (low ohms), maximum current from the built-in battery causes a low reading, whereas an open circuit prevents any current from flowing. Different meters have different ways of indicating infinity resistance, or a reading higher than the scale allows. For example, most meters read "OL" meaning "over limit," whereas others may show a number 1 or 3 on the left side of the display. See figures 4–6 through 4–8. See figure 4–9 for a summary of meter hookup. To summarize open and zero readings, remember:

$0.00 \ \Omega$ means zero resistance

OL means an open circuit (no current flows)

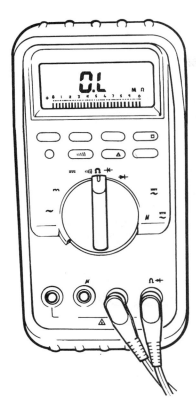

FIGURE 4–7 Typical digital multimeter showing "OL" (over limit) on the readout with the ohms (Ω) unit selected. This usually means that the unit being measured is open (infinity resistance) and has no continuity.

THE MEANING OF INPUT IMPEDANCE

Input impedance is a term used to describe the internal resistance of a test instrument. The term covers more than just the resistance of the tester; it includes all inductances (coils) and capacitance (condensers or capacitors) inside the tester that oppose current flow through the test instruments. Impedance is measured in ohms, the same as resistance. An older style of needle-type voltmeter may have only 1000 ohms of impedance. This means that when the meter is connected to a circuit to measure its voltage, the meter itself becomes another conductor (resistance) connected to the circuit in parallel.

A good-quality digital meter should have more than 10 million (10,000,000) ohms of internal impedance.

NOTE: The input impedance of any meter can be measured by using another meter and measuring the resistance on the voltmeter scale.

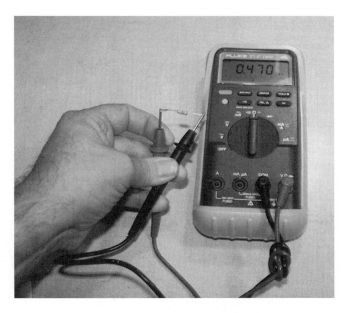

FIGURE 4–8 Ohmmeter measuring a 470-ohm resistor.

Remember, the resistance of any meter is only effective when the meter is set on the *voltmeter* scales. When a technician uses the ohmmeter scales, the meter is applying a voltage to the component being tested through its test leads. When a technician uses the ammeter scales, current can flow freely through the meter. This is the major reason why most automobile manufacturers recommend testing *voltage* at selected points instead of resistance or current.

ELECTRICAL UNIT PREFIXES

Electrical units are measured in numbers such as 12 volts, 150 amperes, and 470 ohms. Large units more than a 1000 may be expressed in kilo units. *Kilo* means 1000.

$$1100 \text{ volts} = 1.1 \text{ kilovolts (kV)}$$

$$4700 \text{ ohms} = 4.7 \text{ kiloohms (k}\Omega)$$

If the value is more than 1 million (1,000,000), then the prefix *mega* (M) is often used. For example,

$$1,100,000 \text{ volts} = 1.1 \text{ megavolts (MV)}$$

$$4,700,000 \text{ ohms} = 4.7 \text{ megaohms (M}\Omega)$$

Sometimes a circuit conducts so little current that a smaller unit of measure is required. Small units of measure of 1/1000 are called **milli** (m).

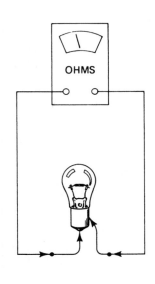

AMMETER	VOLTMETER	OHMMETER
1. Connected in series IN a circuit according to polarity.	1. Connected in parallel to a circuit or part of a circuit according to polarity.	1. Has its own supply of power.
2. Measures current flow.	2. Measures voltage drop: This is the difference between voltage at its two leads.	2. USED ONLY WHEN UNIT IS DISCONNECTED from its original circuit.
3. Used in a closed circuit.	3. Used in a closed circuit.	3. Measures resistance directly on meter.
		4. Low ohms means continunity.
		5. Infinity reading means open circuit.

ALWAYS USE A LARGE ENOUGH AMMETER AND VOLTMETER

FIGURE 4–9 Summary of test meter hookup.

The micro is represented by the Greek letter mu (μ). One microampere is one millionth (1/1,000,000). To summarize:

Mega (M) = 1,000,000 (decimal point 6 places to the right = 1 $\underset{123456}{000000}$)

Kilo (K) = 1000 (decimal point 3 places to the right = 1 $\underset{123}{000}$)

Milli (m) = 1/1000 (decimal point 3 places to the left = 0. $\underset{321}{001}$)

Micro (μ) = 1/1,000,000 (decimal point 6 places to the left = 0. $\underset{654321}{000001}$)

HINT: Lowercase m equals a small unit, milli, whereas a capital M represents a large unit (mega).

These prefixes can be confusing because most digital meters can express values in more than one prefix, especially if the meter is auto ranging. For example, an ammeter reading may show 36.7 mA on auto ranging. When the scale is changed to amperes (A in the window of the display), the number displayed will be 0.037 A. Note that the resolution of the value is reduced.

HINT: Always check the face of the meter display for the unit being measured. To best understand what is being displayed on the face of a digital meter, select a manual scale and move the selector until *whole units appear,* such as A for amperes instead of mA for milliamperes.

◄ TECH TIP ►

FUSE YOUR METER LEADS

Most digital meters include an ammeter capability. When a technician reads amperes, the leads of the meter must be changed from volts or ohms (V or Ω) to amperes (A) or milliamperes (mA) or microamperes (μA).

A common problem may then occur the next time that voltage is measured. Although the technician may switch the selector to read volts, often the leads are not switched back to the volt or ohm position. Because the ammeter lead position results in zero ohms of resistance to current flow through the meter, the meter or the fuse inside the meter will be destroyed if the meter is connected to a battery. Many meter fuses are expensive and difficult to find.

To solve this problem, simply solder an inline blade fuse holder into one meter lead. See figures 4–10 and 4–11. Do not think that this fuse is necessary just for beginners. Experienced technicians often get in a hurry and forget to switch the lead. A blade fuse is faster, easier, and less expensive to replace than a meter fuse or the meter itself. Also, if the soldering is done properly, the addition of an inline fuse holder and fuse does not increase the resistance of the meter leads. All meter leads have some resistance. If the meter is measuring very low resistance, simply touch the two leads together and read the resistance (usually just a couple of tenths of an ohm). Simply subtract the resistance of the leads from the resistance of the component being measured.

HOW TO READ DIGITAL METERS

Getting to know and use a digital meter takes time and practice. The first step is to read, understand, and follow all safety and operational instructions that come with the meter. The use of the meter usually involves the following steps.

Step #1. Select the proper unit of electricity for what is being measured: volts, ohms (resistance), or amperes (amount of current flow). If the meter is not auto ranging, select the proper scale for the anticipated reading. For example, if a 12-volt battery is being measured, select a meter reading range that is higher than

FIGURE 4–10 Note the blade-type fuse holder soldered in series with one of the meter leads. A 10-ampere fuse helps protect the internal meter fuse (if equipped) and the meter itself from damage that might result from excessive current flow if accidentally used incorrectly.

FIGURE 4–11 Tie a knot in the test leads near the meter to help prevent the leads from becoming tangled.

the voltage but not too high. A 20- or 30-volt range will accurately show the voltage of a 12-volt battery. If a 1000-volt scale is selected, a 12-volt reading may not be accurate.

Step #2. Place the meter leads into the proper input terminals.

1. The black lead usually is inserted into the common (com) terminal. This meter lead usually stays in this location for *all* meter functions.
2. The red lead is inserted into the volt, ohm, or diode check terminal, usually labeled "V Ω," when voltage, resistance, or diodes are being measured.
3. When current flow in amperes is being measured, most digital meters require that the red test lead be inserted in the ammeter terminal, usually labeled "A" or "mA."

CAUTION: If the meter leads are inserted into the ammeter terminals, even though the selector is set to volts, the meter may be damaged or an internal fuse may blow if the test leads touch both terminals of a battery. See the tech tip about installing an inline fuse in the meter lead.

Step #3. Measure the component being tested. Carefully note the decimal point and the unit on the face of the meter.

- *Correct scale.* A 12-volt battery is measured with a low-voltage scale.
- *Incorrect scale.* A 12-volt battery is measured with a high-voltage scale selected. Use of the incorrect scale results in a reading of 0.012.

Correct Scale	*Incorrect Scale*
12-volt battery	12-volt battery
12.0	.012
set on low voltage scale	set on high voltage scale

If a 12-volt battery is measured with an auto-ranging meter, the correct reading of 12.0 is given. Note that "Auto" and "V" should be showing on the face of the meter.

Step #4. Interpret the reading. This is especially difficult on auto-ranging meters, where the meter itself selects the proper scale.

- *Example #1.* A voltage drop is being measured. The specifications indicate a maximum voltage

◄ **TECH TIP** ►

ANALOG METERS ARE NOT DEAD

When computers became standard equipment on most vehicles during the early 1980s, service technicians were instructed to use only digital test meters for testing.

Although digital multitesters must be used in most diagnoses, the old analog meters can be very useful in the following cases:

1. *Analog dwell meter.* For General Motors computerized carburetion systems (Computer Command Control or CCC), the blue wire with the green connector can be used to monitor the activity of the mixture control solenoid in the carburetor.
2. *Analog voltmeter.* Can be used for retrieving Ford trouble code information when connected to the underhood diagnostic connector.
3. *Analog ohmmeter.* An analog ohmmeter has a higher output through the test leads than does a high-impedance digital meter. This permits most analog ohmmeters to forward bias diodes and check units such as the General Motors torque converter clutch solenoid with accuracy. Digital meters cannot be used because the diode in the circuit gives unclear results. See figures 4–12 and 4–13 for details.

drop of 0.2 volt. The meter reads "AUTO" and "43.6 mV."

This reading means that the voltage drop is 0.0436 volts, or 43.6 millivolts (mV), which is far lower than 0.2 volt (200 millivolts). Because the number showing on the meter face is much larger than the specifications, many beginning technicians are led to believe that the voltage drop is excessive.

HINT: Pay attention to the units displayed on the meter face and convert to whole units.

- *Example #2.* A spark plug wire is being measured. The reading should be less than 10,000 ohms for each foot in length if the wire is okay. The wire being tested is 3 feet long (maximum al-

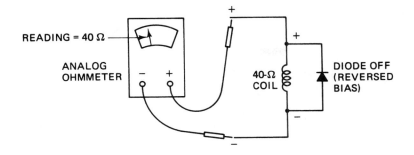

READING = 40 Ω

ANALOG OHMMETER

40-Ω COIL

DIODE OFF (REVERSED BIAS)

FIGURE 4–12 An analog (needle-type) ohmmeter should be used to test solenoids that also have diodes connected across the windings for high-voltage spike protection. The true resistance (40 ohms) of the coil is read when the test leads are connected as illustrated.

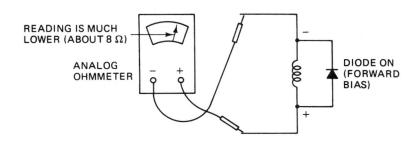

READING IS MUCH LOWER (ABOUT 8 Ω)

ANALOG OHMMETER

DIODE ON (FORWARD BIAS)

FIGURE 4–13 When the test leads are reversed from the terminals illustrated in figure 4–12, the diode becomes forward biased and conducts. The resulting parallel circuit splits the current flow from the meter, and the effective resistance (as read by the meter) is greatly reduced.

lowable resistance is 30,000 ohms). The meter reads "AUTO" and "14.85 KΩ." This reading is equivalent to 14,850 ohms.

HINT: When converting from K ohms to ohms, make the decimal point a comma.

Because this reading is well below the specified maximum allowable, the spark plug wire is okay.

TEST LIGHTS

A test light is simply a light bulb with two wires attached. See figure 4–14. It is used to test for low-voltage (6- to 12-volt) current. Battery voltage cannot be seen or felt and can be detected only with test equipment. See figures 4–15 and 4–16.

A test light can be purchased or homemade. A purchased test light could be labeled as follows:

1. As a 6- to 12-volt test light
2. As a static timing light (because a test light can be used to set timing on point-type ignition systems)

Do not purchase a test light designed for household current (110 or 220 volts). It will not light with 12 volts.

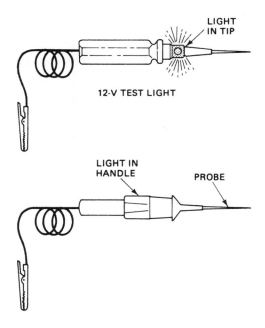

LIGHT IN TIP

12-V TEST LIGHT

LIGHT IN HANDLE

PROBE

FIGURE 4–14 Examples of probe-type test lights.

CONTINUITY TEST LIGHTS

A continuity light is similar to a test light but includes a battery. A continuity light lights whenever connected to both ends of a wire that has continuity, or is not broken. See figure 4–17.

CAUTION: The use of a continuity test light is not recommended on any electronic circuit. Because a continuity light contains a battery and applies voltage, it may harm delicate electronic components.

HOMEMADE TEST LIGHTS

The easiest way to make a test light is to use a #194 bulb, the type commonly used for side marker lights. This push-in style of bulb can easily have its exposed con-

FIGURE 4–16   A test light being used to check for current being available at the field terminal of an alternator.

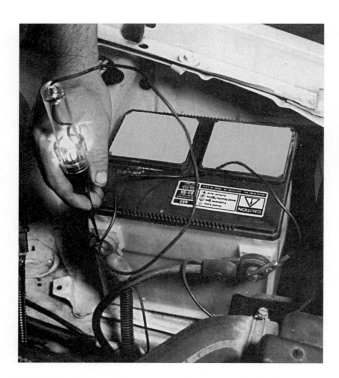

FIGURE 4–15   Always test the test light before using! Connecting the test light across the vehicle battery assures the technician that the leads and bulb are functioning before further testing with the test light.

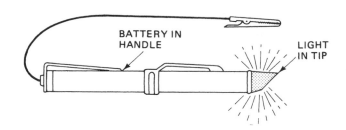

FIGURE 4–17   A continuity light should not be used on computer circuits because the applied voltage can damage delicate electronic components or circuits.

FIGURE 4–18   Homemade test light. A #194 bulb is the type normally used for side marker lights and is readily available at most automotive supply stores.

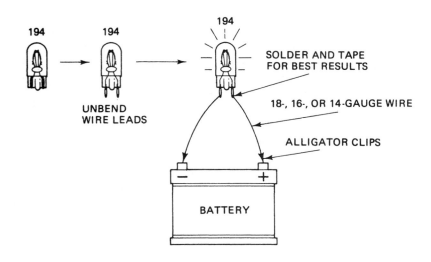

nector wires straightened and test leads connected. See figure 4–18.

LED TEST LIGHT

Another type of test light uses an LED instead of a standard automotive bulb for a visual indication of voltage. An LED test light only requires about 25 milliamperes (0.025 amperes) to light, and therefore, it can be used on electronic circuits as well as on standard circuits. See figure 4–19 for construction details.

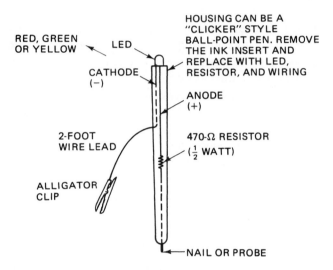

FIGURE 4–19 High-impedance test light. An LED test light can be easily made using low-cost components and an old ink pen. With the 470-ohm resistor in series with the LED, this tester only draws 0.025 amperes (25 milliamperes) from the circuit being tested. This low current draw helps assure the technician that the circuit or component being tested will not be damaged by excessive current flow.

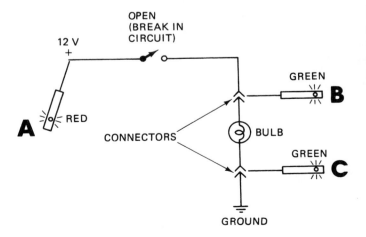

LOGIC PROBE

A logic probe is an electronic device that lights up a red (usually) LED if the probe is touched to battery voltage. If the probe is touched to ground, a green (usually) LED lights. See figure 4–20. A logic probe can "sense" the difference between high and low voltage levels—hence the term *logic*. A typical logic probe can also light another light (a "pulse" light) whenever there is a change in voltage levels. This feature is helpful whenever checking for a variable voltage output from a computer or ignition sensor.

A logic probe must be first connected to a power source (vehicle battery). This connection powers the probe and gives the probe a reference low (ground). If the circuit being tested does not use the same ground (reference low) as the probe uses for its power source, an auxiliary ground connection from the logic probe must be used. The logic probe uses this auxiliary ground as the reference low signal for the circuit being tested. See figure 4–21 for a diagram of a homemade logic probe.

Most logic probes also make a distinctive sound for each high- and low-voltage level. This makes troubleshooting easier when probing connectors or component terminals. A sound (usually a beep) is heard whenever the probe tip is touched to a voltage source that is changing. The changing voltage also usually lights the pulse light on the logic probe. Therefore, the probe can be used to check components such as pickup coils, Hall-effect sensors, magnetic sensors, and many other circuits. See the appropriate chapters for testing procedures.

NOTE: Most logic probes are *not* high impedance and may be damaging to some circuits.

FIGURE 4–20 A logic probe will show green (in this example) if a ground is detected such as at *B* and *C*. A standard (or LED) test light would only indicate to a technician a lack of power at *B* and could not determine if *C* was, in fact, connected to a ground.

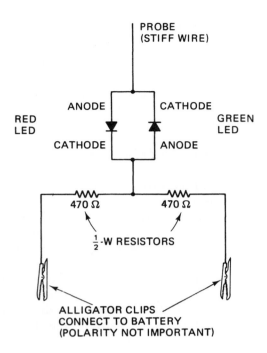

FIGURE 4–21 A schematic for a homemade logic probe. To use, connect the alligator (also called gator) clips to the vehicle battery. If voltage is probed, the red LED will light. If a ground is probed, the green LED will light.

JUMPER WIRES

A jumper wire is simply a length of wire, usually with alligator clips attached to both ends. It is used to conduct current directly to a component from the battery or to bypass a suspected defective component. See figure 4–22. For safety, install a 5-ampere fuse in the jumper wire to protect against accidental damage.

SUMMARY

1. *Digital multimeter* is abbreviated as *DMM*. *DVOM* stands for *digital volt-ohm-milliammeter*.
2. A high-impedance digital meter is *required* to be used on any computer-related circuit or component.
3. Ammeters measure current and must be connected in series in the circuit.
4. Voltmeters measure voltage and are connected in parallel.
5. Ohmmeters measure resistance of a component and must be connected in parallel, with the circuit or component disconnected from power.
6. Logic probes can indicate the presence of ground, as well as power.

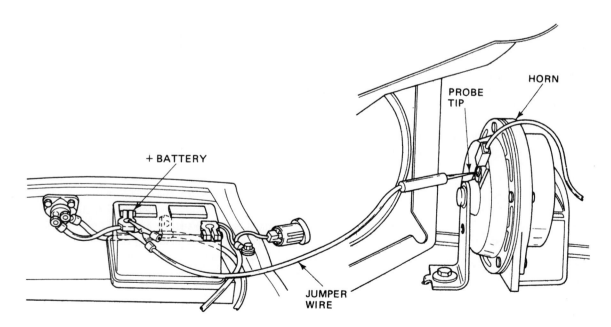

FIGURE 4–22 Using a jumper wire to test the operation of a horn. If the horn works when connected to the positive terminal of the battery, the horn itself and its ground connection are okay. An inline fuse should be used on all jumper wires to prevent possible electrical damage to the unit being tested or the vehicle's electrical system.

REVIEW QUESTIONS

1. Explain why most digital meters are called high-impedance meters.

2. Describe how an ammeter should be connected to an electrical circuit.

3. Explain why an ohmmeter must be connected to a disconnected circuit or component.

4. Discuss the differences between a test light and a logic probe.

MULTIPLE-CHOICE QUESTIONS

1. Most analog (needle-type) meters use what type of movement?
   a. D'Arsonval
   b. High-impedance
   c. Ohmmeter type
   d. Both a and b

2. A meter used to measure amperes is called _____ .
   a. An amp meter
   b. An ampmeter
   c. An ammeter
   d. A coulomb meter

3. A voltmeter should be connected to the circuit being tested _____ .
   a. In series
   b. In parallel
   c. Only when no power is flowing
   d. Both a and c.

4. An ohmmeter should be connected to the circuit being tested _____ .
   a. In series
   b. In parallel
   c. Only when no power is flowing
   d. Both b and c

5. A high-impedance meter is a meter that _____ .
   a. Measures a high amount of current flow
   b. Measures a high amount of resistance
   c. Can measure a high voltage
   d. Has a high internal resistance

6. A logic probe is more useful than a test light because _____ .
   a. A logic probe will indicate when a ground is probed
   b. A logic probe will indicate a power side of a circuit
   c. A logic probe will indicate when a changing voltage is being probed
   d. Both a and c

7. When using a jumper wire for testing, be certain _____ .
   a. To use a fused jumper wire to prevent possible electrical damage
   b. Never to bypass resistances in the circuit
   c. To only bypass circuit control units
   d. All of the above

8. The highest amount of resistance that can be read by the meter set to the 2-KΩ scale is _____ .
   a. 2000 ohms
   b. 200 ohms
   c. 200 KΩ (200,000 ohms)
   d. 20,000,000 ohms

9. If a digital meter face shows 0.93 when set to read K ohms, the reading means _____ .
   a. 93 ohms
   b. 930 ohms
   c. 9300 ohms
   d. 93,000 ohms

10. A reading of 432 shows on the face of the meter set to the millivolt scale. The reading means _____ .
   a. 0.432 volts
   b. 4.32 volts
   c. 43.2 volts
   d. 4320 volts

◀ Chapter 5 ▶

WIRING, CIRCUIT DIAGRAMS, AND TROUBLESHOOTING

OBJECTIVES

After studying chapter 5, the reader will be able to

1. Explain the wire gauge number system.
2. Describe how fusible links protect electrical circuits.
3. Discuss wiring schematics.
4. List the steps for performing a proper wire repair.

Today's vehicles contain miles of wire and hundreds of connections. The service technician has to be able to read and understand wiring diagrams to be able to diagnose and repair electrical problems.

AUTOMOTIVE WIRING

Most automotive wire is made from strands of copper covered by insulating plastic. Copper is an excellent conductor of electricity, reasonably priced, and very flexible. Even copper can break when moved repeatedly, and therefore, most copper wiring is constructed of multiple small strands that allow for repeated bending and moving without breaking. Solid copper wire is generally used for components such as starter armature and alternator stator windings that do not bend or move during normal operation.

GAUGE SIZE

Wiring is sized and purchased according to gauge size as assigned by the **American wire gauge (AWG) system**. AWG numbers can be confusing because as the gauge number *increases*, the size of the conductor wire *decreases*. Therefore, a 14-gauge wire is smaller than a 10-gauge wire. The greater the amount of current (in amperes), the larger the conducting wire (the smaller the gauge number) required.

EXAMPLES OF APPLICATIONS FOR WIRE GAUGE SIZES

Following are general applications for the most commonly used wire gauge sizes. Always check installation instructions or the manufacturer's specifications for wire gauge size before replacing any automotive wiring.

20–22 gauge: radio speaker wires

18 gauge: small bulbs and short leads

16 gauge: taillights, gas gauge, turn signals, windshield wipers

14 gauge: horn, radio power lead, headlights, cigarette lighter, brake lights

12 gauge: headlight switch to fuse box, rear window defogger, power windows and locks

10 gauge: ammeter, generator or alternator to battery

Some manufacturers indicate on the wiring diagrams the wire sizes measured in square millimeters (mm^2) of cross-sectional area. The following chart gives conversions or comparisons between metric and AWG gauge sizes. Notice that the metric wire size increases with size (area), whereas the AWG gauge size gets smaller with larger-size wire.

Metric Size (mm^2)	AWG Gauge
0.22	24
0.35	22
0.50	20
0.80	18
1.00	16
2.00	14
3.00	12
5.00	10
8.00	8
13.00	6
19.00	4
32.00	2

The gauge number should be decreased (wire size increased) with increased lengths of wire. See figure 5–1. For example, a trailer may require 14-gauge wire to light all the trailer lights, but if the wire required is more than 25 feet long, 12-gauge wire should be used. If the length is more than 50 feet, the wire size should be increased further, to 10 gauge, to prevent excessive voltage drops due to the connecting wires. Most automotive wire, except for spark plug wire, is often called **primary wire** because it is designed to operate at or near battery voltage (named for the voltage range used in the primary ignition circuit).

BRAIDED GROUND STRAPS

All vehicles use ground straps between the engine and body and/or between the body and the negative terminal of the battery. Many of the engine-to-body straps are braided and uninsulated as shown in figure 5–2. It is not necessary to insulate a ground strap because it does not matter if it touches metal because it already attaches to ground. Braided ground straps are more flexible than stranded wire. Because the engine is free to move slightly on its mounts, the braided ground strap is able

Wire Gauge Selection Chart

1. Measure wire length. When a return ground wire is used, measure both wires.
2. Find the correct wire gauge by matching the amperage, at the correct voltage, with the wire length or the next larger footage on the chart.

Note: This chart is based upon a 10% maximum voltage drop, for 5% voltage drop, use double the measure wire length.

12 Volt Amps	WIRE GAUGE REQUIRED—BY LENGTH OF CIRCUIT IN FEET														
	3'	5'	7'	10'	15'	20'	25'	30'	40'	50'	60'	70'	80'	90'	100'
1	20	20	20	20	20	20	20	20	20	20	20	20	20	20	20
1.5	20	20	20	20	20	20	20	20	20	20	20	20	18	18	18
2	20	20	20	20	20	20	20	20	20	18	18	16	16	16	16
3	20	20	20	20	20	20	20	20	18	18	16	16	14	14	14
4	20	20	20	20	20	20	20	18	16	16	14	14	14	14	12
5	20	20	20	20	20	20	18	18	16	14	14	14	12	12	12
6	20	20	20	20	20	18	18	16	16	14	14	12	12	12	12
7	20	20	20	20	20	18	16	16	14	14	12	12	12	10	10
8	20	20	20	20	18	16	16	14	14	12	12	12	10	10	10
10	20	20	20	20	18	16	14	14	12	12	10	10	10	10	8
12	20	20	20	18	16	14	14	14	12	10	10	10	8	8	8
15	20	20	20	18	16	14	12	12	10	10	10	8	8	8	6
20	20	20	18	16	14	12	12	10	10	8	8	8	6	6	6
24	20	18	16	14	14	12	10	10	8	8	8	6	6	6	4
30	18	16	16	14	12	10	10	10	8	8	6	6	6	4	4
36	16	14	14	14	12	10	10	8	8	6	6	4	4	4	4
50	14	14	14	12	10	8	8	6	6	4	4	4	2	2	2
100	14	12	10	8	8	6	6	4	4	2	2	1	0	0	2/0
150	12	10	8	6	6	4	4	2	2	1	0	2/0	2/0	3/0	3/0
200	10	8	8	6	4	2	2	2	1	0	2/0	3/0	4/0	4/0	4/0

— WHEN MECHANICAL STRENGTH IS A FACTOR, USE NEXT LARGER WIRE GAUGE

FIGURE 5–1 Wire gauge selection chart.

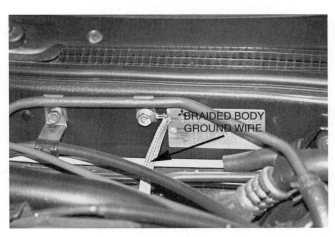

FIGURE 5–2 All lights and accessories ground to the body of the vehicle. Body ground wires such as this one are needed to conduct all of the current from these components back to the negetive terminal of the battery. The body ground wire connects the body to the engine. Most battery negative cables attach to the engine.

to flex without breaking. The braided strap also dampens out some radio-frequency interference that otherwise might be transmitted through standard stranded wiring. High-frequency electricity tends to travel on the

◀ TECH TIP ▶

THE GROUND WIRE IN THE KIT

Since the early 1990s, automatic transmissions have been electronically shifted. The vehicle computer operates solenoids to control shifting and operation of the torque converter clutch. Because all of these solenoids ground to the case of the transmission or transaxle, a poor ground can cause improper shifting. Some transmission suppliers are now including a braided ground strap as part of the transmission repair (overhaul) kit. Often the original factory ground strap has corroded or broken. Even if the original still looks okay, additional ground wires will simply improve the chances of a proper ground connection. Therefore, before removing or replacing any electrically or electronically operated component, try connecting another ground strap first. It may save you lots of time and money.

outside of the wire instead of through the center or core of the conductor. This phenomenon is called the **skin effect**. Because the outside surfaces of the small wires used in braided straps cross and connect to each other, any induced high-frequency interference is shorted out and not transferred. This is the reason why many radio installation kits include braided ground straps.

NOTE: Body ground wires are necessary to provide a path for the lights and accessories that ground to the body to flow to the negative battery terminal.

BATTERY CABLES

Battery cables are the largest wires used in the automotive electrical system. The cables are usually 4-gauge, 2-gauge, or 1-gauge wires. Wires larger than 1 gauge are called 0 gauge (pronounced ought). Larger cables are labeled 2/0 or 00 (called double ought) and 3/0 or 000 (triple ought). Six-volt electrical systems require battery cables two sizes larger than those for 12-volt electrical systems.

JUMPER CABLES

Jumper cables are 4- to 2/0-gauge electrical cables with large clamps attached, used to connect a vehicle that has a discharged battery to a vehicle that has a good battery. Good-quality jumper cables are necessary to prevent excessive voltage drops caused by the cable's resistance. Aluminum wire jumper cables should not be used, because even though aluminum is a good electrical conductor (although not as good as copper), it is less flexible and can crack and break when bent or moved repeatedly. The size should be 4 gauge or larger. Ought-gauge welding cable can be used to construct an excellent set of jumper cables using welding clamps on both ends. Welding cable is usually constructed of many very fine strands of wire, which allows for easier bending of the cable because the strands of fine wire can slide against each other inside the cable.

FUSES

Fuses should be used in every circuit to protect the wiring from overheating and damage caused by excessive current flow as a result of a short circuit or other malfunction.

The symbol for a fuse is a wavy line between two points: $\sigma\!\!\sim\!\!\omega$. A fuse is constructed of a fine tin conductor inside a glass, plastic, or ceramic housing. The tin is designed to melt and open the circuit if excessive current flows through the fuse. Each fuse is rated according to its maximum current-carrying capacity.

Many fuses are used to protect more than one circuit of the automobile. See figure 5–3. A typical example is the fuse for the cigarette lighter that also supplies many other circuits.

NOTE: The SAE term for a cigarette lighter is *cigar lighter* because the diameter of the heating element is large enough for a cigar. The term *cigarette lighter* will be used throughout this book because it is the most commonly used term.

The cigarette lighter fuse may also be used to protect the courtesy lights, clock, and other circuits. Therefore, a fault in one circuit can cause the fuse to melt, which will prevent the operation of all other circuits that are protected by the fuse.

GLASS FUSES

Standard glass tube or ceramic fuses are rated according to maximum current and size. Glass tube fuses are generally all 1/4 inch in diameter, with lengths of 1 1/4, 1 7/8, 3/4, and 5/8 inches. There are many different sizes and time-delay factors designed into each of the various manufacturers' fuses. Fuses manufactured under the standards established by the Society of Fuse Engineers

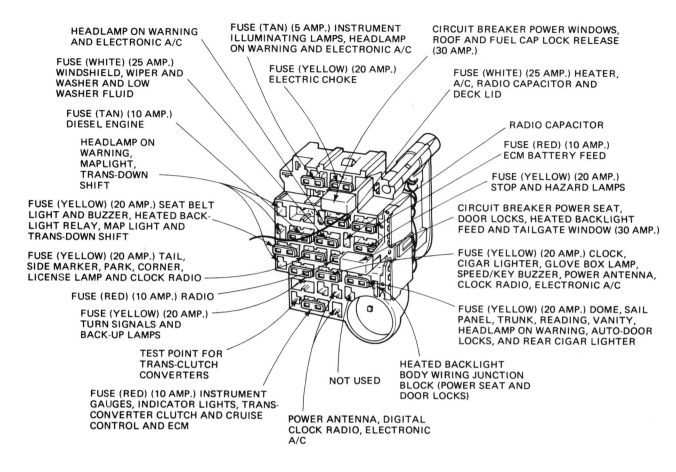

HEADLAMP ON WARNING
AND ELECTRONIC A/C

FUSE (WHITE) (25 AMP.)
WINDSHIELD, WIPER AND
WASHER AND LOW
WASHER FLUID

FUSE (TAN) (10 AMP.)
DIESEL ENGINE

HEADLAMP ON
WARNING,
MAPLIGHT,
TRANS-DOWN
SHIFT

FUSE (YELLOW) (20 AMP.) SEAT BELT
LIGHT AND BUZZER, HEATED BACK-
LIGHT RELAY, MAP LIGHT AND
TRANS-DOWN SHIFT

FUSE (YELLOW) (20 AMP.) TAIL,
SIDE MARKER, PARK, CORNER,
LICENSE LAMP AND CLOCK RADIO

FUSE (RED) (10 AMP.) RADIO

FUSE (YELLOW) (20 AMP.)
TURN SIGNALS AND
BACK-UP LAMPS

TEST POINT FOR
TRANS-CLUTCH
CONVERTERS

FUSE (RED) (10 AMP.) INSTRUMENT
GAUGES, INDICATOR LIGHTS, TRANS-
CONVERTER CLUTCH AND CRUISE
CONTROL AND ECM

FUSE (TAN) (5 AMP.) INSTRUMENT
ILLUMINATING LAMPS, HEADLAMP
ON WARNING AND ELECTRONIC A/C

FUSE (YELLOW) (20 AMP.)
ELECTRIC CHOKE

NOT USED

POWER ANTENNA, DIGITAL
CLOCK RADIO, ELECTRONIC
A/C

CIRCUIT BREAKER POWER WINDOWS,
ROOF AND FUEL CAP LOCK RELEASE
(30 AMP.)

FUSE (WHITE) (25 AMP.) HEATER,
A/C, RADIO CAPACITOR AND
DECK LID

RADIO CAPACITOR

FUSE (RED) (10 AMP.)
ECM BATTERY FEED

FUSE (YELLOW) (20 AMP.)
STOP AND HAZARD LAMPS

CIRCUIT BREAKER POWER SEAT,
DOOR LOCKS, HEATED BACKLIGHT
FEED AND TAILGATE WINDOW (30 AMP.)

FUSE (YELLOW) (20 AMP.) CLOCK,
CIGAR LIGHTER, GLOVE BOX LAMP,
SPEED/KEY BUZZER, POWER ANTENNA,
CLOCK RADIO, ELECTRONIC A/C

FUSE (YELLOW) (20 AMP.) DOME, SAIL
PANEL, TRUNK, READING, VANITY,
HEADLAMP ON WARNING, AUTO-DOOR
LOCKS, AND REAR CIGAR LIGHTER

HEATED BACKLIGHT
BODY WIRING JUNCTION
BLOCK (POWER SEAT AND
DOOR LOCKS)

FIGURE 5–3   Typical automotive fuse panel.

◀ **TECH TIP** ▶

THE EIGHTY PERCENT RULE

The maximum anticipated current flow through
a circuit should be approximately 80% of the
fuse rating for that circuit. For example, if an
automotive circuit is designed for a maximum
current of 12 amperes, a 15-ampere fuse should
be used to protect the circuit (80% of 15 amperes is 12 amperes: 15 × 0.80 = 12). Circuit
breakers also usually adhere to the 80% rule.
The 80% rule can also be used to calculate the
current in a circuit if the amperage rating of the
fuse is known:

Fuse rating × 0.80 = current in circuit

(SFE) vary in length according to amperage rating. SFE
fuses usually are longer as amperage rating increases.
See figure 5–4. The fuses manufactured by the
Bussmann Manufacturing Division of McGraw-Edison
Company (Buss fuses) are the same length for each type
regardless of amperage rating. Some common Buss fuse
types include the following:

AGA, formerly 1AG

AGW, formerly 7AG

AGC, formerly 3AG

AGY, formerly 9AG

AGX, formerly 8AG

The letters used are a Bussmann identification code and
have no other meaning.

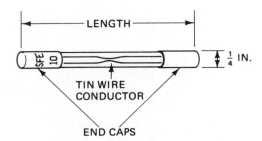

FIGURE 5–4   Most glass automotive fuses are the same diameter, but the length varies depending on the type of fuse.

Certain fuses are designed to allow an overload for varying lengths of time. Some fuses are designed to delay "blowing" to allow for the starting current, usually accompanying the starting of electric motors such as the blower motor or the windshield wiper motor. Other fuses are designed to be "quick blow" and immediately open the circuit upon detecting any current flow higher than the fuse rating. Because each fuse is selected to meet a wide range of operating conditions, temperatures, shocks, and vibrations, it is important to replace a blown fuse with the correct type (for example, SFE, AGA, or AGC) and amperage rating.

BLADE FUSES

Colored blade-type fuses have been used since 1977. The color of the plastic of blade fuses indicates the maximum current flow measured in amperes. The following chart lists the color and the amperage rating.

Amperage Rating	Color
1	Dark green
2	Gray
2.5	Purple
3	Violet
4	Pink
5	Tan
6	Gold
7.5	Brown
9	Orange
10	Red
14	Black
15	Blue
20	Yellow
25	White
30	Green

All blade fuses are the same size regardless of amperage rating. See figure 5–5.

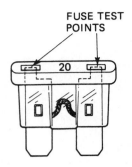

FIGURE 5–5   Blade-type fuses can be tested through openings in the plastic at the top of the fuse.

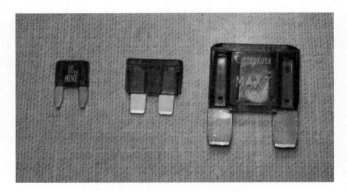

FIGURE 5–6   Maxi fuse on the right and mini fuse on the left. A standard blade fuse is in the center.

MINI FUSES

To save space, many vehicles use mini (small) blade fuses. Not only do they save space, but they also allow the vehicle design engineer to fuse individual circuits instead of grouping many different components to one fuse. This improves customer satisfaction because if one component fails, it only affects that one circuit without stopping electrical power to several other circuits as well. This makes troubleshooting a lot easier too, because each circuit is separate. See figure 5–6.

The following chart lists the amperage rating and corresponding fuse color for mini fuses.

Amperage Rating	Color
5	Tan
7.5	Brown
10	Red
15	Blue
20	Yellow
25	Natural
30	Green

FIGURE 5–7 To test a fuse, use a test light to check for power at the power side of the fuse. The ignition switch may have to be on (run) before some fuses receive power. Use the test points as illustrated in figure 5–5.

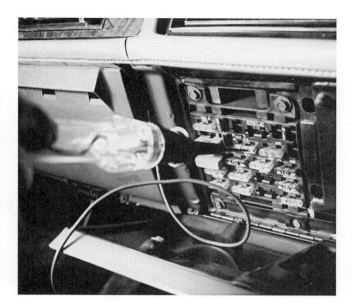

FIGURE 5–8 If the fuse is good, the test light should light on both sides (power side and load side) of the fuse.

MAXI FUSES

Maxi fuses are a large version of blade fuses used to replace fusible links in many vehicles. Maxi fuses are rated up to 80 amperes or more.

The following chart lists the amperage rating and corresponding color for maxi fuses.

Amperage Rating	Color
20	Yellow
30	Green
40	Amber
50	Red
60	Blue
70	Brown
80	Natural

TESTING FUSES

It is important to test the condition of a fuse if the circuit being protected by the fuse does not operate. Most blown fuses can be detected quickly because the center conductor is melted. Fuses can also fail and open the circuit because of a poor connection in the fuse itself or in the fuse holder. Therefore, just because a fuse "looks okay" does not mean that it *is* okay. All fuses should be tested with a test light. The test light should be connected to

◀ **DIAGNOSTIC STORY** ▶

THE 7-HOUR FUSE TEST

A technician spent 7 hours troubleshooting an older-model Toyota on which the "charge" light remained on whenever the engine was running. Other technicians had replaced both the alternator and the voltage regulator. After hours of troubleshooting, the problem was discovered to be the fuse for the charging circuit. The fuse had been checked by removing the fuse and checking it with an ohmmeter. It did have continuity. However, when placed back in the circuit, the fuse would not conduct enough amperes for the circuit to operate. The fuse was corroded inside the end caps, yet looked perfect on the outside. Replacing the fuse restored proper operation of the alternator, voltage regulator, and charge light. *Always* test fuses in the fuse panel with a test light.

first one side of the fuse and then the other. A test light should light on both sides. See figures 5–7 and 5–8.

CIRCUIT BREAKERS

Circuit breakers are used to prevent harmful overload (excessive current flow) in a circuit by opening the circuit and stopping the current flow to prevent overheating and possible fire caused by hot wires or electrical

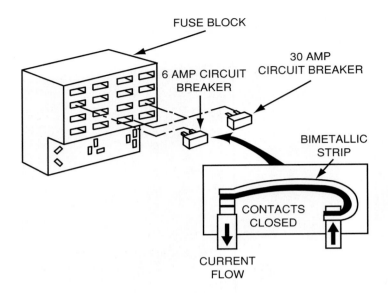

FUSE BLOCK

6 AMP CIRCUIT BREAKER

30 AMP CIRCUIT BREAKER

BIMETALLIC STRIP

CONTACTS CLOSED

CURRENT FLOW

FIGURE 5–9 Typical blade circuit breaker fits into the same space as a blade fuse. If excessive current flows through the bimetallic strip, the strip bends and opens the contacts and stops current flow. When the circuit breaker cools, the contacts close again, completing the electrical circuit.

components. Circuit breakers are mechanical units that open the circuit by means of the heating effect of two different metals (bimetallic), which deform and open a set of contact points that work in the same manner as an "off" switch. See figure 5–9.

Circuit breakers, therefore, are reset when the current stops flowing, which causes the bimetallic strip to cool and the circuit to close again. A circuit breaker is used in circuits that could affect the safety of the passengers if a conventional nonresetting fuse were used. The headlight circuit gives an excellent example of the use of a circuit breaker rather than a fuse. A short or grounded circuit anywhere in the headlight circuit could cause excessive current flow, and therefore the opening of the circuit. A sudden loss of headlights at night could have disastrous results. A circuit breaker, however, would open and close the circuit rapidly, thereby protecting the circuit from overheating and also providing sufficient current flow to maintain at least partial headlight operation.

Circuit breakers are also used for other circuits wherein conventional fuses could not provide for the surges of high current commonly found in those circuits. Examples are the circuits for the following accessories:

1. Power seats
2. Power door locks
3. Power windows

PTC CIRCUIT PROTECTORS

Positive temperature coefficient (PTC) circuit protectors are solid-state (without moving parts). Like all other circuit protection devices, these are installed in se-

ries in the circuit being protected. If excessive current flows, the temperature and resistance of the PTC increase.

This increased resistance reduces current flow (amperes) in the circuit and may cause the electrical component in the circuit not to function correctly. For example, when a PTC circuit protector is used in a power window circuit, the increased resistance causes the operation of the power window to be much slower than normal.

Unlike circuit breakers or fuses, PTC circuit protection devices do not open the circuit, but rather provide a very high resistance between the PTC circuit protector and the component. See figure 5–10. In other words, voltage will be available to the component. This fact has lead to a lot of misunderstanding about how these circuit protection devices actually work. It is even more confusing when the circuit is opened and the PTC circuit protector is allowed to cool. Then when the circuit is turned back on, the component may operate normally for a short time until the PTC circuit protector again gets hot because of too much current flow and its resistance again increases to limit current flow.

For example, if an 8-ampere PTC circuit protector is used when powering up a blower motor that draws 12 amperes, the blower motor will operate normally for a short time until the PTC device gets warm. As the PTC circuit protector gets hot, the blower motor will start to run slower because of the reduced current flow. Eventually the motor will stop, once the PTC device has caused resistance to climb to a certain level. As long as voltage is applied, the PTC circuit protector will be hot and current will be restricted. In other words, the PTC circuit protector will not reset until voltage is removed from the circuit. PTC circuit protectors are used in almost all speakers, cellular phones, and other automotive and nonautomotive electronic equipment.

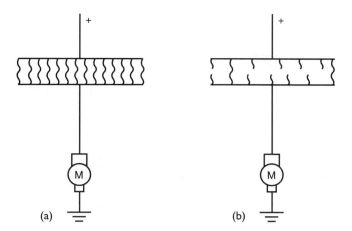

FIGURE 5–10 *(a)* Normal operation of a PTC circuit protector in a power window motor circuit. Note the many conducting paths. With normal current flow, temperature of the PTC circuit protector remains normal. *(b)* When current exceeds the amperage rating of the PTC circuit protector, the polymer material that makes up the electronic circuit protector increases in resistance. As shown here, a high-resistance electrical path still exists even though the motor will stop operating as a result of the very low current flow through the very high resistance. The circuit protector will not reset or cool down until voltage is removed from the circuit.

The electronic control unit (computer) used in most vehicles today incorporates thermal overload protection devices. Therefore, whenever a component fails to operate, do not blame the computer. The current control device is controlling current flow to protect the computer. Components that do not operate correctly should be checked for proper resistance and current draw.

FUSIBLE LINKS

A fusible link is a type of fuse that consists of a short length of standard copper-strand wire covered with a special nonflammable insulation. This wire is usually four wire sizes smaller than the wire of the circuits it protects. The special thick insulation over the wire may make the wire look larger than other wires of the same gauge number. See figure 5–11.

If excessive current flow (caused by a short to ground or a defective component) occurs, the fusible link will melt in half and open the circuit to prevent a fire hazard. Some fusible links are identified with tags at the junction between the fusible link and the standard chassis wiring. These tags are labeled "fusible link" and represent only the junction. Fusible links are the backup system for circuit protection. All current except

◀ **TECH TIP** ▶

LOOK FOR THE "GREEN CRUD"

Corroded connections are a major cause of intermittent electrical problems and open circuits. The usual sequence of conditions is as follows:

1. Heat causes expansion. This heat can be from external sources such as connectors being too close to the exhaust system. Another possible source of heat is a poor connection at the terminal, causing a voltage drop and heat due to the electrical resistance.
2. Condensation is created when a connector cools. The moisture caused by the condensation causes rust and corrosion.

The solution is as follows: If corroded connectors are noticed, the terminal should be cleaned and the condition of the electrical connection to the wire terminal end(s) confirmed. Many automobile manufacturers recommend using a dielectric silicone or lithium-based grease inside connectors to prevent moisture from getting into and attacking the connector.

the current used by the starter motor flows through fusible links and then through individual circuit fuses. It is possible that a fusible link will melt and not blow a fuse. Fusible links are installed as close to the battery as possible so that they can protect the wiring and circuits coming directly from the battery. See figure 5–12.

TERMINALS AND CONNECTORS

A **terminal** is a metal fastener attached to the end of a wire. The term *connector* usually refers to the plastic portion that snaps or connects together. Wire terminal ends usually snap into and are held in a connector. Male and female connectors can then be snapped together, thereby completing an electrical connection.

A typical repair often involves removing a wire's terminal from a connector and replacing that terminal on the end of the lead (wire). Terminals are usually retained in a connector by a locking tang or tab that must be depressed to release the terminal end from the plastic connector. See figures 5–13 through 5–15.

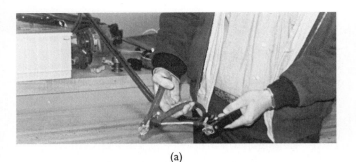

(a)

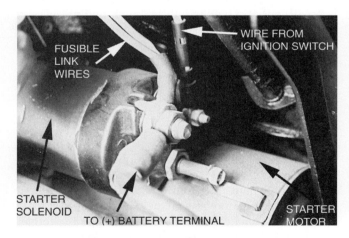

(b)

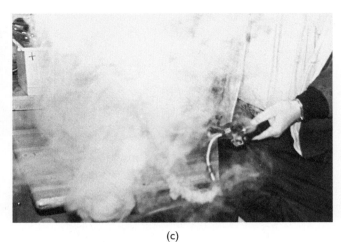

(c)

(d)

FIGURE 5–11 *(a)* Testing a fusible link by connecting a battery to each end with jumper cables. *(b)* After about 1 to 2 seconds, smoke starts to roll out from around the insulation. *(c)* After about 5 seconds, smoke fills the area as the wire inside finally melts and breaks (opens) the circuit. *(d)* The fusible link afterward. Notice that the special high-temperature insulation is unharmed even though the copper conductor has melted in half.

FIGURE 5–12 Fusible links conduct electrical current from the battery or starter terminal (as illustrated) to the fuse panel. Notice that two wires are used. Each wire is four gauge sizes smaller (higher number) than the size in the circuits they are protecting.

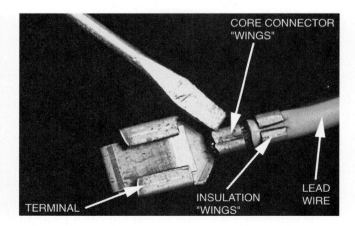

FIGURE 5–13 Wire with terminal illustrating typical terms used to describe leads and fastening parts.

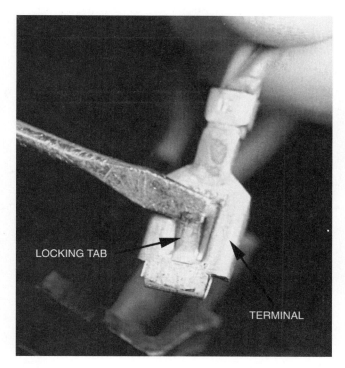

FIGURE 5–14 The locking tab part of a terminal is designed to snap into a plastic connector. This locking tab must be depressed before removing the terminal (with attached lead) from the connector.

WIRE AND CABLE

Even though many technicians use the terms *wire* and *cable* interchangeably, there is a slight difference. A **cable** is usually defined as a bundle of wires; a **wire** is generally defined as a single electrical conductor; and a **lead** is any wire or cable carrying a current. Common usage usually defines a conductor 4 gauge (AWG) or larger (smaller number) as a *cable*, and a conductor smaller (larger number) than 4 gauge as a *wire*. The term *lead* is a safe term to use under any circumstance.

SOLDER

Solder is an alloy of tin and lead used to make a good electrical contact between two wires or connections in an electrical circuit. The solder itself is made from an alloy of tin and lead. However, a flux must be used to help clean the area and to help make the solder flow. Therefore, solder is made with a resin (rosin) contained in the center, and this is called **rosin-core solder**. An acid-core solder is also available but should only be used for soldering sheet metal. Solder is available with

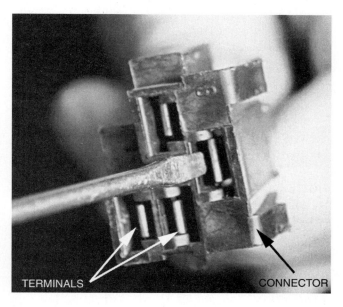

FIGURE 5–15 To release a terminal from a plastic connector, insert a small screwdriver or pick into an entry channel to depress the locking tab.

various percentages of tin and lead in the alloy. Ratios are used to identify these various types of solder, with the first number in the ratio denoting the percentage of tin in the alloy and the second number giving the percentage of lead. The most commonly used solder is 50/50, which means that 50% of the solder is tin and the other 50% is lead. The percentages of each alloy primarily determine the melting point of the solder:

> 60/40 solder (60% tin/40% lead) melts at 361° F (183° C).
>
> 50/50 solder (50% tin/50% lead) melts at 421° F (216° C).
>
> 40/60 solder (40% tin/60% lead) melts at 460° F (238° C).

NOTE: The melting points stated here can vary depending on the purity of the metals used.

Because of the lower melting point, 60/40 solder is the most highly recommended solder to use, followed by 50/50.

WIRE REPAIR PROCEDURE

Many manufacturers recommend that all wiring repairs be soldered. See figures 5–16 through 5–24 for a photo sequence on soldering and using heat shrink tubing.

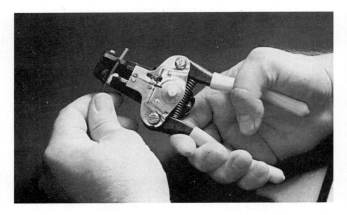

FIGURE 5–16 Wire-stripping pliers. This type of pliers can grasp the wire insulation and strip the insulation off of wire of a wide range of gauge sizes.

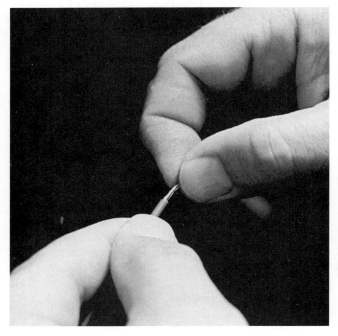

FIGURE 5–17 After stripping the insulation from the end of the wire, twist the strands of wire together in preparation for soldering.

FIGURE 5–18 Always use rosin-core solder for electrical or electronic soldering. Also, use small-diameter solder for small soldering irons. Only use large-diameter solder for large-diameter (large-gauge) wire and higher-wattage soldering irons (guns).

FIGURE 5–19 Before soldering, make certain that the tip of the soldering iron (or gun) has a coating of solder. This process is called "tinning" the soldering iron and helps the transfer of heat to the wire being soldered.

FIGURE 5–20 The stripped, twisted wires are then twisted into a tight spiral and soldered. Be certain to use the soldering iron to heat the wire and to allow the hot wire to melt the solder. This splice is generally acceptable; however, the ends of the wire should not overhang the insulation. This overhang could cut through the tape or heat shrink tubing covering the splice.

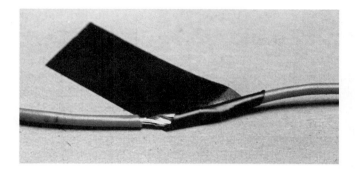

FIGURE 5–21   Taping the soldered splice.

FIGURE 5–22   Close-up view of heat shrink tubing. When heated, this plastic insulating tubing shrinks to about one-half of its original diameter.

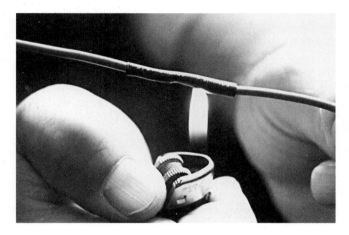

FIGURE 5–23   After sliding and centering the tubing over the splice, heat the tubing until it makes a tight seal over the splice. (Note: For best results, do *not* allow the flame of the match or lighter to contact the shrink tubing. It can burn as well as shrink.)

CRIMP-AND-SEAL CONNECTORS

The use of crimp-and-seal connectors is recommended by many vehicle manufacturers as the method for wire repair. Crimp-and-seal connectors are *not* simply butt

FIGURE 5–24   A butane soldering tool. The cap has a built-in striker to light a converter in the tip of the tool. This handy soldering tool produces the equivalent of 60 watts of heat. It operates for about ½ hour on one charge from a commonly available butane refill dispenser.

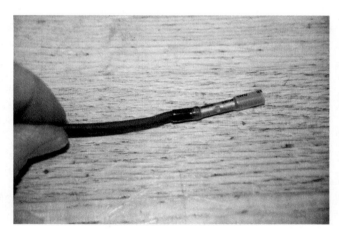

FIGURE 5–25   A crimp-and-seal connector. The left side has been gently crimped and heated. Note how the connector has shrunk down around the wire. The heat has also released a thermal sealant that forms an effective environmental seal around the wire.

connectors. Crimp-and-seal connectors contain a sealant *and* shrink tubing in one piece. See figure 5–25.

The usual procedure specified for making a wire repair using a crimp-and-seal connector is as follows:

- *Step #1.* Strip the insulation from the ends of the wire about 5/16 inch, or 8 millimeters.
- *Step #2.* Select the proper size of crimp-and-seal connector for the gauge of wire being repaired. Insert the wires into the splice sleeve and crimp.

■ *Step #3.* Apply heat to the connector until the sleeve shrinks down around the wire and a small amount of sealant is observed around the ends of the sleeve.

ALUMINUM WIRE REPAIR

Since the mid-1970s, many automobile manufacturers have used plastic-coated solid aluminum wire for some body wiring. Because aluminum wire is brittle and can break as a result of vibration, it is only used where there is no possible movement of the wire, such as along the floor or sill area. This section of wire is stationary, and the wire changes back to copper at a junction terminal after the trunk or rear section of the vehicle, where movement of the wiring may be possible.

If any aluminum wire must be repaired or replaced, the following procedure should be used to be assured of a proper repair. The aluminum wire is usually found protected in a plastic conduit. This conduit is then normally slit, after which the wires can easily be removed for repair.

■ *Step #1.* Carefully strip only about 1/4 inch (6 mm) of insulation from the aluminum wire, being careful not to nick or damage the aluminum wire case.

■ *Step #2.* Use a crimp connector to join two wires together. Do *not* solder an aluminum wire repair. Solder will not readily adhere to aluminum because the heat causes an oxide coating on the surface of the aluminum.

■ *Step #3.* The spliced, crimped connection must be coated with petroleum jelly to prevent corrosion.

■ *Step #4.* The coated connection should be covered with shrinkable plastic tubing or wrapped with electrical tape to seal out moisture.

WIRING DIAGRAMS

Automotive manufacturers' service manuals include wiring diagrams of all the electrical circuits. These wiring diagrams may include all circuits combined on several large foldout sheets, or they may be broken down to show individual circuits. All circuit diagrams include the power-side wiring of the circuit and all splices, connectors, electrical components, and ground return paths. The gauge and color of the wiring are also included on most wiring diagrams.

FIGURE 5–26   The center wire is a solid-color wire, meaning that the wire has no other identifying tracer or stripe color. The two end wires could be labeled "WHT/BRN," indicating a white wire with a brown tracer or stripe.

CIRCUIT INFORMATION

Many wiring diagrams include numbers and letters near components and wires that may cause confusion to readers of the diagram. Most letters used near or on a wire are to identify the color or colors of the wire. The first color or color abbreviation is the color of the wire insulation, and the second color (if mentioned) is the color of the strip or tracer on the base color. See figure 5–26.

Wires with different-color tracers are indicated by both colors with a slash (/) between them. For example, BRN/WHT means a brown wire with a white stripe or tracer.

Abbreviation	Color
BRN	Brown
BLK	Black
GRN	Green
WHT	White
PPL	Purple
PNK	Pink
TAN	Tan
BLU	Blue
YEL	Yellow
ORN	Orange
DK BLU	Dark blue
LT BLU	Light blue
DK GRN	Dark green
LT GRN	Light green
RED	Red
GRY	Gray

Figure 5–27 illustrates a rear side marker bulb circuit diagram wherein ".8" indicates the metric wire gauge size in square millimeters (mm^2) and "PPL" indicates a solid purple wire.

The wire diagram also shows that the color of the wire changes at the number C210. This stands for "connector #210" and is used for reference purposes. The symbol for the connection can vary depending on the manufacturer. The color change from purple (PPL) to

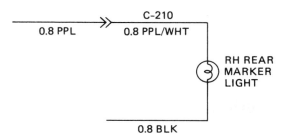

FIGURE 5–27 Typical section of a wiring diagram. Notice that the wire color changes at connection C210. The ".8" represents the metric wire size in square millimeters.

purple with a white tracer (PPL/WHT) is not important except for knowing where the wire changes color in the circuit. The wire gauge has remained the same on both sides of the connection (0.8 square millimeters or 18 gauge). The ground circuit is the ".8 BLK" wire.

Figure 5–28 shows electrical and electronic symbols that are used in wiring and circuit diagrams.

Most General Motors and many other wiring diagrams use three-digit numbers for grounds (G), splices (S), and connectors (C). These numbers are arranged so that the numbers 100 through 199 indicate locations under the hood; 200 through 299 indicate locations under the dash; 300 through 399 indicate locations in the passenger compartment; and 400 through 499 indicate locations in the trunk area. See figure 5–29.

◀ **TECH TIP** ▶

READ THE ARROWS

Wiring diagrams indicate connections by symbols that look like arrows. See figure 5–30. Do *not* read these "arrows" as pointers showing the direction of current flow. Also observe that the power side (positive side) of the circuit is usually the female end of the connector. If a connector becomes disconnected, it will be difficult for the circuit to become shorted to ground or to another circuit because the wire is recessed into the connector.

RELAY TERMINAL IDENTIFICATION

Most automotive relays adhere to common terminal identification. Knowing this terminal information will help in the correct diagnosis and troubleshooting of any circuit containing a relay. See figures 5–31 through 5–33.

◀ **TECH TIP** ▶

DO IT RIGHT—INSTALL A RELAY

Often owners of vehicles, especially owners of pickup trucks and sport utility vehicles (SUVs), want to add additional electrical accessories or lighting. It is tempting to simply splice into an existing circuit. However, whenever another circuit or component is added, the current that flows through the newly added component is added to the current for the original component. This additional current can easily overload the fuse and wiring. Do not simply install a larger-amperage fuse. The wire gauge size was not engineered for the additional current and could overheat.

The solution is to install a relay. A relay uses a small coil to create a magnetic field that causes a movable arm to switch a higher-current circuit on. The typical relay has from 50 to 150 ohms of resistance and requires just 0.24 to 0.08 amperes when connected to a 12-volt source. This small additional current will not be enough to overload the existing circuit. See figure 5–34 for an example of how additional lighting can be added.

The schematic is often printed or embossed on the side of the relay. The terminals are labeled to help the technician test and check for proper operation. The identification of relay terminals also helps when wiring accessories, such as auxiliary lighting, into existing wiring.

Despiking diodes or resistors are connected in parallel across the coil of most automotive relays (terminals 85 and 86).

USING WIRING DIAGRAMS FOR TROUBLESHOOTING

Follow these steps when troubleshooting wiring problems:

- *Step #1.* Verify the malfunction. If, for example, the backup lights do not operate, make certain that the ignition is on (run position) (engine off), with the gear selector in reverse, and check for operation of the backup lights.
- *Step #2.* Check everything else that does or does not operate correctly. For example, if the taillights are also failing to operate, the

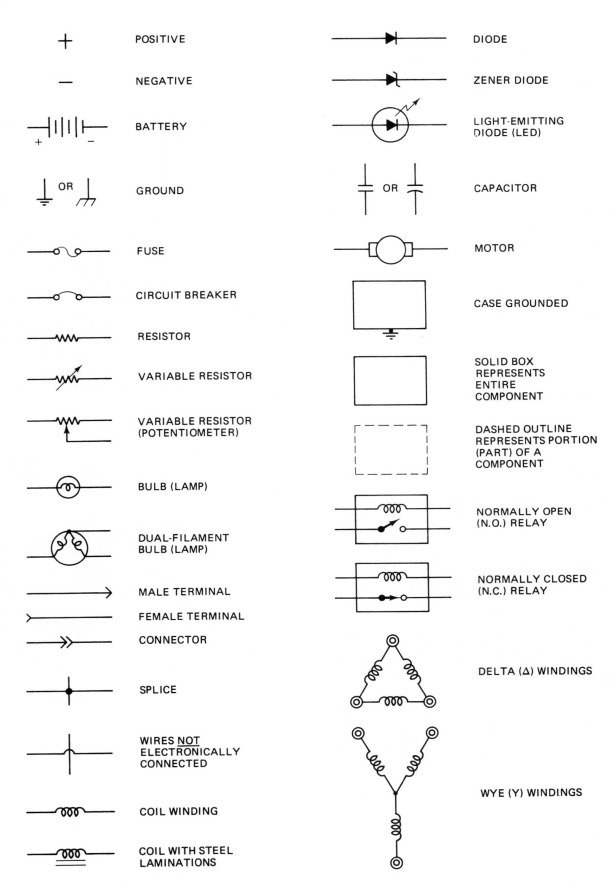

FIGURE 5–28 Typical electrical and electronic symbols used in automotive wiring and circuit diagrams.

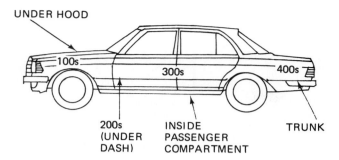

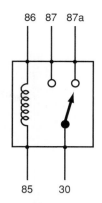

86 87 87a

85 30

86–POWER SIDE OF THE COIL
85–GROUND SIDE OF THE COIL

(MOST RELAY COILS
HAVE BETWEEN
50–150 OHMS
OF RESISTANCE.)

30–COMMON POWER FOR RELAY CONTACTS
87–NORMALLY OPEN OUTPUT (N.O.)
87a–NORMALLY CLOSED OUTPUT (N.C.)

FIGURE 5–29 Connectors (C), grounds (G), and splices (S) are followed by a number generally indicating the location in the vehicle. For example, G209 is a ground connection located under the dash. (Note: Some wiring installed by outside custom body converters, such as in convertible-top conversions, do not adhere to the numbering system described here. Also, some factory grounds, splices, and connectors may not adhere to the general rule because of changes during production.)

TO BATTERY ⟨⟨ TO ELECTRICAL
COMPONENT

FIGURE 5–30 Typical connector. Note that the positive terminal is usually a female connector.

FIGURE 5–31 A relay uses a movable arm to complete a circuit whenever there is a power at terminal **86** and a ground at terminal **85**. A typical relay only requires about $\frac{1}{10}$ ampere through the relay coil. The movable arm then closes the contacts (#30 to #87) and can relay 30 amperes or more.

(a)

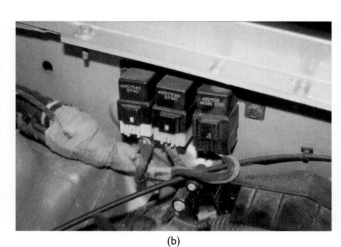

(b)

FIGURE 5–32 (a) Typical relays as found along the inner front fender. (b) Another bank of relays from another brand of vehicle. Relays vary in their outside size and shape, as well as location.

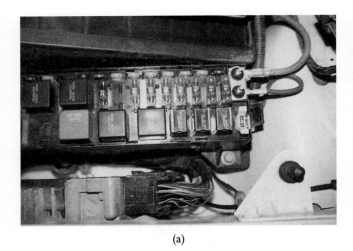

(a)

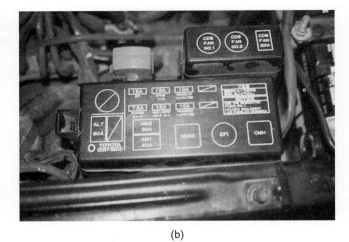

(b)

FIGURE 5–33   *(a)* A power center featuring power cables coming into the right side, with maxi fuses and relays all located together under the hood. The inside cover indentifies the circuit for each component. *(b)* Another example of an underhood power center.

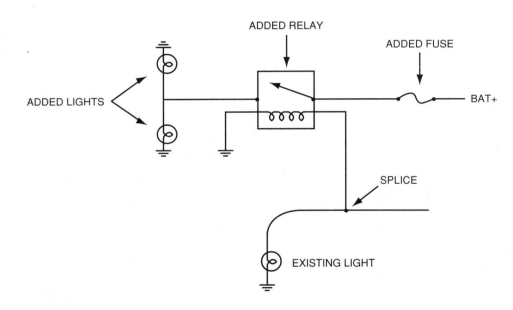

FIGURE 5–34 To add additional lighting, simply tap into an existing light wire and connect a relay. Whenever the existing light is turned on, the coil of the relay is energized. The arm of the relay then connects power from another circuit (fuse) to the auxiliary lights without overloading the existing light circuit.

problem could be a loose or broken ground connection in the trunk area that is shared by both the backup lights and the taillights.

- *Step 3.* Check for voltage at the backup light socket. This can be done using a test light or a voltmeter. See figures 5–35 through 5–37.

If there is voltage available at the socket, the problem is either a defective bulb or a poor ground at the socket or a ground wire connection to the body or frame. If no voltage is available at the socket, consult a wiring diagram for the type of vehicle being tested.

The wiring diagram should show all of the wiring and components included in the circuit. For example, the backup light current must flow through the fuse and ignition switch to the gear selector switch before traveling to the rear backup light socket. As stated in the second step, the fuse used for the backup lights may also be used for other circuits in the vehicle.

The wiring diagram can be used to determine all other components that share the same fuse. If the fuse is blown (open circuit), the cause can be a short in any of the circuits sharing the same fuse. Because the backup light circuit current must be switched on and

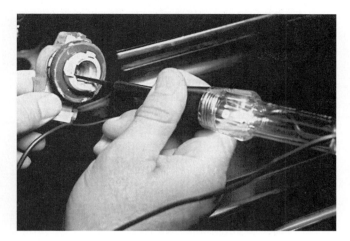

FIGURE 5–35 Checking for current at a backup light socket with a test light.

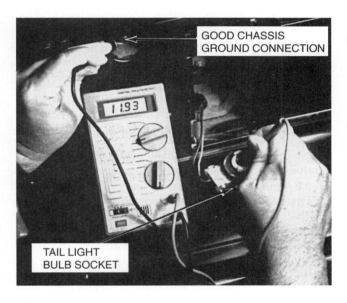

GOOD CHASSIS GROUND CONNECTION

11.93

TAIL LIGHT BULB SOCKET

FIGURE 5–36 Checking for voltage at a backup light socket. The meter reads 11.93 volts, which is satisfactory considering the voltage drops across all wiring connectors and switches before reaching the rear of the vehicle.

off by the gear selector switch, an open in the switch can also prevent the backup lights from functioning.

EUROPEAN WIRING CODES

A circuit diagram is a representation of actual electrical or electronic components using signs and symbols. These symbols are standardized by the Deutsche Industrie Norm (DIN—German Industrial Standard) and the International Electrotechnical Commission (IEC).

FIGURE 5–37 This is the normal amount of grease used by the factory in lamp sockets to help prevent moisture and corrosion damage.

Most European vehicles use code numbers and/or letters to indicate wiring terminals and connections. Trouble-shooting is much easier when the code is identified.

Terminal	Designation
1	Ignition coil negative terminal (tach signal)—green wire
4	Ignition coil high voltage (coil output)
15	Output from ignition switch, battery positive (black wire)
15a	Output at ballast resistor to ignition coil
16	Same as 15 or 15a
30	Alternator output to battery, battery positive (red wire)
31	Ground, battery negative (brown wire)
31b	Alternate ground (brown wire with tracer)
49	Turn signal or flasher input
49a	Turn signal or flasher output
50	Direct starter motor control
53	Wiper motor positive

Terminal	Designation
53a–e	Other wiper-washer leads
54	Brake light power
56	Headlight dimmer switch positive
56a	High beam (white wire or white wire with tracer)
56b	Low beam (yellow wire with or without tracer)
58	Parking lamp positive (gray wire)
61	Charge indicator light
67	Alternator field terminal (also known as DF)
85	Battery positive to relay switching coil
86	Battery negative to relay switching coil
87	Switched relay output
87a	Switched relay output when relay coil not energized (on when 87 is off)
87b	Switched relay output when relay coil energized (on when 87 is on)
B+	Alternator output terminal, battery positive
B−	Ground, battery negative
D+	Charge indicator light; may be positive output terminal of diode trio; also known as 61 (blue wire)
D	Same as D+
D−	Ground, battery negative
DF	Alternator field, control side of field circuit (the "make-and-break" side of the field circuit)
DYN	Same as D+
E	Same as DF
EXC	Exciter; same as DF
F	Field; same as DF
IND	Indicator light; same as 61
M	Ground, battery negative
WL	Indicator light; same as 61
X	Hot when ignition key on except during cranking
+	Auxiliary positive output, used for RFI capacitor, etc.

JAPANESE WIRING CODES

Most Japanese vehicles use code letters to indicate wiring terminals and connections. Circuit knowledge is increased and troubleshooting made easier when the code is known.

Terminal	Designation
A	Alternator output, positive battery voltage-sensing terminal
B	Alternator output, battery positive
E	Ground, earth, battery negative
F	Field, may also be negative input from voltage regulator
IG	Negative input from ignition switch
L	Positive input from indicator light circuit; also positive output to indicator light when charging
N	AC current output, tap onto stator, stator voltage
P	"Pseudo" AC output, connected before a positive diode, used to drive AC device
R	Positive battery input, battery-voltage sensing terminal, used on integral voltage regulator alternators, usually controlled by the ignition switch
S	Positive battery input, similar to R, but usually unswitched connection directly to battery

HEAT AND MOVEMENT

Shorts are commonly caused either by movement, which causes the insulation around wiring to be worn away, or by heat melting the insulation. Whenever checking for a short circuit, first check the wiring susceptible to heat, movement, and damage:

1. **Heat:** wiring near heat sources, such as the exhaust system, cigarette lighter, or alternator
2. **Wire movement:** wiring that moves, such as in areas near the doors, trunk, or hood
3. **Damage:** wiring subject to mechanical injury, such as in the trunk, where heavy objects can move around and smash or damage wiring

LOCATING A SHORT CIRCUIT

A short circuit usually blows a fuse, and a replacement fuse often also blows in the attempt to locate the source of the short circuit. Several methods can be used to locate the short.

Fuse Replacement Method. Disconnect one component at a time and then replace the fuse. If the new fuse blows, continue the process over and over until the location of the short is determined. This method uses many fuses and is *not* a preferred method for finding a short circuit.

Circuit Breaker Method. Another method is to connect an automotive circuit breaker to the contacts of the fuse holder with alligator clips.

NOTE: Circuit breakers are available that plug directly into the fuse panel, replacing a blade-type fuse. See figure 5–38.

The circuit breaker will alternately open and close the circuit, protecting the wiring from possible overheating damage while still providing current flow through the circuit.

NOTE: An HD flasher can also be used in place of a circuit breaker to open and close the circuit. Wires and terminals must be made to connect the flasher unit where the fuse normally plugs in.

All of the components included in the defective circuit should be disconnected one at a time until the circuit breaker stops clicking. The last unit disconnected is the unit causing the short circuit. If the circuit breaker continues to click with all circuit components unplugged, the problem is in the wiring *from* the fuse panel *to* any one of the units in the circuit. Visual inspection of all the wiring or further disconnecting will be necessary to locate the problem.

Ohmmeter Method. The third method uses an ohmmeter connected to the fuse holder and ground. This is the recommended method of finding a short circuit. What is a short circuit? A short circuit is an electrical connection to another wire or to ground before the current flows through some or all of the resistance in the circuit. An ohmmeter will indicate low ohms when connected to a short circuit. An ohmmeter should never be connected to an operating circuit. The correct procedure for locating a short using an ohmmeter is as follows:

1. Connect one lead of an ohmmeter (set to a low scale) to a good clean metal ground and the other lead to the *circuit side* of the fuse holder.

CAUTION: Connecting the lead to the power side of the fuse holder will cause current flow through and damage to the ohmmeter.

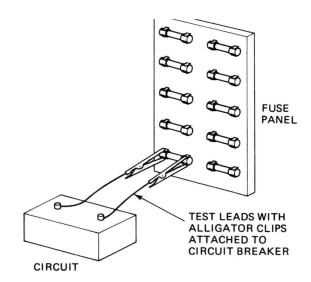

FIGURE 5–38 Replacing a fuse with a circuit breaker in the fuse panel in an attempt to locate the source of a short circuit.

2. The ohmmeter will read zero or almost zero ohms if the circuit is shorted.
3. Disconnect one component in the circuit at a time and watch the ohmmeter. If the ohmmeter reading goes to high ohms or infinity, the component just unplugged was the source of the short circuit.

Gauss Gauge Method. If a short circuit blows a fuse, a special pulsing circuit breaker (similar to a flasher unit) can be installed in the circuit in place of the fuse. Current will flow through the circuit until the circuit breaker opens the circuit. As soon as the circuit breaker opens the circuit, it closes again. This on-and-off current flow creates a pulsing magnetic field around the wire carrying the current. Use a small handheld Gauss gauge to observe this pulsing magnetic field, which is indicated on the gauge as needle movement to the left, then to the right of center. This pulsing magnetic field will register on the Gauss gauge even through the metal body of the vehicle. A needle-type compass can also be used to observe the pulsing magnetic field. See figure 5–39.

ELECTRICAL TROUBLESHOOTING GUIDE

Whenever troubleshooting any electrical component, remember the following hints to find the problem faster and more easily:

1. For a device to work, it must have two things: power and ground. See figures 5–40 and 5–41.

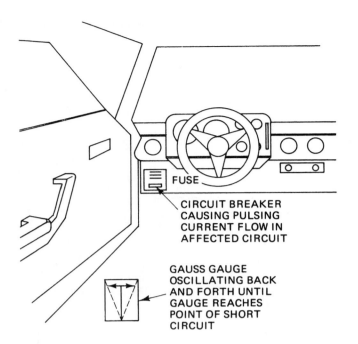

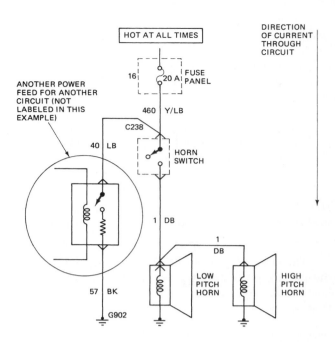

FIGURE 5–39 A Gauss gauge can be used to determine the location of a short circuit.

FIGURE 5–40 Typical Ford horn circuit showing various component parts. The wires are labeled with very brief color abbreviations: Y = yellow, LB = light blue, BK = black, DB = dark blue.

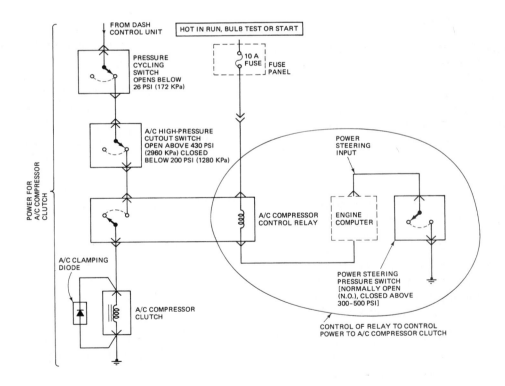

FIGURE 5–41 Typical A/C compressor clutch wiring diagram. Note that the engine computer controls the relay that controls the power (feed) side to the A/C compressor clutch. The power steering pressure switch is an input to the engine computer.

◄ TECH TIP ►

BACKUP BUZZER

All commercial vehicles are required to sound an alarm while backing. This feature is useful for all vehicles in helping to avoid accidents, especially in crowded areas with children. To install, simply splice a buzzer into the backup light circuit. See figure 5–42.

    Install the buzzer where it can be protected from the weather, yet be heard. Sealing the buzzer in a plastic bag is a crude but effective method.

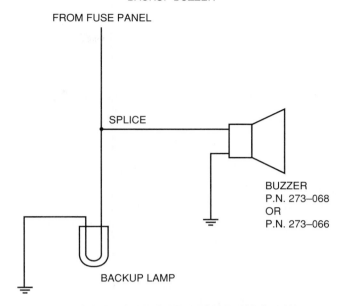

•ALL PART NUMBERS ARE FROM RADIO SHACK

FIGURE 5–42 Backup buzzer.

2. If there is no power to a device, an open power side (blown fuse, etc.) is indicated.

3. If there is power on both sides of a device, an open ground is indicated.

4. If a fuse blows immediately, a grounded power-side wire is indicated.

5. Most electrical faults result from heat or movement.

6. Most non-computer-controlled devices operate by opening and closing the power side of the circuit.

7. Most computer-controlled devices operate by opening and closing the ground side of the circuit.

SUMMARY

1. The higher the gauge size number, the smaller the wire.

2. Metric wire is sized in square millimeters (mm^2).

3. All circuits should be protected by a fuse. The current in the circuit should be about 80% of the fuse rating.

4. Circuit breakers and fusible links are other circuit protection devices.

5. A terminal is the metal end of a wire, whereas a connector is the plastic connection.

6. All wire repair should use either soldering or a crimp-and-seal connector.

7. Relays use a movable arm to conduct a heavy current when activated by a smaller current control circuit.

8. Most wiring diagrams include the wire color, circuit number, and wire gauge.

REVIEW QUESTIONS

1. Describe the AWG wire gauge system and compare it to the metric system.

2. Explain the difference between a wire and a cable.

3. Explain the difference between a terminal and a connector.

4. Discuss how fuses, PTC circuit protectors, circuit breakers, and fusible links protect a circuit.

5. Describe how to perform a wire repair.

MULTIPLE-CHOICE QUESTIONS

1. The higher the AWG number, _____ .
   a. The smaller the wire
   b. The larger the wire
   c. The thicker the insulation
   d. The more strands in the conductor core

2. Metric wire size is measured in units of _____ .
   a. Meters
   b. Cubic centimeters
   c. Square millimeters
   d. Cubic millimeters

3. Which statement is true about fuse ratings?
   a. The fuse rating should be 80% of the maximum current for the circuit.
   b. The fuse rating should be higher than the normal current for the circuit.
   c. Eighty percent of the fuse rating should equal the current in the circuit.
   d. Both b and c.

4. Which statements are true about wire, terminals, and connectors?
   a. Wire is called a lead, and the metal end is a connector.
   b. A connector is usually a plastic piece where terminals lock in.
   c. A lead and a terminal are the same thing.
   d. Both a and c.

5. The type of solder that should be used for electrical work is_____ .
   a. Rosin core
   b. Acid core
   c. 60/40 with no flux
   d. 50/50 with acid paste flux

6. On a wiring diagram, S110 with a ".8 BRN/BLK" means_____ .
   a. Circuit #.8 is spliced under the hood
   b. A connector with 0.8–square millimeter wire
   c. A splice of a brown wire with black stripe, wire size being 0.8 square millimeters (18 gauge AWG)
   d. Both a and b

7. On a German-made vehicle, what is the meaning of the number 30 on a wiring diagram (refer to European wiring codes)?
   a. Output from the ignition switch
   b. Ground, battery negative
   c. Alternator output, battery positive
   d. Charge indicator light circuit

8. On a Japanese-made vehicle, what is the meaning of the letter *L* on a wiring diagram (refer to Japanese wiring codes)?
   a. Alternator output, battery positive
   b. Charge light indicator circuit
   c. Ground, battery negative
   d. Alternator output (AC output)

9. When testing for a short circuit using an ohmmeter, connect one test lead of the ohmmeter to a good ground and connect the other lead to_____ .
   a. The load side of the fuse holder
   b. The power side of the fuse holder
   c. Another good ground
   d. Both a and b

10. If a component such as a dome light has power (voltage) on both the power side and the ground side of the bulb, this indicates_____ .
    a. A defective (open) bulb
    b. A short to ground
    c. A defective (shorted) bulb
    d. An open ground-side circuit

◀ Chapter 6 ▶

DIAGNOSING AND TROUBLESHOOTING LIGHTING AND SIGNALING CIRCUITS

OBJECTIVES

After studying chapter 6, the reader will be able to

1. Determine which replacement bulb to use on a given vehicle.
2. Describe how turn signals work.
3. Use a bulb chart.
4. Discuss troubleshooting procedures for lighting and signaling circuits.

The lighting and signaling circuits represent two of the most frequently serviced automotive electrical areas.

LIGHTING

Exterior lighting is controlled by the headlight switch, which is connected directly to the battery on most vehicles. Therefore, if lights are left on, it can drain the battery. Most headlight switches contain a built-in circuit breaker. If excessive current flows through the headlight circuit, the circuit breaker will momentarily open the circuit, then close it again. The result is headlights that flicker on and off rapidly. This feature allows the headlights to function, as a safety measure, in spite of current overload.

NOTE: Flickering on and off is misunderstood by many drivers and technicians. Because flickering is rapid, many people believe that the problem is caused by a loose headlight or by a defective voltage regulator.

The headlight switch controls the following lights on most vehicles:

1. Headlights
2. Taillights
3. Side marker lights
4. Front parking lights
5. Dash lights
6. Interior (dome) light(s)

NOTE: Because these lights can easily drain the battery if accidentally left on, many newer vehicles control these lights through the vehicle's computer. The computer keeps track of the time the lights are on and can turn them off if the time is excessive. The computer can control either the power side or the ground side of the circuit.

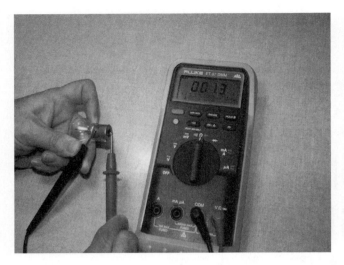

FIGURE 6–1 This single-filament bulb is being tested with a digital multimeter set to read resistance in ohms. The reading of 1.3 ohms is the resistance of the bulb when cold. As soon as current flows through the filament, the resistance increases about 10 times. It is the initial surge of current flowing through the filament when the bulb is cool that causes many bulbs to fail in cold weather as a result of the reduced resistance. As the temperature increases, the resistance increases.

BULB NUMBERS

The number used on automotive bulbs is called the bulb **trade number,** as recorded with the American National Standards Institute (ANSI), and the number is the same regardless of manufacturer. Amber-colored bulbs that use natural amber glass are indicated with an *NA* (for *natural amber*) at the end of the number (for example, #1157NA). A less expensive amber bulb that uses painted glass is labeled with only the letter *A* for *amber* (for example, #1157A).

The trade number also identifies the size, shape, number of filaments, and amount of light produced. The amount of light produced is measured in **candlepower.** For example, the candlepower of a #1156 bulb, commonly used for backup lights, is 32. A #194 bulb, commonly used for dash or side marker lights, is rated at only 2 candlepower. The amount of light produced by a bulb is determined by the resistance of the filament wire, which also affects the amount of current (in amperes) required by the bulb. See figures 6–1 and 6–2.

It is important that the correct trade number of bulb always be used for replacement to prevent circuit or component damage. The correct replacement bulb for your vehicle is usually listed in the owner's manual or service manual. See figure 6–3 and the bulb table.

FIGURE 6–2 Close-up of a dual-filament (double-filament) bulb (#1157) that failed. Notice that one filament (top) broke from its mounting and melted onto the lower filament. This bulb caused the dash lights to come on whenever the brakes were applied.

DOUBLE CONTACT
1157/2057 BULBS

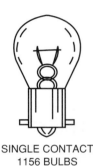

SINGLE CONTACT
1156 BULBS

WEDGE
194 BULB

FIGURE 6–3 Number 1157 or 2057 bulbs are typically used for taillights and front parking lights. These bulbs contain both a low-intensity filament for taillights or parking lights and a high-intensity filament for brake lights and turn signals.

Typical Automotive Light Bulbs

Trade number	Design volts	Design amperes	Watts: $P = I \times E$
37	14.0	0.09	1.3
37E	14.0	0.09	1.3
51	7.5	0.22	1.7

Trade number	Design volts	Design amperes	Watts: $P = I \times E$	Trade number	Design volts	Design amperes	Watts: $P = I \times E$
53	14.4	0.12	1.7	1073	12.8	1.80	23.0
55	7.0	0.41	2.9	1076	12.8	1.80	23.0
57	14.0	0.24	3.4	1129	6.4	2.63	16.8
57X14.0	0.24	3.4		1133	6.2	3.91	24.2
63	7.0	0.63	4.4	1141	12.8	1.44	18.4
67	13.5	0.59	8.0	1142	12.8	1.44	18.4
68	13.5	0.59	8.0	1154	6.4	2.63/0.75	16.8/4.5
70	14.0	0.15	2.1	1156	12.8	2.10	26.9
73	14.0	0.08	1.1	1157	12.8	2.10/0.59	26.9/7.6
74	14.0	0.10	1.4	1157A	12.8	2.10/0.59	26.9/7.6
81	6.5	1.02	6.6	1157NA	12.8	2.10/0.59	26.9/7.6
88	13.0	0.58	7.5	1176	12.8	1.34/0.59	17.2/7.6
89	13.0	0.58	7.5	1195	12.5	3.00	37.5
90	13.0	0.58	7.5	1196	12.5	3.00	37.5
93	12.8	1.04	13.3	1445	14.4	0.13	1.9
94	12.8	1.04	13.3	1816	13.0	0.33	4.3
158	14.0	0.24	3.4	1889	14.0	0.27	3.8
161	14.0	0.19	2.7	1891	14.0	0.24	3.4
168	14.0	0.35	4.9	1892	14.4	0.12	1.7
192	13.0	0.33	4.3	1893	14.0	0.33	4.6
194	14.0	0.27	3.8	1895	14.0	0.27	3.8
194E-1	14.0	0.27	3.8	2033	13.5	0.22	3.0
194NA	14.0	0.27	3.8	2057	12.8	2.10/0.48	26.9/6.1
209	6.5	1.78	11.6	2057NA	12.8	2.10/0.48	26.9/6.1
211-2	12.8	0.97	12.4	2322-1	12.0	0.16	2.0
212-2	13.5	0.74	10.0	2721	12.0	0.10	1.2
214-2	13.5	0.52	7.0	2821	12.0	4.00	3.0
561	12.8	0.97	12.4	2825	12.0	0.42	5.0
562	13.5	0.74	10.0	3057	12.8	0.16	2.1
563	13.5	0.52	7.0	3157	12.0	1.10	12.8
631	14.0	0.63	8.8	3796	12.0	6.00	2.0
880	12.8	2.10	27.0	3893	12.0	3.00	4.0
881	12.8	2.10	27.0	3894	12.0	4.00	3.0
906	13.0	0.69	9.0	3898	12.0	6.00	2.0
912	12.8	1.00	12.8	3966	12.0	4.00	3.0
1003	12.8	0.94	12.0	5004	12.0	4.00	3.0
1004	12.8	0.94	12.0	5006	6.0	1.20	5.0
1034	12.8	1.80/0.59	23.0/7.6	5007	12.0	2.40	5.0

Continued

Trade number	Design volts	Design amperes	Watts: $P = I \times E$
5008	12.0	1.20	10.0
6418	12.0	0.42	5.0
6428	12.0	0.25	3.0
6461	12.0	0.83	10.0
7230	12.0	2.40	5.0
7301	12.0	3.75	45.0
7309	12.0	2.92	35.0
7506	12.0	0.60	21.0
7527	12.0	0.69	18.0
7528	12.0	2.40	5.0
7533	12.0	0.80	15.0
9004 H*	12.8	5.00/35.00	65.0/45.0
9005 H†	12.8	5.00	65.0
9006 H‡	12.8	4.30	55.0
26736	12.0	0.83	10.0
64150 H1	12.0	4.50	55.0
64151 H3	12.0	4.50	55.0
64152 H1	12.0	8.30	100.0
64153 H3	12.0	8.30	100.0
64173 H2	12.0	4.50	55.0
64174 H2	12.0	8.30	100.0
64185 H4	12.0	2.90	35.0
64193 H4	12.0	5.00	60.0
P25-1	13.5	1.86	25.1
P25-2	13.5	1.86	25.1
R19/5	13.5	0.37	5.1
R19/10	13.5	0.74	10.0
W10/3	13.5	0.25	3.4

*High and low beam.
†High beam only.
‡Low beam only.

#1157 BULBS VERSUS #2057 BULBS

Vehicles built after the early 1980s use a bulb for the taillights that has a slightly lower candlepower than was previously used. The newer trade numbers include #2358, #2457, #2057, and #3057. These bulbs provide a 10:1 ratio between the brightness of the brake lights and the brightness of the taillights. Even though a #1157 will fit in the place of a #2057 and work correctly regarding the operation of the turn signals, this ratio between brightnesses made the bulb number change necessary.

◄ TECH TIP ►

HEAVY-DUTY AUTOMOTIVE BULBS

Many automotive bulbs have the same operating parameters (same wattage, voltage, amperage, and candlepower), yet have different trade numbers. Some numbers are for standard duty, whereas others have heavier filament wire or additional filament support, which qualifies them for a different trade number. A fleet-duty designation represents some increase in durability, and a heavy-duty designation identifies the most severe-service bulb.

Regular	Fleet duty	Heavy duty
53	182	1445 or 53X
57	293	1895
67	97	97
68	96	96
69	98	631
90	99	—
93	1093	—
158	193	194
161	184	—
1003	105	—
1004	104	—
1034	198	1157
1034A	—	1157NA/1157A
1073	199	1156
1141	1159	—
1889/1891	1893	1893
4000	—	4040
6014	—	6015

Therefore, if the specification for your vehicle gives a trade number listed under the "regular" heading, you can safely switch to the trade number of bulb listed under the "fleet duty" or "heavy duty" heading. For best operation of turn signals and consistent brightness of bulbs, the switch of trade numbers should include all similar bulbs of the type being replaced.

NOTE: Trade #2358, #2457, and #3057 are wedge-type bulbs and are interchangeable because they all have the same specifications. The problem of possible wrong interchange involves the use of #1157 instead of #2057.

HEADLIGHT SWITCHES

The headlight switch operates the exterior and interior lights of most vehicles. The headlight switch is connected directly to the battery through a fusible link and has power to it at all times. This is called being "hot" all the time. A circuit breaker is built into most headlight switches to protect the headlight circuit. See figure 6–4. The interior dash lights can be dimmed manually by rotating the headlight switch knob, which controls a vari-

able resistor (called a **rheostat**) built into the headlight switch.

The rheostat drops the voltage sent to the dash lights. Whenever there is a voltage drop (increased resistance), there is heat. A coiled resistance wire is built into a ceramic holder that is designed to insulate the rest of the switch from the heat and allow heat to escape. Continual driving with the dash lights dimmed can result in the headlight switch knob getting hot to the touch. This is normal, and the best prevention is to increase the brightness of the dash lights to reduce the amount of heat generated in the switch. The headlight switch also contains a built-in circuit breaker that will rapidly turn the headlights on and off in the event of a short circuit. This prevents a total loss of headlights. If the headlights are rapidly flashing on and off, check the entire headlight circuit for possible shorts. The circuit breaker controls only the headlights. The other lights

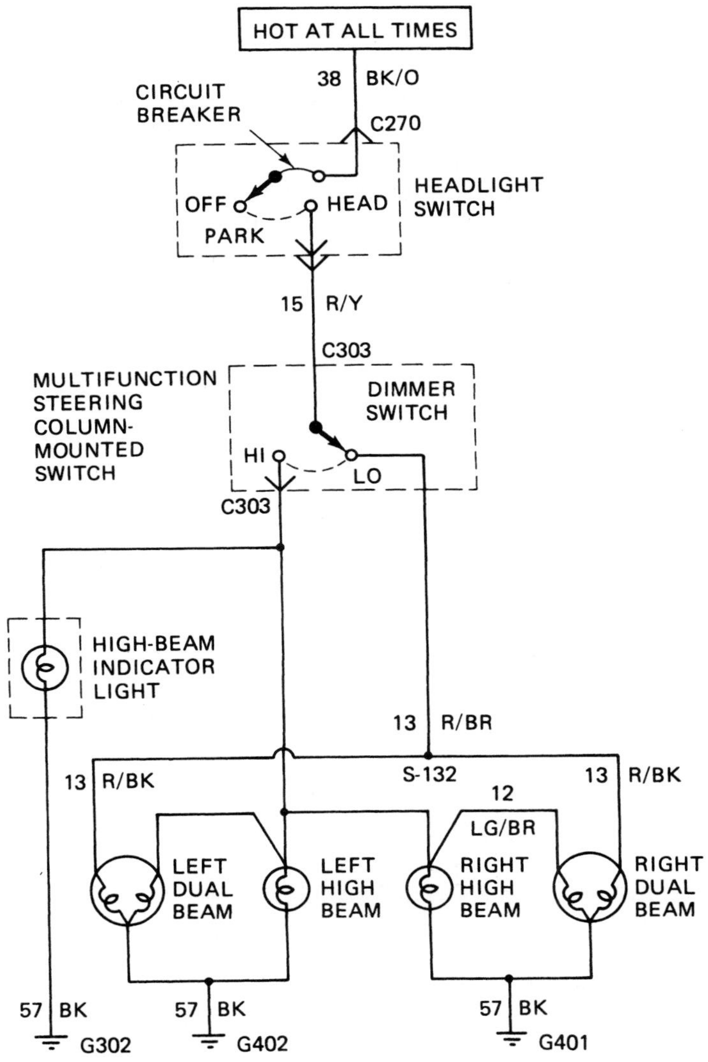

FIGURE 6–4 Typical headlight circuit diagram. Note that the headlight switch is represented by a dotted outline indicating that other circuits (such as dash lights) also operate from the switch.

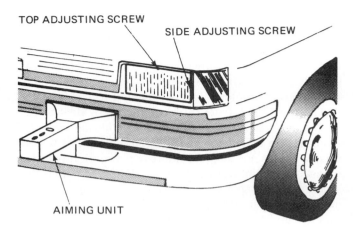

TOP ADJUSTING SCREW
SIDE ADJUSTING SCREW
AIMING UNIT

FIGURE 6–5   All vehicles sold in the United States have to have provision for the use of mechanical aiming devices. Even the halogen bulb units with plastic or glass lenses have locating points and adjustment screws.

controlled by the headlight switch (taillights, dash lights, and parking lights) are fused separately. Flashing headlights may also be caused by a failure in the built-in circuit breaker, requiring replacement of the switch assembly.

REMOVING A HEADLIGHT SWITCH

Most dash-mounted headlight switches can be removed by first removing the dash panel. However, to get the dash panel off, the headlight switch knob usually has to be removed. Some knobs can be removed by depressing a small clip in a notch in the knob itself. Other headlight switch knobs are removed by depressing a spring-loaded release, which allows for removal of the entire headlight switch knob and shaft.

Headlight switches mounted on the steering column are removed as part of the turn signal and wiper switch assembly. Many can be easily removed, whereas others require the removal of the steering wheel and so forth. See the service information for the exact year and model on which you are working in order to be assured of the correct procedure.

SEALED-BEAM HEADLIGHTS

Low-beam headlights contain two filaments: one for low beam and the other for high beam. High-beam headlights contain only one filament. Headlights are standardized so that they can be replaced by sealed-beam

◄ **TECH TIP** ►

THE SWITCH TRICK

Many vehicles equipped with halogen replaceable headlight bulbs in aerodynamic headlights use a #9004 bulb. These bulbs have both a high- and low-beam filament. However, only the low-beam filament is used on the outboard lens and only the high-beam filament is used on the inboard position. If a low-beam filament should fail, simply switch the bulb with the high-beam bulb. The high-beam bulb has a low-beam filament that has never been used, and the low-beam bulb has an unused high-beam filament.

units that can be purchased at most auto parts stores. Because low-beam headlights also contain a high-beam filament, the entire headlight assembly must be replaced if either filament is defective.

A sealed-beam headlight can be tested with an ohmmeter. A good bulb should cause the ohmmeter to indicate low ohms between the ground terminal and both power-side (hot) terminals. If either the high-beam or the low-beam filament is burned out, the ohmmeter will indicate infinity (OL). See figures 6–5 through 6–7 regarding headlight aiming.

COMPOSITE HEADLIGHTS

Composite headlights are constructed using a replaceable bulb and a fixed lens cover that is part of the vehicle. The replaceable bulbs are usually bright halogen bulbs. Halogen bulbs get very hot during operation (between 500° and 1300° F [260° and 700° C]). It is important never to touch the glass of any halogen bulb with bare fingers because the natural oils of the skin on the glass bulb can cause the bulb to break when it heats during normal operation.

HALOGEN SEALED-BEAM HEADLIGHTS

Halogen sealed-beam headlights are brighter and more expensive than normal headlights. Because of their extra brightness, it is common practice to have only two headlights on at any one time because the candlepower output would exceed the maximum U.S.

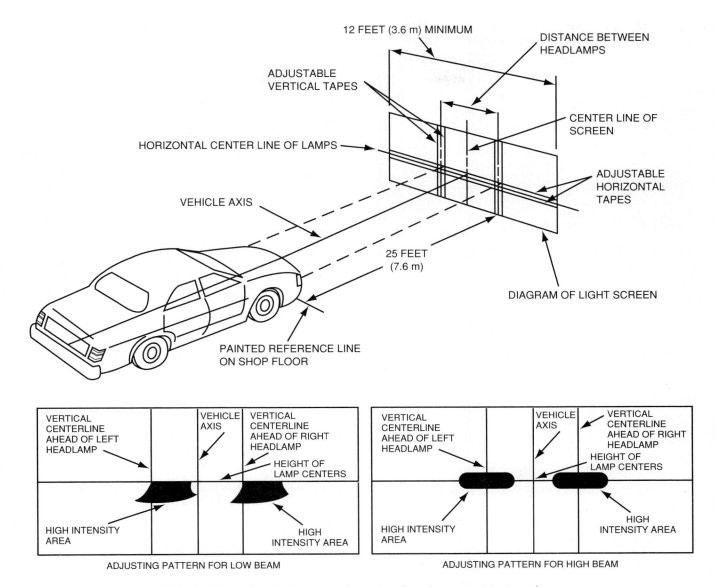

FIGURE 6–6   Typical headlight-aiming diagram as found in a service manual.

federal standards if all four halogen headlights were on. Therefore, before trying to repair the problem that only two of the four lamps are on, check with the owner's manual or shop manual for proper operation.

CAUTION: Do not attempt to wire all headlights together. The extra current flow could overheat the wiring from the headlight switch through the dimmer switch and to the headlights. The overloaded circuit could cause a fire.

HIGH-INTENSITY DISCHARGE HEADLIGHTS

High-intensity discharge (HID) headlights produce a distinctive blue-white light that is crisper, clearer, and brighter than light produced by a halogen headlight. Unlike a halogen bulb, the HID bulb has no filament. It creates light from an electrical discharge between two electrodes in a gas-filled arc tube. It produces twice the light with less electrical input than conventional halogen bulbs.

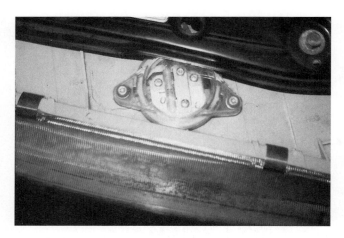

FIGURE 6–7 Many composite headlights have a built-in bubble to make aiming easy and accurate.

◄ TECH TIP ►

DIAGNOSE BULB FAILURE

Halogen bulbs can fail for various reasons. Some of the causes for halogen bulb failure, along with their indications, are as follows:

Gray color—low voltage to bulb (check for corroded socket or connector)

White (cloudy) color—indication of an air leak

Broken filament—usually caused by excessive vibration

Blistered glass—indication that someone has touched the glass

NOTE: Never touch the glass ampule of any halogen bulb. The oils from your fingers can cause unequal heating of the glass during operation leading to a shorter than normal service life.

The HID lighting system consists of the discharge arc source, igniter, ballast, and headlight assembly. The two electrodes are contained in a tiny quartz capsule filled with xenon gas, mercury, and metal halide salts. The lights and support electronics are expensive, but they should last the life of the vehicle unless physically damaged.

DAYLIGHT RUNNING LIGHTS

Daylight running lights (DRL) involve operating the headlights (usually at reduced current and voltage) whenever the vehicle is running. Canada has required daylight running lights on all new vehicles since 1989. DRLs have reduced accidents where used.

Daylight running lights usually use a control module that turns on *either* the low-beam or the high-beam lamps. The lights on some vehicles come on whenever the engine starts. Some vehicles will turn on the lamps when the engine is running, but delay their operation until a signal from the vehicle speed sensor indicating that the vehicle is moving.

To avoid having the lights on during servicing, some systems will turn off the headlights whenever the parking brake is applied. Others will only light the headlights when the vehicle is in a drive gear. See figure 6–8.

CAUTION: Most factory daylight running lights operate the headlights at reduced intensity. These are not designed to be used at night. Normal intensity of the headlights (and operation of the other external lamps) is actuated by turning on the headlights as usual.

DIMMER SWITCHES

The headlight switch controls the power or hot side of the headlight circuit. The current is then sent to the dimmer switch, which allows current to flow to either the high-beam or the low-beam filament of the headlight bulb. An indicator light lights on the dash whenever the bright lights are selected.

The dimmer switch can be either foot operated on the floor or hand operated on the steering column. The popular steering column switches are actually attached to the *outside* of the steering column on most vehicles and are spring-loaded. To replace most of these types of dimmer switches, the steering column needs to be lowered slightly to gain access to the switch itself, which is also adjustable for proper lever operation.

TURN (DIRECTIONAL) SIGNALS

A turn signal flasher unit is a metal or plastic can containing a switch that opens and closes the turn signal circuit. See figure 6–9. This turn signal flasher unit is usually installed in a metal clip attached to the dash panel to allow the "clicking" noise of the flasher to be

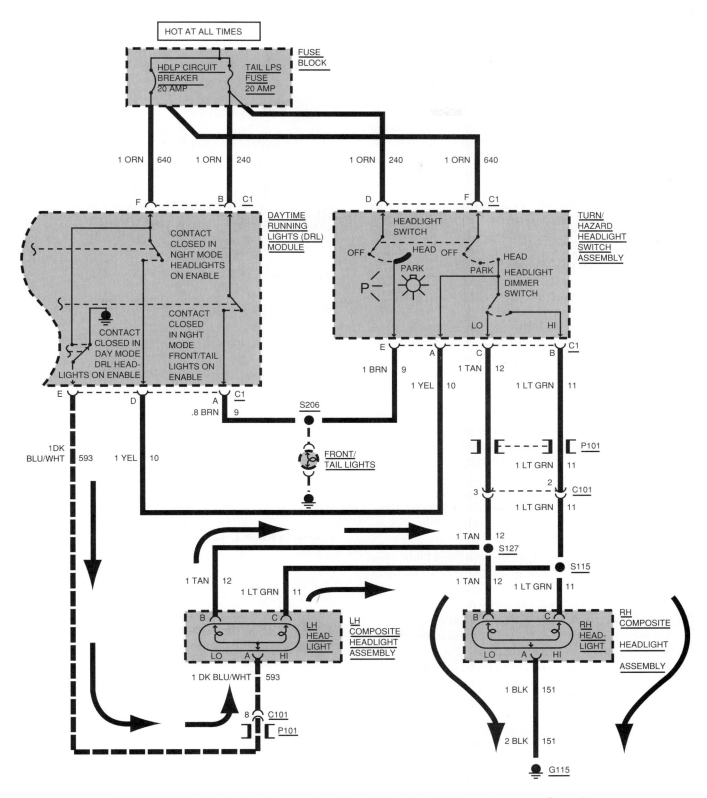

FIGURE 6–8 Typical daylight running lights (DRL) circuit. Follow the arrows from the DRL module through both headlights. Notice that the left and right headlights are connected in series, resulting in increased resistance, less current flow, and dimmer than normal lighting. When the normal headlights are turned on, both headlights receive full battery voltage, with the left headlight grounding through the DRL module.

heard by the driver. The turn signal flasher is designed to transmit the current to light the front and rear bulbs on only one side at a time.

The United States Department of Transportation (DOT) regulation requires that the driver be alerted when a turn signal bulb is not working. This is achieved by using a series-type flasher unit. The flasher unit requires current flow through two bulbs (one in the front and one in the rear) in order to flash. If one bulb burns out, the current flow through only one bulb is not sufficient to make the unit flash; it will be a steady light. These turn signal units are often called DOT flashers.

When the turn signal flasher unit is old, the lights will flash more slowly (both sides equally). The contact points inside the flasher unit may become corroded and pitted, requiring higher voltage to operate. To restore normal operation, replace the turn signal flasher unit. Other common turn signal problems and possible solutions include the following:

Problem	Possible Causes and/or Solutions
1. Slow flashing on both sides equally	1. Replace the worn flasher unit. Check the battery and the charging voltage to be certain that the charging circuit and battery are supplying high-enough voltage for proper operation of the turn signals. (See chapter 11.)
2. Slow or no flashing on one side only	2. Replace the defective bulb, or clean poor connections on the front or rear bulbs on the side that does not work.
3. Turn signals not flashing on either side	3. The most likely cause is a defective flasher unit, in which case replacement will be necessary. However, defective bulbs or connections on *both* sides could also be the cause.

Most turn signal flasher units are mounted in a metal clip that is attached to the dash. The dash panel acts as a sounding board, increasing the sound of the flasher unit. Most four-way hazard flasher units are plugged into the fuse panel. Some two-way turn signal flasher units are also plugged into the fuse panel. How do you know for sure where the flasher unit is located? With both the turn signal and the ignition on, listen and/or feel for the clicking of the flasher unit. Some service manuals also give general locations for the placement of flasher units.

FIGURE 6–9 Two styles of two-prong flashers.

HAZARD FLASHERS

Hazard flasher units are usually plugged into the fuse panel and are designed to flash four or more bulbs safely and at the same flashing speed regardless of the number of bulbs used in the lighting circuit.

Therefore, if trailer lights are connected to the taillights, the flasher unit for the four-way hazard flasher should be used in place of the standard turn signal flasher. However, the regular (DOT) turn signal flasher *cannot* be used for the four-way hazard flashers. The result would be the very rapid flashing of the hazard flasher and damage to the flasher itself.

COURTESY LIGHTS

Courtesy lights is a generic term generally used for interior lights, including overhead (dome) and under-the-dash (courtesy) lights. These interior lights can be operated by rotating the headlight switch knob fully counterclockwise (left) or by operating switches located in the doorjambs of the vehicle doors. There are two types of circuits commonly used for these interior lights. Most manufacturers, except Ford, use the door switches to ground the courtesy light circuit. Many Ford vehicles use the door switches to open and close the power side of the circuit.

Many newer vehicles operate the interior lights through the vehicle computer or through an electronic module. Because the exact wiring and operation of these units differ, consult the service literature for the exact model on which you are working.

ILLUMINATED ENTRY

Some vehicles are equipped with illuminated entry, whereby the interior lights are turned on for a given amount of time whenever the outside door handle is operated while the doors are locked. Most vehicles equipped with illuminated entry also light the exterior door keyhole. Some vehicles equipped with body computers use the door handle electrical switch of the illuminated entry circuit to "wake up" the power supply for the body computer.

FIBER OPTICS

Fiber optics is the transmission of light through special plastic (polymethyl methacrylate) that keeps the light rays parallel even if the plastic is tied in a knot. These strands of plastic are commonly used in automotive applications as indicators for the driver that certain lights are functioning. For example, some vehicles are equipped with fender-mounted units that light whenever the lights or turn signals are operating. Plastic fiber-optic strands, which often look like standard electrical wire, transmit the light at the bulb to the indicator on top of the fender so that the driver can determine if a certain light is operating. Fiber-optic strands can also be run like wires to indicate the operation of all lights on the dash or console. Fiber optic strands are also commonly used to light ashtrays, outside

door locks, and other areas where a small amount of light is required. The source of the light can be any normally operating light bulb. A special bulb clip is usually used to retain the fiber-optic plastic tube near the bulb.

FEEDBACK

When current that lacks a good ground goes backward along the power side of the circuit in search of a return path (ground) to the battery, this reverse flow is called **feedback** or **reverse-bias** current flow. Feedback can cause other lights or gauges to work that should not be working.

AN EXAMPLE OF FEEDBACK

A customer complained that when the headlights were on, the left turn signal indicator light on the dash remained on. The cause was found to be a poor ground connection for the left front parking light socket. The front parking light bulb is a dual filament: one filament for the parking light (dim) and one filament for the turn signal operation (bright). A corroded socket did not

◄ **TECH TIP** ►

SERVICE MANUAL DIAGNOSIS

It used to be that if a technician could see the schematic of the circuit being diagnosed, then the problem could be corrected. From the schematic or wiring diagram, the technician could see where voltage should be at various parts of the circuit. Not anymore! Many of today's vehicles use a computer to control almost everything, including interior lights. The old switches by the door simply signal the computer that a door has been opened. The computer controls the lighting to help guard against accidental battery drain. For example, in the event that the vehicle door has been left open, the computer can open the circuit and prevent a dead battery.

The schematic rarely shows exactly how the circuit works. However, most service manuals walk you through the diagnosis. With a service manual (or service disk if on compact disk with read-only memory [CD-ROM]), the technician is not lost. Always follow the procedures exactly! Even if the service procedure sounds long and involved, the procedure *will* lead you to the correct diagnosis.

◄ **TECH TIP** ►

LIGHTS-ON BUZZER

Many vehicles are not equipped with a buzzer or beeper to notify the driver that the lights are on. Here is an easy-to-install, simple buzzer that can be added to any vehicle.

The basic principle on which it operates is the fact that most ignition fuses "go to ground" when the ignition is turned off. Therefore, the power side (+) of the buzzer is powered by a light fuse (circuit) and the ground side (−) connects to the ignition fuse. Therefore, if the lights are on and the ignition switch is off, the buzzer gets both a power and a ground and the buzzer sounds. See figure 6–10.

NOTE: Due to the resistance in some ignition-controlled circuits, it may be necessary to try several different ignition-controlled fuses until a fuse is found that will permit the buzzer to operate.

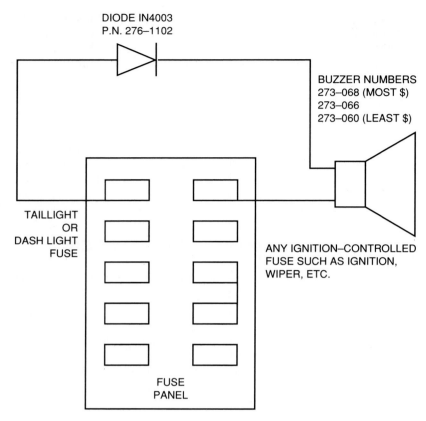

* ALL PART NUMBERS ARE FROM RADIO SHACK

FIGURE 6–10   Lights-on buzzer circuit. The buzzer will sound when the ignition is turned off if the lights are on.

provide a good enough ground to conduct all of the current required to light the dim filament of the bulb.

The two filaments of the bulb share the same ground connection and are electrically connected. When all of the current could not flow through the bulb's ground in the socket, it caused a feedback or reversed its flow through the other filament, looking for ground. The turn signal filament is electrically connected to the dash indicator light; therefore, the reversed current on its path toward ground could light the turn signal indicator light. Cleaning or replacing the socket usually solves the problem if the ground wire for the socket is making a secure chassis ground connection.

LIGHTING SYSTEM TROUBLESHOOTING GUIDE

The following list will assist technicians in troubleshooting lighting systems.

Problem	*Possible Causes and/or Solutions*
1. One headlight dim	**1.** Check for poor ground connection on body.
2. One headlight out (dim or bright)	**2.** Possible burned-out headlight filament. Check the headlight with an ohmmeter. There should be a low-ohm reading between the power-side connection and the ground terminal of the bulb.
3. Both high- and low-beam headlights out	**3.** Check for burned-out bulbs. Check for voltage at the wiring connector to the headlights (possible open circuit to the headlights or open [defective] dimmer switch).
4. All headlights inoperative	**4.** Possible burned-out filaments in all headlights. Check for proper charging system voltage. Possible defective dimmer switch. Possible defective headlight switch.
5. Slow turn signal operation	**5.** Possible defective flasher unit. Possible high resistance in sockets or ground wire connections. Possible incorrect bulb numbers.

6. Turn signals operating on one side only

6. Possible burned-out bulb on affected side. Possible poor ground connection or defective socket on affected side. Possible incorrect bulb number on affected side.

7. Interior light(s) inoperative

7. Possible burned-out bulb(s). Possible open in the power-side circuit (blown fuse). Possible open in doorjamb switch(es).

8. Interior lights on all the time

8. Possible shorted doorjamb switch. Possible headlight switch turned fully counterclockwise.

9. Brake lights inoperative

9. Possible defective brake switch. Possible defective turn signal switch. Possible burned-out brake light bulbs. Possible open circuit or poor ground connection.

10. Hazard warning lights inoperative

10. Possible defective hazard flasher unit. Possible open in hazard circuit.

11. Hazard warning lights blinking too rapidly

11. Possible incorrect flasher unit. Possible shorted wiring to front or rear lights. Possible incorrect bulb numbers.

SUMMARY

1. Automotive bulbs are identified by trade numbers.
2. The trade number is the same regardless of manufacturer for the exact same bulb specification.
3. Daylight running lights (DRL) light the headlights, usually at reduced intensity, whenever the engine is running or the vehicle is moving.
4. High-intensity discharge (HID) headlights are brighter and have a blue tint.
5. One defective turn signal bulb causes the turn signal on the affected side to stop blinking (flashing).

REVIEW QUESTIONS

1. Explain why the exact same trade number of bulb should be used as a replacement.
2. Explain why you should not touch a halogen bulb with your fingers.
3. Describe how to diagnose a turn signal operating problem.
4. Discuss how to aim headlights on a vehicle equipped with aerodynamic-style headlights.

MULTIPLE-CHOICE QUESTIONS

1. Technician A says that the bulb trade number is the same for all bulbs of the same size. Technician B says that a dual-filament bulb has different candlepower ratings for each filament. Which technician is correct?
   a. A only
   b. B only
   c. Both a and b
   d. Neither a nor b

2. Two technicians are discussing flasher units. Technician A says that a DOT-approved flasher unit should be used only for turn signals. Technician B says that a variable-load flasher will function for turn signal usage, although it will not warn the driver if a bulb burns out. Which technician is correct?
   a. A only
   b. B only
   c. Both a and b
   d. Neither a nor b

3. Interior overhead lights (dome lights) are operated by doorjamb switches that _____ .
   a. Complete the power side of the circuit
   b. Complete the ground side of the circuit
   c. Move the bulb(s) into contact with the power and ground
   d. Either a or b depending on application

4. Electrical feedback is usually a result of _____ .
   a. Too high a voltage in a circuit
   b. Too much current (in amperes) in a circuit
   c. Lack of a proper ground
   d. Both a and b

5. Which bulb is brightest? (Refer to the bulb table.)
   a. #194
   b. #168
   c. #194NA
   d. #57

6. If a #1157 bulb were to be installed in a left front parking brake socket instead of a #2057 bulb, what would be the most likely result?

   a. The left turn signal would flash faster.

   b. The left turn signal would flash slower.

   c. The left parking light would be slightly brighter.

   d. The left parking light would be slightly dimmer.

7. A technician replaced a #1157NA with a #1157A bulb. Which is the most likely result?

   a. The bulb is brighter because the #1157A candlepower is higher.

   b. The amber color of the bulb is a different shade.

   c. The bulb is dimmer because the #1157A candlepower is lower.

   d. Both b and c.

8. A customer complained that every time he turned on his vehicle's lights, the left-side turn signal indicator light on the dash remained on. The most likely cause is _____.

   a. A poor ground to the parking light (or taillight) bulb on the *left* side

   b. A poor ground to the parking light (or taillight) bulb on the *right* side causing current to flow to the left-side lights

   c. A defective (open) parking light (or taillight) bulb on the left side

   d. A defective (open) parking light (or taillight) bulb on the right side

DIAGNOSING AND TROUBLESHOOTING DASH INSTRUMENTATION

OBJECTIVES

After studying chapter 7, the reader will be able to

1. Discuss how a fuel gauge works.
2. Explain how to use a service manual to troubleshoot a malfunctioning dash instrument.
3. Describe how to use the bulb test position to help diagnose problems.
4. List the various types of dash instrument displays.

Dash instruments are the main source of information for the driver regarding vehicle operation.

ANALOG DASH INSTRUMENTS

Dash instruments are either analog or digital. This section describes only the operation and testing of **analog-type** (also called **needle-type**) dash instruments. (The next section will discuss digital instruments.) There are two basic types of gauges used: the **electromagnetic** and the **thermoelectric.** General Motors uses the electromagnetic type, whereas Ford, Chrysler, and American Motors usually use the thermoelectric type. The type used, if unknown, can usually be determined by looking at the fuel gauge with the ignition off.

If the gauge reads the fuel level with the ignition off, it is an electromagnetic gauge. If the gauge falls to empty with the ignition off, the gauge is thermoelectric. All dash instruments on a vehicle work in the same way as the fuel gauge; only the function being measured is different.

Thermoelectric Gauges

A thermoelectric gauge uses electrical current flow through the meter, controlled by a **sending unit** or **sensor,** to heat a curved bimetallic strip. As the current flow increases, the heat generated inside the gauge causes the indicator needle to swing toward the right.

This type of gauge moves very slowly, which is an advantage because turns and hills do not affect the readings of the fuel gauge, for example, and the needle tends to remain steady. However, a thermoelectric gauge is very sensitive to battery voltage variations. Therefore, to maintain accuracy, thermoelectric-type gauges use an **instrument voltage regulator** (IVR). An IVR maintains instrument voltage at an average of 5 volts. See figure 7–1.

The regulator uses a bimetallic strip and an electric heating coil, which will alternately open and close (pulse) a contact, which produces the average 5 volts for all instrument gauges. To prevent radio interference caused by the pulsation from the regulator, a small coil

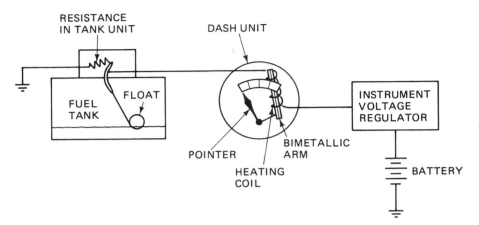

FIGURE 7–1 A thermoelectric fuel gauge has 5 volts coming from the instrument voltage regulator (IVR). The IVR is shared by all other dash instruments. Electronic gauges use the same sensor (sending unit), but use electronic circuits to control needle movement or digital display.

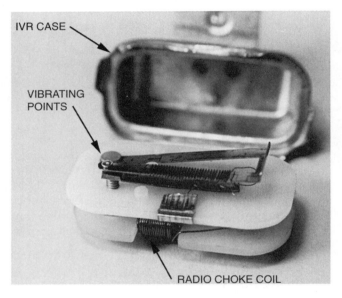

FIGURE 7–2 Instrument voltage regulator. Vibrating points maintain current through the instruments at 5 volts. The radio choke prevents radio interference created by the pulsing current flow.

of wire called a **radio choke** is installed in the power lead going to the IVR. If *all* dash instruments are functioning incorrectly, as when all are reading high or low, the usual cause is the instrument voltage regulator located on the back of the instrument panel. See figure 7–2.

Electromagnetic Gauges

Electromagnetic dash instruments use small electromagnetic coils that are connected to a sending unit for such things as fuel level, water temperature, and oil pressure. The resistance of the sensor varies with what is being measured. See figure 7–3 for typical electromagnetic fuel gauge operation.

◀ **TECH TIP** ▶

GET A SERVICE MANUAL AND USE IT

Today's electronic circuits are often too complex to show on a wiring diagram. Instead, all of the electronics are simply indicated as a solid box with "electronic module" printed on the diagram. Even if all of the electronic circuitry were shown on the wiring diagram, it would require the skill of an electronic engineer to determine exactly how the circuit was designed to work. Study figure 7–4. Note that the grounding for the "check oil" dash indicator lamp is accomplished through an electronic buffer. The exact conditions, such as amount of time since the ignition was shut off, are unknown to the technician. To correctly diagnose problems with this type of circuit *requires* that the technicians read, understand, and follow the written diagnostic procedures specified by the vehicle manufacturer.

COMPUTER-CONTROLLED INSTRUMENT PANELS

Many instrument panels are operated by electronic control units that communicate with the engine control computer for engine data such as revolutions per minute (RPM) and engine temperature. These electronic instrument panels (IPs) use the voltage change from varying-resistance sensors, such as that of the fuel gauge to determine fuel level. Therefore, even though the sensor in the fuel tank is the same, the display itself may be computer controlled. Because all

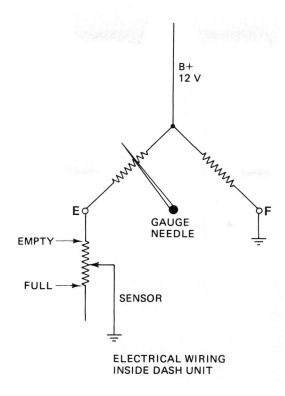

ELECTRICAL WIRING
INSIDE DASH UNIT

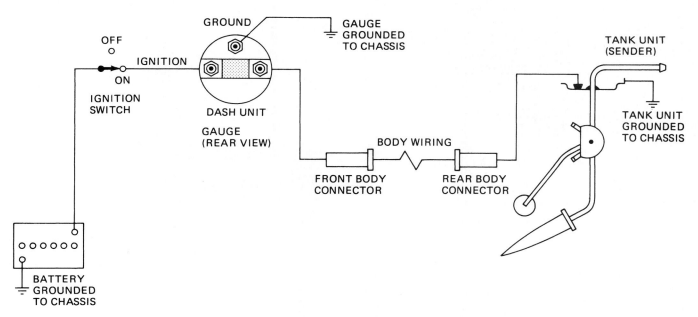

TYPICAL FUEL GAUGE SYSTEM SCHEMATIC

FIGURE 7–3 Electromagnetic fuel gauge wiring. If the sensor wire is unplugged and grounded, the needle should point to "E" (empty). If the sensor wire is unplugged and held away from ground, the needle should point to "F" (full).

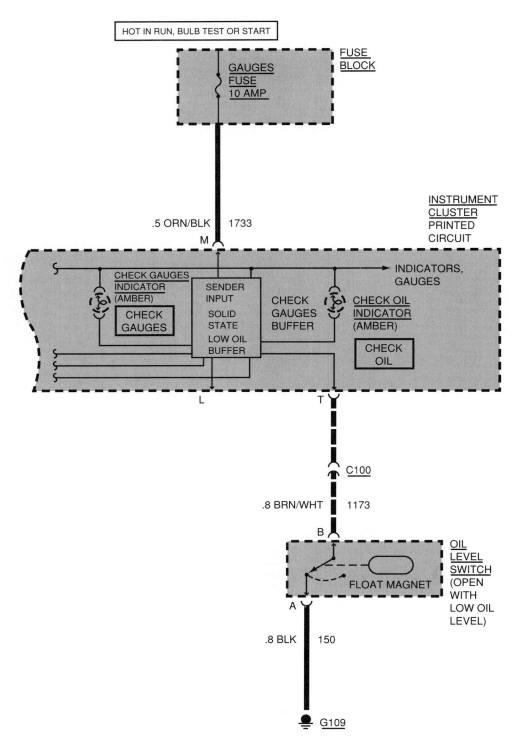

FIGURE 7–4 The ground for the "check oil" indicator lamp is controlled by the electronic low-oil buffer. Even though this buffer is connected to an oil level sensor, the buffer also takes into consideration the amount of time the engine has been stopped and the temperature of the engine. The only way to properly diagnose a problem with this circuit is to use the procedures specified by the vehicle manufacturer. Besides, only the engineer that designed the circuit knows for sure how it is supposed to work.

sensors' inputs are interconnected, the technician should always follow the factory-recommended diagnostic procedures.

DASH INSTRUMENTS

With electromagnetic gauges, if the resistance of the sensor is low, the meter reads low. If the resistance of the sensor is high, the meter reads high.

NOTE: Thermoelectric gauges are opposite from electromagnetic gauges and read low when resistance is high. The following procedures are given for electromagnetic gauges and should be reversed for working on thermoelectric gauges.

When a technician is troubleshooting a fuel gauge, if the power wire is unplugged from the tank unit with the ignition on, the dash unit should move toward full (high resistance). If the power lead is touched to a ground (low resistance), the fuel gauge should register empty. The same operation can be used with oil pressure and water temperature gauges.

TELLTALE LAMPS

Telltale lamps (often called **idiot lights**) warn the driver of system failure. Whenever the ignition is turned on, all warning lamps come on as a bulb check.

The charging system warning lamp may be labeled "CHARGE," "GEN," or "ALT" and will light if the charging system voltage is lower than battery voltage. Complete operation of the charging system and the warning lamp circuit is discussed in chapter 11.

The oil pressure lamp operates through use of an oil pressure sensor unit, which is screwed into the engine block, and which grounds the electrical circuit and lights the dash warning lamp in the event of low oil pressure (3 to 7 psi [20 to 50 kilopascals (kPa)]). Normal oil pressure is generally between 10 and 60 psi (70 and 400 kPa).

OIL PRESSURE LAMP

To test the operation of the oil pressure warning circuit, unplug the wire from the oil pressure sending unit, usually located near the oil filter, with the ignition switch on. With the wire disconnected from the sending unit, the warning lamp should be off. If the wire is touched to

◄ **TECH TIP** ►

OOPS!

After replacing valve cover gaskets on a Chevrolet V-8, the technician discovered that the oil pressure warning lamp was on. After checking the oil level and finding everything else okay, the technician discovered a wire pinched under the valve cover.

The wire went to the oil pressure sending unit. The edge of the valve cover had cut through the insulation and caused the current from the oil lamp to go to ground through the engine. Normally the oil lamp comes on when the sending unit grounds the wire from the lamp.

The technician freed the pinched wire and covered the cut with silicone sealant to prevent corrosion damage.

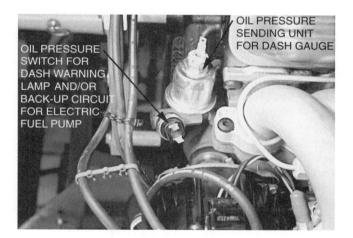

FIGURE 7–5 This engine uses both an oil pressure sensor and an oil pressure switch. The smaller unit is a switch that can turn a light or another unit on and off. The larger unit is a sensor that is a variable-resistance unit that varies with oil pressure and is used for a dash oil pressure gauge.

a ground, the warning lamp should be on. If there is *any* doubt of the operation of the oil pressure warning lamp, always check actual engine oil pressure using a gauge that can be screwed into the opening that is left after unscrewing the oil pressure sending unit. For removing the sending unit, special sockets are available at most auto parts stores, or a 1- or 1¹⁄₁₆-inch six-point socket may be used for most units. See figure 7–5 for the location of typical oil pressure sending units.

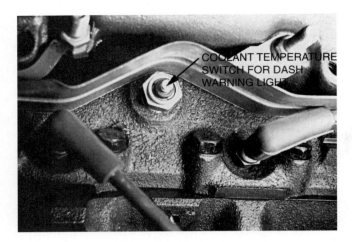

FIGURE 7–6 Coolant temperature switch located on the left (driver's side) cylinder head on this small-block Chevrolet V-8 engine.

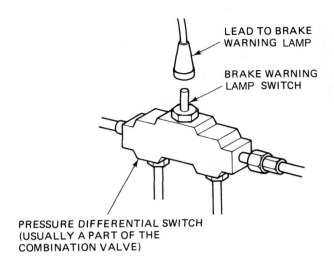

FIGURE 7–7 Typical brake warning lamp switch located on or near the master brake cylinder.

TEMPERATURE LAMP

The "hot" lamp or engine coolant overheat warning lamp warns the driver whenever the engine coolant temperature is between 248° and 258° F (124° C). This temperature is just slightly below the boiling point of the coolant in a properly operating cooling system. To test the hot lamp, disconnect and ground the wire from the water temperature sending unit. The hot lamp should come on. The sensor is located in the engine block, usually near the thermostat. Always check the cooling system operation and the operation of the warning lamp circuit whenever the hot lamp comes on during normal driving. See figure 7–6.

BRAKE WARNING LAMP

All vehicles sold in the United States after 1967 must be equipped with a dual braking system and a dash-mounted warning lamp to signal the driver of a failure in one part of the hydraulic brake system. The switch that operates the warning lamp is called a **pressure differential switch**. This switch is usually the center portion of a multiple-purpose brake part called a **combination valve**. If there is unequal hydraulic pressure in the braking system, the switch usually grounds the 12-volt lead at the switch and the lamp comes on. See figure 7–7.

Unfortunately, the dash warning lamp is often the same lamp as that used to warn the driver that the parking brake is on. The warning lamp is usually operated by using the parking brake lever or brake hydraulic pressure switch to complete the ground for the warning lamp circuit. If the warning lamp is on, first check to see if the parking brake is fully released. If the parking

brake is fully released, the problem could be a defective parking brake switch or a hydraulic brake problem. To test for which system is causing the lamp to remain on, simply unplug the wire from the valve or switch. If the wire on the pressure differential switch is disconnected and the warning lamp remains on, the problem is due to a defective or misadjusted parking brake switch. If, however, the warning lamp goes out when the wire is removed from the brake switch, the problem is due to a hydraulic brake fault that caused the pressure differential switch to complete the warning lamp circuit.

DIGITAL (ELECTRONIC) DASH OPERATION

Mechanical or electromechanical dash instruments use cables, mechanical transducers, and sensors to operate a particular dash instrument. Digital dash instruments use various electric and electronic sensors that activate segments or sections of an electronic display. Most electronic dash clusters use a computer chip and various electronic circuits to operate and control the internal power supply, sensor voltages, and display voltages. Electronic dash display systems may use one or more of the several types of displays: LED, liquid crystal display (LCD), vacuum tube fluorescent (VTF), and cathode ray tube (CRT).

LED Digital Displays

LED stands for *light-emitting diode*. All diodes emit some form of energy during operation, and the LED is a semiconductor that is constructed to release energy in the form of light. Many colors of LEDs can be constructed, but the most popular are red, green, and yellow. Red is difficult to see in direct sunlight; therefore, if an LED is used, most vehicle manufacturers use yellow. Light-emitting diodes can be arranged in a group of seven. Seven-segment LEDs can be used to display both numbers and letters. See figure 7–8.

An LED display requires more electrical power than do other types of electronic displays. A typical LED display requires 30 milliamperes for each *segment;* therefore, each number or letter displayed could require 210 milliamperes (0.210 milliamperes).

Liquid Crystal Displays

Liquid crystal displays (LCDs) can be arranged into a variety of forms, letters, numbers, and bar graph displays. LCD construction consists of a special fluid sandwiched between two sheets of polarized glass. The special fluid between the glass plates will permit light to pass if a small voltage is applied to the fluid through a conductive film laminated to the glass plates.

The light from a very bright halogen bulb behind the LCD shines through those segments of the LCD that have been polarized to let the light through, which then show numbers or letters. Color filters can be placed in front of the display to change the color of certain segments of the display, such as the maximum engine speed on a digital tachometer. LCDs are used on newer-model Chevrolet Corvettes and several other makes and models.

NOTE: Be careful, when cleaning an LCD, not to push on the glass plate covering the special fluid. If excessive pressure is exerted on the glass, the display may be permanently distorted. If the glass breaks, the fluid will escape and could damage other components in the vehicle as a result of its strong alkaline nature. Use only a soft, damp cloth to clean these displays.

The major disadvantage of an LCD digital dash is that the numbers or letters are slow to react or change at low temperatures.

Vacuum Tube Fluorescent Displays

The vacuum tube fluorescent (VTF) display is a popular automotive and household appliance display because it is very bright and can easily be viewed in strong sunlight. The usual VTF display is green, but white is often used for home appliances. The VTF display generates its bright light in a manner similar to that of a TV screen, whereby a chemical-coated light-emitting element called a **phosphor** is hit with high-speed electrons. VTF dis-

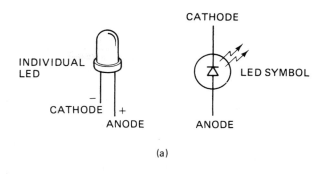

(a)

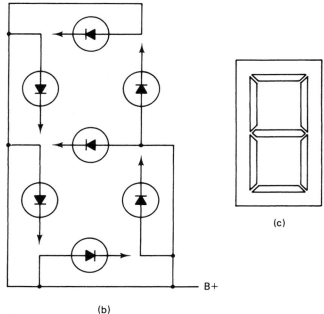

(b)

FIGURE 7–8 *(a)* Symbol and line drawing of a typical light-emitting diode (LED). *(b)* Grouped in seven segments, this array is called a seven-segment LED display with a common anode (positive connection). The dash computer toggles the cathode (negative) side of each individual segment to display numbers and letters. *(c)* When all segments are turned on, the number 8 is displayed.

plays are very bright and must be dimmed by use of dense filters or by controlling the voltage applied to the display. A typical VTF dash is dimmed to 75% brightness whenever the parking lights or headlights are turned on. Some displays use a photocell to monitor and adjust the intensity of the display during daylight viewing. Most VTF displays are green for best viewing under most lighting conditions.

Cathode Ray Tube Displays

A cathode ray tube (CRT) dash display is similar to a television tube and permits the display of hundreds of controls and diagnostic messages in one convenient location.

Using the touch-sensitive cathode ray tube, the driver or technician can select from many different displays, including those of radio, climate, trip, and dash instrument information. All of these functions can be accessed readily by the driver. Further diagnostic information can be displayed on the CRT if the proper combination of air-conditioning controls is touched.

Other Electronic Gauge Displays

Oil pressure, water temperature, and voltmeter readings are other commonly used electronic dash displays. Oil pressure is monitored by a variable-resistance sending unit threaded into an oil passage, usually near the oil filter. A typical oil pressure sending unit will have low resistance when the oil pressure is zero and higher resistance when the oil pressure is high.

Water temperature is also sensed by a variable-resistance sending unit, usually located near the engine's thermostat. Similar to the case with oil pressure, the higher the coolant temperature, the greater the number of segments that will be indicated, based on the resistance of the coolant temperature sensor.

NOTE: The coolant temperature sensor for the dash display is usually a separate sensor from the coolant temperature sensor used by the engine computer.

◄ TECH TIP ►

THE BULB TEST

Many ignition switches have six positions. See figure 7–9.

Notice the bulb test position, the position between "on" and "start." When the ignition is turned to "on" (run), some dash warning lamps are illuminated. When the bulb test position is reached, additional dash warning lamps are often lighted. Technicians often use this ignition switch position to check the operation of fuses that protect various circuits. Dash warning lamps are not all powered by the same fuses. If an electrical component or circuit does not work, the power side (fuse) can be quickly checked by observing the operation of the dash lamps that share a common fuse with the problem circuit. Consult a wiring diagram for fuse information on the exact circuit being tested.

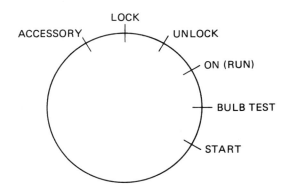

FIGURE 7–9 Typical ignition switch positions. Notice the bulb check position between on (run) and start.

A voltmeter is often included in a digital display, and each segment of the display represents a particular voltage range. A warning lamp is often part of the electronic circuits in the electronic display to warn the driver of high or low battery voltage.

THE "WOW" DISPLAY

When a vehicle equipped with a digital dash is started, all segments of the electronic display are turned on at full brilliance for 1 or 2 seconds. This is commonly called the "WOW" and is used to show off the brilliance of the display. If numbers are part of the display, the number 8 is displayed, because this number uses all segments of a number display. Technicians can also use the WOW display to determine if all segments of the electronic display are functioning correctly.

ELECTRONIC SPEEDOMETERS

Electronic dash displays usually use an electric vehicle speed sensor driven by a small gear on the output shaft of the transmission. These speed sensors contain a permanent magnet and generate a voltage in proportion to the vehicle speed. These speed sensors are commonly called **permanent-magnet** or **PM generators.** See figure 7–10.

The output of a PM generator speed sensor is an AC voltage that varies in frequency and intensity with increasing vehicle speed. The PM generator speed signal is sent to the instrument cluster electronic circuits. These specialized electronic circuits include a buffer amplifier circuit that converts the variable sine wave voltage from the speed sensor to an on-and-off signal that can be used by other electronic circuits to indicate

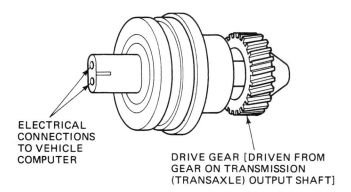

ELECTRICAL
CONNECTIONS
TO VEHICLE
COMPUTER

DRIVE GEAR [DRIVEN FROM
GEAR ON TRANSMISSION
(TRANSAXLE) OUTPUT SHAFT]

FIGURE 7–10 Permanent-magnet generator vehicle speed sensor. The unit is usually driven by a gear on the output section of the transmission or transaxle. Some vehicle speed sensors are driven by a speedometer cable and are used by the vehicle computer (the cable still drives the speedometer).

◀ **DIAGNOSTIC STORY** ▶

THE TOYOTA TRUCK STORY

The owner of a Toyota truck complained that several electrical problems plagued the truck, including the following:

1. The speed (cruise) control would kick out intermittently.
2. The red brake warning lamp would come on, especially during cold weather.

The owner had replaced the parking brake switch, thinking that was the cause of the red brake warning lamp coming on.

An experienced technician checked the wiring diagram on the computer data disc. Checking the warning lamp circuit, the technician noticed that the same wire went to the brake fluid level sensor. The brake fluid was at the minimum level. See figure 7–11. Filling the master cylinder to the maximum level with clean brake fluid solved both problems. The electronics of the speed control stopped operation when the red brake warning lamp was on as a safety measure.

a vehicle's speed. The vehicle speed is then displayed by either an electronic needle-type speedometer or by numbers on a digital display.

(a)

(b)

FIGURE 7–11 (a) The brake fluid reservoir fluid level sensor attaches to the filler cap. (b) Lifting the filler cap reveals a float sensor. When the brake fluid was down to the minimum level, the red brake warning lamp lighted.

ELECTRONIC ODOMETERS

An odometer is a dash display that indicates the total miles traveled by the vehicle. Some dash displays also include a trip odometer that can be reset and used to record total miles traveled on a trip or the distance traveled between fuel stops. Electronic dash displays can use either an electrically driven mechanical odometer or a digital display odometer to indicate miles traveled. A small electric motor called a **stepper motor** is used to turn the number wheels of a mechanical-style odometer. A pulsed voltage is fed to this stepper motor, which moves in relation to the miles traveled. See figure 7–12.

Digital odometers use LED, LCD, or VTF displays to indicate miles traveled. Because total miles must be retained when the ignition is turned off or the battery is

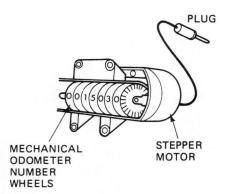

FIGURE 7–12 Some vehicles that use a PM generator for a vehicle speed sensor use a stepper motor to drive a mechanical odometer. The stepper motor receives a signal (pulses) from the vehicle computer and rotates in "steps" corresponding to the distance traveled.

disconnected, a special electronic chip must be used that will retain the miles traveled.

These special chips are called **nonvolatile random access memory** (NVRAM). Nonvolatile means that the information stored in the electronic chip is not lost when electrical power is removed. Some vehicles use a chip called **electronically erasable programmable read-only memory** (EEPROM). Most digital odometers can read up to 999,999.9 kilometers (km), or 621,388 miles; then the display indicates error. If the chip is damaged or exposed to static electricity, it may fail to operate and "error" may appear.

ELECTRONIC SPEEDOMETER AND ODOMETER SERVICE

If the speedometer and odometer fail to operate, the speed sensor should be the first item checked. With the vehicle safely raised off the ground and supported, disconnect the wires from the speed sensor near the output shaft of the transmission. Connect a multitester, set on AC volts, to the terminals of the speed sensor and rotate the drive wheels with the transmission in neutral. A good speed sensor should indicate approximately 2 volts AC if the drive wheels are rotated by hand. If the speed sensor is working, check the wiring from the speed sensor to the dash cluster. If the wiring is good, the dash should be sent to a specialty repair facility. Consult your local dealer for the nearest authorized repair facility.

If the speedometer operates correctly but the mechanical odometer does not work, the odometer stepper motor, the number wheel assembly, or the circuit controlling the stepper motor is defective. If the digital odometer does not operate but the speedometer operates correctly, the dash cluster must be removed and sent to a specialized repair facility. A replacement chip is available only through authorized sources and if the odometer chip is defective, the original number of miles must be programmed into the replacement chip.

NOTE: Some digital odometers only change (update) every 15 miles or whenever the ignition is turned off. Be certain to check for normal operation before attempting to repair the odometer. Digital dash displays that use EEPROM odometer chips are the type most likely to update odometer readings periodically rather than continuously.

ELECTRONIC FUEL LEVEL GAUGES

Electronic fuel level gauges usually use the same fuel tank sending unit as that used on conventional fuel gauges. The tank unit consists of a float attached to a variable resistor. As the fuel level changes, the resistance of the sending unit changes. As the resistance of the tank unit changes, the dash-mounted gauge also changes. The only difference between a digital fuel level gauge and a conventional needle type is in the display. Digital fuel level gauges can be either numerical (indicating gallons or liters remaining in the tank) or a bar graph display. A bar graph consists of light segments, often with each segment corresponding to a gallon of fuel. The electronic circuits inside the cluster light the correct number of gallons remaining or the number of segments, depending on the resistance of the tank sending unit. For example, a typical General Motors tank unit has 90 ohms when the fuel tank is full and 0 ohms when the tank is empty. Therefore, every decrease of 6 ohms will decrease the display one segment if it is sixteen-segment bar graph fuel gauge.

The diagnosis of a problem is the same as that described earlier for conventional fuel gauges. If the tests indicate that the dash unit is defective, usually the *entire* dash gauge assembly must be replaced.

ELECTRONIC DASH INSTRUMENT DIAGNOSIS AND TROUBLESHOOTING

If one or more electronic dash gauges do not work correctly, first check the WOW display that lights all segments to full brilliance whenever the ignition switch is first switched on. If all segments of the display do *not*

◄ TECH TIP ►

THE SOLDERING GUN TRICK

Diagnosing problems with digital or electronic dash instruments can be difficult. Replacement parts are generally expensive and usually not returnable if installed in the vehicle. A popular trick that helps pin down the problem is to use a soldering gun near the PM generator.

A PM generator contains a coil of wire. As the magnet inside revolves, a voltage is produced. It is the *frequency* of this voltage that the dash (or engine) computer uses to calculate vehicle speed.

A soldering gun plugged into 110 volts AC will provide a strong *varying* magnetic field around the soldering gun. This magnetic field is constantly changing at the rate of 60 times per second. This frequency of the magnetic field induces a voltage in the windings of the PM generator. This induced voltage at 60 hertz (Hz) is converted by the computer circuits to a miles-per-hour (mph) reading on the dash.

To test the electronic speedometer, turn the ignition to "on" (engine off) and hold a soldering gun near the PM generator.

CAUTION: The soldering gun tip can get hot, so hold the soldering gun tip away from wiring or other components that may be damaged by the hot tip.

If the PM generator, wiring, computer, and dash are okay, the speedometer should register a speed, usually 54 mph (87 kilometers per hour [km/h]). If the speedometer does not work when the vehicle is driven, the problem is in the PM generator drive.

If the speedometer does not register a speed when the soldering gun is used, the problem could be caused by:

1. A defective PM generator (check the windings with an ohmmeter)
2. Defective (open or shorted) wiring from the PM generator to the computer
3. Defective computer or dash circuit

HINT: Use a pulsing logic probe and apply a pulse to the wiring after unplugging from the PM generator. If the speedometer now registers a speed, the wiring, computer, and dash are okay and, therefore, the PM generator must be defective.

---

operate, the entire electronic cluster must be replaced in most cases. If all segments operate during the WOW display but do not function correctly after the WOW display, the problem is most often a defective sensor or defective wiring to the sensor.

All dash instruments except the voltmeter use a variable-resistance unit as a sensor for the system being monitored. Most new-vehicle dealers are required to purchase essential test equipment, including a test unit that permits the technician to insert various fixed-resistance values in the suspected circuit. For example, if a 45-ohm resistance is put into the fuel gauge circuit that reads from 0 to 90 ohms, a properly operating dash unit should indicate one-half tank. The same tester can produce a fixed signal to test the operation of the speedometer and tachometer. If this type of special test equipment is not available, the electronic dash instruments can be tested using the following procedure:

1. With the ignition switched off, unplug the wire(s) from the sensor for the function being tested. For example, if the oil pressure gauge is not functioning correctly, unplug the wire connector at the oil pressure sending unit.

2. With the sensor wire unplugged, turn the ignition switch on and wait until the WOW display stops. The display for the affected unit should show either fully lighted segments or no lighted segments, depending on the make of the vehicle and the type of sensor.

3. Turn the ignition switch off. Connect the sensor wire lead to ground and turn the ignition switch on. After the WOW display, the display should be the opposite (either fully on or fully off) of the results in step #2.

Testing Results

If the electronic display does function fully on and fully off with the sensor unplugged and then grounded, the problem is a defective sensor. If the electronic display fails to function fully on and fully off when the sensor wire(s) are opened and grounded, the problem is usually in the wiring from the sensor to the electronic dash or is a defective electronic cluster.

CAUTION: Whenever working on or *near* any type of electronic dash display, always wear a wire attached to your wrist (wrist strap) connected to a good body ground, to prevent damaging the electronic dash with static electricity.

MAINTENANCE REMINDER LAMPS

Maintenance reminder lamps indicate that an exhaust emission control device should be tested or replaced. If the vehicle manufacturer cannot prove to the federal government that an emission control device can function correctly for 5 years or 50,000 miles (80,000 kilometers), the owner has to be notified to return to the dealer for service. The services most commonly specified include cleaning or replacing the exhaust gas recirculation (EGR) valve and replacing the oxygen sensor (O2S).

There are numerous ways to extinguish a maintenance reminder lamp. Some require the use of a special

◀ TECH TIP ▶

KISS—KEEP IT STOCK, STUPID!

Whenever larger (or smaller) wheels or tires are installed, the speedometer and odometer calibration are also thrown off. This can be summarized as follows:

1. Larger-diameter tires—The speed showing on the speedometer is slower than actual speed. The odometer reading will show fewer miles than actual.

2. Smaller-diameter tires—The speed showing on the speedometer is faster than actual speed. The odometer reading will show more miles than actual.

General Motors trucks can be recalibrated with a recalibration kit (1988–91) or with a replacement controller assembly called a digital ratio adapter controller (DRAC) located under the dash. It may be possible to recalibrate the speedometer and odometer on earlier models (before 1988) or vehicles that use speedometer cables by replacing the drive gear in the transmission. Check with a speedometer repair company or vehicle dealer for details.

tool. Consult service literature or dealership personnel for the exact procedure for the vehicle being serviced.

SUMMARY

1. Most digital and analog (needle-type) dash gauges use variable-resistance sensors.

2. Dash warning lamps are called idiot lights or telltale lamps.

3. Many electronically operated or computer-operated dash indicators require that a service manual be used to perform accurate diagnosis.

4. Permanent magnet generators produce an AC signal and are used for vehicle speed and wheel speed sensors.

REVIEW QUESTIONS

1. Explain the difference between thermoelectric and electromagnetic dash instruments.

2. Describe LED, LCD, VTF, and CRT dash displays.

3. Discuss how to diagnose a problem with a red brake warning lamp.

4. Explain how to test the dash unit of a fuel gauge.

MULTIPLE-CHOICE QUESTIONS

1. Two technicians are discussing a fuel gauge on a General Motors vehicle. Technician A says that if the ground wire connection to the fuel tank sending unit becomes rusty or corroded, the fuel gauge will read *lower* than normal. Technician B says that if the power lead to the fuel tank sending unit is disconnected from the tank unit and grounded (ignition on), the fuel gauge should go to empty. Which technician is correct?
   a. A only
   b. B only
   c. Both a and b
   d. Neither a nor b

2. If an oil pressure warning lamp on a General Motors vehicle is on all the time, yet the engine oil pressure is normal, the problem could be _____.
   a. A defective (shorted) oil pressure sending unit (sensor)
   b. A defective (open) oil pressure sending unit (sensor)
   c. An open wire between the sending unit (sensor) and the dash warning lamp
   d. Both b and c

3. When the oil pressure drops between 3 and 7 psi, the oil pressure lamp lights by _____.
   a. Opening the circuit
   b. Shorting the circuit
   c. Grounding the circuit
   d. Conducting current to the dash lamp by oil

4. A brake warning lamp on the dash remains on whenever the ignition is on. If the wire to the pressure differential switch (usually a part of a combination valve or built into the master cylinder) is unplugged, the dash lamp goes out. Technician A says that this is an indication of a defective pressure differential switch. Technician B says that the problem is probably due to a stuck parking brake cable switch. Which technician is correct?
   a. A only
   b. B only
   c. Both a and b
   d. Neither a nor b

5. A customer complains that every time the lights are turned on in the vehicle, the dash lights become dim. What is the most probable explanation?
   a. Normal behavior for LED dash displays
   b. Normal behavior for VTF dash displays
   c. Poor ground in lighting circuit causing a voltage drop to the dash lamps
   d. Feedback problem most likely caused by a short to voltage between the headlights and dash display

6. Technician A says that an electromagnetic-type fuel gauge similar to the type used on General Motors vehicles will read full when the resistance of the fuel tank sending unit is high, and empty when the resistance is low. Technician B says that a thermoelectric-type fuel gauge similar to the type used on many Ford and Chrysler vehicles will read empty when the resistance of the fuel tank sending unit is high, and full when the resistance is low. Which technician is correct?
   a. A only
   b. B only
   c. Both a and b
   d. Neither a nor b

7. Technician A says that LCDs may be slow to work at low temperatures. Technician B says that an LCD dash display can be damaged if pressure is exerted on the front of the display during cleaning. Which technician is correct?
   a. A only
   b. B only
   c. Both a and b
   d. Neither a nor b

8. Technician A says that some electronic dashes use an analog speedometer. Technician B says that all electronic dash fuel gauges use a numerical display. Which technician is correct?
   a. A only
   b. B only
   c. Both a and b
   d. Neither a nor b

◀ Chapter 8 ▶

DIAGNOSING AND TROUBLESHOOTING ACCESSORY CIRCUITS

OBJECTIVES

After studying chapter 8, the reader will be able to

1. Explain how many speeds can be achieved with a blower motor.
2. Describe how power door locks and windows operate.
3. Discuss steps to take to eliminate sound system interference.
4. List the safety precautions for working around an airbag.

Electrical accessories provide comfort and assistance to the driver and passengers. The growing list of electrical accessories makes this an area of much concern to vehicle owners and service technicians.

BLOWER MOTOR OPERATION

The same blower motor moves air inside the vehicle for air conditioning, heat, and defrosting or defogging. The fan switch controls the path that the current follows to the blower motor. The motor is usually a permanent-magnet, one-speed motor that operates at its maximum speed with full battery voltage. The switch gets current from the fuse panel with the ignition switch on. The switch directs

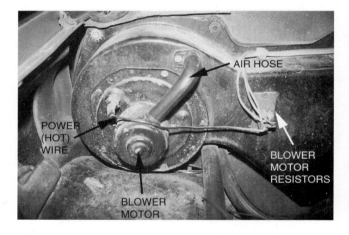

FIGURE 8–1 Typical blower motor installation. The dropping resistors are located near the blower motor to help keep the resistors cool.

full battery voltage to the blower motor for high speed and directs voltage to the blower motor through resistors for lower speeds. See figures 8–1 and 8–2.

BLOWER MOTOR DIAGNOSIS

If the blower motor does not operate at any speed, the problem could be any of the following:

1. A defective ground wire or ground wire connection.
2. A defective blower motor (not repairable; must be replaced)
3. An open circuit in the power-side circuit, including fuse, wiring, or fan switch

If the blower works on lower speeds but not on high speed, the problem is usually an "inline" fuse or high-speed relay that controls the heavy current flow for high-speed operation. The high-speed fuse or relay usually fails as a result of internal blower motor bushing wear, which causes excessive resistance to motor rotation. At slow blower speeds, the resistance is not as noticeable and the blower operates normally. The blower motor is a sealed unit and, if defective, must be replaced as a unit. If the blower motor operates normally at high speed but not at any of the lower speeds, the problem could be melted wire resistors or a defective switch. See figure 8–3.

FIGURE 8–2 Close-up view of blower motor resistors. If they are defective, replacement resistors are purchased as a unit, as shown.

WINDSHIELD WIPERS

The windshield wipers usually use a special two-speed electric motor. General Motors uses many different-shaped wiper motors. Most are compound-wound motors, which are a type of motor with both a **series-wound field** and a **shunt field**, which provides for two different speeds. The wiper switch provides the necessary electrical connections for either speed. Switches in the mechanical wiper motor assembly provide the necessary operation for "parking" and "concealing" of the wipers.

Other wiper motors usually use a permanent-magnet motor with a low-speed brush and a high-speed brush. The brush connects the battery to the internal windings

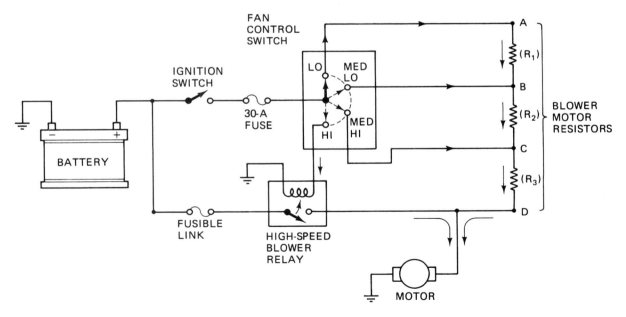

FIGURE 8–3 Typical blower motor circuit with four speeds. The three lowest fan speeds (low, medium low, and medium high) use the blower motor resistors to drop the voltage to the motor and reduce current to the motor. On high, the resistors are bypassed. The "hi" position on the fan switch energizes a relay. This relay supplies the current for the blower on high through a fusible link.

◄ TECH TIP ►

THE 20-AMPERE FUSE TRICK

Most blower motors operate at about 12 amperes on high speed. If the bushings (bearings) on the armature of the motor become worn or dry, the motor turns more slowly. Because a motor also produces **counter EMF** (often abbreviated **CEMF**) as it spins, a slower-turning motor will actually draw more amperes than a fast-spinning motor.

If a blower motor draws too many amperes, the resistors or the blower controlling the electronic circuit can fail. Testing the actual current draw of the motor is sometimes difficult because the amperage often exceeds the permissible amount for most digital meters.

A commonly used trick is to unplug the power lead to the motor (retain the ground on the motor) and use a fused jumper lead with one end connected to the battery's positive terminal and the other end to the motor terminal. Use a 20-ampere fuse in the test lead. Operate the motor for several minutes. If the blower motor is drawing more than 20 amperes, the fuse will blow. Some experts recommend using a 15-ampere fuse. If the 15-ampere fuse blows and the 20-ampere fuse does not, then you know the approximate blower motor current draw.

of the motor, and the two brushes provide for two different motor speeds.

The ground brush is directly opposite the low-speed brush. Off to the side of the low-speed brush is the high-speed brush. When current flows through the high-speed brush, there are fewer turns on the armature between the hot and ground brushes, and therefore the resistance is less. With less resistance, more current flows and the armature revolves faster. See figures 8–4 and 8–5.

Variable-delay wipers (also called **pulse wipers**) use an electronic circuit with a variable resistor that controls the time of the charge and discharge of a capacitor. This charging and discharging of the capacitor controls the circuit for the operation of the wiper motor.

HORNS

Automotive horns are usually wired directly to battery voltage from the fuse panel. The majority of automobiles, except for most Fords, utilize a horn relay. With a relay, the horn button on the steering wheel or column completes a circuit to ground that closes a relay, and the heavy current flow required by the horn then travels from the relay to the horn. See figure 8–6.

Horns are manufactured in several different tones or frequencies ranging between 1800 and 3550 hertz. Vehicle manufacturers can select from various

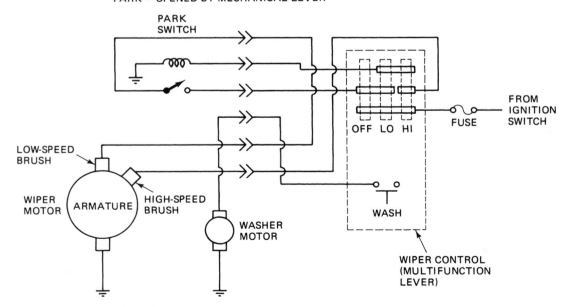

FIGURE 8–4 Typical wiring diagram of a two-speed windshield wiper circuit using a three-brush, two-speed motor. The dashed line for the multifunction lever indicates that the circuit shown is only a part of the total function of the steering column lever.

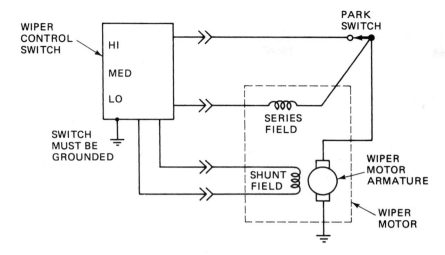

FIGURE 8–5 Typical wiring diagram of a three-speed windshield wiper circuit using a two-brush motor, with both a series and a shunt field coil.

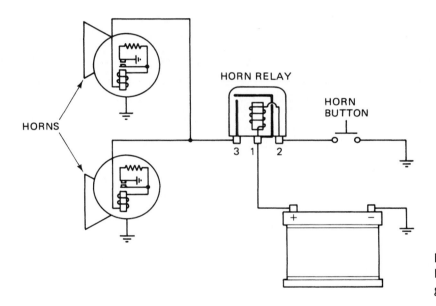

FIGURE 8–6 Typical horn circuit diagram. Note that the horn button completes the ground circuit for the relay.

horn tones for a particular vehicle sound. When two horns are used, each has a different tone when operated separately, yet the sound combines when both are operated.

HORN DIAGNOSIS

To help determine the cause of a horn's not operating, use a jumper wire and connect one end to the positive post of the battery and the other end to the wire terminal of the horn itself. If the horn works, the problem is in the circuit supplying current to the horn. If the horn does not work, the horn itself could be defective or the mounting bracket may not be providing a good ground.

If a replacement horn is required, attempt to use a horn of the same tone as the original. The tone is usually indicated by a number or letter stamped on the body of the horn.

SPEED CONTROL

Speed (cruise) control is a combination of electrical and mechanical components designed to maintain a constant, set vehicle speed without driver pressure on the accelerator pedal. Major components of a typical speed control system include the following:

1. **Servo unit**. The servo unit attaches to the throttle linkage through a cable or chain. The servo unit

◀ TECH TIP ▶

BUMP PROBLEMS

Speed control problem diagnosis can involve a complex series of checks and tests.

The troubleshooting procedures vary from manufacturer to manufacturer (and year to year), so a technician should always consult a service manual for the exact vehicle being serviced.

However, every speed control system uses a brake safety switch (and, if the vehicle has manual transmission a clutch safety switch). The purpose of these safety switches is to ensure that the speed control system is disabled if the brakes are applied. Some systems use redundant brake pedal safety switches, one electrical to cut off power to the system and the other vacuum to bleed vacuum away from the actuating unit.

If the speed control "cuts out" or disengages itself while traveling over bumpy roads, the most common cause is a misadjusted brake (and/or clutch) safety switch(es). Often, a simple readjustment of these safety switches will cure the intermittent speed control disengagement problems.

CAUTION: Always follow manufacturers' recommended safety switch adjustment procedures. If the brake safety switch(es) are misadjusted, it could keep pressure applied to the master brake cylinder, resulting in severe damage to the braking system.

---

controls the movement of the throttle by receiving a controlled amount of vacuum from a control unit.

2. **Transducer**. A transducer is an electrical and mechanical speed-sensing and control unit.

3. **Speed set control**. A speed set control is a switch or control located on the steering column, steering wheel, dash, or console. Many speed control units feature coast, accelerate, and resume functions.

4. **Safety release switches**. Whenever the brake pedal is depressed, the speed control system is disengaged through use of an electrical and vacuum switch, usually located on the brake pedal bracket. Both electrical and vacuum releases are used to be certain that the speed control system is released, even in the event of failure of one of the release switches.

BASIC SPEED CONTROL OPERATION

A typical speed control system can be set only if the vehicle speed is 30 miles per hour or more. In a non-computer-operated system, the transducer contains a low-speed electrical switch that closes whenever the speed-sensing section of the transducer senses a speed exceeding the minimum engagement speed.

An electric solenoid operates a clutch spring wrapped around the rubber clutch and squeezes the rubber clutch whenever the driver-operated engagement switch is activated. The clutch spring is held tight around the rubber clutch and opens and closes vacuum ports that control the amount of vacuum for the vacuum servo attached to the throttle linkage. If the vehicle speed increases, a greater rotary force is exerted on the rubber clutch, which rotates slightly, uncovering vent slots in the vacuum control for the servo, reducing its pull on the throttle linkage. If the vehicle speed is reduced, the force on the rubber clutch is reduced, which closes the vacuum vent for the servo, resulting in a greater vacuum in the servo. This high vacuum exerts a greater opening force on the throttle, and the engine speed is increased. In actual operation, the throttle is moved only enough to maintain a constant road speed regardless of terrain.

NON-COMPUTER-CONTROLLED RESUME-TYPE SPEED CONTROL

Most resume-style non-computer-controlled speed control systems use a two-piece rubber clutch to retain a "mechanical memory" of the vehicle road speed.

Depressing the brake pedal causes a vacuum-release solenoid to release vacuum from the servo unit, and the speed control stops maintaining vehicle speed. When "resume" is pushed, the vacuum solenoid closes and vacuum is again applied to the servo unit. The speed is "remembered" by the position of the split rubber clutch.

COMPUTER-CONTROLLED SPEED CONTROL

Most computer-controlled speed control systems use the vehicle's speed sensor input to the engine control computer for speed reference. Computer-controlled speed control units also use servo units for throttle control, control switches for driver control of speed control functions, and both electrical and vacuum brake pedal release switches.

TROUBLESHOOTING SPEED CONTROL

Speed control system troubleshooting is usually performed using the step-by-step procedure as specified by the vehicle manufacturer. A quick method used by many dealers is to use known-to-be-good components that can be quickly plugged in to check for proper operation.

POWER WINDOWS

Power windows use electric motors to raise and lower door glass. They can be operated by both a **master control switch** located beside the driver and additional **independent switches** for each electric window. Some power window systems use a **lock-out switch** located on the driver's controls to prevent operation of the power windows from the independent switches. Power windows are designed to operate only with the ignition switch in the "on" (run) position. This safety feature of power windows should never be defeated. Some manufacturers use a time delay for accessory power after the ignition switch is turned off. This feature permits the driver and passengers an opportunity to close all windows or operate other accessories for about 10 minutes or until a vehicle door is opened after the ignition has been turned off.

Most power window systems use permanent-magnet electric motors. It is possible to run a PM motor in the reverse direction simply by reversing the polarity of the two wires going to the motor. Most power window motors do not require that the motor be grounded to the body (door) of the vehicle. The ground for all the power windows is most often centralized near the driver's master control switch. The up-and-down motion of the individual window motors is controlled by double-pole, double-throw (DPDT) switches. These DPDT switches have five contacts and permit battery voltage to be applied to the power window motor and to reverse the polarity and direction of the motor. See figure 8–7.

The power window motors rotate a mechanism called a **window regulator**. The window regulator is attached to the door glass and controls opening and closing of the glass. Door glass adjustments such as glass tilt and upper and lower stops are usually the same for both power and manual windows.

TROUBLESHOOTING POWER WINDOWS

Before troubleshooting a power window problem, check for proper operation of all power windows. If one of the **control wires** that run from the independent switch to the master switch is cut (open), the power window may operate in just one direction. The window may go down but not up, or vice versa. However, if one of the **direction wires** that run from the independent switch to the motor is cut (open), the window will not operate in either direction. The direction wires and the motor must be electrically connected to permit operation and change of direction of the electric lift motor in the door.

1. If *both* rear door windows fail to operate from the independent switches, check the operation of the window lockout (if the vehicle is so equipped) and the master control switch.

2. If one window can move in one direction only, check for continuity in the control wires (wires between the independent control switch and the master control switch).

3. If *all* windows fail to work or fail to work occasionally, check, clean, and tighten the ground wire(s) located either behind the driver's interior door panel or under the dash on the driver's side. A defective fuse or circuit breaker could also cause all the windows to fail to operate.

4. If one window fails to operate in both directions, the problem could be a defective window lift motor. The window could be stuck in the track of the door, which could cause the circuit breaker built into the motor to open the circuit to protect the wiring, switches, and motor from damage. To check for a

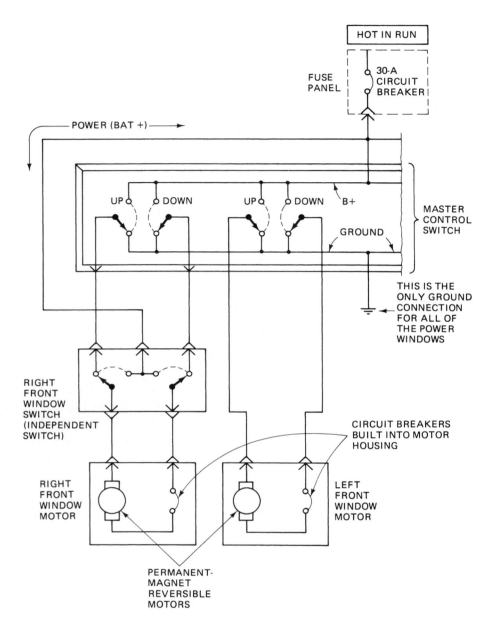

FIGURE 8–7 Typical power window circuit using PM motors. Control of the direction of window operation is achieved by directing the polarity of the current through the nongrounded motors. The *only* ground for the entire system is located at the master control (driver's side) switch assembly.

stuck door glass, attempt to move (even slightly) the door glass up and down, forward and back, and side to side. If the window glass can move slightly in all directions, the power window motor should be able to at least move the glass.

POWER SEATS

A typical power-operated seat includes a reversible electric motor and a transmission assembly that has three solenoids and six **drive cables** that turn the six seat adjusters. A six-way power seat offers seat move-

ment forward and backward, plus seat cushion movement up and down at the front and the rear. See figure 8–8. The drive cables are very similar to speedometer cables because they rotate inside a cable housing and connect the power output of the seat transmission to a gear or screw jack assembly that moves the seat. A **screw jack assembly** is often called a **gearnut** and is used to move the front or back of the seat cushion up and down. Between the electric motor and the transmission is usually a **rubber coupling** that could permit the electric motor to continue to rotate in the event of a jammed seat. This coupling is designed to prevent motor damage.

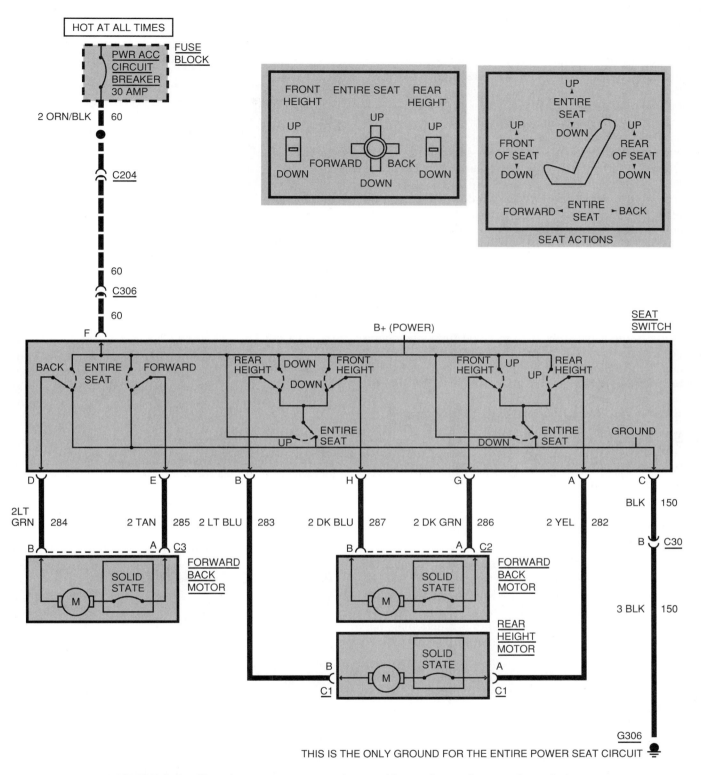

FIGURE 8–8 Typical power seat circuit diagram. Notice that each motor has a built-in electronic (solid state) PTC circuit protector. The seat control switch can change the direction in which the motor(s) run by reversing the direction in which the current flows through the motor.

Most power seats use a permanent-magnet motor that can be reversed by simply reversing the polarity of the current sent to the motor by the seat switch. Most PM motors have a built-in circuit breaker to protect the motor from overheating. Many Ford power seat motors use three separate armatures inside one large permanent-magnet field housing. Some power seats use a series-wound electric motor with two separate field coils, one field coil for each direction of rotation. This type of power seat motor typically uses a relay to control the direction of current from the seat switch to the corresponding field coil of the seat motor. This type of power seat can be identified by the "click" heard whenever the seat switch is changed from up to down or front to back, or vice versa. The click is the sound of the relay switching the field coil current. Some power seats use as many as eight separate PM motors that operate all functions of the seat, including headrest height, seat length, and side bolsters, in addition to the usual six-way power seat functions. Some power seats use a small air pump to inflate a bag or bags in the lower part of the back of the seat, called the **lumbar** because it supports the lumbar section of the spine.

TROUBLESHOOTING POWER SEATS

Power seats are usually wired from the fuse panel to operate all the time without having to turn the ignition switch to "on" (run). If a power seat does not operate or make any noise, the circuit breaker (or fuse, if the vehicle is so equipped) should be checked first.

■ *Step #1.* Check the circuit breaker, usually located on the fuse panel, using a test light. The test light should light on both sides of the circuit breaker even with the ignition off. If the seat relay clicks, the circuit breaker is functioning, but the relay or electric motor may be defective.

■ *Step #2.* Remove the screws or clips that retain the controls to the inner door panel or seat and check for voltage at the seat control.

■ *Step #3.* Also check the ground connection(s) at the transmission and clutch control solenoids (if the vehicle is so equipped). The solenoids must be properly grounded to the vehicle body for the power seat circuit to operate.

If the power seat motor runs but does not move the seat, the most likely fault is a worn or defective rubber clutch sleeve between the electric seat motor and the transmission.

If the seat relay clicks but the seat motor does not operate, the problem is usually a defective seat motor

◀ **TECH TIP** ▶

WHAT EVERY DRIVER SHOULD KNOW ABOUT POWER SEATS

Power seats use an electric motor or motors to move the position of the seat. These electric motors turn small cables that operate mechanisms that move the seat. *Never* place rags, newspapers, or any other object under a power seat. Even ice scrapers can get caught between moving parts of the seat and can often cause serious damage or jamming of the power seat.

or defective wiring between the motor and the relay. If the power seat uses a motor relay, the motor has a double reverse-wound field for reversing the motor direction. This type of electric motor must be properly grounded. Permanent-magnet motors do not require grounding for operation.

HINT: Power seats are often difficult to service because of restricted working room. If the entire seat cannot be removed from the vehicle because the track bolts are covered, attempt to remove the seat from the top of the power seat assembly. These bolts are almost always accessible regardless of seat position.

ELECTRIC POWER DOOR LOCKS

Electric power door locks use either a solenoid or a permanent-magnet motor to lock or unlock all vehicle door locks from a control switch or switches. Large (heavy) solenoids were typically used before the mid-1970s. These solenoids usually used two-wire connections that carried a high-ampere current through a relay controlled by a door lock switch. With a solenoid-style door lock, only one of the two wires is used at any one time. If current flows through one wire to the solenoid, the door locks; the door unlocks when current flows through the other wire to the solenoid. The solenoids must be grounded to the metal of the door to complete the electrical circuit. Because of constant opening and closing of a typical vehicle door, a solenoid-style power door lock frequently vibrates loose from the mounting inside the door and fails to operate because of the poor ground connection with the metal door.

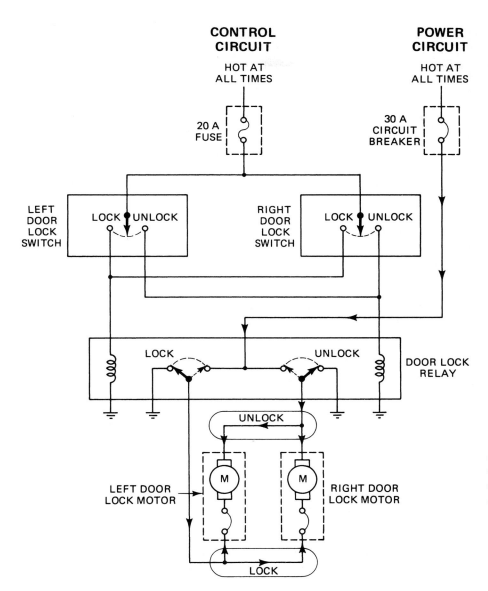

CONTROL CIRCUIT

HOT AT ALL TIMES

20 A FUSE

LEFT DOOR LOCK SWITCH

LOCK UNLOCK

RIGHT DOOR LOCK SWITCH

LOCK UNLOCK

POWER CIRCUIT

HOT AT ALL TIMES

30 A CIRCUIT BREAKER

LOCK UNLOCK

DOOR LOCK RELAY

UNLOCK

LEFT DOOR LOCK MOTOR

RIGHT DOOR LOCK MOTOR

LOCK

FIGURE 8–9 Typical electric power door lock circuit diagram. Note that the control circuit is protected by a fuse, whereas the power circuit is protected by a circuit breaker. As with the operation of power windows, power door locks typically use reversible PM nongrounded electric motors. These motors are geared mechanically to the lock-unlock mechanism.

Most electric door locks use a permanent-magnet reversible electric motor that operates the lock-activating rod. PM reversible motors do not require grounding because, as with power windows, the motor control is determined by the polarity of the current through the two motor wires. Some two-door vehicles do *not* use a power door lock relay because the current flow for only two PM motors can be handled through the door lock switches. However, most four-door vehicles and vans with power locks on rear and side doors use a relay to control the current flow necessary to operate four or more power door lock motors. The door lock relay is controlled by the door lock switch and is commonly the location of the one and only ground connection for the entire door lock circuit. See figure 8–9.

HEATED REAR WINDOW DEFOGGERS

An electrically heated rear window defogger system uses an electrical grid baked on the glass that warms the glass and clears it of fog or frost. The rear window is also called a **backlight**. The rear window defogger system is controlled by a driver-operated switch and a timer relay. The timer relay is necessary because the window grid can draw up to 30 amperes, and continued operation would put a strain on the battery and the charging system. Generally, the timer relay permits current to flow through the rear window grid for only 10 minutes. If the window is still not clear of fog after 10 minutes, the driver can turn the defogger on again, but after the first 10 minutes any additional defogger operation is limited to 5 minutes.

Electric grid-type rear window defoggers can be damaged easily by careless cleaning or scraping of the inside of the rear window glass. Short broken sections of the rear window grid can be repaired using a special epoxy-based electrically conductive material. If more than one section is damaged or if the damaged grid length is greater than approximately 1½ inches (3.8 centimeters), a replacement rear window glass may be required to restore proper defogger operation.

The electrical current through the grids depends, in part, on the temperature of the conductor grids. As the temperature decreases, the resistance of the grids decreases and the current flow increases, helping to warm the rear glass. As the temperature of the glass increases, the resistance of the conductor grids increases and the current flow decreases. Therefore, the defogger system tends to self-regulate the electrical current requirements to match the need for defogging.

NOTE: Some vehicles use the wire grid of the rear window defogger as the radio antenna. Therefore, if the grid is damaged, radio reception can be affected.

TROUBLESHOOTING A HEATED REAR WINDOW DEFOGGER

Troubleshooting a nonfunctioning rear window defogger unit involves using a test light or a voltmeter to check for voltage to the grid. If no voltage is present at the rear window, check for voltage at the switch and relay timer assembly. A poor ground connection on the opposite side of the grid from the power side can also cause the rear defogger not to operate. Because most defogger circuits use an indicator light switch and a relay timer, it is possible to have the indicator light on even if the wires are disconnected at the rear window grid. A voltmeter can be used to test the operation of the rear window defogger grid. See figure 8–10. With the negative test terminal attached to a good body ground, carefully probe the grid conductors. There should be a decreasing voltage reading as the probe is moved from the power ("hot") side of the grid toward the ground side of the grid.

RADIOS

The power feed for automobile radios should be fused to an ignition switch-controlled circuit that permits radio operation only when the ignition switch is in the "on" (run)

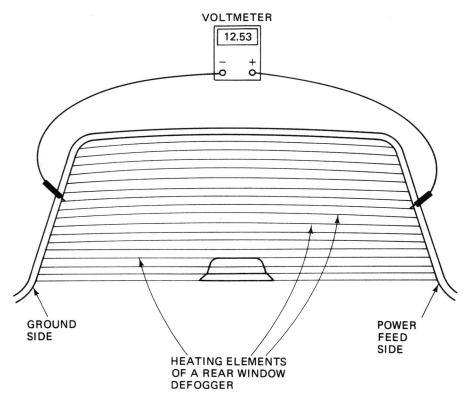

VOLTMETER

12.53

− +

GROUND SIDE

POWER FEED SIDE

HEATING ELEMENTS OF A REAR WINDOW DEFOGGER

FIGURE 8–10 Checking a rear window defogger grid with a voltmeter. As the voltmeter positive lead is moved along the grid (on the inside of the vehicle), the voltmeter reading should steadily decrease as the meter approaches the ground side of the grid.

◀ **TECH TIP** ▶

THE BREATH TEST

It is difficult to test for the proper operation of all grids of a rear window defogger unless the rear window happens to be covered with fog. A common trick that works is to turn on the rear defogger and exhale onto the outside of the rear window glass. In a manner similar to that of people cleaning eyeglasses with their breath, this procedure produces a temporary fog on the glass so that all sections of the rear grids can quickly be checked for proper operation.

or "accessory" position. All radios also use electrical connections for an antenna and for one or more speakers. Most newer radios are called **electronically tuned receiver** (ETR).

AM Reception. **Amplitude modulation** (AM) is a method of varying the carrier signal in such a way as to vary the amplitude or strength of the signal. Frequencies range from 550 to 1600 kilohertz (kHz) and can be received a long distance from the transmitting station because the signal waves are reflected by the atmosphere (ionosphere). The AM method of transmitting is subject to noise and is therefore more sensitive to interference when tuned to weak stations and lack of a properly functioning radio antenna.

FM Reception. **Frequency modulation** (FM) is a method of varying the frequency of the carrier wave to represent the audio broadcast signal. An FM signal is broadcast between 88 and 108 megahertz (MHz), and because the frequency is so high, the signal is *not* reflected by the atmosphere and the range is limited to line-of-sight distances. Because the radio antenna must be "seen" by the transmitting antenna, the signal can easily be blocked by a building or a hill. In cities where the radio signals are strong, the waves can bounce off tall buildings, which can provide reception to areas that are not in sight of the transmitting antenna. FM reception is usually noise free, due to the fact that the radio receives changes in frequency rather than amplitude changes, which often contain noise.

SPEAKERS

Good-quality speakers are the key to a proper-sounding radio or sound system. Replacement speakers should be securely mounted and wired according to the correct **polar-**ity. All speakers used on the same radio or amplifier should have the same internal coil resistance, called **impedance**. If unequal-impedance speakers are used, sound quality may be reduced and serious damage to the radio may result.

The wire used for speakers should be as large a wire (as low a gauge number) as is practical in order to be assured that full power is reaching the speakers. Typical "speaker wire" is about 22 gauge (0.35 square millimeters), yet tests conducted by audio engineers have concluded that increasing the wire gauge to 14 (2.0 square millimeters) or larger greatly improves sound quality. All wiring connections should be soldered after making certain that all speaker connections have the correct polarity.

Be careful when installing additional audio equipment on a General Motors vehicle or on other radio systems that use a two-wire speaker connection called a **floating ground system**. Other systems run only one power (hot) lead to each speaker and ground the other speaker lead to the body of the vehicle.

Regardless of radio speaker connections used, *never* operate any radio without the speakers connected, or a transistor in the radio may be damaged as a result of the open speaker circuit.

ANTENNAS

AM radios operate best with as long an antenna as possible, but FM reception is best when the antenna height is exactly 31 inches (79 centimeters). Most fixed-length antennas are, therefore, exactly this height. Even the horizontal section of a windshield antenna is 31 inches (79 centimeters) long.

A defective antenna will be most noticeable on AM radio reception.

ANTENNA TESTING

If the antenna or lead-in cable is broken (open), FM reception will be heard, but may be weak, and there will be *no* AM reception. An ohmmeter should read infinity between the center antenna lead and the antenna case. For proper reception and lack of noise, the case of the antenna must be properly grounded to the vehicle body. See figure 8–11.

POWER ANTENNAS

Most power antennas use a circuit breaker and a relay to power a reversible electric motor that moves a nylon cord attached to the antenna mast. Some vehicles have a dash-mounted control that can regulate antenna mast

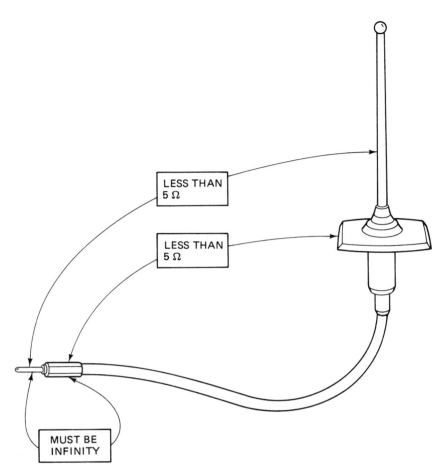

LESS THAN 5 Ω

LESS THAN 5 Ω

MUST BE INFINITY

FIGURE 8–11 If all ohmmeter readings are satisfactory, the antenna is good.

height and/or operation, whereas many operate automatically when the radio is turned on and off. The power antenna assembly is usually mounted between the outer and inner front fender or in the rear quarter panel. The unit contains the motor, a spool for the cord, and upper- and lower-limit switches. The power antenna mast is tested in the same way as a fixed-mast antenna. (An infinity reading should be noted on an ohmmeter when the antenna is tested between the center antenna terminal and the housing or ground.) Except in the case of cleaning or mast replacement, most power antennas are either replaced as a unit or repaired by specialty shops.

Many power antenna problems can be prevented by making certain that the drain holes in the motor housing are not plugged with undercoating, leaves, or dirt. All power antennas should be kept clean by wiping the mast with a soft cloth and lightly oiling with a light oil.

RADIO INTERFERENCE

Radio interference is caused by variations in voltage in the power line or picked up by the antenna. A "whine" that increases in frequency with increasing engine speed is usually referred to as **alternator whine** and is eliminated by installing a radio choke or a filter capacitor in the power feed wire to the radio. See figure 8–12.

Ignition noise is usually a "raspy" sound that varies with the speed of the engine. This noise is usually eliminated by the installation of a capacitor on the positive side of the ignition coil. The capacitor should be connected to the power feed wire to either the radio or the amplifier or both. The capacitor *has* to be grounded. If a standard automotive condenser is not available, use a 470-μF 50-volt electrolytic capacitor, which is readily available from most radio supply stores. A special coaxial capacitor can also be used in the power line. See figure 8–13.

A **radio choke** can also be used to reduce or eliminate radio interference. Again, the radio choke is installed in the power line to the radio equipment. Radio interference being picked up by the antenna can best be eliminated by stopping the source of the interference by making certain that all units containing a coil, such as electric motors, have a capacitor or diode attached to the power-side wire.

Most radio interference complaints come when someone installs an amplifier, power booster, equalizer, or other radio accessory. *A major cause of this interference is the variation in voltage through the ground cir-*

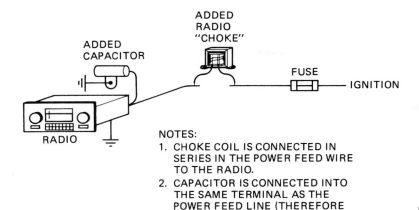

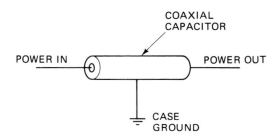

FIGURE 8–13 A coaxial capacitor. Many automobile manufacturers install a coaxial capacitor in the power feed wire to the blower motor to eliminate interference caused by the blower motor.

cuit wires. To prevent or reduce this interference, make sure all ground connections are clean and tight. Placing a capacitor in the ground circuit may also be beneficial.

CAUTION: Amplifiers sold to boost the range or power of an antenna often increase the level of interference and radio noise to a level that disturbs the driver.

◄ TECH TIP ►

THE SEPARATE BATTERY TRICK

Whenever diagnosing sound system interference, try running separate 14-gauge wires from the sound system power lead and ground to a separate battery outside the vehicle. If the noise is still there, the interference is *not* due to an alternator diode or other source in the wiring of the vehicle.

FIGURE 8–12 A radio choke and/or a capacitor can be installed in the power feed lead to any radio, amplifier, or equalizer.

In summary: Radio noise can be broadcast or caused by noise (voltage variations) in the power circuit to the radio. A capacitor and/or a radio choke are the most commonly used components. Two or more capacitors can be connected in parallel to increase the capacity of the original capacitor.

CELLULAR TELEPHONES

Cellular telephones are telephones that can transmit and receive from portable or mobile (vehicle) locations. The power output is relatively low (generally limited to 3 watts of transmitting power). A cellular telephone is able to transmit and receive telephone conversations because of facilities located close together that place, receive, and rebroadcast signals. The mobile phone transmits a signal to the nearest "cell," which is relayed to other cells until received by the cell nearest to its destination (therefore, the term *cellular*).

As the distance between transmitter and receiver increases, the strength of the signal decreases. The signal strength decreases proportionally to the square of the distance. For example, if the distance is doubled, the signal strength is reduced to one-fourth. Therefore, many cells are required in a service area to maintain proper and uninterrupted line-of-sight signal transmissions. See figure 8–14.

TROUBLESHOOTING AND SERVICING CELLULAR TELEPHONES

The power to the cellular telephone should be connected to an ignition feed source from the fuse panel (such as the radio feed fuse). *Do not connect a cellular telephone feed to the blower motor fuse.* The blower motor creates electromagnetic interference on the power feed wire during operation that could affect the operation of the cellular telephone.

1. **Dead spots**. If dead spots occur during transmission, be certain that the operation is inside of the operating range of one or more of the cells.
2. **Static.** Static or interference can be caused by loose connections to the transceiver (transmitter and receiver unit) or in the antenna cables or cords.
3. **Whining noise**. Whining noise in the transceiver is usually due to a defective wiper motor, blower motor, cooling fan motor, or alternator. If these components are known to be good, install a noise filter (capacitor and/or coil in the power feed line). Check the cellular phone operation with the engine off to confirm that the noise is engine related.
4. **Popping noise.** A popping noise during conversation is usually caused by defective spark plug wires or spark plugs. (Check operation of the cellular phone with the engine off to confirm that the noise is engine related.)
5. **Scratchy noise.** A scratchy noise during conversation is usually due to a defective antenna, an antenna too close to the transceiver, or defective control cables.

AIRBAGS

Airbag-type passive restraints are designed to cushion the driver (or passenger, if the passenger side is so equipped) during a frontal collision. Airbags may be known by many different names, including the following:

1. Supplemental restraint system (SRS)
2. Supplemental inflatable restraints (SIR)
3. Supplemental air restraints (SAR)

Most airbags are designed to supplement the safety belts in the event of a collision. Most airbags are designed to be deployed only in the event of a frontal impact within 30 degrees of center. Most airbag systems are *not* designed to inflate during side or rear impact. The force required to deploy a typical airbag is approximately equal to the force of a vehicle hitting a wall at over 10 miles per hour (6 kilometers per hour).

The force required to trigger the sensors within the system prevents accidental deployment if curbs are hit or the brakes are rapidly applied. The system requires a substantial force to deploy the airbag as a measure to help prevent accidental inflation.

Operation

A typical airbag system includes three sensors. See figure 8–15 for the electrical operation. The **squib** is the heating element used to ignite the gas-generating material, usually sodium azide. It requires about 2 amperes of current to heat the heating element to ignite the inflator. Once the inflator is ignited, the nylon bag quickly inflates (in about 30 milliseconds [ms] or 0.030 seconds) with nitrogen gas generated by the inflator. During a real accident, the driver is being thrown forward by the driver's own momentum toward the steering wheel. The strong nylon bag inflates at the same time. Personal injury is reduced by the spreading of the stopping force over the entire upper-body region. The normal collapsible steering column remains in operation and collapses in a collision when equipped with an airbag system. The bag is equipped with two large side vents that allow the bag to deflate immediately after inflation, once the bag has cushioned the occupant in a collision. To cause inflation, the closing of the **arming sensor** is required to provide the power-side voltage to the inflator module. Before the airbag can inflate, however, the squib circuit must also have a ground. The ground is provided through the actuation of either the **forward** or the **passenger discriminating sensor**. In other

FIGURE 8–14   Cellular telephone cells.

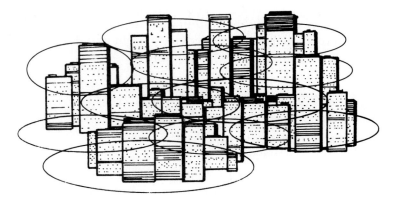

words, two sensors *must* be triggered *at the same time* before the airbag will be deployed.

Sensors

All three sensors are basically switches that complete an electrical circuit when activated. The sensors are basically similar in construction and operation, and the *location* of the sensor determines its name. All airbag sensors are rigidly mounted to the vehicle and *must* be mounted with the arrow pointing toward the front of the vehicle. This ensures that the sensor can detect rapid forward deceleration.

There are three basic styles (designs) of airbag sensors:

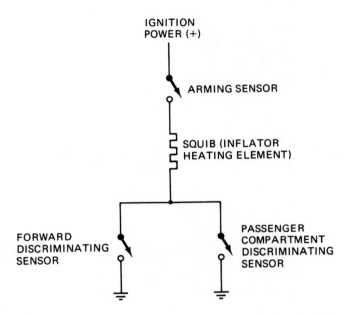

FIGURE 8–15 Typical airbag deployment circuit. Note that both the arming sensor and at least one of the discriminating sensors must be activated at the same time.

1. Magnetically retained gold-plated ball sensor. This sensor uses a permanent magnet to hold a gold-plated steel ball away from two gold-plated electrical contacts. See figure 8–16. If the vehicle (and the sensor) stop rapidly enough, the steel ball is released from the magnet and makes contact with the two gold-plated electrodes. The steel ball only remains in contact with the electrodes for a relatively short time because the steel ball is drawn back into contact with the magnet.

2. Rolled-up stainless steel ribbon-type sensor. This sensor is housed in an airtight package with nitrogen gas inside to prevent harmful corrosion of the sensor parts. See figure 8–17. If the vehicle (and the sensor) stop rapidly, the stainless steel roll "unrolls" and contacts the two gold-plated contacts. Once the force is stopped, the stainless steel roll rolls back into its original shape.

3. Integral sensor. Some vehicles use electronic deceleration sensors built into the inflator module. These sensors measure the rate of deceleration, and, through the computer logic, determine if the airbags should be deployed.

CAUTION: In the event of a collision that causes the airbag to deploy, some vehicle manufacturers require that all sensors be replaced along with the airbag assembly. The force of impact can cause unseen damage inside the sensor and the sensor may not work correctly if used again.

Wiring

By worldwide agreement, all electrical wiring for airbags is yellow. To ensure proper electrical connection to the inflator module in the steering wheel, a coil assembly is used in the steering column. This coil is a

FIGURE 8–16 Airbag magnetic sensor.

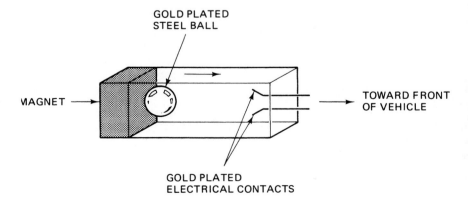

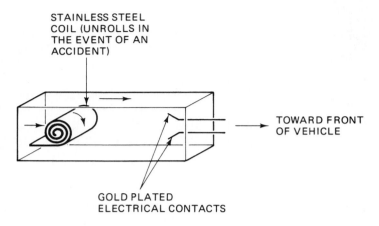

STAINLESS STEEL
COIL (UNROLLS IN
THE EVENT OF AN
ACCIDENT)

TOWARD FRONT
OF VEHICLE

GOLD PLATED
ELECTRICAL CONTACTS

FIGURE 8–17 Airbag ribbon-type sensor.

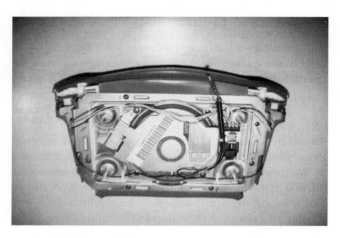

FIGURE 8–18 Underneath a typical driver's airbag module. All airbag wiring connectors are yellow.

FIGURE 8–19 An airbag being deployed as part of a demonstration in an auto laboratory.

copper wire ribbon conductor that operates much like a window shade when the steering wheel is rotated. This coil prevents the lack of continuity between the sensors and the inflator assembly that might result from a horn ring type of sliding conductor. Most airbag systems also include a diagnostic unit that often includes an auxiliary power supply that is used to provide the current to inflate the airbag if the battery is disconnected from the vehicle during a collision. This auxiliary power supply usually involves capacitors that are discharged through the squib of the inflation module. See figures 8–18 through 8–21.

Troubleshooting

The electrical portion of most airbag systems is constantly checked by the circuits within the airbag-energizing power unit or through the vehicles's computer system. The electrical system is monitored by the electronic system by the application of a small signal voltage through the various sensors and components. If continuity exists, a small voltage drop will be measured by the testing circuits. If an open or short circuit occurs, a dash warning light is lighted. Follow exact manufacturer's recommended procedures for accessing and erasing airbag diagnostic trouble codes.

Precautions

Remember the following when working with or around airbags:

1. Always follow all precautions and warning stickers on vehicles equipped with airbags.

FIGURE 8–20 Typical passenger-side airbag inflator module with door opened.

2. In the event of a collision in which the bag(s) were deployed, the inflator module *and* all sensors usually must be replaced to ensure proper future operation of the system.

3. Avoid using a self-powered test light around the yellow airbag wiring. Even though it is highly unlikely, a self-powered test light could provide the necessary current to accidentally set off the inflator module and create an airbag deployment.

4. Use care when handling the inflator module section when it is removed from the steering wheel. Always hold the inflator away from your body.

5. If handling a deployed inflator module, always wear gloves and safety glasses to avoid the possibility of skin irritation from the sodium hydroxide dust that remains after deployment.

6. Never jar or strike a sensor. The contacts inside of the sensor may be damaged, preventing the proper operation of the airbag system in the event of a collision.

7. When mounting a sensor in a vehicle, make certain that the arrow on the sensor is pointing toward the front of the vehicle. Also be certain that the sensor is securely mounted.

ANTILOCK BRAKE SYSTEM ELECTRICAL COMPONENT TROUBLESHOOTING

Most antilock brake system (ABS) electrical components are serviced by replacement only. For example, if an open circuit is detected in one wheel speed sensor wiring harness, the wiring harness section is usually re-

FIGURE 8–21 A typical electronic control unit for an airbag system.

placed. Other commonly replaced ABS components include relays and wheel speed sensors. Most wheel speed sensors are not adjustable, but some vehicles do provide for adjustment. See figures 8–22 through 8–24.

ELECTRICAL ACCESSORY TROUBLESHOOTING GUIDE

The following list will assist technicians in troubleshooting electrical accessory systems.

Blower Motor Problem	*Possible Cause and/or Solutions*
1. Blower motor does not operate.	1. Possible blown fuse. Possible poor ground connection on blower motor. Possible defective motor (use a jumper wire connected between positive terminal of the battery and the blower motor power lead connection [lead disconnected] to check for blower motor operation).
2. Blower motor operates only on high speed.	2. Possible open in the speed control resistors located in the air box near the blower motor. Possible stuck or defective high-speed relay. Possible defective blower motor control switch.

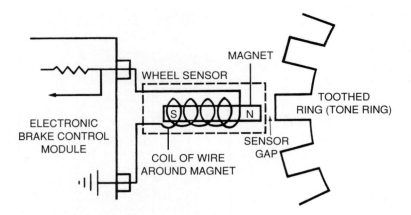

FIGURE 8–22 Typical wheel speed sensor.

3. Blower motor operates in lower speed(s) only—no high speed	**3.** Possible defective high-speed relay or blower high-speed fuse. Check for possible normal operation if the rear window defogger is not in operation; some vehicles electrically prevent simultaneous operation of the high-speed blower and rear window defogger to help reduce the electrical loads.

NOTE: If the high-speed fuse blows a second time, check the current draw of the motor and replace the blower motor if the current draw is above specifications.

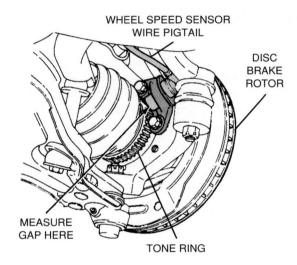

FIGURE 8–23 The gap between the toothed ring and the wheel speed sensor is important for proper operation.

Windshield Wiper or Washer Problem — *Possible Cause and/or Solutions*

1. Windshield wipers are inoperative.	**1.** Possible blown fuse. Possible poor ground on the wiper motor or the control switch. Possible defective motor.
2. Windshield wipers operate on high speed only.	**2.** Possible defective switch. Possible defective motor assembly. Possible poor ground or low speed on the wiper control switch.
3. Windshield washers are inoperative.	**3.** Possible defective switch. Possible empty reservoir or clogged lines or discharge nozzles. Possible poor ground on the washer pump motor.

Horn Problem — *Possible Causes and/or Solutions*

1. Horn(s) are inoperative.	**1.** Possible poor ground on horn(s). Possible defective relay (if used). Possible open circuit in the steering column. Possible defective horn (use a jumper wire connected between the positive terminal of the battery and the horn [horn wire disconnected] to check for proper operation of the horn).
2. Horn(s) produce low volume or wrong sound.	**2.** Possible poor ground at horn. Possible incorrect frequency of horn.

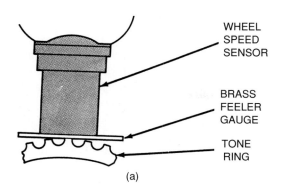

(a)

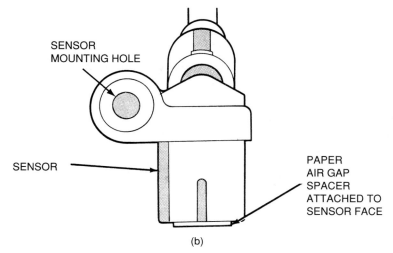

(b)

10X MULTIPLIER*

FIGURE 8–24 *(a)* Always use a nonferrous (brass or plastic) feeler (thickness) gauge when measuring the gap between the toothed ring and the wheel speed sensor. Because the sensor contains a magnet, a steel feeler gauge would stick to the sensor itself and a true "feel" for the actual gap would be difficult to obtain. *(b)* Sometimes a sensor is equipped with a paper spacer that is the exact thickness of the spacing required between the toothed ring and the sensor. If so equipped, the sensor is simply installed with the paper touching the toothed wheel. A typical gap ranges from 0.020 to 0.050 inches (0.5 to 1.3 millimeters).

FIGURE 8–25 A 10-times multiplier.

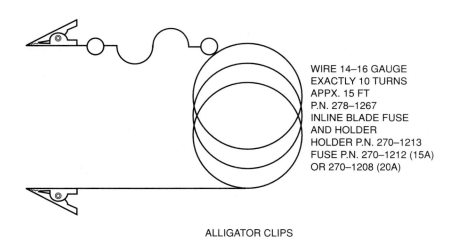

WIRE 14–16 GAUGE
EXACTLY 10 TURNS
APPX. 15 FT
P.N. 278–1267
INLINE BLADE FUSE
AND HOLDER
HOLDER P.N. 270–1213
FUSE P.N. 270–1212 (15A)
OR 270–1208 (20A)

ALLIGATOR CLIPS
P.N. 270–349

*ALL PART NUMBERS ARE FROM RADIO SHACK

3. Horn blows all the time.

3. Possible stuck horn relay (if used). Possible short to ground in the wire to the horn button.

Speed (Cruise) Control Problem

Possible Causes and/or Solutions

1. Speed (cruise) control is inoperative.

1. Possible broken speedometer cable. Possible blown fuse. Possible defective or misadjusted electrical or vacuum safety switch near the brake pedal arm. Possible lack of engine vacuum to servo or transducer. Possible defective transducer. Possible defective speed control switch.

2. Speed (cruise) control speed is incorrect or variable.

2. Possible misadjusted activation cable or chain. Possible defective or pinched vacuum hose. Possible binding of speedometer cable (remove and lubricate). Possible misadjustment of transducer.

Power Window Problem

Possible Causes and/or Solutions

1. Power windows are inoperative.

1. Possible defective (blown) blower fuse (circuit breaker). Possible defective relay (if used). Possible poor ground for master control switch. Possible poor connections at switch(es) or motor(s). Possible open circuit (usually near the master control switch). Possible defective lockout switch.

2. One power window is inoperative.

2. Possible defective motor. Possible defective or open control switch. Possible open or loose wiring to the switch or the motor.

3. Only one power window can be operated from the master switch.

3. Poor connection or open circuit in the control wire(s).

Power Seat Problem

Possible Causes and/or Solutions

1. Power seats are inoperative —no click or noise.

1. Possible defective circuit breaker. Possible poor ground at the switch or relay (if used). Possible open in the wiring between the switch and relay (if

used). Possible defective switch. Possible defective solenoid(s) or wiring. Possible defective door switch.

2. Power seats are inoperative —click is heard.

2. Check for "flex" in the cables from the motor(s) to check for motor operation. If flex is felt, the motor is trying to operate the gearnut or the screw jack. Check for possible binding or obstruction. Possible defective motor (the click is generally the relay sound). Possible defective solenoids(s) or wiring to the solenoid(s).

3. All power seat functions are operative except one.

3. Possible defective motor. Possible defective solenoid or wiring to the solenoid.

Electric Power Door Lock Problem

Possible Causes and/or Solutions

1. Power door locks are inoperative.

1. Possible defective circuit breaker, fuse, or wiring to the switch(es) or relay (if used). Possible defective relay (if used). Possible defective switch(es). Possible defective door lock solenoid or ground for solenoid (if solenoid operated). Possible open in the wiring to the door lock solenoid or the motor. Possible mechanical obstruction of the door lock mechanism.

2. Only one door lock is inoperative.

2. Possible defective switch. Possible poor ground on the solenoid (if solenoid operated). Possible defective door lock solenoid or motor. Possible poor electrical connection at the motor or solenoid.

Rear Window Defogger Problem

Possible Causes and/or Solutions

1. Rear window defogger is inoperative.

1. Check for proper operation by performing breath test and/or voltmeter check at the power side of the rear window grid. Possible defective relay or timer assembly. Possible defective switch. Possible open ground connection at the rear window grid.

2. Rear window defogger cleans only a portion of the rear window.

2. The most common cause of partial operation of a heated rear window defogger is a broken grid wire(s) or poor electrical connections at either the power side or the ground side of the wire grid.

NOTE: If there is an open circuit (power side or ground side), the dash indicator light will still operate in most cases.

SUMMARY

1. Most blower motors use resistors wired in series to control blower motor speed.

2. Most windshield wipers use a three-brush two-speed motor.

3. Most power windows and power door locks use a permanent-magnet motor that has a built-in circuit breaker and is reversible. The control switches and relays direct the current through the motors.

4. The current flow through a rear window defogger is often self-regulating. As the temperature of the grid increases, its resistance increases, reducing current flow. Some rear window defoggers are also used as radio antennas.

5. Airbags use a sensor(s) to determine if the rate of deceleration is enough to cause bodily harm. All airbag wiring is yellow. When working around an

◀ **TECH TIP** ▶

THE 10-TIMES MULTIPLIER

Measuring a small amount of current (in amperes) with a starting and charging unit is possible if you use a 10-times multiplier. See figure 8–25.

Connect a coil of wire with exactly ten turns in series with the component being measured, such as a blower motor. Since the current flows through the multiplier exactly 10 times, the ampere probe will read the 10-times value. Simply divide by 10 to get the actual reading.

For example, if the blower motor is set to "high," the starting and charging tester will read about 120 amperes. Divide by 10 and the true reading of 12 amperes (120/10 = 12). This 10-times multiplier is easy to make out of insulated wire and makes current measurements quick and easy. This method is especially useful for those circuits (such as the blower motor circuit) wherein the current flow exceeds the 10-ampere rating of most digital multimeters.

airbag, disconnect the wiring connectors to help prevent accidental deployment.

REVIEW QUESTIONS

1. Explain why a defective blower motor draws more current (amperes) than a good motor.

2. Describe how power door locks on a four-door vehicle can function with only one ground wire connection.

3. Explain how a rear window defogger can regulate how much current flows through the grids based on temperature.

4. List the safety precautions to follow whenever working around an airbag.

MULTIPLE-CHOICE QUESTIONS

1. Technician A says that a defective high-speed blower motor relay prevents high-speed blower operation, yet allows normal operation at low speeds. Technician B says that a defective (open) blower motor resistor can prevent low-speed blower operation, yet permit high-speed operation. Which technician is correct?
   a. A only
   b. B only
   c. Both a and b
   d. Neither a nor b

2. With most windshield wiper systems,_____ .
   a. Both the motor and the control switch must be grounded
   b. No ground is necessary if PM motors are used
   c. Only the motor unit itself must be properly grounded
   d. The only ground is located at the control unit (switch) if PM motors are used

3. Technician A says that a misadjusted brake switch could cause the speed control to be inoperative. Technician B says that a defective low-speed switch (non-computer-controlled speed control) or defective vehicle speed sensor (computer-controlled speed control) could cause the speed control to be inoperative. Which technician is correct?

   a. A only
   b. B only
   c. Both a and b
   d. Neither a nor b

4. Technician A says that a defective ground connection at the master control switch (driver's side) could cause the failure of all power windows. Technician B says that if one control wire is disconnected, all windows will fail to operate. Which technician is correct?

   a. A only
   b. B only
   c. Both a and b
   d. Neither a nor b

5. A typical six-way power seat _____ .

   a. Uses six separate PM nongrounded electric motors
   b. Uses one or three motors (depending on manufacturer)
   c. Uses six separate grounded electric motors only
   d. Uses two electric motors and a three-way direct-acting solenoid-controlled transmission device

6. When checking the operation of a rear window defogger with a voltmeter, _____ .

   a. The voltmeter should be set to read AC volts
   b. The voltmeter should read close to battery voltage anywhere along the grid
   c. Voltage should be available anytime at the power side of the grid because the control circuit just completes the ground side of the heater grid circuit
   d. The voltmeter should indicate decreasing voltage when the grid is tested across the width of the glass

7. PM motors used in power windows, mirrors, and seats can be reversed by_____ .

   a. Sending current to a reversed field coil
   b. Reversing the polarity of the current to the motor
   c. Using a reverse relay circuit
   d. Using a relay and a two-way clutch

8. Technician A says that a radio can receive AM signals, but not FM signals, if the antenna is defective. Technician B says that a good antenna should give a reading of about 500 ohms when tested with an ohmmeter between the center antenna wire and ground. Which technician is correct?

   a. A only
   b. B only
   c. Both a and b
   d. Neither a nor b

9. When a cellular telephone is being installed or serviced, the power lead connection should *never* be connected to _____ .

   a. A power tap close to the battery
   b. An ignition-controlled circuit such as the radio feed circuit
   c. The blower motor circuit
   d. The rear defogger or power door lock circuit

10. If only one power door lock is inoperative, a possible cause includes _____ .

    a. A poor ground connection at the power door lock relay
    b. A defective motor (or solenoid)
    c. A defective (open) circuit breaker for the power circuit
    d. A defective (open) fuse for the control circuit

◀ Chapter 9 ▶

BATTERIES AND BATTERY TESTING

OBJECTIVES

After studying chapter 9, the reader will be able to

1. Describe how a battery works.
2. List the precautions necessary whenever working with batteries.
3. Explain how to safely charge a battery.
4. Discuss how to perform a battery drain test.

Everything electrical in a vehicle is supplied current from the battery. The battery is one of the most important parts of a vehicle.

PURPOSE OF A BATTERY

The primary purpose of an automotive battery is to provide a source of electrical power for starting and for electrical demands that exceed generator output. The battery also acts as a stabilizer to the voltage for the entire electrical system. The battery is a voltage stabilizer because it acts as a reservoir where large amounts of current (amperes) can be removed quickly during starting and replaced gradually by the alternator during charging.

The battery *must* be in good (serviceable) condition before the charging system and the cranking system can be tested. For example, if a battery is discharged, the cranking circuit (starter motor) could test as being defective because the battery voltage might

drop below specifications. (See the description of the general voltmeter test in chapter 11.) The charging circuit could also test as being defective because of a weak or discharged battery. It is important to test the vehicle battery before further testing of the cranking or charging system.

BATTERY CONSTRUCTION

Most automotive battery cases (containers or covers) are constructed of polypropylene, a thin (approximately 0.08 inches [2.0 millimeters] thick), strong, and lightweight plastic. Containers for industrial batteries and some truck batteries are constructed of a hard, thick rubber material.

Inside the case there are six cells (for a 12-volt battery). Each cell has positive and negative plates. Built into the bottom of many batteries are ribs that support the lead-alloy plates and provide a space for sediment to settle. This space prevents spent active material from causing a short circuit between the plates at the bottom of the battery, and it is called the **sediment chamber.** Some maintenance-free batteries do not have a sediment chamber, but enclose the plates in an envelope-type separator that prevents material from settling to the bottom of the battery case. See figure 9–1.

Maintenance free is a term used to describe batteries that use little water during normal service because of the alloy material used to construct the battery plate grids. Maintenance-free batteries are also called **low-water loss batteries.**

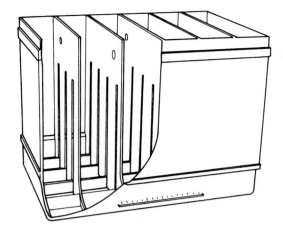

FIGURE 9–1   Typical polypropylene plastic battery case.

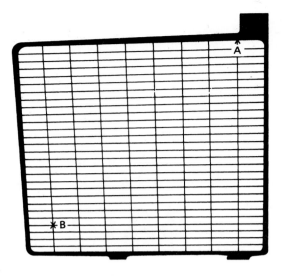

FIGURE 9–3

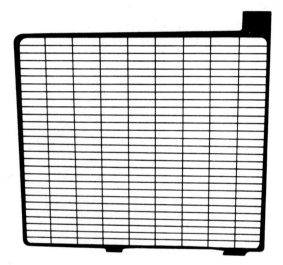

FIGURE 9–2   Lead-alloy grid. The active battery materials are "pasted" onto these grids.

Grids

Each positive and negative plate in a battery is constructed on a framework or **grid** made primarily of lead. Lead is a soft material and must be strengthened for use in an automotive battery grid. Adding antimony or calcium to the pure lead adds strength to the lead grids. See figure 9–2. Battery grids hold the active material and provide the electrical pathways for the current created in the plate.

Maintenance-Free versus Standard Battery Grids

A normal battery uses up to 5% **antimony** in the construction of the plate grids to add strength. However, the greater the amount of antimony, the greater the

amount of gassing (hydrogen gas and oxygen gas released), and therefore the more water the battery will use. Maintenance-free batteries use **calcium** instead of antimony because 0.2% calcium has the same strength as 6% antimony. A typical lead-calcium grid uses only 0.09% to 0.12% calcium.

Low-maintenance batteries use a low percentage of antimony (about 2% to 3%) or use antimony only in the positive plates and use calcium for the negative plates. *The percentages that make up the alloy of the plate grids constitute the major difference between standard and maintenance-free batteries.* The chemical reactions that occur inside each battery are identical regardless of the type of material used to construct the grid plates.

Radial Grid Design

Some batteries use a grid design with only vertical and horizontal strips. The battery plate creates electrical energy from chemical energy, and this current must flow from where it is generated (for example, location *B* in figure 9–3) to where it is connected to the outside battery post (indicated by point *A*). The current must move over and up along the grid strips to reach point *A*.

With a radial grid design (radial means branching out from a common center), the current generated near point *B* in figure 9–4 can travel directly to point *A*. Therefore, a grid with a radial design has lower resistance and can provide more current more rapidly than can the non-radial-grid design used in conventional batteries. The radial spokes act as a superhighway system enabling the current to travel from all areas of the grid to the battery post.

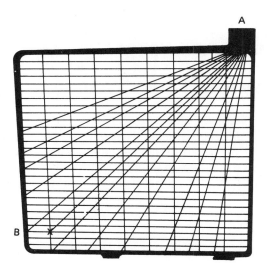

FIGURE 9–4 Radial design battery grids permit lower resistance for current generated at point *B* to reach point *A*. Point *A* is where the grid is joined to other grids by connector plates.

Positive Plates

The positive plates have **lead dioxide (peroxide)** placed onto the grid framework. This process is called **pasting**. This active material can react with the sulfuric acid of the battery and is dark brown in color.

Negative Plates

The negative plates are pasted with a pure **porous lead** called **sponge lead** and are gray in color.

Separators

The positive and the negative plates must be installed alternately next to each other without touching. Nonconducting **separators** are used, which allow room for the reaction of the acid with both plate materials, yet insulate the plates to prevent shorts. These separators are porous (with many small holes) and have ribs facing the positive plate. Some batteries also use a glass fiber between the positive plate and the separator to help prevent the loss of the active material from the grid plate. Separators can be made from resin-coated paper, porous rubber, fiberglass, or expanded plastic. Many batteries use envelope-type separators that encase the entire plate and help prevent any material that may shed from the plates from causing a short circuit between plates at the bottom of the battery.

Cells

Cells are constructed of positive and negative plates with insulating separators between each plate. Most batteries use one more negative plate than positive plate in each cell. Many newer batteries use the same number of positive and negative plates. A cell is also called an **element.** Each cell is actually a 2-volt battery, regardless of the number of positive or negative plates used. The greater the number of plates used in each cell, the greater the amount of *current* that can be produced. Typical batteries contain four positive plates and five negative plates per cell. A 12-volt battery contains six cells connected in series, which produce the 12 volts (6 $\times$ 2 = 12) and contain fifty-four plates (9 plates per cell $\times$ 6 cells). If the same 12-volt battery had five positive plates and six negative plates, for a total of eleven plates per cell (5 + 6), or sixty-six plates (11 plates $\times$ 6 cells), it would have the same voltage, but the amount of current that the battery could produce would be increased. The capacity of a battery is determined by the amount of active plate material in the battery and the area of the plate material exposed to the liquid, called electrolyte, in the battery.

Partitions

Each cell is separated from the other cells by **partitions**, which are made of the same material as that used for the outside case of the battery. Electrical connections between cells are provided by lead connectors that loop over the top of the partition and connect the plates of the cells together. Many batteries connect the cells directly through the partition connectors, which provides the shortest path for the current and the lowest resistance. See figure 9–5. Older-style truck and industrial batteries commonly used connectors that extended through the top of the case and over and then down through the case to connect the cells.

Electrolyte

The **electrolyte** used in automotive batteries is a solution (liquid combination) of 36% sulfuric acid and 64% water. This electrolyte is used for both lead-antimony and lead-calcium (maintenance-free) batteries. The chemical symbol for this sulfuric acid solution is H_2SO_4

- H = Symbol for hydrogen (the subscript 2 means that there are two atoms of hydrogen)

- S = Symbol for sulfur

- O = Symbol for oxygen (the subscript 4 indicates that there are four atoms of oxygen)

This electrolyte is sold premixed in the proper proportion and is factory installed or added to the battery when the battery is sold. Additional electrolyte must *never* be added to any battery after the original electrolyte fill. It is normal for some water (H_2O) to escape during charging as a result of the **gassing** that is produced by the chemical reactions. Only pure distilled water should be added to a battery. If distilled water is not available, clean drinking water can be used.

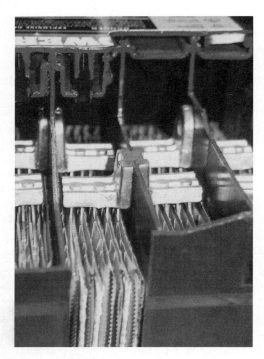

FIGURE 9–5   Photo of a cutaway battery showing the connection of the cells to each other through the partition.

HOW A BATTERY WORKS

A fully charged lead-acid battery has a positive plate of lead dioxide (peroxide) and a negative plate of lead surrounded by a sulfuric acid solution (electrolyte). The difference in potential (voltage) between lead peroxide and lead in acid is approximately 2.1 volts.

Discharging

The positive plate lead dioxide (PbO_2) combines with the SO_4 from the electrolyte and releases its O_2, into the electrolyte, forming H_2O. The negative plate also combines with the SO_4 from the electrolyte and becomes lead sulfate ($PbSO_4$). See figure 9–6.

The Fully Discharged State

When the battery is fully discharged, both the positive and the negative plates are $PbSO_4$ (lead sulfate) and the electrolyte has become water (H_2O). It is usually not possible for a battery to become 100% discharged. However, as the battery is being discharged, the plates and electrolyte approach the completely dead situation. There is also the danger of freezing when a battery is discharged, because the electrolyte is mostly water.

FIGURE 9–6   Chemical reaction for a lead-acid battery that is fully *charged* being discharged by the attached electrical load.

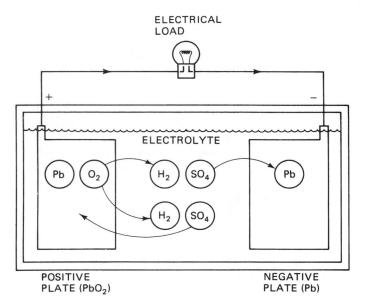

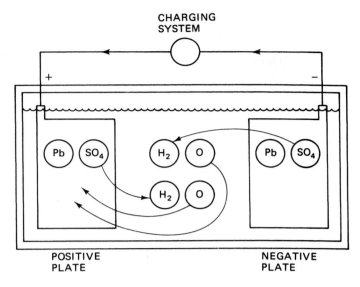

FIGURE 9–7   Chemical reaction for a lead-acid battery that is fully *discharged* being charged by the attached generator.

Charging

During charging, the sulfate (acid) leaves both the positive and the negative plates and returns to the electrolyte, where it becomes normal-strength sulfuric acid solution. The positive plate returns to lead dioxide (PbO_2) and the negative plate is again pure lead (Pb). See figure 9–7.

SPECIFIC GRAVITY

The amount of sulfate in the electrolyte is determined by the electrolyte's **specific gravity**. Specific gravity is the ratio of the weight of a given volume of a liquid to the weight of an equal volume of water. In other words, the more dense the material (liquid), the higher its specific gravity. Pure water is the basis for this measurement and is given a specific gravity of 1000 at 80° F. Pure sulfuric acid has a specific gravity of 1.835; the *correct* concentration of water and sulfuric acid (called electrolyte—64% water, 36% acid) is 1.260 to 1.280 at 80° F. The higher the battery's specific gravity, the more fully it is charged. See figure 9–8.

CHARGE INDICATORS

Some batteries are equipped with a built-in state-of-charge indicator. This indicator is simply a small ball-type hydrometer that is installed in one cell. This hydrometer uses a plastic ball that floats if the electrolyte is dense enough (which is when the battery is about 65% to 75% charged). When the ball floats, it appears in the hydrometer's sight glass, changing its color. See figures

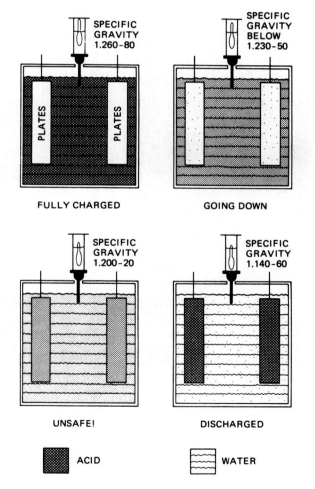

FIGURE 9–8   As the battery becomes discharged, the specific gravity of the battery acid decreases.

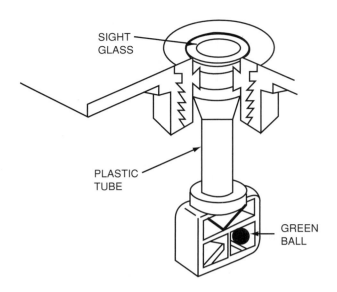

FIGURE 9–9 Typical battery charge indicator. If the specific gravity is low (battery discharged), the ball drops away from the reflective prism and the sight glass is dark. When the battery is charged enough, the ball floats and reflects the color of the ball (usually green) back up through the sight glass.

FIGURE 9–10 Cutaway of the battery showing the charge indicator. If the electrolyte level drops below the bottom of the prism, the sight glass shows clear (light). Most battery manufacturers warn that if the electrolyte level is low on a sealed battery, the battery must be replaced. Attempting to charge a battery that has a low electrolyte level can cause a buildup of gases and possibly an explosion.

9–9 and 9–10. Because the hydrometer is only testing one cell (out of six on a 12-volt battery), and because the hydrometer ball can easily stick in one position, it should not be trusted to give accurate information about a battery's state of charge.

SPECIFIC GRAVITY VERSUS STATE OF CHARGE AND BATTERY VOLTAGE

Values of specific gravity, state of charge, and battery voltage at 80° F (27° C) are given in the following table.

Specific gravity	State of charge	Battery voltage
1.265	Fully charged	12.6 or higher
1.225	75% charged	12.4
1.190	50% charged	12.2
1.155	25% charged	12.0
Lower than 1.120	Discharged	11.9 or lower

CAUSES AND TYPES OF BATTERY FAILURE

Most batteries have a useful service life of 2 to 5 years. However, proper care can help increase the life of a battery and abuse can shorten the life. The major cause of premature battery failure is overcharging. The automotive charging circuit, consisting of an alternator (generator), voltage regulator, and connecting wires, must be operating correctly to prevent damage to the battery. Charging voltages higher than 15.5 volts can damage a battery by warping the plates as a result of the heat of overcharging. See figure 9–11.

Overcharging also causes the active material to disintegrate and fall out of the supporting grid framework. Vibration or bumping can also cause internal damage similar to that caused by overcharging. It is important, therefore, to ensure that all automotive batteries are securely clamped down in the vehicle. The shorting of cell plates can occur without notice. If one of the six cells of a 12-volt battery is shorted, the resulting voltage of the battery is only 10 volts ($12 - 2 = 10$). With only 10 volts available, the starter *usually* will not be able to start the engine.

BATTERY HOLD-DOWNS

All batteries must be attached securely to the vehicle to prevent battery damage. Normal vehicle vibrations can cause the active materials inside the battery to shed. Battery hold-down clamps or brackets help reduce vi-

FIGURE 9–11 Battery that was accidentally left over the weekend, on a battery charger that was set for high-charge rate. Note how the plates warped and the top blew off.

bration, which can greatly reduce the capacity and life of any battery.

WHAT CAUSES A BATTERY TO WEAR OUT

Every automotive battery has a limited service life of approximately 2 to 5 years. During the life of a battery, the active material sheds from the surface of the positive plates. This gradually limits the power of the battery. This cycling can also cause the negative plates to become soft, which will also cause eventual battery failure.

BATTERY RATINGS

Batteries are rated according to the amount of current they can produce under specific conditions.

Cold Cranking Amperes. Every automotive battery must be able to supply electrical power to crank the engine in cold weather and still provide battery voltage high enough to operate the ignition system for starting. The cold cranking power of a battery is the number of amperes that can be supplied by a battery at $0°$ F $(-18°$ C) for 30 seconds while the battery still maintains a voltage of 1.2 volts per cell or higher. This means that the battery voltage would be 7.2 volts for a 12-volt battery and 3.6 volt for a 6-volt battery. The cold cranking performance rating is called **cold cranking amperes** (CCA). Try to purchase a battery with the highest CCA for the money. See

vehicle manufacturers' specifications for recommended battery capacity.

Reserve Capacity. The **reserve capacity** rating for batteries is *the number of minutes* for which the battery can produce 25 amperes and still have a battery voltage of 1.75 volts per cell (10.5 volts for a 12-volt battery). This rating is actually a measurement of the time for which a vehicle can be driven in the event of a charging system failure.

WHAT DETERMINES BATTERY CAPACITY

The capacity of any battery is determined by the amount of active material in the battery. A battery with a large number of thin plates can produce high current for a short period. If a few thick plates are used, the battery can produce low current for a long period. A trolling motor battery used for fishing needs to supply a low current for a long period of time. An automotive battery is required to produce a high current for a short period for cranking. Therefore, every battery is designed for a specific application.

DEEP CYCLING

Deep cycling is almost fully discharging a battery and then completely recharging it. Golf cart batteries are an example of lead-acid batteries that must be designed to be deep cycled. A golf cart must be able to cover two eighteen-hole rounds of golf and then be fully recharged overnight. Because charging is hard on batteries because the internal heat generated can cause plate warpage, these specially designed batteries use thicker plate grids, which resist warpage. Normal automotive batteries are not designed for repeated deep cycling.

HYBRID BATTERIES

A hybrid battery is a battery that uses two different alloys in the plate grids. The positive plates are usually of a low-antimony (2% to 3%) alloy, whereas the negative plates are of a calcium alloy. This hybrid (combining two types of construction) is a battery with lower water usage and corrosion than that of a lead-antimony battery, with improved deep-cycling capacity.

BATTERY COUNCIL INTERNATIONAL (BCI) GROUP SIZES

The Battery Council International organization has established battery group size designations. See the following chart.

BCI group size	Inches L	W	H	Millimeters L	W	H
21	8 3/16	6 13/16	8 3/4	208	173	222
22F	9 1/2	6 7/8	8 5/16	241	175	211
22HF	9 1/2	6 7/8	9	241	175	229
22NF	9 7/16	5 1/2	8 15/16	240	140	227
22NL	9 1/4	5 1/4	7 13/16	235	133	198
22R	9	6 7/8	8 5/16	229	175	211
23	10 3/4	6 7/8	8 7/16	273	175	214
24	10 1/4	6 13/16	8 7/8	260	173	225
24F	10 3/4	6 13/16	9	273	173	229
24H	10 1/4	6 13/16	9 3/8	260	173	238
24R	10 1/4	6 13/16	9	260	173	229
24T	10 1/4	6 13/16	9 3/4	260	173	248
25	9 1/16	6 7/8	8 7/8	230	175	225
26	8 3/16	6 13/16	7 3/4	208	173	197
27	12 1/16	6 13/16	8 7/8	306	173	225
27F	12 1/2	6 13/16	8 15/16	318	173	227
27H	11 3/4	6 13/16	9 1/4	298	173	235
27HF	12 1/2	6 13/16	9 3/16	318	173	233
28	10 5/16	6 13/16	9 7/16	261	173	240
29HR	13 1/8	6 13/16	9 1/8	333	173	232
29NF	13	5 1/2	8 15/16	330	140	227
33	13 3/8	6 13/16	9 1/2	339	173	240
34	10 1/4	6 13/16	7 13/16	260	173	200
35	9 1/16	6 7/8	8 7/8	230	175	225
41	11 9/16	6 7/8	6 7/8	293	175	175
42	9 9/16	6 13/16	6 13/16	243	173	173
43	13 1/8	6 7/8	8 1/16	334	175	205
44	16 7/16	6 7/8	8 1/16	418	175	205
45	9 7/16	5 1/2	8 15/16	240	140	227
46	10 3/4	6 13/16	9	273	173	229
47	9 11/16	6 7/8	7 1/2	246	175	190
48	12 1/16	6 7/8	7 9/16	306	175	192

BCI group size	Inches L	W	H	Millimeters L	W	H
49	15	6 7/8	7 9/16	381	175	192
53	13	4 11/16	8 1/4	330	119	210
54	7 3/8	6 1/16	8 3/8	186	154	212
55	8 5/8	6 1/16	8 3/8	218	154	212
56	10 1/16	6 1/16	8 3/8	254	154	212
57	8 1/16	7 1/4	7	204	183	177
58	9 7/16	7 1/4	7	239	183	177
60	13 1/16	6 5/16	8 7/8	332	160	225
61	7 9/16	6 1/16	8 7/8	192	162	225
62	8 15/16	6 1/16	8 7/8	226	162	225
63	10 3/16	6 1/16	8 7/8	258	162	225
64	11 11/16	6 1/16	8 7/8	296	162	225
65	11 3/8	7 1/2	7 9/16	288	190	192
70	8 3/16	7 1/16	7 3/4	208	179	196
71	8 3/16	7 1/16	8 1/2	208	179	216
72	9 1/16	7 1/16	8 1/4	230	179	210
73	9 1/16	7 1/16	8 1/2	230	179	216
74	10 1/4	7 1/4	8 3/4	260	184	222
75	9 1/16	7 1/16	7 3/4	230	179	196
76	13 1/8	7 1/16	8 1/2	333	179	216
77	12 1/16	7 1/4	8 3/4	306	184	222
78	10 1/4	7 1/16	7 3/4	260	179	196

The original designations (the numbers in the 20s) were becoming very confusing because of the additional letters used to describe various sizes. Letters and their meanings include the following:

F (e.g., 22F)—usually designates use on Ford vehicles or the reversing end-to-end of positive and negative posts

H (e.g., 24H)—designates greater height than normal for the group

R (e.g., 22R)—designates the reversing side-to-side of positive and negative posts

N—designates narrower width than normal for the group

L—designates greater length than normal for the group

T (e.g., 24T)—designates greater height than an H rating

All letters were added to the original group sizes to satisfy vehicle manufacturer need for a battery close to a standard size, but with one or two changes. Notice in the chart that some groups have two letters added to the group number, such as 22NL, meaning group 22, but narrower (N) and longer (L) than a standard 22 group size.

When General Motors and Delco batteries started using side post batteries, BCI assigned a new designated group number sequence rather than add additional letters to existing group numbers. The numbers in the 70s represent side post batteries. The 50s represent the reversed post design commonly used by Ford products.

BATTERY SERVICE SAFETY CONSIDERATIONS

Batteries contain acid and release explosive gases (hydrogen and oxygen) during normal charging and discharging cycles. To help prevent physical injury or damage to the vehicle, always adhere to the following safety procedures:

1. Whenever working on any electrical component on a vehicle, disconnect the negative battery cable from the battery. When the negative cable is disconnected, all electrical circuits in the vehicle will be open which will prevent accidental electrical contact between an electrical component and ground. Any electrical spark has the potential to cause explosion and personal injury.
2. Wear eye protection whenever working around any battery.
3. Wear protective clothing to avoid skin contact with battery acid.
4. Always adhere to all safety precautions as stated in the service procedures for the equipment used for battery service and testing.
5. Never smoke or use an open flame around any battery.

BATTERY MAINTENANCE

Most new-style batteries are of a maintenance-free design that uses lead-calcium instead of lead-antimony plate grid construction. Because lead-calcium batteries do not release as much gas as do the older-style lead-antimony batteries, there is less consumption of water during normal service. Also, with less gassing, less corrosion is observed on the battery terminals, wiring, and support trays. Side terminal battery design has also reduced the self-discharge that can often occur as a re-

sult of dirt and moisture on the top of the battery, which provide a conductive path for the current to flow between the terminals that can lead to battery discharge.

Battery maintenance includes making certain that the battery case is clean and checking and adding clean water, if necessary. Distilled water is recommended by all battery manufacturers, but if distilled water is not available, clean ordinary drinking water, low in mineral content, can be used. Because water is the only thing in a battery that is consumed, acid should never be added to a battery. Battery electrolyte is an exact mixture of acid and water (64% water and 36% acid). Some of the water in the electrolyte escapes during the normal operation of charging and discharging, but the acid content of the electrolyte remains in the battery. Adding electrolyte simply increases the acid content of the electrolyte and will shorten the life of the battery. Do not overfill a battery, because normal bubbling (gassing) of the electrolyte will cause the electrolyte to escape and start corrosion on the battery terminals, hold-down brackets, and battery tray. Fill batteries to the indicator that is approximately 1½ inches (3.8 centimeters) from the top of the filler tube. Another method is to fill the battery until the water becomes "puckered," indicating that the electrolyte level is even with the bottom of the filler tube. This puckering of water in a tube is called the **meniscus**. See figures 9–12 and 9–13.

The battery should also be secured with a hold-down bracket to prevent vibration from damaging the plates inside the battery. The hold-down bracket should be snug

◄ TECH TIP ►

DYNAMIC VERSUS OPEN CIRCUIT VOLTAGE

Open circuit voltage is the voltage (usually of a battery) that exists *without* a load being applied. **Dynamic voltage** is the voltage of the power source (battery) with the circuit in operation. A vehicle battery, for example, may indicate that it has 12.6 volts or more, but that voltage may drop when the battery is put under a load such as cranking the engine. If the battery voltage drops too much, the starter motor will rotate more slowly and the engine may not start.

If the dynamic voltage is lower than specified, the battery may be weak or defective or the circuit may be defective, resulting in too much current being drawn from the battery. See chapter 10 for further starting circuit information and testing.

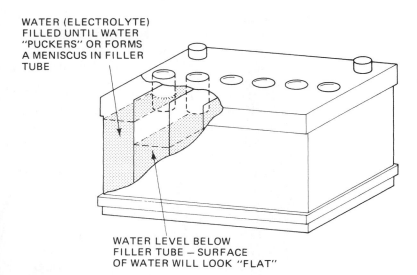

WATER (ELECTROLYTE) FILLED UNTIL WATER "PUCKERS" OR FORMS A MENISCUS IN FILLER TUBE

WATER LEVEL BELOW FILLER TUBE — SURFACE OF WATER WILL LOOK "FLAT"

FIGURE 9–12

FIGURE 9–13 Many maintenance-free batteries can be opened to check the electrolyte level without damaging the battery. Notice the surface dirt, which could cause the battery to self-discharge.

enough to prevent battery movement, yet not so tight as to cause the case to crack. Factory-original hold-down brackets are often available through local automobile dealers, and universal hold-down units are available through local automotive parts stores.

Battery cable connections should be checked and cleaned to prevent voltage drop at the connections. One of the most common reasons for an engine not starting is loose or corroded battery cable connections. Replacement battery cable terminal ends are available at most automotive parts stores.

BATTERY VOLTAGE TEST

Testing the battery voltage with a voltmeter is a simple method for determining the state of charge of any battery. See figure 9–14. The voltage of a battery does not neces-

sarily indicate whether or not the battery can perform satisfactorily, but it does indicate to the technician more about the battery's condition than does a simple visual inspection. A battery that "looks good" may not be good. This test is commonly called an **open circuit battery voltage test** because it is conducted with an open circuit—with no current flowing and no load applied to the battery.

1. If the battery has just been charged or the vehicle has recently been driven, it is necessary to remove the surface charge from the battery before testing. A surface charge is a charge of higher-than-normal voltage that is just on the surface of the battery plates. The surface charge is quickly removed whenever the battery is loaded and therefore does not accurately represent the true state of charge of the battery.

2. To remove the surface charge, turn the headlights on high beam (brights) for 1 minute, then turn the headlights off and wait 2 minutes.

3. With the engine and all electrical accessories off, and the doors shut (to turn off the interior lights), connect a voltmeter to the battery posts. Connect the red positive lead to the positive post and the black negative lead to the negative post. See figure 9–15.

NOTE: If the meter reads negative, the battery has been reverse charged (has reversed polarity) and should be replaced, or the meter has been connected incorrectly.

---

4. Read the voltmeter and compare the results with the state-of-charge chart following. The voltages shown are for a battery at or near room temperature (70° to 80° F, 21° to 27° C).

(a)

(b)

FIGURE 9–14 *(a)* A battery with only 9 volts is definitely discharged and must be recharged before it can be tested. *(b)* This dirty battery is slightly discharged.

FIGURE 9–15 Testing the open circuit voltage (no load on the battery) with a digital multitester. For an accurate state-of-charge indication, the headlights should be turned on for 1 minute to remove the surface charge.

Battery voltage (V)	State of charge
12.6 or higher	100% charged
12.4	75% charged
12.2	50% charged
12.0	25% charged
11.9 or lower	Discharged

HYDROMETER TESTING

If the battery has removable filler caps, the specific gravity of the electrolyte can also be checked. This test can also be performed on most maintenance-free batteries because the filler caps are removable from most maintenance-free batteries except for those produced by Delco battery. The specific gravity test indicates the state of charge of the battery and can indicate a defective battery if the specific gravity of one or more cells varies by more than 0.050 from the value of the highest-reading cell.

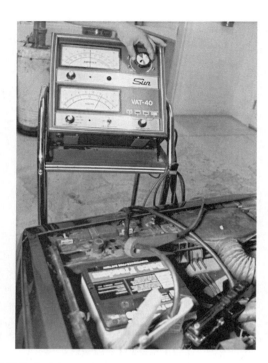

FIGURE 9–16   A Sun Electric VAT-40 (volt amp tester, model 40) connected to a battery for load testing. The technician turns the load knob until the ammeter registers an amperage reading equal to one-half of the battery's CCA rating. The load is maintained for 15 seconds, and the voltage of the battery should be higher than 9.6 volts at the end of the time period *with the load still applied.*

Specific gravity	Battery voltage (V)	State of charge
1.265	12.6 or higher	100% charged
1.225	12.4	75% charged
1.190	12.2	50% charged
1.155	12.0	25% charged
Lower than 1.120	11.9 or lower	Discharged

BATTERY LOAD TESTING

The most accurate test to determine the condition of any battery is the **load test**. Most automotive starting and charging testers use a carbon pile to create an electrical load on the battery. The amount of the load is determined by the original capacity of the battery being tested. The capacity is measured in cold cranking amperes, which is the number of amperes that a battery can supply at 0° F (−18° C) for 30 seconds. An older type of battery rating is called the **ampere-hour rating**. *The proper electrical load to be used to test a battery is one-half of the CCA rating or 3 times the ampere-hour rating, with a*

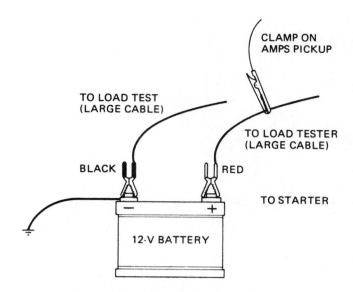

FIGURE 9–17   Typical battery load tester hookup.

minimum of a 150-ampere load. Apply the load for a full 15 seconds and observe the voltmeter at the end of the 15-second period while the battery is still under load. A good battery should indicate above 9.6 volts. Many battery manufacturers recommend performing the load test twice, using the first load period to remove the surface charge on the battery and the second test to provide a truer indication of the condition of the battery. Wait 30 seconds between tests to allow time for the battery to recover. See figures 9–16 and 9–17.

If the battery fails the load test, recharge the battery and retest. If the load test is failed again, replacement of the battery is required.

BATTERY CHARGING

If the state of charge of a battery is low, it must be recharged. It is best to slow-charge any battery to prevent possible overheating damage to the battery. See figure 9–18 for the recommended charging rate. *Remember, it may take 8 hours or more to charge a fully discharged battery.* The initial charge rate should be about 35 amperes for 30 minutes to help start the charging process. Fast-charging a battery increases the temperature of the battery and can cause warping of the plates inside the battery. Fast-charging also increases the amount of gassing (release of hydrogen and oxygen), which can create a health and fire hazard. The battery temperature should not exceed 125° F (hot to the touch). *Most batteries should be charged at a rate equal to 1% of the battery's CCA rating.*

Fast charge: 15 amperes maximum

Slow charge: 5 amperes maximum

BATTERY CHARGING GUIDE
(6-Volt and 12-Volt Batteries)
Caution:Do Not Use for Low Water Loss Batteries
Recommended Rate and Time for Fully Discharged Condition

Rated Battery Capacity (Reserve Minutes)	Slow Charge	Fast Charge
80 Minutes or Less	10 hrs. @ 5 Amperes 5 hrs. @ 10 Amperes	2.5 hrs. @ 20 Amperes 1.5 hrs. @ 30 Amperes
Above 80 to 125 Minutes	15 hrs. @ 5 Amperes 7.5 hrs. @ 10 Amperes	3.75 hrs. @ 20 Amperes 1.5 hrs. @ 50 Amperes
Above 125 to 170 Minutes	20 hrs. @ 5 Amperes 10 hrs. @ 10 Amperes	5 hrs. @ 20 Amperes 2 hrs. @ 50 Amperes
Above 170 to 250 Minutes	30 hrs. @ 5 Amperes 15 hrs. @ 10 Amperes	2.5 hrs. @ 20 Amperes 3 hrs. @ 50 Amperes
Above 250 Minutes	24 hrs. @ 10 Amperes	6 hrs. @ 40 Amperes 4 hrs. @ 60 Amperes

FIGURE 9–18 Battery-charging guide (6-volt and 12-volt batteries).

◀ TECH TIP ▶

IT COULD HAPPEN TO YOU!

The owner of a Toyota replaced the battery. After replacing the battery, the owner noted that the "airbag" amber warning lamp was lit and the radio was locked out. The owner had purchased the vehicle used from a dealer and did not know the four-digit security code needed to unlock the radio. Determined to fix it, the owner tried three four-digit numbers, hoping that one of them would work. However, after three tries, the radio became permanently disabled.

Frustrated, the owner went to a dealer. It cost more than $300 to fix the problem. A special tool was required to easily reset the airbag lamp. The radio had to be removed and sent out of state to an authorized radio service center and then reinstalled in the vehicle.

Therefore, before disconnecting the battery, please check with the owner to be certain that the owner has the security code for a security-type radio. A "memory saver" may be needed to keep the radio powered up when the battery is being disconnected. See figure 9–19.

JUMP-STARTING

To jump-start another vehicle with a dead battery, connect good-quality copper jumper cables as indicated in figure 9–20. The last connection made should always be on the engine block or an engine bracket as far from the battery as possible. It is normal for a spark to be created when the jumper cables finally complete the jumping circuit, and this spark could cause an explosion of the gases around the battery. Many newer vehicles have special ground connections built away from the battery just for the purpose of jump-starting. Check the owner's manual or service manual for the exact location.

BATTERY DATE CODES

All major battery manufacturers stamp codes on the battery case that give the date of manufacture and other information. Most battery manufacturers use a number to indicate the year of manufacture and a letter to indicate the month of manufacture, skipping the letter *I* because it can be confused with the number 1. For example:

A = January

B = February

C = March

D = April

E = May

F = June

G = July

H = August

J = September

K = October

L = November

M = December

The shipping date from the manufacturing plant is usually indicated by a sticker on the end of the battery. Almost every battery manufacturer uses just one letter and one number to indicate the month and year. For example, a shipping sticker with an "E5" indicates that the battery was shipped in May 1995. See figure 9–21.

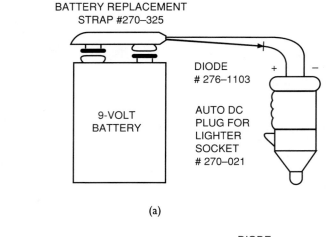

(a)

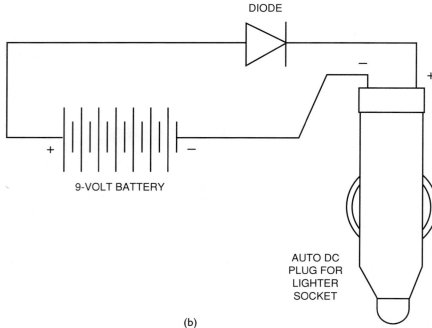

(b)

FIGURE 9–19 *(a)* Memory saver. The part numbers represent components from Radio Shack. *(b)* a schematic drawing of the same memory saver. Some experts recommend using a 12-volt lantern battery instead of a small 9-volt battery to help ensure that there will be enough voltage in the event that a door is opened while the vehicle battery is disconnected. Interior lights could quickly drain a small 9-volt battery.

BATTERY MANUFACTURERS' CODES

Johnson Control

Johnson Control (formerly Globe Battery) is maker of most of the following batteries:

Sears

Standard Oil

Interstate

Battery Associates

NAPA

Motorcraft

TBC (Tire Battery Corporation)

Farm and Fleet

Wal-Mart

A build code of Y J 9 B J 6 on their batteries is interpreted as follows:

Y = Plant location

J = Special code

9 = Manufacturer's process code

B = February (the letter *I* is used here)

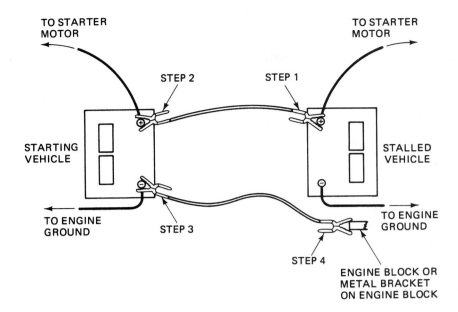

FIGURE 9–20 Jumper cable usage guide.

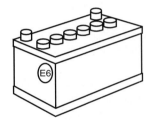

FIGURE 9–21 Typical battery shipping stickers with the month (E = May) and year (6 = 1996) the battery was shipped from the factory.

J = Day of the month (begins with 1 through 9, and then *A* through *W* is used for 10–31)

6 = Year

(February 19, 1996)

A seventh identification code is sometimes used for the shift code. An eighth identification code is sometimes used for the line code.

General Battery Company

General Battery Company (GBC)—formerly Prestolite—is maker of most of the following batteries:

Goodyear

Big A Auto Parts

NAPA (some)

Firestone

Titan

Prestolite

A **build code** of B 29 6 3 C R 3 is interpreted as follows:

B = Shift

29 = Day of the month

6 = Year

3 = Month

C = Type

R = Manufacturing code

3 = Plant location

(March 29, 1996)

Exide

Exide is maker of most of the following batteries:

Western Auto

Chrysler (Mopar)

A build code of Lo 23 B 5 B 1 is interpreted as follows:

Lo = Plant location

23 = Day of the month

B = Month

5 = Year

B = Paste line

1 = Shift

(February 23, 1995)

Delco

Plant locations given for Delco are the following:

I = Indiana

G = Georgia

K = Kansas

N = New Jersey

F = France

Z = Canada

C = California

A build code of 6 B I 17 is interpreted as follows:

6 = Year

B = Month

I = Plant location

17 = Day of the month

(February 17, 1996, in Indiana)

GNB

GNB (formerly Gould National Battery) is maker of most of the following batteries:

Champion Batteries

Power Breed

Action Pack

A build code of 6 A 01 H is interpreted as follows:

6 = Year

A = Month

01 = Day of the month

H = Manufacturer code

(January 1, 1996)

East Penn Manufacturing Company

East Penn Manufacturing Company is maker of the following batteries:

DEKA

Federal

Lynx

Start Rite

A build code of 6 234 6 is interpreted as follows:

6 = Year

234 = Day of the year

6 = Manufacturer code

(August 21, 1996)

NOTE: This form of the day of the year is called the **Julian date.**

BATTERY DRAIN TEST

The **battery drain test** determines if some component or circuit in a vehicle or truck is causing a drain on the battery when everything is off. This test is also called the **ignition off draw** (IOD) or **parasitic load** test. This test should be performed whenever one of the following conditions exists:

1. Whenever a battery is being charged or replaced (a battery drain could have been the cause for charging or replacing the battery)
2. Whenever the battery is suspected of being drained

PROCEDURE FOR BATTERY DRAIN TEST

Following is the procedure for performing the battery drain test using a test light:

1. Make certain that all lights, accessories, and ignition are off.
2. Check all vehicle doors to be certain that the interior courtesy (dome) lights are off.
3. Disconnect the *negative* battery cable as illustrated in figure 9–22.
4. Connect the test light to the disconnected battery cable end and the battery post as illustrated in figure 9–22.
5. The test light should *not* be on. If the light is on, the battery can be drained in a period of several hours.

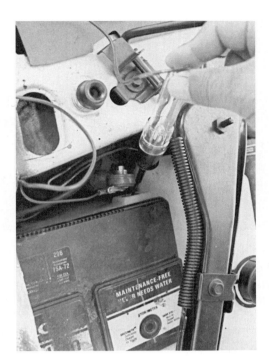

FIGURE 9–22 Performing a battery drain test using a test light. One end of the test light is connected to the battery terminal and the other end to the disconnected battery cable end. Either battery cable can be used, but it is recommended that the negative battery cable be the one disconnected to avoid the possibility of a spark between the vehicle body and the positive terminal of the battery.

NOTE: Many electronic components do draw a slight amount of current from the battery all the time with the ignition off. These components include: (1) digital clocks; (2) radios electronically tuned for station memory and clock circuits (if the vehicle is equipped); (3) the engine control computer (if the vehicle is equipped), through slight diode leakage; and (4) the alternator, through slight diode leakage. These components may cause a voltmeter to read full battery voltage if it is connected between the negative battery terminal and the removed end of the negative battery cable. Using a voltmeter to measure battery drain is *not* recommended by most vehicle manufacturers. The high internal resistance of the voltmeter results in an *irrelevant reading* that does not give the technician the information on whether or not a problem exists.

BATTERY DRAIN TESTING USING AN AMMETER

The ammeter method is the most accurate way to test for a possible battery drain. Connect an ammeter in series between the terminal of the battery and the discon-

◀ **DIAGNOSTIC STORY** ▶

PARK ON THE NORTH OR PARK ON THE SOUTH?

A vehicle owner complained to a dealer service department that every time he parked his vehicle on the north side of the street, his vehicle would fail to start the next morning because of a dead battery. Whenever he parked on the south side of the street, the battery would not be drained and the vehicle always started. The service technician learned that the owner lived on a steep hill and that whenever he parked with the vehicle facing downhill, the battery was drained. The cause of the battery drain was discovered to be a trunk light switch that was operated by mercury (liquid metal). The switch had to be level, or current would flow through the switch to the bulb. The technician rewired the trunk light and used a contact-type switch instead of the mercury switch to prevent future problems.

nected cable. See figure 9–23. (Normal battery drain is 0.020 to 0.030 amperes and any drain greater than 0.050 amperes should be found and corrected.)

Many digital multimeters have an ammeter scale that can be used to safely and accurately test for an abnormal parasitic electrical drain.

CAUTION: Be certain to use an ammeter that is rated to read the anticipated amperage.

FINDING THE SOURCE OF THE DRAIN

If there is a drain, check and temporarily disconnect the following components:

1. Light under the hood. Some lights under the hood are hot all the time and light by means of a mercury switch whenever the hood is opened.
2. Glove compartment light.
3. Trunk light.

If, after disconnecting all three of these components, the battery drain can still light the test light or

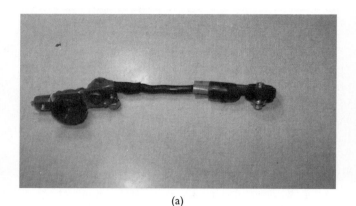

(a)

(b)

FIGURE 9–23 *(a)* Parasitic load tool. *(b)* After connecting the shutoff tool, start the engine and operate all accessories. Stop the engine and turn everything off. Connect the ammeter across the shutoff switch in parallel. Wait 20 minutes. This time allow all electronic circuits to "time out" or shut down. Open the switch—all current now will flow through the ammeter. A reading greater than specified (usually greater than 50 milliamperes [0.05 amperes]) indicates a problem that should be corrected.

draws more than 50 milliamperes, disconnect one fuse at a time from the fuse box until the test light goes out. If the test light goes out after one fuse is disconnected, the source of the drain is located in that particular circuit, as labeled on the fuse box. Continue to disconnect the *power-side* wire connectors from each component included in that particular circuit until the test light goes off. The source of the battery drain can then be traced to an individual component or part of one circuit.

WHAT TO DO IF A BATTERY DRAIN STILL EXISTS AFTER ALL THE FUSES ARE DISCONNECTED

If all the fuses have been disconnected and the drain still exists, the source of the drain has to be between the battery and the fuse box. The most common sources of drain under the hood include the following:

1. The alternator. Disconnect the alternator wires and retest. If the test light is now off, the problem is a defective diode(s) in the alternator. (See chapter 11 for details.)
2. The starter solenoid (relay) or wiring near its components. These are also a common source of battery drain, due to high current flows and heat, which can damage the wire or insulation.

HIDDEN BATTERIES

Many vehicle manufacturers today place the battery under the backseat (Olds Aurora, Buick Riviera) or under the front fender. Often, the battery is not visible even if it is located under the hood.

Whenever testing or jump-starting a vehicle, look for a battery access point as shown in figure 9–24.

BATTERY TROUBLESHOOTING GUIDE

The following list will assist technicians in troubleshooting batteries.

Problem	Possible Causes and/or Solutions
1. Headlights are dim.	1. Discharged battery or poor connections on the battery, engine, or body.
2. Solenoid clicks.	2. Discharged battery or poor connections on the battery or the engine.
3. Engine is slow cranking.	3. Discharged battery, high-resistance battery cables, or defective starter or solenoid.

◀ TECH TIP ▶

WHY SHOULD A DISCHARGED BATTERY BE RECHARGED OR REPLACED BEFORE FURTHER TESTING?

A discharged or defective battery has lower voltage potential than a good battery that is at least 75% charged. This lower battery voltage cannot properly power the starter motor without causing excessive current flow (in amperes) to the starter. This excessive current flow through the starter can damage the starter *and* cause starter tests to indicate a defective starter when the real problem is a weak battery. A weak battery could also prevent the charging voltage from reaching the voltage regulator cutoff point. This lower voltage could be interpreted as indicating a defective alternator and/or voltage regulator. If the vehicle continues to operate with low system voltage, the stator winding in the alternator can be overheated, causing alternator failure.

FIGURE 9–24 Typical access to positive battery connector for a battery that is hidden or not mounted under the hood.

4. Battery will not accept a charge.

5. Battery is using water.

4. If the battery is a maintenance-free type, attempt to fast-start the battery for several hours. If the battery still will not accept a charge, replace the battery.

5. Check the charging system for too high a voltage. If the voltage is normal, the battery is showing signs of gradual failure. Load test and replace the battery if necessary.

◀ TECH TIP ▶

BATTERY STORAGE ON CONCRETE?

All batteries should be stored in a cool, dry place when not in use. Many technicians have been warned not to store or place a battery on concrete. According to battery experts, it is the temperature difference between the top and the bottom of the battery that causes a difference in the voltage potential between the top (warmer section) and the bottom (colder section). It is this difference in temperature that causes self-discharge to occur.

In fact, submarines cycle seawater around their batteries to keep all sections of the battery at the same temperature to help prevent self-discharge.

Therefore, always store or place batteries up off the floor and in a location where the entire battery can be kept at the same temperature, avoiding extreme heat and freezing temperatures.

Concrete cannot drain the battery directly, because the case of the battery is a very good electrical insulator.

◀ TECH TIP ▶

AMPERES-TO-VOLTS CONVERTER

The voltage drop across a 1-ohm resistor is the same as the amount of current flowing through the resistor. This fact can be used to measure a small current flow using just a voltmeter. See figure 9–25.

If measuring parasitic draw, connect one end of a 1-ohm resistor to the negative terminal of the battery and the other end to the disconnected negative cable. Connect a voltmeter to the same ends of the resistor. If the battery draw is 0.02 amperes, the voltmeter will read 0.02 volts.

This tool is useful if an ammeter is not available.

CAUTION: The 1-ohm resistor shown in the figure is rated at 10 watts, meaning that less than 1 ampere should be used when using this tool.

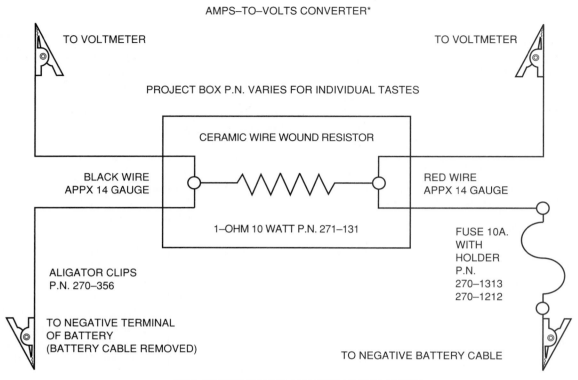

FIGURE 9–25   Amperes-to-volts converter.

SUMMARY

1. Maintenance-free batteries use lead-calcium grids instead of lead-antimony grids to reduce gassing.

2. When a battery is being discharged, the acid (SO_4) is leaving the electrolyte and being deposited on the plates. When the battery is being charged, the acid (SO_4) is forced off the plates and back into the electrolyte.

3. Batteries are rated according to CCA and reserve capacity.

4. All batteries should be securely attached to the vehicle with hold-down brackets to prevent vibration damage.

5. Batteries can be tested with a voltmeter to determine the state of charge. A battery load test loads the battery to one-half of its CCA rating. A good battery should be able to maintain above 9.6 volts for the entire 15-second test period.

6. A battery drain test should be performed if the battery runs down.

REVIEW QUESTIONS

1. Explain why discharged batteries can freeze.

2. Identify the two most commonly used battery rating methods.

3. Describe the results of a voltmeter test of a battery and its state of charge.

4. List the steps for performing a battery load test.

5. Explain how to perform a battery drain test.

MULTIPLE-CHOICE QUESTIONS

1. When a battery becomes completely discharged, both positive and negative plates become _____ and the electrolyte becomes _____ .
   a. H_2SO_4; Pb
   b. $PbSO_4$; H_2O
   c. PbO_2; H_2SO_4
   d. $PbSO_4$; H_2SO_4

2. A fully charged 12-volt battery should indicate_____.
   a. 12.6 volts or higher
   b. A specific gravity of 1.265 or higher
   c. 12 volts
   d. Both a and b

3. Deep cycling means _____ .
   a. Overcharging the battery
   b. Overfilling or underfilling the battery with water
   c. The battery is fully discharged and then recharged
   d. The battery is overfilled with acid (H_2SO_4)

4. Reserve capacity for batteries, means _____ .
   a. The number of *hours* the battery can supply 25 amperes and remain higher than 10.5 volts.
   b. The number of *minutes* the battery can supply 25 amperes and remain higher than 10.5 volts.
   c. The number of *minutes* the battery can supply 20 amperes and remain higher than 9.6 volts.
   d. The number of *minutes* the battery can supply 10 amperes and remain higher than 9.6 volts.

5. Many vehicle manufacturers recommend that a special electrical connector be installed between the battery and the battery cable when testing for _____ .
   a. Battery drain (parasitic drain)
   b. Specific gravity
   c. Battery voltage
   d. Battery charge rate

6. The maximum allowable difference between the highest and lowest hydrometer (specific gravity) reading is _____ .
   a. 0.010
   b. 0.020
   c. 0.050
   d. 0.50

7. A battery high-rate discharge (load capacity) test is being performed on a 12-volt battery. Technician A says that a good battery should have a voltage reading of above 9.6 volts while under load at the end of the 15-second test. Technician B says that the battery should be discharged (loaded to 2 times its CCA rating). Which technician is correct?
   a. A only
   b. B only
   c. Both a and b
   d. Neither a nor b

8. When charging a maintenance-free (lead-calcium) battery _____ .
   a. The initial charging rate should be about 35 amperes for 30 minutes
   b. The battery may not accept a charge for several hours, yet may still be a good (serviceable) battery
   c. The battery temperature should not exceed 125° F (hot to the touch)
   d. All of the above

9. Normal battery drain (parasitic drain) with a vehicle with many computer and electronic circuits is _____.
   a. 20 to 30 milliamperes
   b. 2 to 3 amperes
   c. 150 to 300 milliamperes
   d. None of the above

10. Whenever jump-starting _____ .
    a. The last connection should be the positive post of the dead battery
    b. The last connection should be the engine block of the dead vehicle
    c. The alternator must be disconnected on both vehicles
    d. Both a and c

◀ Chapter 10 ▶

CRANKING SYSTEM OPERATION AND SERVICE

OBJECTIVES

After studying chapter 10, the reader will be able to

1. Describe how the cranking circuit works.
2. Explain how to disassemble and reassemble a starter motor and solenoid.
3. Discuss how to test the cranking circuit.
4. Describe how to perform cranking system testing procedures.

For any engine to start, it must be rotated. It is the purpose and function of the cranking circuit to create the necessary power and transfer it from the battery to the starter motor that rotates the engine.

CRANKING CIRCUIT

The cranking circuit includes those mechanical and electrical components required to crank the engine for starting. The cranking force in the early 1900s was the driver's arm. Modern cranking circuits include the following:

1. *Starter motor.* The starter is normally a 0.5- to 2.6-horsepower (0.4- to 2.0-kilowatt) electric motor that can develop nearly 8 horsepower (6 kilowatts) for a very short time when first cranking a cold engine.
2. *Battery.* The battery must be of the correct capacity and be at least 75% charged to provide the nec-

essary current and voltage for correct operation of the starter.
3. *Starter solenoid or relay.* The high current required by the starter must be able to be turned on and off. A large switch would be required if the current were controlled by the driver directly. Instead, a small current switch (ignition switch) operates a solenoid or relay that controls the high starter current.
4. *Starter drive.* The starter drive uses a small gear that contacts the engine flywheel gear and transmits starter motor power to rotate the engine.
5. *Ignition switch.* The ignition switch and safety control switches control the starter motor operation. See figure 10–1.

The engine is cranked by an electric motor that is controlled by a key-operated ignition switch. The ignition switch will not operate the starter unless the automatic transmission is in neutral or park. This is to prevent an accident that might result from the vehicle moving forward or rearward when the engine is started. Many automobile manufacturers use an electric switch called a **neutral safety switch** that opens the circuit between the ignition switch and the starter to prevent starter motor operation unless the gear selector is in neutral or park. The safety switch can either be attached to the steering column inside the vehicle near the floor or on the side of the transmission.

Many neutral safety switches can be adjusted by loosening the hold-down screws and moving the switch slightly to be certain that the engine will crank only with

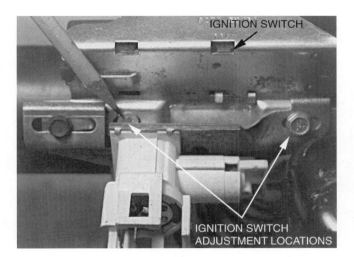

FIGURE 10–1 Adjustment location for a typical steering column–mounted ignition switch. This style of ignition switch is mounted on top of the steering column behind the dash panel and operated by a rod from the key switch.

the transmission in the neutral and park positions. Many manufacturers use a mechanical blocking device in the steering column to prevent the driver from turning the key switch to the start position unless the gear selector is in neutral or park. Many manual transmission vehicles also use a safety switch to permit cranking only if the clutch is depressed.

HOW THE STARTER MOTOR WORKS

A starter consists of a main field housing, one end of which is called a **commutator-end** (or **brush-end**) **housing** and the other end of which is called a **drive-end housing.** The drive-end housing contains the drive pinion gear, which meshes with the engine flywheel gear teeth to start the engine. The commutator-end plate supports the end containing the starter brushes. **Through-bolts** hold the three components together. See figure 10–2.

A starter motor uses electromagnetic principles to convert electrical energy from the battery (up to 500 amperes) to mechanical power (up to 8 horsepower [6 kilowatts]) to crank the engine. The steel housing of the starter motor contains four electromagnets that are connected directly to the positive post of the battery to provide a strong magnetic field inside the starter. Current for the starter is controlled by a solenoid or relay that is controlled by the driver-operated ignition switch. The four electromagnets use heavy copper or aluminum wire wrapped around a soft-iron core. The core is contoured to fit against the rounded internal surface of the starter

◀ **TECH TIP** ▶

WATCH THE DOME LIGHT

Whenever diagnosing any starter-related problem, open the door of the vehicle and observe the brightness of the dome or interior light(s).

The brightness of any electrical lamp is proportional to the voltage.

Normal operation of the starter results in a slight dimming of the dome light.

Observation	Problem
Light remains bright	Usually an open circuit in the control circuit
Light goes out or almost goes out	Usually a shorted or grounded armature of field coils inside the starter

frame. The soft-iron cores are called **pole shoes.** Two of the four pole shoes are wrapped with copper wire in one direction to create a north pole magnet, and the other two pole shoes are wrapped in the opposite direction to create a south pole magnet. These magnets, when energized, create strong magnetic fields inside the starter housing and therefore are called **field coils.** The soft-iron cores (pole shoes) are often called **field poles.**

Inside the field coils is an **armature** that is supported with bushings at both ends, which permit it to rotate. The armature is constructed of thin, circular disks of steel laminated together and wound lengthwise with heavy-gauge insulated copper wire. The laminated iron core supports the copper loops of wire around the armature and helps concentrate the magnetic field produced by the coils. The ends of the copper armature windings are soldered to **commutator segments.** The electrical current that passes through the field coils is then connected to the commutator of the armature by brushes that can move over the segments of the rotating armature. These brushes are made of a combination of copper and carbon. The copper is a good conductor material, and the carbon added to the starter brushes helps provide the graphite-type lubrication needed to reduce wear of the brushes and the commutator segments.

The starter uses four brushes—two brushes to transfer the current from the field coils to the armature, and two brushes to provide the ground return path for the current that flows through the armature. See figure 10–3. Therefore, there are two **hot brushes**

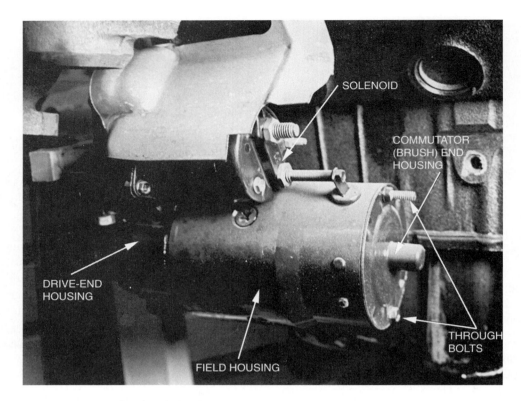

FIGURE 10–2   Typical solenoid-operated starter installation.

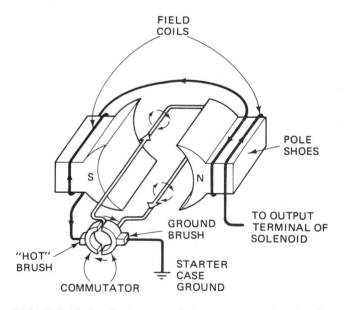

FIGURE 10–3   Series-wound electric motor showing the basic operation with only two brushes: one hot brush and one ground brush. The current flows through both field coils, then through the hot brush and through the loop winding of the armature before reaching ground through the ground brush.

◀ **TECH TIP** ▶

DON'T HIT THAT STARTER!

In the past, it was common to see service technicians hitting a starter in their effort to diagnose a no-crank condition. Often the shock of the blow to the starter aligned or moved the brushes, armature, and bushings. Many times, the starter functioned after being hit—even if only for a short time.

However, most of today's starters use permanent-magnet fields, and the magnets can be easily broken if hit. A magnet that is broken becomes two weaker magnets. Some early PM starters used magnets that were glued or bonded to the field housing. If struck with a heavy tool, the magnets could be broken, with parts of the magnet falling onto the armature and into the bearing pockets, making the starter impossible to repair or rebuild.

in holders, which are insulated from the housing, and two **ground brushes,** which usually use bare, stranded copper wire connections to the brushes. The ground brush holders are not insulated and attach directly to the field housing.

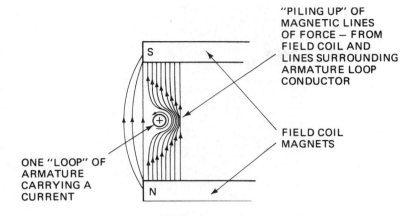

"PILING UP" OF MAGNETIC LINES OF FORCE — FROM FIELD COIL AND LINES SURROUNDING ARMATURE LOOP CONDUCTOR

FIELD COIL MAGNETS

ONE "LOOP" OF ARMATURE CARRYING A CURRENT

FIGURE 10–4 The interaction of the magnetic fields of the armature loops and field coils creates a stronger magnetic field on the right side of the conductor, causing the armature loop to move toward the left.

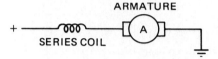

ARMATURE

+ SERIES COIL A

FIGURE 10–6 Wiring diagram illustrating the construction of a series-wound electric motor. Notice that all of the current flows through the field coils, then through the armature (in series) before reaching ground.

FIGURE 10–5 High-torque armatures can often be identified by the size and shape of the armature loops. The armature on the right has square cross-sectional armature loops and is a high-torque unit.

The current travels through the brushes and into the armature windings, where other magnetic fields are created around each copper wire loop in the armature. The two strong magnetic fields created inside the starter housing create the force that rotates the armature.

HOW MAGNETIC FIELDS TURN AN ARMATURE

One of the basic principles of electromagnetism is that a magnetic field surrounds every conductor carrying a current. The strength of the magnetic field is increased as the current flow (in amperes) is increased.

Inside the starter housing there is a strong magnetic field created by the field coil magnets. The armature, a conductor, is installed inside this strong magnetic field, with very little clearance between the armature and the field coils.

The two magnetic fields act together, and their lines of force "bunch up" or are strong on one side of the armature loop wire and become weak on the other side of

the conductor. This causes the conductor (armature) to move from the area of strong magnetic field strength toward the area of weak magnetic field strength. See figure 10–4. This causes the armature to rotate. This rotation force (torque) is increased as the current flowing through the starter motor increases. The torque of a starter is determined by the strength of the magnetic fields inside the starter. Magnetic field strength is measured in ampereturns. If the current or the number of turns of wire are increased, the magnetic field strength is increased. All starters are designed for the starting torque required to crank a particular engine at any temperature. Be certain that a replacement or rebuilt starter is the correct starter for the engine. See figure 10–5 for an example of one of the differences between a high-torque starter and a standard starter motor.

TYPES OF STARTER MOTORS

Starter motors must provide high power at low starter motor speeds to crank an automotive engine at all temperatures and at the cranking speed required for the engine to start (60 to 250 engine RPM). Electric motors are classified according to the internal electrical motor connections. The method used determines the power-producing characteristics of the electric motor. Many starter motors are series wound, which means that the current flows first through the field coils, then in series through the armature, and finally to a ground through the ground brushes. See figure 10–6.

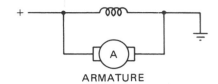

FIGURE 10–7 Wiring diagram illustrating the construction of a shunt-type electric motor. Shunt-type electric motors have the field coils in parallel (or shunt) across the armature as shown.

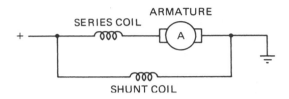

FIGURE 10–8 A compound motor is a combination of series and shunt types, using part of the field coils connected electrically in series with the armature and some in parallel (shunt).

Series Motors

A series motor develops its maximum torque at the initial start (zero RPM) and develops less torque as the speed increases. A series motor is commonly used for an automotive starter motor because of its high-starting power characteristics. A series starter motor develops less torque at high RPM because a current is produced in the starter itself that acts against the current from the battery. Because this current works against battery voltage, it is called **counter electromotive force** or **CEMF.** This counter EMF is produced by electromagnetic induction (see chapter 1) in the armature conductors, which are cutting across the magnetic lines of force formed by the field coils. This induced voltage operates against the applied voltage supplied by the battery, which reduces the strength of the magnetic field in the starter.

Because the power (torque) of the starter depends on the strength of the magnetic fields, the torque of the starter decreases as the starter speed increases. It is also characteristic of series-wound motors to keep increasing in speed under light loads. This could lead to the destruction of the starter motor unless controlled or prevented.

Shunt Motors

Shunt-type electric motors have the field coils in parallel (or shunt) across the armature as shown in figure 10–7. A shunt motor does not decrease in torque at higher motor RPM because the CEMF produced in the armature does not decrease the field coil strength. A shunt motor, however, does not produce as high a starting torque as that of a series-wound motor, and is not used

FIGURE 10–9 Chrysler starter motor showing starter drive and gear-reduction gear.

for starters. Many small electric motors used in automotive blower motors, windshield wipers, power windows, and power seats use permanent magnets rather than electromagnets. Because these permanent magnets maintain a constant field strength, the same as a shunt-type motor, they have similar operating characteristics. To compensate for the lack of torque, all PM starters use gear reduction to multiply starter motor torque. Permanent-magnet starter motors were developed by General Motors for automotive use in the mid-1980s. The permanent magnets used are an alloy of neodymium, iron, and boron. This magnet is almost 10 times more powerful than permanent magnets used previously.

Compound Motors

A compound-wound, or compound, motor has the operating characteristics of a series motor *and* a shunt-type motor because some of the field coils are connected to the armature in series, and some (usually only one) field coils are connected directly to the battery in parallel (shunt) with the armature. See figure 10–8.

Compound-wound starter motors are commonly used in Ford, Chrysler, and some GM starters. The shunt-wound field coil is called a **shunt coil** and is used to limit the maximum speed of the starter. Because the shunt coil is energized as soon as the battery current is sent to the starter, it is used to engage the starter drive on Ford positive-engagement starters.

GEAR-REDUCTION STARTERS

Gear-reduction starters are used by many automotive manufacturers. The purpose of the gear reduction (typically, from 2:1 to 4:1) is to increase starter motor speed and provide the torque multiplication necessary to crank an engine. See figure 10–9. As a series-wound motor in-

FIGURE 10–10 Starter drive unit. Notice the tapered end of the pinion gear and the internal bushing.

creases in rotational speed, the starter produces less power, and less current is drawn from the battery because the armature generates greater CEMF as the starter speed increases. However, a starter motor's maximum torque occurs at zero RPM and torque decreases with increasing RPM. A smaller starter using a gear-reduction design can produce the necessary cranking power with reduced starter amperage requirements. Lower current requirements mean that smaller battery cables can be used. General Motors permanent-magnet starters use a planetary gear set (a type of gear reduction) to provide the necessary torque for starting. Also see the tech tip about not hitting a permanent-magnet starter.

STARTER DRIVES

A starter drive includes a small pinion gear that meshes with and rotates the larger gear on the engine for starting. The pinion gear must engage with the engine gear slightly *before* the starter motor rotates, to prevent serious damage to either the starter gear or the engine, but must be disengaged after the engine starts. The ends of the starter pinion gear are tapered to help the teeth mesh more easily without damaging the flywheel ring gear teeth. See figure 10–10. The ratio of the number of teeth on the engine gear to the number on the starter pinion is between 15:1 and 20:1. A typical small starter pinion gear has 9 teeth that turn an engine gear with 166 teeth. This provides an 18:1 gear reduction. This means that the starter motor is rotating approximately 18 times faster than the engine. Normal cranking speed for the engine is 200 RPM. This means that the starter motor speed is 18 times faster, or 3600 starter RPM (200 × 18 = 3600). If the engine started and was accelerated to

FIGURE 10–11 Cutaway view of rollers, springs, and notches of a typical overrunning clutch.

2000 RPM (normal cold engine speed), the starter would be destroyed by the high speed (36,000 RPM) if the starter were not disengaged from the engine.

Older-model starters (made before the early 1960s) often used a Bendix drive mechanism, which used inertia to engage the starter pinion with the engine flywheel gear. Inertia is the tendency of a stationary object to remain stationary, because of its weight, unless forced to move. On these older-model starters, the small starter pinion gear was attached to a shaft with threads, and the weight of this gear caused it to be spun along the threaded shaft and mesh with the flywheel whenever the starter motor spun. If the engine speed was greater than the starter speed, the pinion gear was forced back along the threaded shaft and out of mesh with the flywheel gear. The Bendix drive mechanism has generally not been used since the early 1960s.

All starter drive mechanisms use a type of one-way clutch that allows the starter to rotate the engine, but that turns freely if the engine speed is greater than the starter motor speed. This clutch is called an **overrunning clutch,** and it protects the starter motor from damage if the ignition switch is held in the start position after the engine starts. The overrunning clutch, which is built in as a part of the starter drive unit, uses steel balls or rollers installed in tapered notches. See figure 10–11. This taper forces the balls or rollers tightly into the notch when rotating in the direction necessary to start the engine. Whenever the engine rotates faster than the starter pinion, the balls or rollers are forced out of the narrow tapered notch, allowing the pinion gear to turn freely (to overrun).

The spring between the drive tang or pulley and the overrunning clutch and pinion is called a **mesh spring,**

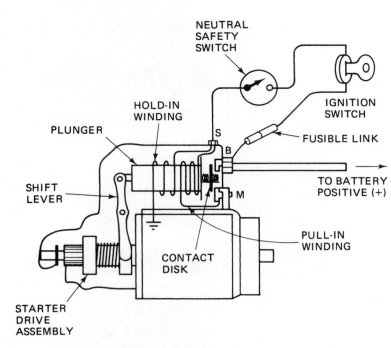

FIGURE 10–12 Wiring diagram of a typical starter solenoid. Notice that both the pull-in winding and the hold-in winding are energized when the ignition switch is first turned to the "start" position. As soon as the solenoid contact disk makes electrical contact with both the B and M terminals, the battery current is conducted to the starter motor and electrically neutralizes the pull-in winding.

and it helps to cushion and control the engagement of the starter drive pinion with the engine flywheel gear. This spring is also called a **compression spring** because the starter solenoid or starter yoke compresses the spring and the spring tension causes the starter pinion to engage the engine flywheel.

SYMPTOMS OF A DEFECTIVE STARTER DRIVE

A starter drive is generally a very dependable unit and does not require replacement unless defective or worn. The major wear occurs in the overrunning clutch section of the starter drive unit. The steel balls or rollers wear and often do not wedge tightly into the tapered notches as is necessary for engine cranking.

A worn starter drive can cause the starter motor to operate freely and not rotate the engine. Therefore, the starter makes a "whining" noise. The whine indicates that the starter motor is operating and that the starter drive is not rotating the engine flywheel. The entire starter drive is replaced as a unit. The overrunning clutch section of the starter drive cannot be serviced or repaired separately because the drive is a sealed unit. Starter drives are most likely to fail intermittently at first and then gradually more frequently, until replacement becomes necessary to start the engine. Intermittent starter drive failure (starter whine) is often most noticeable during cold weather.

STARTER DRIVE OPERATION

The starter drive (pinion gear) must be moved into mesh with the engine ring gear before the starter motor starts to spin. Most automotive starters use a solenoid or the magnetic pull of the shunt coil in the starter to engage the starter pinion.

POSITIVE-ENGAGEMENT STARTERS

Positive-engagement starters, used on many Ford engines, utilize the shunt coil winding of the starter to engage the starter drive. The high starting current is controlled by an ignition switch–operated starter solenoid, usually mounted near the positive post of the battery. When this control circuit is closed, current flows through a hollow coil (called a **drive coil**) that attracts a **movable pole shoe.** The movable metal pole shoe is attached to and engages the starter drive with a lever (called the **plunger lever**).

As soon as the starter drive has engaged the engine flywheel, a tang on the movable pole shoe "opens" a set of contact points. The contact points provide the ground return path for the drive coil operation. After these grounding contacts are opened, all of the starter current can flow through the remaining three field coils and through the brushes to the armature, causing the starter to operate.

The movable pole shoe is held down (which keeps the starter drive engaged) by a smaller coil on the inside of the main drive coil. This coil is called the **holding coil,** and it is strong enough to hold the starter drive engaged while permitting the flow of the maximum possible current to operate the starter. If the grounding contact points are severely pitted, the starter may not operate the starter drive or the starter motor because of the resulting poor ground for the drive coil. If the contact points are bent or damaged enough to prevent them from opening, the starter will "clunk" the starter drive into engagement but will not allow the starter motor to operate.

SOLENOID-OPERATED STARTERS

A starter solenoid is an **electromagnetic switch** containing two separate, but connected, electromagnetic windings. This switch is used to engage the starter drive and control the current from the battery to the starter motor. See figure 10–12.

The two internal windings contain approximately the same number of turns but are made from different-gauge wire. Both windings together produce a strong magnetic field that pulls a metal plunger into the solenoid. The plunger is attached to the starter drive through a **shift fork lever**. When the ignition switch is turned to the start position, the motion of the plunger into the solenoid causes the starter drive to move into mesh with the flywheel ring gear. The heavier-gauge winding (called the **pull-in winding**) is needed to draw the plunger into the solenoid. The lighter-gauge winding (called the **hold-in winding**) produces enough magnetic force to keep the plunger in position. The main purpose of using two separate windings is to permit as much current as possible to operate the starter and yet provide the strong magnetic field required to move the starter drive into engagement. The instant the plunger is drawn into the solenoid enough to engage the starter drive, the plunger makes contact with a metal disk that connects the battery terminal post of the solenoid to the motor terminal. This permits full battery current to flow through the solenoid to operate the starter motor. The contact disk also electrically disconnects the pull-in winding. The solenoid *has* to work to supply current to the starter. Therefore, if the starter motor operates at all, the solenoid is working, even though it may have high external resistance that could cause slow starter motor operation.

STARTING SYSTEM TROUBLESHOOTING

The proper operation of the starting system depends on a good battery, good cables and connections, and a good starter motor. Because a starting problem can be caused by a defective component anywhere in the starting circuit, it is important to check for the proper operation of each part of the circuit to diagnose and repair the problem quickly.

◄ **TECH TIP** ►

VOLTAGE DROP IS RESISTANCE

Many technicians have asked why they should measure voltage drop when they can easily measure the resistance using an ohmmeter. Think of a battery cable with all the strands of the cable broken, except for one. If an ohmmeter is used to measure the resistance of the cable, the reading would be very low—probably less than 1 ohm. The cable, however, is not capable of conducting the amount of current necessary to crank the engine. In less severe cases, several strands can be broken and affect the operation of the starter motor. Although the resistance of the battery cable will not indicate any increased resistance, the restriction to current flow will cause heat and a drop of voltage available at the starter. Because resistance is not effective until current flows, measuring the voltage drop (differences in voltage between two points) is the most accurate method of determining the true resistance in a circuit.

How much is too much? According to Bosch Corporation, all electrical circuits should have a maximum of 3% loss of the voltage of the circuit to resistance. Therefore, in a 12-volt circuit, the maximum loss of voltage in cables and connections should be 0.36 volts ($12 \times 0.03 = 0.36$ volts). The remaining 97% of the circuit voltage (11.64 volts) is available to operate the electrical device (load). Just remember

Low voltage drop = low resistance
High voltage drop = high resistance

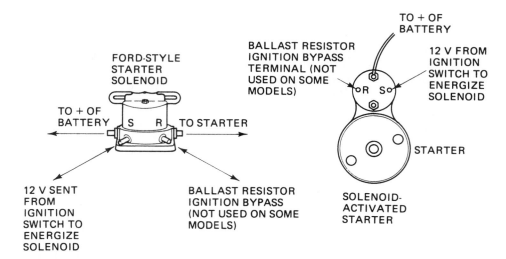

FIGURE 10–13 A typical Ford solenoid on the left, and a typical GM solenoid on the right.

IMPORTANT: Starter remanufacturers state that the single most common cause of starter motor failure is low battery voltage. When battery voltage drops, additional current (amperes) must flow through the starter to maintain the balance of electrical power. Since electrical power is amperes times volts, a drop in battery voltage causes the increase in starter amperage draw.

VOLTAGE-DROP TESTING

Voltage drop is the drop in voltage that occurs when current is flowing through a resistance. For example, a voltage drop is the difference between voltage at the source and the voltage at the electrical device. The higher the voltage drop, the greater the resistance in the circuit. Even though voltage-drop testing can be performed on any electrical circuit, the most common areas of testing include the cranking and charging circuit wiring and connections.

A high voltage drop (high resistance) in the cranking circuit wiring can cause slow engine cranking with less than normal starter amperage drain as a result of the excessive circuit resistance. If the voltage drop is high enough, such as could be caused by dirty battery terminals, the starter may not operate. A typical symptom of high resistance in the cranking circuit is a "clicking" of the starter solenoid.

Voltage-drop testing of the wire involves connecting any voltmeter (on the low scale) to the suspected high-resistance cable ends and cranking the engine. See figures 10–13 through 10–17.

NOTE: Before a difference in voltage (voltage drop) can be measured between the ends of a battery cable, current must be flowing through the cable. *Resistance is not effective unless current is flowing.* If the engine is not being cranked, current is not flowing through the battery cables and the voltage drop cannot be measured.

Crank the engine with a voltmeter connected to the battery and record the reading. Crank the engine with the voltmeter connected across the starter and record the reading. If the difference in the two readings exceeds 0.5 volts, perform the following steps to determine the exact location of the voltage drop.

- *Step 1.* Connect the positive voltmeter test lead to the most positive end of the cable being tested. The most positive end of a cable is the end closest to the positive terminal of the battery.

- *Step 2.* Connect the negative voltmeter test lead to the other end of the cable being tested. With no current flowing through the cable, the voltmeter should read zero because there is the same voltage at both ends of the cable.

- *Step 3.* Crank the engine. The voltmeter should read less than 0.2 volts.

- *Step 4.* Evaluate the results. If the voltmeter reads zero, the cable being tested has no resistance and is good. If the voltmeter reads higher than 0.2 volts (200 millivolts), the cable has excessive resistance and should be replaced. However, before replacing the cable, make certain that the connections at both ends of the cable being tested are clean and tight.

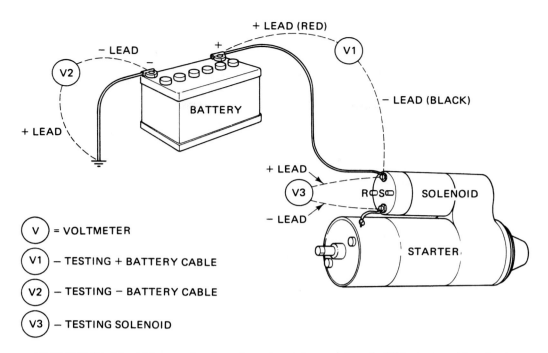

V = VOLTMETER

V1 – TESTING + BATTERY CABLE

V2 – TESTING – BATTERY CABLE

V3 – TESTING SOLENOID

FIGURE 10–14 Voltmeter hookups for voltage-drop testing of a GM-type cranking circuit.

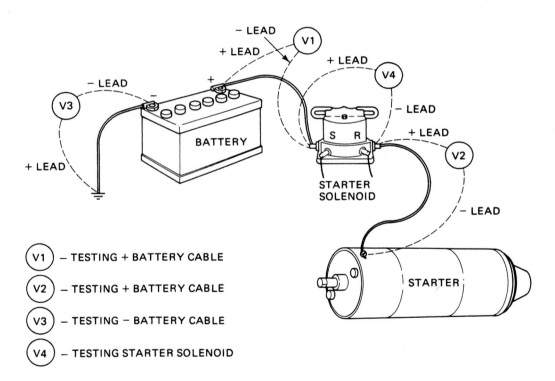

V1 – TESTING + BATTERY CABLE

V2 – TESTING + BATTERY CABLE

V3 – TESTING – BATTERY CABLE

V4 – TESTING STARTER SOLENOID

FIGURE 10–15 Voltmeter hookups for voltage-drop testing of a Ford-type cranking circuit.

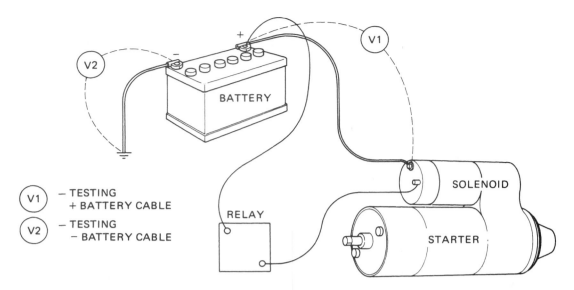

V1 — TESTING
+ BATTERY CABLE

V2 — TESTING
− BATTERY CABLE

FIGURE 10–16 Voltmeter hookups for voltage-drop testing of a Chrysler-type cranking circuit.

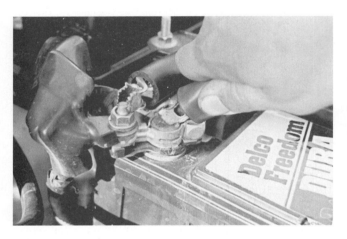

FIGURE 10–17 Using the voltmeter leads from a starting and charging test unit to measure the voltage drop between the battery terminal (red lead) and the cable end (black lead). The engine must be cranked to cause current to flow through this connection.

◄ TECH TIP ►

TOO HOT!

If a cable or connection is hot to the touch, there is electrical resistance in the cable or connection. The resistance changes electrical energy into heat energy. Therefore, if a voltmeter is not available, touch the battery cables and connections while cranking the engine. If any cable or connection is hot to the touch, it should be cleaned or replaced.

◄ DIAGNOSTIC STORY ►

BATTERY CABLE HEAT AND COUNTER EMF

Battery cables can overheat when there is excessive current flow through the cable. The amount of current (in amperes) is determined by the power required to operate the starter motor. A typical problem involved a vehicle driven to Florida from Michigan. The battery cables overheated when the driver tried to start the vehicle. At a service center, some technicians believed that the cause of the overheated cables was an oversized battery, which is often used in vehicles from northern climates. Although it is true that a smaller battery can be used in warmer climates, a large battery does absolutely no harm and, in fact, generally lasts longer than a smaller battery. The cause of the problem was discovered (by testing) to be a defective starter motor that rotated too slowly. The too-slow rotation of the starter meant that the starter was not producing the normal amount of counter EMF (CEMF). The overall result was a tremendous increase in current being drawn from the battery, and it was this extra current flow that overheated the battery cables.

◄ **TECH TIP** ►

WHY DOES A WEAK BATTERY CAUSE AN INCREASE IN THE STARTER CURRENT?

A starter motor requires a certain amount of *power* to start an engine. What is power? Power expressed in electrical terms is amperes times volts (Power = $I \times E$). The power required to start an engine remains the same even if the battery voltage decreases. For example:

Good battery	Weak battery
11.0 V during cranking	9.8 V during cranking
190 A	213 A
Power = 11.0 × 190	Power = 9.8 × 213
= 2090 W	= 2090 W

Notice that the power required for the starter motor to crank the engine is the same (2090 watts). However, the good battery can maintain 11.0 volts while supplying the necessary current for starter operation (190 amperes). A weak battery decreases in voltage while supplying the high current required for cranking. The *power* required by the starter to crank an engine is constant. If the battery voltage decreases, the amount of current must *increase* to compensate for the drop in voltage. Notice that the required current is increased from 190 amperes (good battery) to 213 amperes for the weak battery. Therefore, to get accurate test results, a battery that is known to be good and that is at least 75% charged should be used during starter testing.

CONTROL CIRCUIT TESTING

The control circuit for the starting circuit includes the battery, ignition switch, neutral or clutch safety switch, and starter solenoid. Whenever the ignition switch is rotated to the start position, current flows through the ignition switch and the neutral safety switch and activates the solenoid. High current then flows directly from the battery through the solenoid and to the starter motor. Therefore, an open or break anywhere in the control circuit will prevent the operation of the starter motor. See figure 10–18. If a starter is inoperative, first check for voltage at the *S* (start) terminal of the starter solenoid.

See figure 10–19. Some newer models with antitheft controls use a relay to open this control circuit to prevent starter operation.

SPECIFICATIONS FOR A STARTER AMPERAGE TEST

Before performing a starter amperage test, be certain that the battery is sufficiently charged (75% or more) and capable of supplying adequate starting current. A starter amperage test should be performed whenever the starter fails to operate normally (is slow in cranking) or as part of a routine electrical system inspection. Some service manuals specify normal starter amperage for starter motors being tested on the vehicle; however, most service manuals only give the specifications for bench testing a starter without a load applied. These specifications are helpful in making certain that a repaired starter meets exact specifications, but they do not apply to starter testing on the vehicle. If exact specifications are not available, the following can be used as general specifications for testing a starter on the vehicle:

> Four- or six-cylinder engines: 150 amperes maximum
>
> V-8 engines (except for GM V-8s): 200 amperes maximum
>
> GM V-8 engines: 250 amperes maximum

Excessive current draw may indicate one or more of the following:

1. Low battery voltage (discharged or defective battery)
2. Binding of starter armature as a result of worn bushings
3. Oil too thick (viscosity too high) for weather conditions
4. Shorted or grounded starter windings or cables
5. Tight or seized engine
6. High-resistance battery cables or connections (caused by loose or corroded terminals, for example)
7. High resistance in the starter motor (usually caused by excessively worn brushes)

STARTER OVERHAUL

To remove the starter motor from the vehicle, first remove the negative battery cable from the battery to prevent any possible shorts from causing personal injury or property damage. Because most starter motors must be removed from underneath, the vehicle must be safely raised and supported. Remove attaching bolts, nuts, and braces. Before disconnecting the wiring, mark or tag the location of all wiring connections. See figures 10–20 through 10–31.

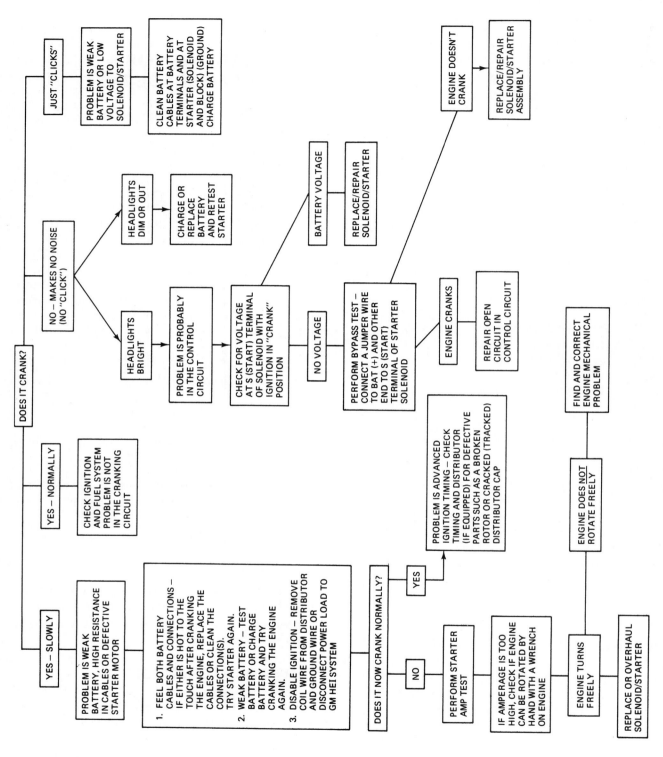

FIGURE 10–18 Starter diagnosis chart.

170

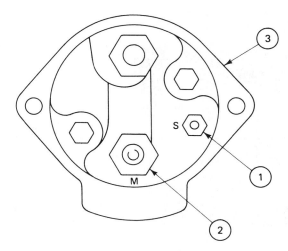

FIGURE 10–19 GM solenoid ohmmeter check. The reading between 1 and 3 (S terminal and ground) should be 0.4 to 0.6 ohms (hold-in winding). The reading between 1 and 2 (S terminal and M terminal) should be 0.2 to 0.4 ohms (pull-in winding).

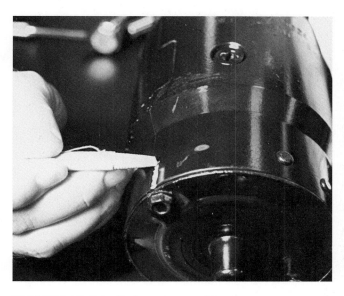

FIGURE 10–20 Before disassembly of any starter, mark the location of the through-bolts on the field housing. This makes reassembly easier.

THE STARTER THAT CROAKED AND THE JUMPING BATTERY CABLES

Once upon a time a vehicle would not start (crank). A technician at first hoped that the problem was a simple case of loose or corroded battery terminal connections; but after the technician cleaned the cables, the starter still did not make any noise at all when the ignition switch was turned to the start position. The technician opened the vehicle door and observed the dome (interior) light. The light was bright, indicating that the battery voltage was relatively high and that the battery should be adequately charged to crank the engine. However, when the technician turned the ignition switch to the start position, the dome light went out completely! This indicated that the battery voltage went down considerably.

NOTE: It is normal for the dome light to dim during cranking as a result of the lowered battery voltage during cranking. However, the voltage should not drop below 9.6 volts, which normally will still provide adequate voltage to light the dome light dimly.

The technician then arranged the two battery cables so that they were parallel for a short distance and repeated the test. As soon as the ignition switch was turned to the start position, the battery cables jumped toward each other. The technician knew that the starter had a shorted or grounded field coil or armature. This provided a direct path to ground for the starter current, which resulted in a substantially greater amount of current (in amperes) leaving the battery than would normally occur with a good starter. This amount of current drain lowered the battery voltage so much that the dome light did not light.

Why did the battery cables jump? The battery cables jumped because the high current flow created a strong magnetic field around each cable. Because one cable is positive and the other cable is negative, the magnetic fields were of opposite polarity and were attracted toward each other.

FIGURE 10–21 If a through-bolt is also used as a stud for a support bracket or heat shield, mark with two marks to distinguish where each through-bolt goes.

FIGURE 10–23 Rotate the solenoid to remove it from the starter housing. (CAUTION: The plunger return spring exerts a force on the solenoid and may cause personal injury if not carefully released.)

FIGURE 10–22 Removing the solenoid from the starter on a GM-type starter assembly.

FIGURE 10–24 The brushes should be replaced if worn to less than 50% of their original length. Replace if less than ½ inch long (13 millimeters).

FIGURE 10–25 Notice that most starter motors use some method, such as the one used with this GM starter, to ensure proper alignment of the various parts.

FIGURE 10–26 Most older-style starter field coils were retained by large attaching screws through the field housing. Newer, smaller-style starters use a press-fit to retain the field coils (shoes) in the field housing. If the field windings show signs of burned insulating varnish, replace the starter with a remanufactured unit. The cost to rewind field coils often exceeds the cost of a replacement starter.

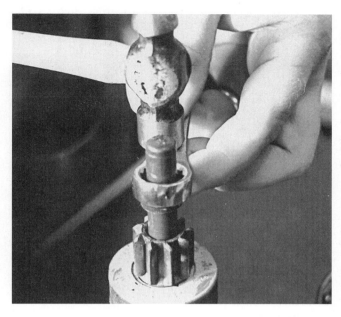

FIGURE 10–27 To replace the starter drive unit, the retainer and clip must be removed from the armature shaft. A box-end wrench and a hammer can be used to pop the retainer off of the spring clip.

FIGURE 10–28 View of armature shaft after the retainer is removed from around the spring clip.

FIGURE 10–29 A special tool provides an easy way to remove or replace this spring clip retainer. The armature should be tested on a growler and replaced if defective. Replacement armatures seldom come equipped with starter drive units.

FIGURE 10–30 Two pliers can be used to snap the retainer over the spring clip if a special tool is not available.

TESTING STARTER ARMATURES

Because the loops of copper wire are interconnected in the armature of a starter, an armature can be accurately tested only by use of a **growler**. A growler is a 110-volt AC test unit that generates an alternating (60-hertz) magnetic field around an armature. A starter armature is placed into the V-shaped top portion of a laminated soft-iron core surrounded by a coil of copper wire. When the growler is plugged into a 110-volt outlet and switched on, the moving magnetic field creates an alternating current in the windings of the armature.

FIGURE 10–31 A worn shift fork such as this one should be replaced. The wear occurs when the fork is being forced against the rotating starter drive when the ignition switch is released.

GROWLER TEST FOR SHORTED ARMATURE WINDINGS

Place the armature on the growler and turn the growler on.

CAUTION: Do not turn the growler on without an armature, or the growler will be damaged.

While rotating the armature by hand, gently place a hacksaw blade along the top of the armature. If any loop of the armature is *shorted*, the hacksaw blade will vibrate. If an armature is shorted (copper-to-copper connection), it must be replaced or rewound by a specialist. The hacksaw vibrates because the alternating current creates an alternating electromagnet in the armature. If only one loop is shorted, it does not create the magnetic pull on the hacksaw blade in one direction and the blade vibrates.

TESTING THE ARMATURE FOR GROUNDS

Built into growlers is a 110-volt test light with two test leads. Touch one lead to all segments (copper strips separated by mica insulation) of the commutator and touch the other test lead to the steel armature shaft or armature steel core. The test light should *not* light. If the test light is on, the armature is *grounded* (shorted to ground) and must be replaced.

TESTING THE ARMATURE FOR OPENS

An *open* in an armature is usually observed visually as a loop that is broken or unsoldered where it connects to the commutator segments. An open is usually caused by overheating of the starter due to excessive cranking time, or by a shorted or grounded armature. A loose or broken solder connection can often be repaired by resoldering the broken connection using rosin-core solder. Many armatures can be tested on some growlers using a pickle fork–shaped test probe.

NOTE: If the armature is open, shorted (copper to copper), or grounded (copper to steel), the armature must be repaired or replaced. The cost of a replacement armature often exceeds the cost of a replacement starter.

ARMATURE SERVICE

If the armature tests okay, the commutator should be measured and machined on a lathe, if necessary, to be certain that the surface is smooth and round. Some manufacturers recommend that the insulation between the segments of the armature (mica or hard plastic) be **undercut.** Mica is harder than copper and will form raised "bumps" as the copper segments of the commutator wear. Undercutting the mica permits a longer service life for this type of starter armature.

TESTING STARTER MOTOR FIELD COILS

With the armature removed from the starter motor, the field coils should be tested for opens and grounds. A powered test light or an ohmmeter can be used. To test for a grounded field coil, touch one lead of the tester to a field brush (insulated or hot) and the other end to the starter field housing. The ohmmeter should indicate infinity (no continuity), and the test light should *not* light. If there is continuity, replace the field coil housing assembly.

NOTE: Many starters use removable field coils, and these coils must be rewound using the proper equipment and insulating materials. Usually, the cost involved in replacing defective field coils exceeds the cost of a replacement starter.

The ground brushes should show continuity to the starter housing.

STARTER BRUSH INSPECTION

Starter brushes should be replaced if the brush length is less than one-half of its original length (less than $^1/_2$ inch [13 millimeters]). On some models of starter motors, the field brushes are serviced with the field coil assembly and the ground brushes with the brush holder. Many starters use brushes that are held in with screws and are easily replaced, whereas other starters may require soldering to remove and replace the brushes.

BENCH TESTING

Every starter should be tested before installation in a vehicle. The usual method includes clamping the starter in a vise to prevent rotation during operation and connecting heavy-gauge jumper wires (minimum 4 gauge) to a battery known to be good and the starter. The starter motor should rotate as fast as specifications indicate and not draw more than the free-spinning amperage permitted. A typical amperage specification for a starter being tested on a bench (not installed in a vehicle) usually ranges from 60 to 100 amperes.

STARTER DRIVE-TO-FLYWHEEL CLEARANCE

For the proper operation of the starter and absence of abnormal starter noise, there must be a slight clearance between the starter pinion and the engine flywheel ring gear. Many starters use shims (thin metal strips) between the flywheel and the engine block mounting pad to provide the proper clearance.

NOTE: Some manufacturers use shims under the starter drive-end housings during production. Other manufacturers *grind* the mounting pads at the factory for proper starter pinion gear clearance. If *any* GM starter is replaced, the starter pinion *must* be checked and corrected as necessary to prevent starter damage and excessive noise.

If the *clearance is too great*, the starter will produce a high-pitched whine during cranking.

If the *clearance is too small*, the starter will produce a high-pitched whine *after* the engine starts, just as the ignition key is released.

NOTE: The major cause of broken drive-end housings on starters is too small a clearance. If the clearance cannot be measured, it is better to put a shim between the engine block and the starter than to leave one out and chance breaking a drive-end housing.

If the clearance is excessive (0.060 inches or more) and there are no shims under the starter, the starter clearance can be reduced by shimming only under the outboard starter mounting bolt. A 0.015-inch shim used under the outboard bolt will decrease the clearance by approximately 0.010 inches.

GROUND WIRE CURRENT FLOW

Low voltage can kill a starter. Therefore, before installing a new or rebuilt starter in a vehicle, be sure that both the positive cable and the negative cable are in good condition. Here is the reason why. All electrical power must have a complete path from the power source, through the electrical loads, and back to the power source. This statement is true of all circuits, whether series, parallel, or series-parallel type.

◄ **TECH TIP** ►

REUSE DRIVE-END HOUSING TO BE SURE

Most General Motors starter motors use a pad mount and attach to the engine with bolts through the drive-end (nose) housing. Many times when a starter is replaced on a GM vehicle, the starter makes noise because of improper starter pinion-to-engine flywheel ring gear clearance. Instead of spending a lot of time shimming the new starter, simply remove the drive-end housing from the original starter and install it on the replacement starter. Because the original starter did not produce excessive gear engagement noise, the replacement starter will also be okay. Reuse any shims that were used with the original starter. This sure beats having to remove and reinstall the replacement starter several times until the proper clearance is determined.

As the current flows through resistances and loads (such as bulbs and coils), its voltage decreases because of the resistance (electrical load) in the circuit. Amperes is the unit of electricity that actually does the work in a circuit. The greater the current flow, the more electrical power is available. Because current flow is actually a measure of the number of electrons making the trip through a circuit, this same number of electrons must also return to the power source. The electrical pressure (voltage) on the return (ground) wires is low (almost zero), but the current in amperes must still flow back to the battery.

The battery ground (negative) cable must be just as large as the positive cable because just as many amperes return as leave the battery.

Still not convinced?

Connect a starting-charging testing unit to a vehicle. Instead of connecting the ampere probe around the positive cable, connect it around the ground cable (all cables should be within the ampere probe if more than one ground cable is connected to the battery terminal).

All ammeter readings should be the same if taken on the positive or negative cables of the battery.

NOTE: Most starting-charging testing units use an arrow on the ammeter probe to show polarity. Reversing the direction in which the arrow points is often necessary to read the correct polarity (positive or negative) on the tester display.

Starting System Troubleshooting Guide

The following list will assist technicians in troubleshooting starting systems.

Problem	Possible Cause
1. Starter motor whines.	1. Possible defective starter drive. Worn starter drive engagement yoke. Defective flywheel.
2. Starter rotates slowly.	2. Possible high resistance in the battery cables or connections. Possible defective or discharged battery. Possible worn starter bushings, causing the starter armature to drag on the field coils. Possible worn starter brushes or weak brush springs. Possible defective (open or shorted) field coil.

◀ TECH TIP ▶

LIGHTS ON TO CRANK

This simple theft deterrent uses a relay to prevent the engine from cranking unless the parking lights are turned on first. See figure 10–32.

To install this low-cost device, simply cut the wire that supplies voltage from the ignition switch to the starter solenoid.

HINT: This wire can be cut near the ignition switch (under the dash) or under the hood anywhere along the path from the starter to the ignition switch.

Connect each end of the cut wire to the power terminal of the relay (usually labeled 30 and 87). Splice into a side marker lamp (or other easy-to-access light). Run the wire to one terminal of the relay coil and ground the other end of the relay coil.

When the lights are turned on, current flows through the relay coil and creates an electromagnet that moves the movable arm inside the relay, allowing the engine to crank as normal.

NOTE: The lights do not have to remain on to operate the vehicle— just to crank (start) the engine. Be sure to remember to turn off the lights when you stop to prevent a dead battery.

---

3. Starter fails to rotate.

3. Possible defective ignition switch or neutral safety switch, or open in the starter motor control circuit. Possible shorted field coils. Possible defective starter armature. Possible open in the power circuit between the battery and the starter. Possible defective starter solenoid.

4. Starter produces grinding noise.

4. Possible defective starter drive unit. Possible defective flywheel. Possible incorrect distance between the starter pinion and the flywheel. Possible cracked or broken starter drive-end housing.

SUMMARY

1. All starter motors use the principle of magnetic interaction between the field coils attached to the housing and the magnetic field of the armature.

2. Proper operation of the starter motor depends on the battery being at least 75% charged and the battery cables being of the correct size (gauge) and having no more than a 0.2-volt drop.

3. Voltage-drop testing includes cranking the engine, measuring the drop in voltage from the battery to the starter, and measuring the drop in voltage from the negative terminal of the battery to the engine block.

4. The cranking circuit should be tested for proper amperage draw.

5. An open in the control circuit can prevent starter motor operation.

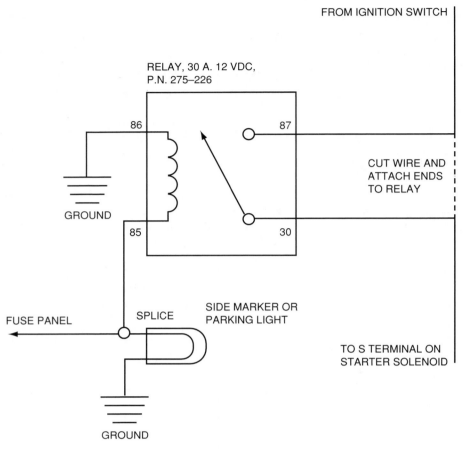

LIGHTS–ON–TO–CRANK THEFT DETERRENT*

FROM IGNITION SWITCH

RELAY, 30 A. 12 VDC,
P.N. 275–226

86

87

CUT WIRE AND
ATTACH ENDS
TO RELAY

GROUND

85

30

FUSE PANEL

SPLICE

SIDE MARKER OR
PARKING LIGHT

TO S TERMINAL ON
STARTER SOLENOID

GROUND

*ALL PART NUMBERS ARE FROM RADIO SHACK

FIGURE 10–32 This simple theft deterrent circuit will prevent the engine from cranking unless the lights are turned on first. The lights do *not* have to remain on after the engine starts.

REVIEW QUESTIONS

1. List the parts of the cranking circuit.

2. Describe the difference between the control circuit and the power circuit sections of a typical cranking circuit.

3. Explain how to perform a voltage-drop test of the cranking circuit.

4. List the steps necessary to overhaul a starter.

MULTIPLE-CHOICE QUESTIONS

1. Starter motors operate on the principle that _____.
   a. The field coils rotate in the opposite direction from the armature
   b. Opposite magnetic poles repel
   c. Like magnetic poles repel
   d. The armature rotates from a strong magnetic field toward a weaker magnetic field

2. Series-wound electric motors _____.
   a. Produce electrical power
   b. Produce maximum power at zero RPM
   c. Produce maximum power at high RPM
   d. Use a shunt coil

3. Technician A says that a defective solenoid can cause a starter whine. Technician B says that a defective starter drive can cause a starter whining noise. Which technician is correct?

   a. A only

   b. B only

   c. Both a and b

   d. Neither a nor b

4. The instant the ignition switch is turned to the start position, _____.

   a. Both the pull-in winding and the hold-in winding are energized

   b. The hold-in winding is energized

   c. The pull-in winding is energized

   d. The starter motor starts to rotate before energizing the starter pinion gear

5. Technician A says that a discharged battery (lower than normal battery voltage) is harmful to the starter motor. Technician B says that a discharged battery or dirty (corroded) battery cables can cause solenoid clicking. Which technician is correct?

   a. A only

   b. B only

   c. Both a and b

   d. Neither a nor b

6. Slow cranking by the starter can be caused by all *except* the following: _____.

   a. A low or discharged battery

   b. Corroded or dirty battery cables

   c. Engine mechanical problems

   d. An open neutral safety switch

7. If the starter "whines" when engaged, a possible cause is _____.

   a. A worn or defective starter drive

   b. A defective solenoid

   c. An open pull-in winding

   d. A worn leather armature break

8. If the clearance between the starter pinion and the engine flywheel is too great, _____.

   a. The starter will produce a high-pitched whine during cranking

   b. The starter will produce a high-pitched whine after the engine starts

   c. The starter drive will not rotate at all

   d. The solenoid will not engage the starter drive unit

CHARGING SYSTEM OPERATION, DIAGNOSIS, AND SERVICE

OBJECTIVES

After studying chapter 11, the reader will be able to

1. Describe how an alternator works.
2. Discuss the various alternator test procedures.
3. Explain how to disassemble an alternator and test its component parts.
4. Discuss how to check the wiring from the alternator to the battery.

All vehicles operate electrical components by taking current from the battery. It is the purpose and function of the charging system to keep the battery fully charged.

PRINCIPLES OF GENERATOR OPERATION

All electrical generators use the principle of electromagnetic induction to generate electrical power from mechanical power. Electromagnetic induction (see chapter 1 for details) involves the generation of an electrical current in a conductor when the conductor is moved through a magnetic field. The amount of current generated can be increased by the following factors:

1. Increasing the *speed* of the conductor through the magnetic field
2. Increasing the *number* of conductors passing through the magnetic field
3. Increasing the *strength* of the magnetic field

ALTERNATING-CURRENT GENERATORS (ALTERNATORS)

An AC generator generates an alternating current when the current changes polarity during the generator's rotation. However, a battery cannot "store" alternating current; therefore, this alternating current is changed to direct current (DC) by diodes inside the generator. Diodes are one-way electrical check valves that permit current to flow in only one direction. Most manufacturers call an AC generator an **alternator**.

ALTERNATOR CONSTRUCTION

An alternator is constructed of a two-piece cast-aluminum housing. Aluminum is used because of its light weight, nonmagnetic properties, and heat transfer properties needed to help keep the alternator cool. A front ball bear-

◀ **TECH TIP** ▶

ALTERNATOR HORSEPOWER AND ENGINE OPERATION

Many technicians are asked how much power certain accessories require. A 100-ampere alternator requires about 2 horsepower from the engine. One horsepower is equal to 746 watts. Watts are calculated by multiplying amperes times volts.

$$\text{Power in watts} = 100 \text{ A} \times 14.5 \text{ V}$$
$$= 1450 \text{ W}$$
$$1 \text{ hp} = 746 \text{ W}$$

therefore, 1450 watts is about 2 horsepower.

Allowing about 20% for mechanical and electrical losses adds another 0.4 horsepower. Therefore, whenever anybody asks how much power it takes to produce 100 amperes from an alternator, the answer is about 2.4 horsepower.

Many alternators delay the electrical load to prevent the engine from stumbling whenever a heavy electrical load is applied. The voltage regulator or vehicle computer is capable of gradually increasing the output of the alternator over a period of up to several minutes. Even though 2 horsepower does not sound like much, a sudden demand for 2 horsepower from an idling engine can cause the engine to run rough or stall. The difference in part numbers of various alternators is often an indication of the time interval over which the load is applied. Therefore, the use of the wrong replacement alternator could cause the engine to stall!

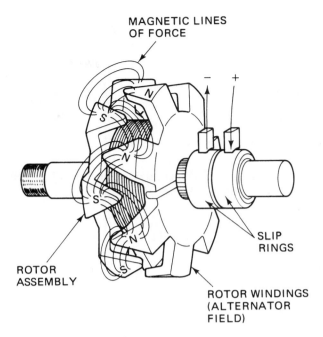

FIGURE 11–1 Rotor assembly of a typical alternator (AC generator). Current through the slip rings causes the "fingers" of the rotor to become alternating north and south magnetic poles. As the rotor revolves, these magnetic lines of force induce a current in the stator windings.

ing is pressed into the front housing (called the **drive-end** [DE] housing) to provide the support and friction reduction necessary for the belt-driven rotor assembly. The rear housing (called the **slip ring end** [SRE]) usually contains a roller-bearing support for the rotor and mounting for the brushes, diodes, and internal voltage regulator (if the alternator is so equipped).

ROTORS

The rotor creates the magnetic field of the alternator and produces a current by electromagnetic induction in the stationary stator windings. This differs from a DC generator, wherein the field current is created in the sta-

tionary field windings and the current is generated in the rotating armature. The alternator rotor is constructed of many turns of copper wire coated with a varnish insulation wound over an iron core. The iron core is attached to the rotor shaft. See figure 11–1.

At both ends of the rotor windings are heavy-gauge metal plates bent over the windings with triangular fingers called **poles.** These pole fingers do not touch, but alternate or interlace. When current flows through the rotor windings, the metal pole pieces at each end of the rotor become electromagnets. Whether a north or a south pole magnet is created depends on the *direction* in which the wire coil is wound. Because the pole pieces are attached to each end of the rotor, one pole piece will be a north pole magnet. The other pole piece is on the opposite end of the rotor and therefore is viewed as being wound in the opposite direction, creating a south pole. Therefore, the rotor fingers are alternating north and south magnetic poles. The magnetic fields are created between the alternating pole piece fingers. These individual magnetic fields produce a current by electromagnetic induction in the stationary stator windings.

The current necessary for the field (rotor) windings is conducted through **slip rings.** The current to the field is conducted through the slip rings with carbon brushes. The maximum-rated alternator output in amperes is largely dependent on the number and gauge of the windings of the rotor. Substituting rotors from one alternator in another can greatly affect maximum output. Many commercially rebuilt alternators are tested and have a sticker put on them indicating their tested output. The original rating stamped on the housing is then ground off.

ALTERNATOR BRUSHES

The current for the field is controlled by the voltage regulator and is conducted to the slip rings through carbon brushes. The brushes conduct only the field current (approximately 2 to 5 amperes) and therefore tend to last longer than the brushes used on a DC generator, where all of the current generated in the generator must flow through the brushes.

STATORS

Supported between the two halves of the alternator housing are three copper wire windings wound on a laminated metal core. See figure 11–2. As the rotor revolves, its moving magnetic field induces a current in the windings of the stator.

◄ TECH TIP ►

THE SNIFF TEST

Whenever checking the charging system, one of the first things that a technician should do is to sniff (smell) the alternator! If the alternator smells like a dead rat (rancid), the stator windings have been overheated by trying to charge a discharged or defective battery. If the battery voltage is continuously low, the voltage regulator will continue supplying full-field current to the alternator. The voltage regulator is designed to cycle on and off to maintain a narrow charging system voltage range.

If the battery voltage is continually below the cutoff point of the voltage regulator, the alternator is continually producing current in the stator windings. This constant charging can often overheat the stator and burn the insulating varnish covering the stator windings. If the alternator fails the sniff test, the technician should replace the stator and other alternator components that are found to be defective *and* replace or recharge and test the battery.

DIODES

Diodes are constructed of a semiconductor material (usually silicon) and operate as a one-way electrical check valve that permits the current to flow in only one direction. Alternators use six diodes (one positive and one negative for each of the three stator windings) to convert alternating current to direct current. The symbol for a diode is shown in figure 11–3.

HOW AN ALTERNATOR WORKS

A rotor inside an alternator is turned by a belt and drive pulley by the engine. The magnetic field of the rotor generates a current in the windings of the stator by electromagnetic induction. See figure 11–4.

Field current flowing through the slip rings to the rotor creates an alternating north and south pole on the rotor, with a magnetic field between each finger of

FIGURE 11–2   Stator being removed from a GM SI AC generator.

FIGURE 11–3   Diode symbol.

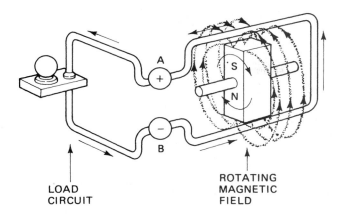

FIGURE 11–4 Magnetic lines of force cutting across a conductor induce a voltage and current in the conductor.

the rotor. The induced current in the stator windings is an alternating current because of the alternating magnetic field of the rotor. The induced current starts to increase as the magnetic field starts to induce current in each winding of the stator. The current then peaks when the magnetic field is the strongest and starts to decrease as the magnetic field moves away from the stator winding. Therefore, the current generated is described as being of a **sine wave** pattern (figure 11–5). As the rotor continues to rotate, this sine wave current is induced in each of the three windings of the stator.

Because each of the three windings generates a sine wave current, as shown in figure 11–6, the resulting currents combine to form a three-phase voltage output.

The current induced in the stator windings connects to diodes (one-way electrical check valves) that permit

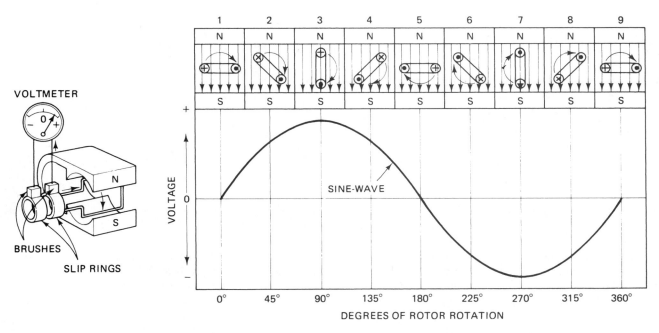

FIGURE 11–5 Sine wave voltage curve created by one revolution of a winding rotating in a magnetic field.

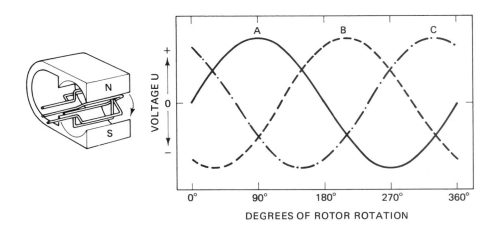

FIGURE 11–6 When three windings (A, B, and C) are present in a stator, the resulting current generation is represented by the three sine waves. The voltages are 120° out of phase. The connection of the individual phases produces a three-phase alternating voltage.

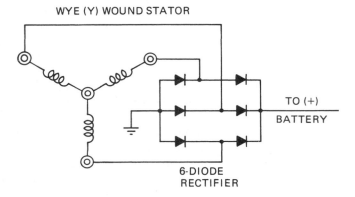

FIGURE 11–7 Wye-connected stator winding.

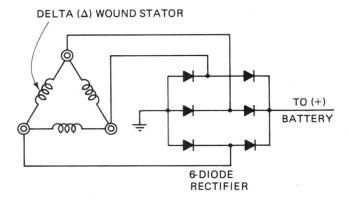

FIGURE 11–8 Delta-connected stator winding.

the alternator output current to flow in only one direction. Most alternators contain six diodes, one pair of a positive and a negative diode for each of the three stator windings.

WYE-CONNECTED STATORS

The **Y** (pronounced "wye" and generally so written) **type** or star pattern (figure 11–7) is the most commonly used alternator stator winding connection. The output current with a wye-type stator connection is constant over a broad alternator speed range.

Current is induced in each winding by electromagnetic induction from the rotating magnetic fields of the rotor. In a wye-type stator connection the currents must combine because two windings are always connected in series. The current produced in each winding is added to the other windings' current and then flows through the diodes to the alternator output terminal. One-half of the current produced is available at the neutral junction (usually labeled "STA" for stator). The voltage at this center point is used by some alternator manufacturers (especially Ford) to control the charge indicator light or is used by the voltage regulator to control the rotor field current.

DELTA-CONNECTED STATORS

The **delta winding** is connected in a triangular shape, as shown in figure 11–8. (Delta is a Greek letter shaped like a triangle.) Current induced in each winding flows to the diodes in a parallel circuit. More current can flow through two parallel circuits than can flow through a series circuit (as in a wye-type stator connection).

Delta-connected stators are used on alternators where high output at high alternator RPM is required. The delta-connected alternator can produce 73% more current than the same alternator with wye-type stator

◀ **TECH TIP** ▶

THE HAND CLEANER TRICK

Lower than normal alternator output could be the result of a loose or slipping drive belt. All belts (V and serpentine multigroove) use an interference angle between the angle of the V's of the belt and the angle of the V's on the pulley. A belt wears this interference angle off the edges of the V of the belt. As a result, the belt may start to slip and make a squealing sound even if tensioned properly.

A common trick to determine if the noise is belt related is to use grit-type hand cleaner or scouring powder. With the engine off, sprinkle some powder onto the pulley side of the belt. Start the engine. The excess powder will fly into the air, so get away from under the hood when the engine starts. If the belts are now quieter, you know that it was the glazed belt that made the noise.

NOTE: Often, the noise sounds exactly like a noisy bearing. Therefore, before you start removing and replacing parts, try the hand cleaner trick.

Often, the grit from the hand cleaner will remove the glaze from the belt and the noise will not return. However, if the belt is worn or loose, the noise will return and the belt should be replaced. A fast alternative method to see if the noise is from the belt is to spray water from a squirt bottle at the belt with the engine running. If the noise stops, the belt is the cause of the noise. The water quickly evaporates, and therefore, unlike the gritty hand cleaner, water just finds the problem—it does not provide a short-term fix.

connections. For example, if an alternator with a wye-connected stator can produce 32 amperes, the *same* alternator with delta-connected stator windings can produce 73% more current, or 55 amperes (32 × 1.73 = 55). The delta-connected alternator, however, produces lower current at low speed and must be operated at high speed to produce its maximum output.

HINT: General Motors delta-wound alternators can easily be identified by the location of the amperage output stamping on the *front* of the drive-end housing facing the drive pulley. Wye-wound GM alternators are stamped on top of the drive-end housing near the small pivot-end ear.

ALTERNATOR OUTPUT

The output voltage and current of an alternator depend on several factors:

1. *Speed of rotation.* Alternator output is increased with alternator rotational speed up to the alternator's maximum possible ampere output. Alternators normally rotate at a speed 2 to 3 times faster than engine speed, depending on the relative pulley sizes used for the belt drive.
2. *Number of conductors.* A high-output alternator contains more turns of wire in the stator windings. Stator winding connections (whether wye or delta) also affect the maximum alternator output.
3. *Strength of the magnetic field.* If the magnetic field is strong, a high output is possible because the current generated by electromagnetic induction is dependent on the number of magnetic lines of force that are cut.
   a. The strength of the magnetic field can be increased by increasing the number of turns of conductor wire wound on the rotor. A higher-output alternator has more turns of wire than does an alternator with a low-rated output.
   b. The strength of the magnetic field also depends on the current through the field coil (rotor). Because magnetic field strength is measured in ampere-turns, the greater the amperage or the number of turns, or both, the greater the alternator output.

ALTERNATOR VOLTAGE REGULATION

An automotive alternator must be able to produce electrical pressure (voltage) higher than battery voltage to charge the battery. Excessively high voltage can dam-

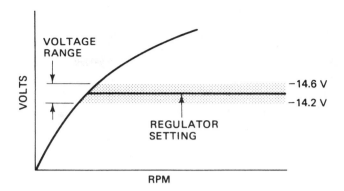

FIGURE 11–9 Typical voltage regulator voltage range.

age the battery, electrical components, and the lights of a vehicle. If no (zero) amperes of current existed throughout the field coil of the alternator (rotor), alternator output would be zero because without field current a magnetic field does not exist. The field current required by most automotive alternators is under 3 amperes. It is the *control* of the *field* current that controls the output of the alternator. Current for the rotor flows from the battery through the brushes to the slip rings. After generator output begins, the voltage regulator controls the current flow through the rotor. See figure 11–9. The voltage regulator simply opens the field circuit if the voltage reaches a predetermined level, then closes the field circuit again as necessary to maintain the correct charging voltage.

BATTERY CONDITION AND CHARGING VOLTAGE

If the automotive battery is discharged, its voltage will be lower than the voltage of a fully charged battery. The alternator will supply charging current, but it may not reach the maximum charging voltage. For example, if a vehicle is jump-started and run at a fast idle (2000 RPM), the charging voltage may be only 12.0 volts. As the battery becomes charged and the battery voltage increases, the charging voltage will also increase, until the voltage regulator limit is reached; then the voltage regulator will start to control the charging voltage. A good, but discharged, battery should be able to convert into chemical energy all the current the alternator can produce. As long as alternator voltage is higher than battery voltage, current will flow from the alternator (high pressure, high voltage) to the battery (lower pressure, lower voltage). Therefore, if a voltmeter is connected to a discharged battery with the engine running, it may indicate charging voltage that is lower than normally acceptable.

In other words, the condition and voltage of the battery *do* determine the charging rate of the alternator. It is often stated that the battery is the true "voltage regulator" and that the voltage regulator simply acts as the upper-limit voltage control. This is the reason that all charging system testing *must* be performed with a known-to-be-good battery, at least 75% charged, to be assured of accurate test results. If a discharged battery is used during charging system testing, tests could mistakenly indicate a defective alternator and/or voltage regulator.

TEMPERATURE COMPENSATION

All voltage regulators (mechanical or electronic) provide a method for increasing the charging voltage slightly at low temperatures and for lowering the charging voltage at high temperatures. A battery requires a higher charging voltage at low temperatures because of the resistance to chemical reaction changes. However, the battery would be overcharged if the charging voltage were not reduced during warm weather. Electronic voltage regulators use a temperature-sensitive resistor in the regulator circuit. This resistor is called a **thermistor,** and it provides lower resistance as the temperature increases. A thermistor is used in the electronic circuits of the voltage regulator to control charging voltage over a wide range of under-the-hood temperatures.

NOTE: Voltmeter test results may vary according to temperature. Charging voltage tested at 32° F (0° C) will be higher than for the same vehicle tested at 80° F (27° C) because of the temperature compensation factors built into voltage regulators.

A AND B FIELD CIRCUITS

When testing the charging circuit, most test equipment requires the technician to select either A or B field type. An A circuit is the most commonly used. This type of circuit has an *external* ground, or is grounded by the voltage regulator. See figure 11–10. All electronic voltage regulators use A circuits because the controlling transistor(s) control a lower-voltage current opening and closing the ground return path.

In a B-circuit field, the voltage regulator controls (open and closes) the power side of the field circuit, and the circuit is grounded inside the generator or alternator. Therefore, a B circuit is internally grounded. See figure 11–11.

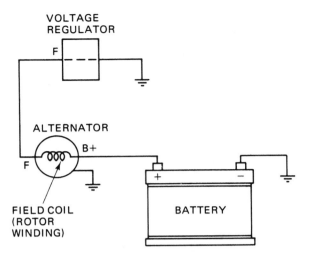

FIGURE 11–10   Diagram of an A-type field circuit.

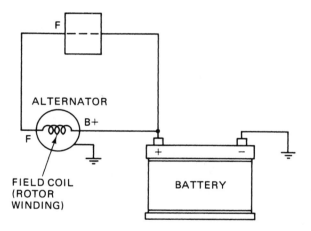

FIGURE 11–11   Diagram of a B-type field circuit.

ELECTRONIC VOLTAGE REGULATORS

Electronic voltage regulators have been used since the early 1970s. The electronic circuit of the voltage regulator cycles between 10 and 7000 times per *second* as needed to accurately control the field current through the rotor, and therefore control the alternator output. The control of the field current is accomplished by opening and closing the *ground* side of the field circuit through the rotor of the alternator. Electronic voltage regulators also use many resistors to help reduce the current through the regulator, and the resulting heat must be dissipated into the air to prevent damage to the diodes and transistors. Whether mounted inside the alternator or externally under the hood, electronic voltage regulators are mounted where normal airflow can keep the electronic components cool.

HOW AN ELECTRONIC VOLTAGE REGULATOR WORKS

The zener diode is a major electronic component that makes voltage regulation possible. A zener diode blocks current flow until a specific voltage is reached, then it permits current to flow. Alternator voltage from the stator and diodes is first sent through a thermistor, which changes resistance with temperature, and then to a zener diode. Whenever the upper-limit voltage is reached, the zener diode conducts current to a transistor, which then opens the field (rotor) circuit. All the current stops flowing through the alternator's brushes, slip rings, and rotor, and no magnetic field is formed. Without a magnetic field, an alternator does not produce current in the stator windings. When no voltage is applied to the zener diode, current flow stops and the base of the transistor is turned off, closing the field circuit. The magnetic field is thus restored in the rotor. The rotating magnetic fields of the rotor induce a current in the stator, which is again controlled if the output voltage exceeds the designed limit as determined by the zener diode breakdown voltage. Depending on the alternator RPM, vehicle electrical load, and state of charge of the battery, this controlled switching on and off can occur between 10 and 7000 times per second. See figure 11–12.

COMPUTER-CONTROLLED ALTERNATORS

Beginning in the mid-1980s, General Motors introduced a smaller, yet high-output series of alternators. These alternators are called the charging system (CS) series. See figure 11–13. After the letters *CS*, in the identification system, are found numbers indicating the *outside diameter* in millimeters of the stator laminations. Typical sizes, designations, and outputs include the following:

CS-121,	5-SI	74 A
CS-130,	9-SI	105 A
CS-144,	17-SI	120 A

These alternators feature two cooling fans (one internal) and terminals designed to permit connections to an on-board body computer through terminals L and F.

The reduced-size alternators also feature ball bearings front and rear, and totally soldered internal electrical connections. The voltage is controlled either by the body computer (if the vehicle is so equipped) or by the built-in voltage regulator. The voltage regulator switches the field voltage on and off at a fixed frequency of about 400 times per second. Voltage is controlled by varying the on and off time of the field current. See figure 11–14 for the wiring diagram for a typical computer-controlled Chrysler alternator.

CHARGING SYSTEM TESTING AND SERVICE

The charging system can be tested as part of a routine vehicle inspection or to determine the reason for a "no charge" or reduced-charging circuit performance. All 12-volt automotive alternator systems use the voltage regulator to control the current through the rotor of the alternator. The rotor creates a magnetic field whenever there is a complete circuit through the brushes and slip rings of the rotor. If there is no current through the rotor, there is no alternator output. Whenever the rotor is energized, the entire rotor shaft and the alternator bearings become magnetized. Technicians often use this information to help diagnose a no-charging problem. With the engine running, use a screwdriver or other metallic object to test for magnetism at the rear bearing of the alternator. See figure 11–15.

NOTE: The front bearing is also magnetized, but testing for magnetism of the front bearing with the engine running can be dangerous.

If the rear bearing *is* magnetized, then the following facts are known:

1. The voltage regulator is working.
2. The alternator brushes are working.
3. The rotor in the alternator is producing a magnetic field.

If the rear bearing is *not* magnetized, then one or more of the following problems exist:

1. The voltage regulator is not working.
2. The alternator brushes are worn or stuck, and they are not making good electrical contact with the rotor slip rings.
3. The alternator rotor could be defective.

No automotive alternator can produce charging current if the rotor is not producing a magnetic field. It is this rotating magnetic field created in the rotor that induces current in the stator windings. Therefore, by

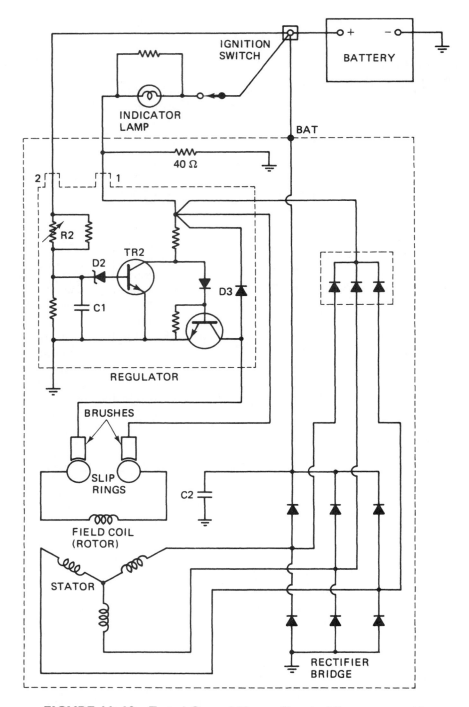

FIGURE 11–12 Typical General Motors SI-style AC generator with an integral voltage regulator. Voltage present at terminal 2 is used to reverse bias the zener diode (D2) that controls TR2. The hot brush is fed by the ignition current (terminal 1) plus current from the diode trio.

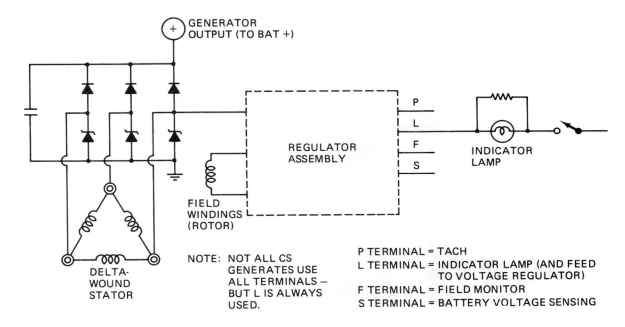

FIGURE 11–13 General Motors CS generator. Notice the use of zener diodes in the rectifier to help control any high-voltage surges that could affect delicate computer circuits. If a high-voltage surge does occur, the zener diode(s) will be reversed biased and the potentially harmful voltage will be safely conducted to ground.

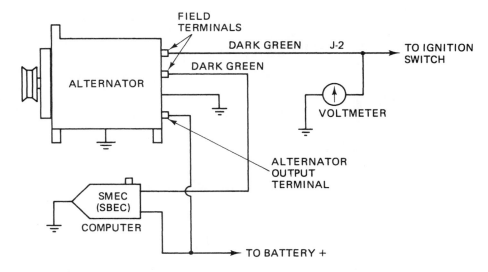

FIGURE 11–14 The alternator field (rotor) current is controlled by the computer. SMEC stands for *single-module engine controller*. SBEC stands for *single-board engine controller*.

FIGURE 11–15 If the rear bearing is magnetized, the voltage regulator, alternator brushes, and rotor are functioning.

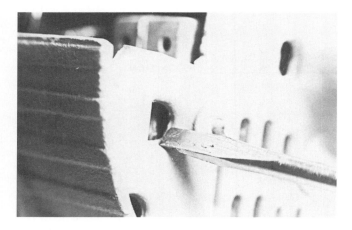

FIGURE 11–16 To full-field an internal regulator GM alternator, insert a screwdriver through the test hole (usually D-shaped).

checking for a magnetized rear bearing, the technician can better determine where the charging system problem is located. If, for example, the rear bearing is magnetized, yet the "charge" ("GEN") light is on and the alternator is not charging, the problem has to be inside the alternator (diodes, stator, etc.).

If the rear bearing is not magnetized, then a procedure for bypassing the voltage regulator should be used to determine if the alternator is capable of producing its designed output. This procedure is called "full-fielding" the alternator. See figures 11–16 through 11–25 for examples of procedures and connections necessary to full-field various charging systems.

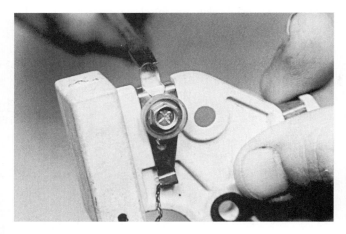

FIGURE 11–17 The screwdriver (as shown in figure 11–16) grounds the tab on the ground brush, thereby providing full current flow through the brushes and rotor.

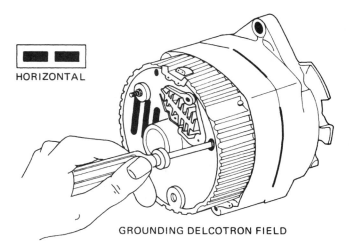

GROUNDING DELCOTRON FIELD

FIGURE 11–18 A GM alternator with an internal voltage regulator can be identified by the horizontal plug-in connector.

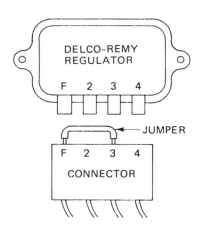

FIGURE 11–19 Connections required to full-field a GM alternator with an external voltage regulator.

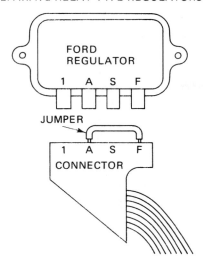

JUMPER

CONNECTOR

FIGURE 11-20 Connections required to full-field a Ford alternator with an external voltage regulator.

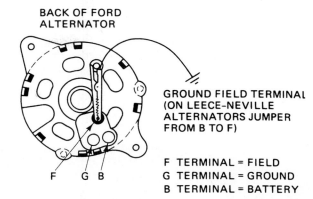

BACK OF FORD ALTERNATOR

GROUND FIELD TERMINAL (ON LEECE-NEVILLE ALTERNATORS JUMPER FROM B TO F)

F TERMINAL = FIELD
G TERMINAL = GROUND
B TERMINAL = BATTERY

FIGURE 11-21 Jumper wire connections required to full-field a Ford (or Leece-Neville) alternator with an internal electronic voltage regulator.

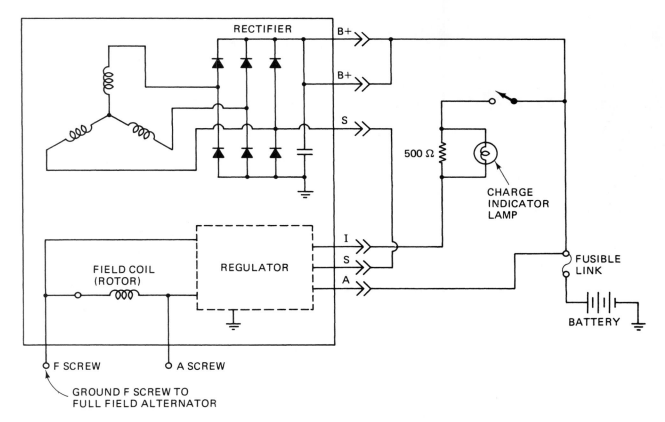

FIGURE 11-22 Wiring diagram of a Ford integral alternator and regulator (IAR) assembly.

AC VOLTAGE CHECK

A good alternator should *not* produce any AC voltage. It is the purpose of the diodes in the alternator to rectify all AC voltage into DC voltage. The procedure to check for AC voltage includes the following steps:

- *Step #1.* Set the digital meter to read AC volts.
- *Step #2.* Start the engine and operate it at 2000 RPM (fast idle).
- *Step #3.* Connect the voltmeter leads to the positive and negative battery terminals.
- *Step #4.* Turn on the headlights to provide an electrical load on the alternator.

NOTE: A higher, more accurate reading can be obtained by touching the meter lead to the output terminal of the alternator.

FIGURE 11–23 Typical Ford IAR alternator installation. Notice the labeled terminals I, S, and A. White chalk was rubbed over the letters to help make them more visible for photographing.

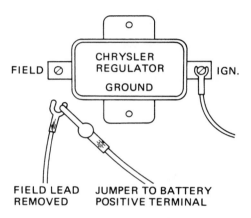

FIGURE 11–24 Connections required to full-field a Chrysler alternator with a mechanical voltage regulator.

FIGURE 11–25 Connections required to full-field a Chrysler alternator with an electronic voltage regulator.

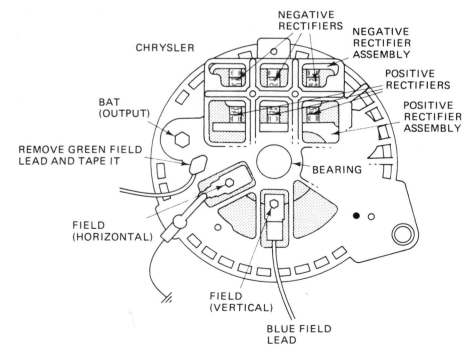

The results should be interpreted as follows: If the diodes are good, the voltmeter should read *less* than 0.4 volts AC. If the reading is over 0.5 volts AC, the rectifier diodes are defective.

NOTE: This test will *not* test for a defective diode trio.

CHARGING SYSTEM VOLTAGE-DROP TESTING

For the proper operation of any charging system, there must be good electrical connections between the battery positive terminal and the alternator output terminal. The alternator must also be properly grounded to the engine block.

Many manufacturers of vehicles run the lead from the output terminal of the alternator to other connectors or junction blocks that are electrically connected to the positive of the battery. If there is high resistance (a high voltage drop) in these connections or in the wiring itself, the battery will not be properly charged.

Whenever there is a suspected charging system problem (with or without a charge indicator light on), simply follow these steps to measure the voltage drop of the insulated (power-side) charging circuit:

- *Step #1.* Start the engine and run it at a fast idle (about 2000 engine RPM).
- *Step #2.* Turn on the headlights to ensure an electrical load on the charging system.
- *Step #3.* Using any voltmeter, connect the positive test lead (usually red) to the output terminal of the alternator. Attach the negative test lead (usually black) to the positive post of the battery.

The results should be interpreted as follows:

1. If there is less than a 0.2-volt reading, then all wiring and connections are satisfactory.
2. If the voltmeter reads higher than 0.2 volts, there is excessive resistance (voltage drop) between the alternator output terminal and the positive terminal of the battery.
3. If the voltmeter reads battery voltage (or close to battery voltage), there is an open circuit between the battery and the alternator output terminal.

To determine whether the alternator is correctly grounded, maintain the engine speed at 2000 RPM with the headlights on. Connect the positive voltmeter lead to the case of the alternator and the negative voltmeter lead to the negative terminal of the battery. The voltmeter should read less than 0.2 volts if the alternator is properly grounded. If the reading is over 0.2 volts, connect one end of an auxiliary ground wire to the case of the alternator and the other end to a good engine ground. See figure 11–26.

GM SI TEST LIGHT TEST

All General Motors SI (System Integration [internal voltage regulator]) series Delcotron generators (alternators) can be easily tested using a standard 6- to 12-volt

◀ **TECH TIP** ▶

"2 TO 4"

Most voltage-drop specifications range between 0.2 and 0.4 volts. Generally, if the voltage loss (voltage drop) in a circuit exceeds 0.5 volts (½ volt), the wiring in that circuit should be repaired or replaced. During automotive testing, it is sometimes difficult to remember the exact specification for each test; therefore, the technician can simply remember "2 to 4" and that any voltage drop over that indicates a problem.

◀ **TECH TIP** ▶

USE JUMPER CABLES AS A DIAGNOSTIC TOOL

Whenever diagnosing an alternator charging problem, try using jumper cables to connect the positive and negative terminals of the alternator directly to the positive and negative terminals of the battery. If a definite improvement is noticed, the problem is in the *wiring* of the vehicle. High resistance, due to corroded connections or loose grounds, can cause low alternator output, repeated regulator failures, slow cranking, and discharged batteries. A voltage-drop test of the charging system can also be used to locate excessive resistance (high voltage drop) in the charging circuit, but using jumper wires (cables) is often faster and easier.

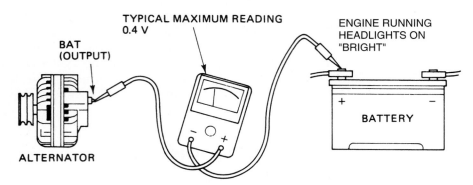

VOLTAGE DROP – INSULATED CHARGING CIRCUIT

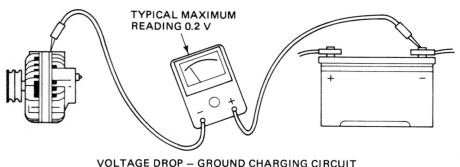

VOLTAGE DROP – GROUND CHARGING CIRCUIT

FIGURE 11–26 Voltmeter hookup to test the voltage drop of the charging circuit.

test light. The SI series generators were first used in the early 1970s and use an internal voltage regulator. See figure 11–27.

Normal Operation

The following steps outline the procedure for testing an SI series alternator for normal operation:

- *Step #1.* With the ignition on (engine off), a test light should be bright if touched to the "BAT" terminal or #2 terminal.

> **NOTE:** Terminal #2 is the battery-sensing terminal. On many GM applications, a jumper wire simply connects the "BAT" terminal to terminal #2.

The test light should be dim when touched to terminal #1. Terminal #1 is the wire from the dashboard warning light. The test light should be dim because of the voltage drop across the dashboard light bulb.

- *Step #2.* With the engine running, touching any of the three terminals should produce a bright test light. The "BAT" terminal and terminal #2 should both cause a bright light because both of these are battery voltage sources. Terminal #1 should also light the test light brightly because when the generator is producing a current, the internal voltage rises and applies an opposing voltage on the dash light bulb, which causes current to stop flowing through the bulb and the charge light to go out.

Problems and Possible Causes

If the test light is not on at all on terminal #1 (brown or tan wire), the problem is an open circuit in the wiring between the dash and the alternator.

If the test light is bright on terminal #1 with the key turned to "on" and the engine off, the most likely cause is a defective (open) voltage regulator.

If the test light does not light on either the "BAT" terminal or #2 terminal, an open circuit exists between the positive post of the battery and the alternator. Check the condition of all fusible links.

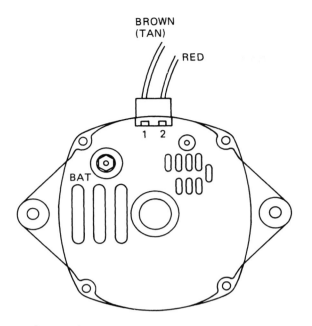

FIGURE 11–27 Typical GM SI alternator. Note the location and wire color used for terminal #1 and #2.

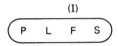

FIGURE 11–28 Typical GM CS alternator wiring plug identification. Note that terminal F is sometimes terminal I on some alternators.

GM CS SERIES AC GENERATORS

A General Motors CS series generator requires only two wires to operate—the battery "bat" feed and the wire to the L terminal.

The CS series generators are designed to operate as a stand-alone generator or be controlled by a vehicle computer system. See figure 11–28 for terminal identification.

The P terminal is connected directly to the stator that produces about one-half of the system alternating current and is used as a tachometer signal. *P* is used because it is an abbreviation for *pseudo*, meaning alternating (not straight) output. Terminal S is the sensing terminal for true battery voltage. F is the computer-sensing terminal. The computer monitors this terminal and sets trouble codes and alerts the driver if there is a charging system malfunction. The letter *I* is sometimes used instead of *F*, and this terminal is used as a backup voltage source to the voltage regulator if the L terminal circuit is lost.

DIAGNOSING PROBLEMS WITH THE GM CS SERIES

If the charge indicator light is on in the dash, unplug the connector (which can have up to four wires connected). Start the engine and observe the dash charge light. If the light is still on, there is a short to ground in the L wire circuit between the generator and the dash. If the charge light is out, check for voltage at the L terminal. If there is voltage available at the L terminal (remember, the connector is still unplugged from the generator), the problem is in the generator, if charging is not occurring.

If there is no voltage available at the L terminal, apply a voltage through a standard test light to the L terminal of the generator. This supplies the power for the regulator. (This is not full-fielding the generator, but simply supplies power to the internal regulator.) If the generator output is now normal, the problem is in the wiring to the L terminal of the generator. Check all fuses, all fusible links, and the charge light indicator bulb.

ALTERNATOR OUTPUT TEST

A charging circuit may be able to produce correct charging circuit voltage, but not be able to produce adequate amperage output. If in doubt about charging system output, first check the condition of the alternator drive belt. With the engine off, attempt to rotate the fan of the alternator with your hands. Replace or tighten the drive belt if the alternator fan can be rotated by hand. See figure 11–29 for typical test equipment hookup.

The testing procedure for alternator output is as follows:

- *Step #1.* Connect the starting and charging test leads according to the manufacturer's instructions.
- *Step #2.* Turn the ignition switch on (engine off) and observe the ammeter. This is the ignition circuit current, it should be about 2 to 8 amperes.
- *Step #3.* Start the engine and operate it at 2000 RPM (fast idle). Turn the load increase control slowly to obtain the highest reading on the ammeter scale. Note the ampere reading.
- *Step #4.* Total the amperes from steps #2 and #3. Results should be within 10% (or 15 amperes) of the rated output. Rated output may be stamped on the alternator as shown in figure 11–30.

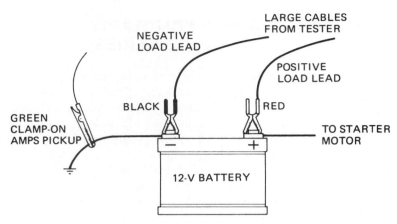

Test lead connections for testing the starting system, charging system, voltage regulator, and diode stator.

FIGURE 11–29 Typical hookup of a starting and charging tester.

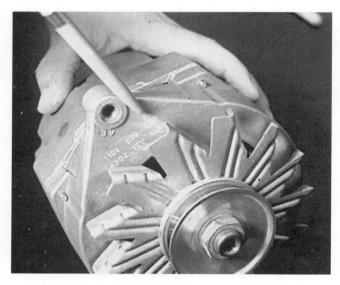

FIGURE 11–30 The amperage rating of most GM alternators is stamped on the drive-end housing either facing the front (pulley side) or on top behind the small threaded mounting lug.

If the alternator output is less than within 10% of its rated output, perform the same test as just described, but this time bypass the voltage regulator and provide a full-field current to the rotor (field) of the alternator.

NOTE: When applying a load to the battery with a carbon pile tester during an alternator output test, do not permit the battery voltage to drop below 12 volts. Most alternators will produce their maximum output (in amperes) above 13 volts.

ALTERNATOR IDENTIFYING COLORS

The following table gives output ratings associated with various identifying colors used by Ford and Chrysler.

Manufacturer	Color	Rating (A)
Chrysler	Violet	41
	Red	41
	Blue	41
	Bronze	41
	Natural	50
	Green	50
	Yellow	60
	Brown	65
	Brown	78
	Black	65
	Yellow	100‡
Ford	Orange	40*
	Black	65*
	Green	60*
	Black	70†
	Red	100†

*Rear terminal.

†Side terminal.

‡Larger housing than 60 ampere.

FIGURE 11–31 Whenever connecting an inductive ammeter probe, be certain that the pickup is over *all* wires. The probe will work equally well over either all positive or all negative cables, because all current leaving a battery must return.

NOTE: Some alternators of different-color tags or insulators have the same rated output because of different color codes used in different years of production or for different vehicle applications. Not every alternator is marked to indicate its output rating. When load testing any alternator, always check the manufacturer's specification for the vehicle being tested.

HOW TO DETERMINE MINIMUM REQUIRED ALTERNATOR OUTPUT

All charging systems must be able to supply the electrical demands of the electrical system. If lights and accessories are used constantly and the alternator cannot supply the necessary ampere output, the battery will be drained. To determine the minimum electrical load requirements, connect an ammeter in series with either battery cable.

NOTE: If using an inductive-pickup ammeter, be certain that the pickup is over *all* the wires leaving the battery terminal. See figure 11–31. Failure to include the small body ground wire from the negative battery terminal to the body or the small positive wire (if testing from the positive side) will *greatly decrease* the current flow readings.

◄ **TECH TIP** ►

BIGGER IS NOT ALWAYS BETTER

Many technicians are asked to install a higher-output alternator to allow the use of emergency equipment or other high-amperage equipment such as a high-wattage sound system.

Although many higher-output units can be physically installed, it is important not to forget to upgrade the wiring and the fusible link(s) in the alternator circuit.

Failure to upgrade the wiring could lead to overheating. The usual failure locations are at junctions or electrical connectors.

After connecting an ammeter correctly in the battery circuit, turn on all lights and accessories (with the engine off) that are likely to be used continuously, as follows:

1. Turn ignition to "on" (run)—do not start the engine.
2. Turn the heat selector to air conditioning (if the vehicle is so equipped).
3. Turn the blower motor to high speed.
4. Turn the headlights on bright.
5. Turn on the radio.
6. Turn on the windshield wipers.
7. Turn on any other accessories that may be used continuously (do not operate the horn, power door locks, or other units that are not used for more than a few seconds).

Observe the ammeter. The current indicated (normally 30 amperes or more) is the electrical load that the alternator must be able to exceed to keep the battery fully charged. The minimum acceptable alternator output is 5 amperes greater than the accessory load. For example, if the measured continuous electrical load was 36 amperes, the *minimum* acceptable alternator output is 41 amperes (36 + 5 = 41).

ALTERNATOR DISASSEMBLY

If testing has confirmed that there are alternator problems, remove the alternator from the vehicle *after* disconnecting the *negative* battery cable. This will prevent the occurrence of damaging short circuits. Mark the case with a scratch or with chalk to ensure proper reassembly of the alternator case. See figure 11–32.

NOTE: Most alternators of a particular manufacturer can be used on a variety of vehicles, which may require wiring connections placed in various locations. For example, a Chevrolet and an Oldsmobile alternator may be identical except for the position of the rear section containing the electrical connections. The four through-bolts that hold the two halves together are equally spaced; therefore, the rear alternator housing *can* be reinstalled in any one of four positions to match the wiring needs of various models. See figure 11–33.

After the through-bolts have been removed, carefully separate the two halves; the stator windings stay with the rear case. The rotor can be inspected and tested while attached to the front housing. See figures 11–34 through 11–36.

TESTING THE ROTOR

The slip rings on the rotor should be smooth and round (within 0.002 inch of being perfectly round). If grooved, the slip rings can be machined to provide a suitable surface for the brushes. Do not machine beyond the minimum slip ring dimension as specified by the manufacturer.

If the slip rings are discolored or dirty, they can be cleaned with 400-grit or fine emery (polishing) cloth. The rotor must be turned while being cleaned to prevent flat spots on the slip rings.

FIGURE 11–32 Always mark the case of the alternator before disassembly to be assured of correct reassembly.

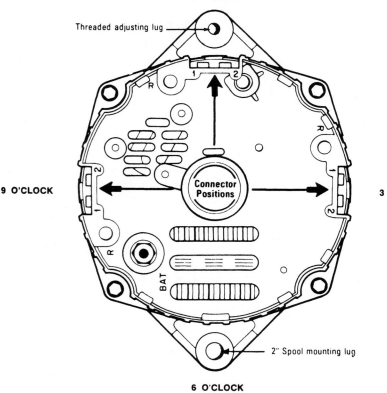

FIGURE 11–33 Explanation of Delco clock positions. Because the four through-bolts are equally spaced, it is possible for an alternator to be installed in one of four different clock positions. The connector position is determined by viewing the alternator from the diode end with the threaded adjusting lug in the up or 12 o'clock position. Select the 3 o'clock, 6 o'clock, 9 o'clock, or 12 o'clock position to match the unit being replaced.

FIGURE 11–34 Remove the drive pulley from a GM alternator by holding a ⁵⁄₁₆-inch hex (Allen) wrench in a vise with a ¹⁵⁄₁₆-inch box-end wrench.

FIGURE 11–35 Alternative method of removing the front pulley from a GM alternator. Gently place the rotor in a vise after removing the brush-end frame housing. The vise will hold the rotor while the front nut is removed.

The field coil continuity in the rotor can be checked by touching one test lead of a 110-volt (15-watt bulb) tester on each slip ring. The test light should light. A more accurate method is to measure the resistance between the slip rings using an ohmmeter. Typical resistance values include the following:

GM:	2.4 to 3.5 ohms
Ford:	3.0 to 5.5 ohms
Chrysler:	3.0 to 6.0 ohms

FIGURE 11–36 To separate the halves of most alternators, remove the through-bolts and gently pry between the stator metal laminations and the front drive-end housing.

The resistance values listed here are typical only; exact specifications for the alternator being tested should be consulted before condemning a rotor. Ohmmeters can also vary in accuracy. See figure 11–37.

1. If the resistance is below specification, the rotor is shorted.
2. If the resistance is above specification, the rotor connections are corroded or open.

Rotor inspection specifications often include an acceptable amperage current. With an ammeter connected in series with the battery, connect one test lead directly to the positive post of the battery and one slip ring. Connect the other test lead between the negative post of the battery and the other slip ring. Current will flow through the field windings of the rotor and create a magnetic field. Compare the ammeter reading with the manufacturer's specifications (usually between 1.8 and 4.5 amperes). If the current draw is above specification, the rotor is shorted. If the current draw is below specification, the rotor has high resistance or corroded connections or an open rotor winding.

If the rotor is found to be open, shorted (copper to copper), or grounded (copper to steel), the rotor must be replaced or repaired by a specialized shop. Loose connections at the rotor slip rings may be repaired by resoldering.

TESTING AN ALTERNATOR ROTOR USING AN OHMMETER

CHECKING FOR GROUNDS
(SHOULD READ INFINITY IF ROTOR IS <u>NOT</u> GROUNDED)

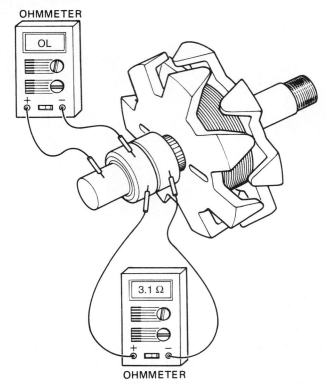

CHECKING FOR OPENS (IF INFINITY)
CHECKING FOR SHORTS (IF LOWER THAN SPECIFICATIONS)

FIGURE 11–37 Testing an alternator rotor using an ohmmeter.

NOTE: The cost of a replacement rotor may exceed the cost of an entire rebuilt alternator. Be certain, however, that the rebuilt alternator is rated at the same output as the original or higher.

TESTING THE STATOR

The stator must be disconnected from the diodes (rectifiers) before testing. Because all three windings of the stator are electrically connected (either wye or delta), a powered (110- or 12-volt) test light or an ohmmeter can be used to check a stator. There should be low resistance at all three stator leads (continuity), and the test light *should light*. There should *not* be continuity (in other words, there should be infinity ohms, or the test light should *not* light) when the stator is tested between any stator lead and the metal stator core. If there is continuity, the stator *is grounded* (short to ground) and must be repaired or replaced. See figure 11–38. Because the resistance is very

low for a normal stator, it is generally *not* possible to test for a *shorted* (copper-to-copper) stator. A shorted stator will, however, greatly reduce alternator output.

If all alternator components test okay and the output is still low, substitute a known-to-be-good stator and retest. If the stator is black or smells burned, check the vehicle for a discharged or defective battery. If battery voltage never reaches the voltage regulator cutoff point, the alternator will be continuously producing current in the stator windings. This continuous charging often overheats the stator.

If the stator is open, an ohmmeter cannot detect this if the stator is Delta wound. The ohmmeter will still indicate low resistance because all three windings are electrically connected. See figure 11–39.

TESTING THE DIODE TRIO

Many alternators are equipped with a diode trio. A diode is an electrical one-way check valve that permits current to flow in only one direction. Trio means three.

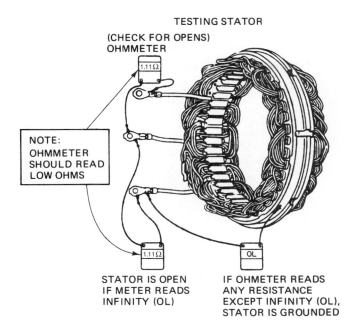

TESTING STATOR

(CHECK FOR OPENS)
OHMMETER

NOTE:
OHMMETER
SHOULD READ
LOW OHMS

STATOR IS OPEN
IF METER READS
INFINITY (OL)

IF OHMETER READS
ANY RESISTANCE
EXCEPT INFINITY (OL),
STATOR IS GROUNDED

FIGURE 11–38 If the ohmmeter reads infinity between any two of the three stator windings, the stator is open and, therefore, defective. The ohmmeter should read infinity between any stator lead and the steel laminations. If the reading is less than infinity, the stator is grounded. Stator windings can be tested if shorted because the normal resistance is very low.

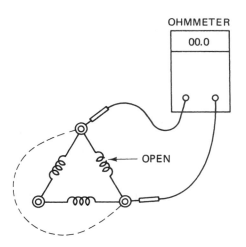

OHMMETER

00.0

OPEN

FIGURE 11–39 An open in a delta-wound stator cannot be detected using an ohmmeter.

A diode trio is three diodes connected together. See figure 11–40. The diode trio is connected to all three stator windings. The current generated in the stator flows through the diode trio to the internal voltage regulator. The diode trio is designed to supply current for the field (rotor) and turns off the charge indicator light whenever the alternator voltage equals or exceeds the battery voltage. If one of the three diodes in the diode trio

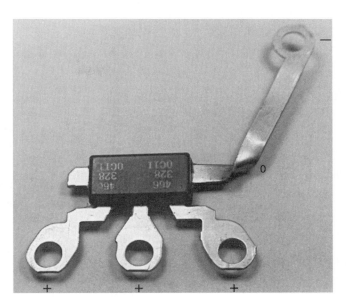

FIGURE 11–40 Typical diode trio. If one leg of a diode trio is open, the alternator may produce close to normal output, but the charge indicator light on the dash will be on dimly. The plus signs indicate the anodes, and the minus sign indicates the cathode terminal of the diodes.

is defective (usually open), the alternator may produce close to normal output; however, the charge indicator light will be on dimly.

A diode trio should be tested with a digital multimeter. The meter should be set to the *diode-check* position. The multimeter should indicate 0.5 to 0.7 volts one way and "OL" (over limit) after reversing the test leads and touching all three connectors of the diode trio.

TESTING THE RECTIFIER BRIDGE (DIODES)

Alternators are equipped with six diodes to convert the alternating current (AC) generated in the stator windings into direct current (DC) for use by the vehicle's battery and electrical components. The six diodes include three positive diodes and three negative diodes (one positive and one negative for each winding of the stator). These diodes can be individual diodes or grouped into a positive and a negative rectifier, each containing three diodes. All six diodes can be combined into one replaceable unit called a **rectifier bridge.** The rectifier(s) (diodes) should be tested using a multimeter that is set to "diode check" or "ohms."

Because a diode (rectifier) should allow current to flow in only one direction, each diode should be tested to determine if the diode allows current flow in one direction and blocks current flow in the opposite direction. To

FIGURE 11–41 Testing a GM alternator rectifier bridge containing six diodes in one unit. Notice that the test leads are connected to the top finned heat sink and the copper diode connector (not the stud). The test leads should be reversed and all six diodes tested.

FIGURE 11–42 Diodes being soldered to the stator on a Ford alternator.

◀ **TECH TIP** ▶

CHANGING PARTS TO LABOR

If a remanufactured alternator is installed on a vehicle, the technician usually gets paid only for the R & R (remove and replace) time to replace the unit. On a flat-rate or commission basis, the amount of time for each operation is published in time guides. The technician can receive a higher amount of flat-rate pay (for more time) if the alternator is repaired instead of being replaced as a unit. The customer also benefits, because the total bill is often lower than if the entire unit were replaced. Of course if severe damage is found inside the alternator, it still may be less expensive to replace the entire unit.

Many service facilities do not repair components because this operation requires a higher skill level of technician. Also, component parts may not be as readily available as complete replacement units. If all conditions are equal, it is still better to repair what you have and conserve resources by adhering to the "using it up and wearing it out" philosophy.

The technician benefits because the R & R time is the same for both methods, and additional time is paid for testing, servicing, and replacing defective components. Once experienced, the technician should spend little time testing and replacing only those components that are found to be defective.

test many alternator diodes, it may be necessary to unsolder the stator connections. Accurate testing is not possible unless the diodes are separated electrically from other alternator components. See figure 11–41. Connect the leads to the leads of the diode (pigtail and housing of the rectifier bridge). Read the meter. Reverse the test leads. A good diode should have high resistance (OL) one way (reverse bias) and low voltage drop (0.5 to 0.7 volts) the other way (forward bias).

An ohmmeter can also be used. If the ohmmeter reads low ohms (low voltage drop) in both directions, the diode is shorted. If the ohmmeter reads high ohms (OL) in both directions, the diode is open. Open or shorted diodes must be replaced. Most alternators group or combine all positive and all negative diodes in the one replaceable rectifier component. General Motors Delcotron alternators use a replaceable rectifier bridge containing all six diodes in one unit combined with a finned heat sink. Some Ford and other alternators also use six diodes in a single replaceable bridge. See figure 11–42.

TESTING THE VOLTAGE REGULATOR

Even though the voltage regulator can be tested on the vehicle with the engine running, the internal voltage regulator can also be tested using a special tester. See figure 11–43.

NOTE: On a GM alternator, the insulated screw is not installed in the correct location, either unregulated (maximum) output or zero output is the result.

FIGURE 11–43 Testing a GM SI internal voltage regulator using a voltage regulator tester. This tester can be used to test most internal and external electronic voltage regulators by using the appropriate adapter harness and test leads.

FIGURE 11–44 A brush holder assembly shown assembled in the alternator. The brush retainer is actually a straightened-out paper clip.

BRUSH HOLDER REPLACEMENT

Alternator carbon brushes often last for many years and require no scheduled maintenance. The life of the alternator brushes is extended because they conduct only the field (rotor) current, which is normally only 2 to 5 amperes. The alternator brushes should be inspected whenever the alternator is disassembled and should be replaced whenever worn to less than ½ inch in length. Alternator brushes are spring loaded, and if the springs are corroded or damaged, the brushes will not be able to keep constant contact with the slip rings of the rotor. If the brushes do not contact the slip rings, field current cannot create the magnetic field in the rotor that is necessary for current generation. Brushes are commonly purchased assembled together in a brush holder. After the brushes are installed (usually retained by two or three screws) and the rotor is installed in the alternator housing, a brush retainer pin can be pulled out through an access hole in the rear of the alternator, allowing the brushes to be pressed against the slip rings by the brush springs. See figure 11–44.

BEARING SERVICE AND REPLACEMENT

The bearing of an alternator must be able to support the rotor and reduce friction. An alternator must be able to rotate at up to 15,000 RPM and withstand the forces created by the drive belt. The front bearing is usually a ball bearing type and the rear is a smaller roller bearing. The front bearing is located under a retainer and pressed into the front alternator case. The pulley must be removed before the rotor can be separated from the case. Chrysler alternator press-fit pulleys must be removed using a puller, whereas Ford and General Motors alternators use a nut to hold the drive pulley to the rotor. The front pulley can be removed from most GM alternators by using a $^{15}/_{16}$-inch wrench while holding the rotor shaft to keep it from rotating using a $^{5}/_{16}$-inch hex (Allen) wrench.

The old or defective bearing can sometimes be pushed out of the front housing and the replacement pushed in by applying pressure with a socket or pipe against the outer edge of the bearing (outer race). Replacement bearings are usually prelubricated and sealed. Adding additional grease could cause overheating of the bearing by reducing heat transfer from the bearing surfaces to the alternator housing. Many alternator front bearings must be removed from the rotor using a special puller.

ALTERNATOR ASSEMBLY

After testing or servicing, the alternator rectifier(s), regulator, stator, and brush holder must be reassembled. If the brushes are internally mounted, insert a wire through the holes in the brush holder and in the alternator SRE frame to retain the brushes for reassembly. Install the rotor and drive-end frame in proper alignment with the mark made on the outside of the alternator housing. Install the through-bolts. Before removing the wire pin holding the brushes, spin the alternator pulley. If the alternator is noisy or not rotating freely, the alternator can easily be disassembled again to check for the cause. After making certain the alternator is free to rotate, remove the brush holder pin and spin the alternator again by hand. The noise level may be slightly higher with the brushes released onto the slip rings.

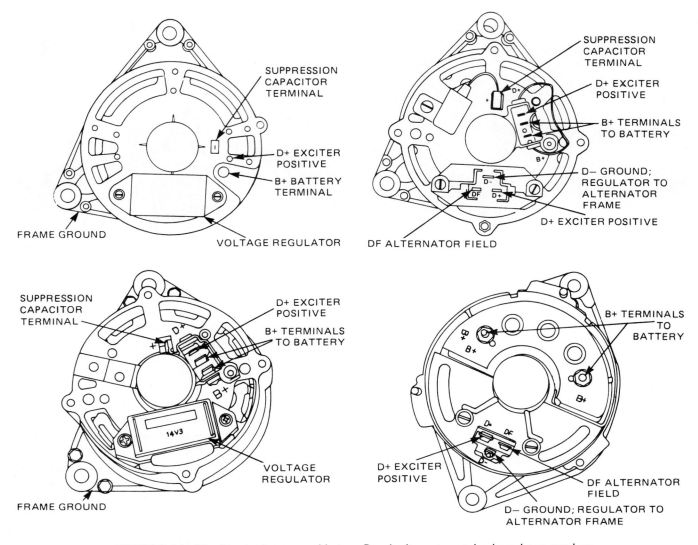

FIGURE 11–45 Bosch alternators. Various Bosch alternator styles have been used on various models and years of Audi, BMW, Mercedes, Porsche, Volvo, and VW vehicles. (*Courtesy of Arrow Automotive Industries*)

Alternators should be tested on a bench tester, if available, before they are reinstalled on a vehicle. When installing the alternator on the vehicle, be certain that all mounting bolts and nuts are tight. The battery terminal should be covered with a plastic or rubber protective cap to help prevent accidental shorting to ground, which could seriously damage the alternator.

REMANUFACTURED ALTERNATORS

Remanufactured or rebuilt alternators are totally disassembled and rebuilt. Even though there are many smaller rebuilders who may not replace all worn parts, the major national remanufacturers *totally* remanufacture the alternator. Old alternators (called **cores**) are totally disassembled and cleaned. Both bearings are replaced and all components tested. Rotors are rewound to original specifications if required. The rotor windings are not counted but are rewound on the rotor "spool," using the correct-gauge copper wire, to the *weight* specified by the original manufacturer. New slip rings are replaced as required and soldered to the rotor spool windings and machined. The rotors are also balanced and measured to ensure that the outside diameter of the rotor meets specifications. An undersized rotor will produce less alternator output because the field must be close to the stator windings for maximum output. *Individual* diodes (within the rectifiers) are re-

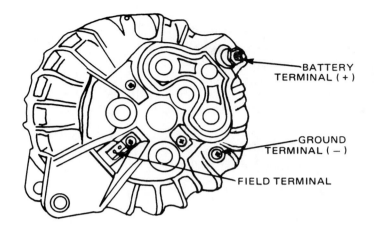

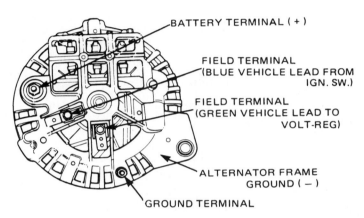

FIGURE 11–46   Chrysler alternators. (*Courtesy of Arrow Automotive Industries*)

placed if required. Every alternator is then assembled and tested for proper output, boxed, and shipped to a warehouse. Individual parts stores (called **jobbers**) purchase parts from various regional or local warehouses.

ALTERNATOR DRAWINGS

See figures 11–45 through 11–59 for line drawings of alternators produced by most of the manufacturers. These drawings can help identify the exact model being tested or serviced. All electrical connector identifications are also included to aid in troubleshooting charging system problems. Consult service literature for exact servicing procedures for the vehicle being serviced. See chapter 5 for circuit code letter designations for European and Japanese wiring connectors.

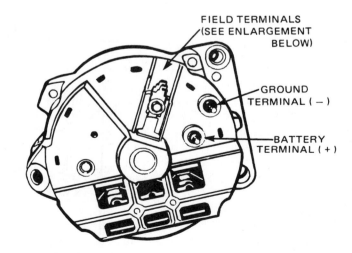

FIGURE 11–47   Chrysler 100-amperes alternator. (*Courtesy of Arrow Automotive Industries*)

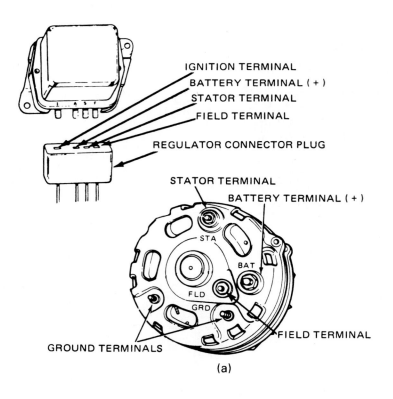

(a)

(b)

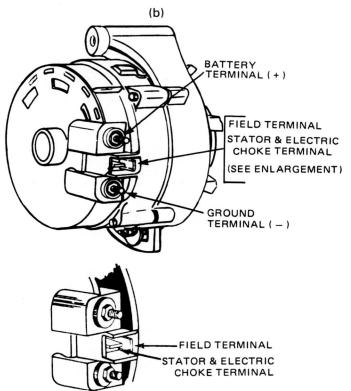

FIGURE 11–48 Ford alternators. A, Rear terminal alternator. B, Side terminal alternator. (*Courtesy of Arrow Automotive Industries*)

FORD

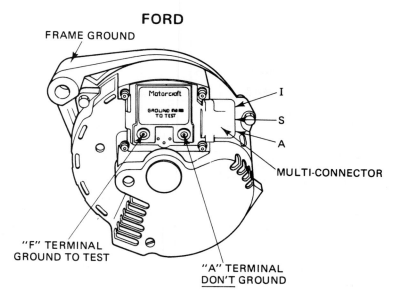

FRAME GROUND

Motorcraft
GROUND ■■■
TO TEST

I

S

A

MULTI-CONNECTOR

"F" TERMINAL
GROUND TO TEST

"A" TERMINAL
DON'T GROUND

USES INTEGRAL ELECTRONIC VOLTAGE REGULATOR "A"-TYPE CIRCUIT

FIGURE 11–49 Ford IAR alternator. (*Courtesy of Arrow Automotive Industries*)

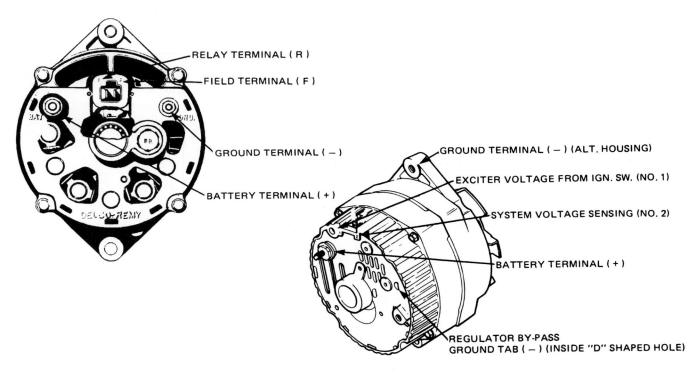

RELAY TERMINAL (R)

FIELD TERMINAL (F)

GROUND TERMINAL (–)

BATTERY TERMINAL (+)

GROUND TERMINAL (–) (ALT. HOUSING)

EXCITER VOLTAGE FROM IGN. SW. (NO. 1)

SYSTEM VOLTAGE SENSING (NO. 2)

BATTERY TERMINAL (+)

REGULATOR BY-PASS
GROUND TAB (–) (INSIDE "D" SHAPED HOLE)

FIGURE 11–50 General Motors (Delcotron) alternator. (*Courtesy of Arrow Automotive Industries*)

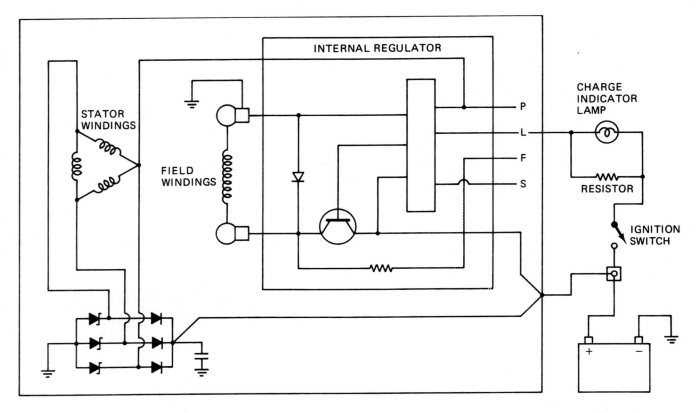

USES INTEGRAL REGULATOR (B-TYPE)
P TERMINAL = STATOR CONNECTION (TACHOMETER CONNECTION ON SOME MODELS)
L CHARGE INDICATOR LAMP (USED ON ALL VEHICLES) (COMPUTER CONTROLLED ON SOME MODELS)
F FIELD POSITIVE (DIAGNOSTICS ON SOME MODELS)
S BATTERY SENSING TERMINAL (SOME MODELS)

FIGURE 11–51   General Motors Delcotron CS alternator. (*Courtesy of Arrow Automotive Industries*)

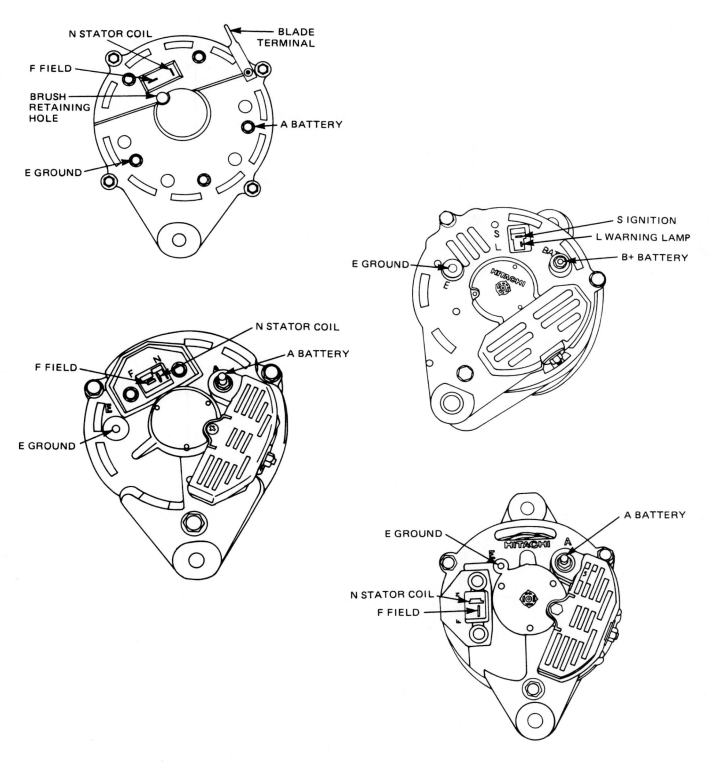

FIGURE 11–52 Hitachi alternators. Used on various models and years of Honda, Nissan (Datsun), and Subaru vehicles. *(Courtesy of Arrow Automotive Industries)*

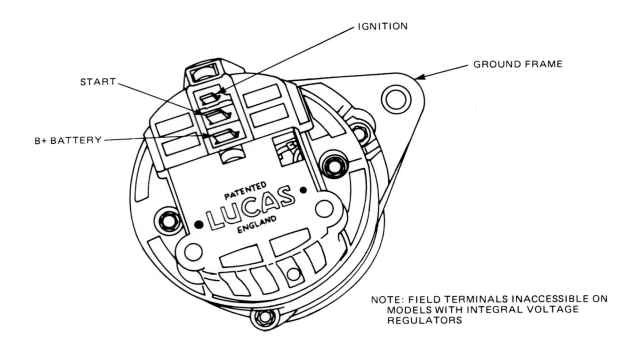

IGNITION

START

B+ BATTERY

GROUND FRAME

PATENTED
LUCAS
ENGLAND

NOTE: FIELD TERMINALS INACCESSIBLE ON
MODELS WITH INTEGRAL VOLTAGE
REGULATORS

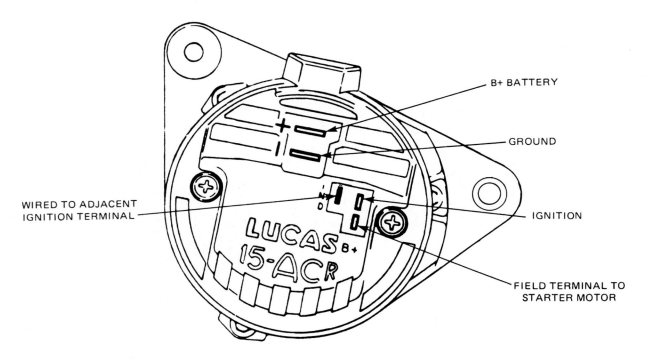

B+ BATTERY

GROUND

WIRED TO ADJACENT
IGNITION TERMINAL

IGNITION

LUCAS
15-ACR

FIELD TERMINAL TO
STARTER MOTOR

FIGURE 11–53   Lucas alternators. Used on various makes and years of British-built vehicles. (*Courtesy of Arrow Automotive Industries*)

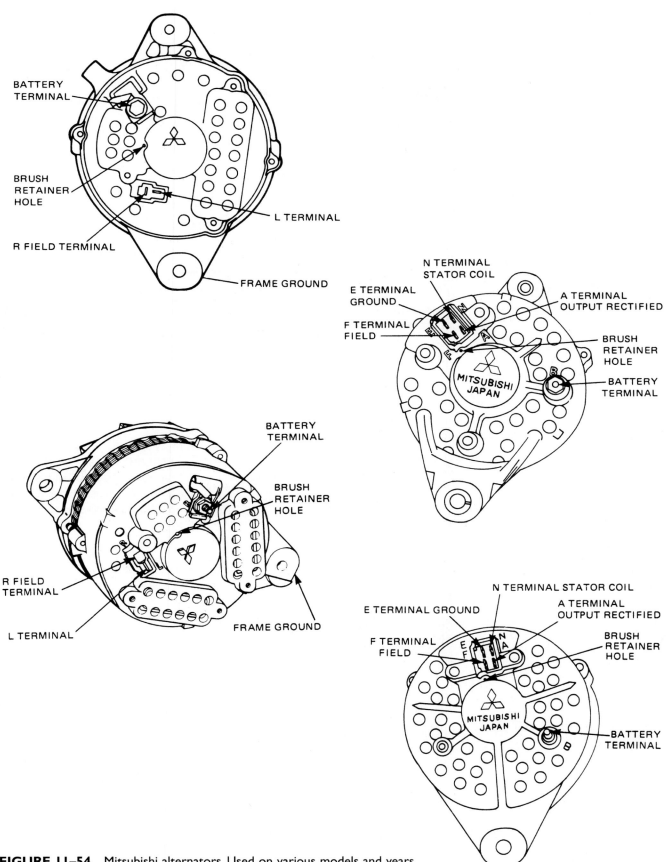

FIGURE 11–54 Mitsubishi alternators. Used on various models and years of Chrysler, Mazda, and Mitsubishi vehicles. *(Courtesy of Arrow Automotive Industries)*

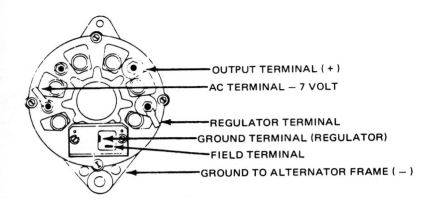

OUTPUT TERMINAL (+)
AC TERMINAL – 7 VOLT

REGULATOR TERMINAL
GROUND TERMINAL (REGULATOR)
FIELD TERMINAL
GROUND TO ALTERNATOR FRAME (–)

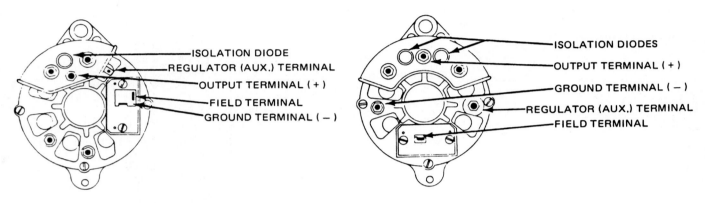

ISOLATION DIODE
REGULATOR (AUX.) TERMINAL
OUTPUT TERMINAL (+)
FIELD TERMINAL
GROUND TERMINAL (–)

ISOLATION DIODES
OUTPUT TERMINAL (+)
GROUND TERMINAL (–)
REGULATOR (AUX.) TERMINAL
FIELD TERMINAL

FIGURE 11–55 Motorola alternators. Used on American Motors, Jeep, and other vehicles. (*Courtesy of Arrow Automotive Industries*)

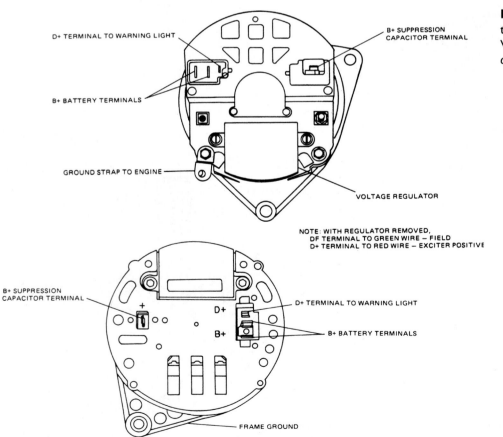

D+ TERMINAL TO WARNING LIGHT

B+ SUPPRESSION CAPACITOR TERMINAL

B+ BATTERY TERMINALS

GROUND STRAP TO ENGINE

VOLTAGE REGULATOR

NOTE: WITH REGULATOR REMOVED,
DF TERMINAL TO GREEN WIRE – FIELD
D+ TERMINAL TO RED WIRE – EXCITER POSITIVE

FIGURE 11–56 Motorola alternators. Used on Audi, Mercedes, VW, and Porsche vehicles. (*Courtesy of Arrow Automotive Industries*)

B+ SUPPRESSION CAPACITOR TERMINAL

D+
B+

D+ TERMINAL TO WARNING LIGHT

B+ BATTERY TERMINALS

FRAME GROUND

NOTE: WITH REGULATOR REMOVED,
DF TERMINAL TO GREEN WIRE – FIELD
D+ TERMINAL TO RED WIRE – EXCITER POSITIVE

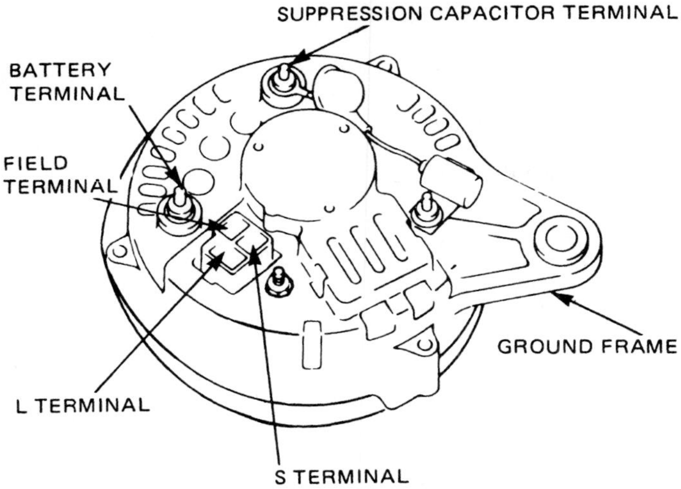

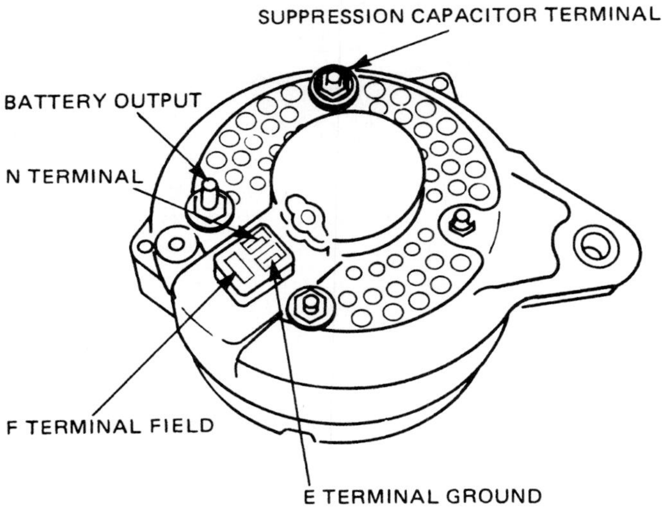

SUPPRESSION CAPACITOR TERMINAL

BATTERY TERMINAL

FIELD TERMINAL

GROUND FRAME

L TERMINAL

S TERMINAL

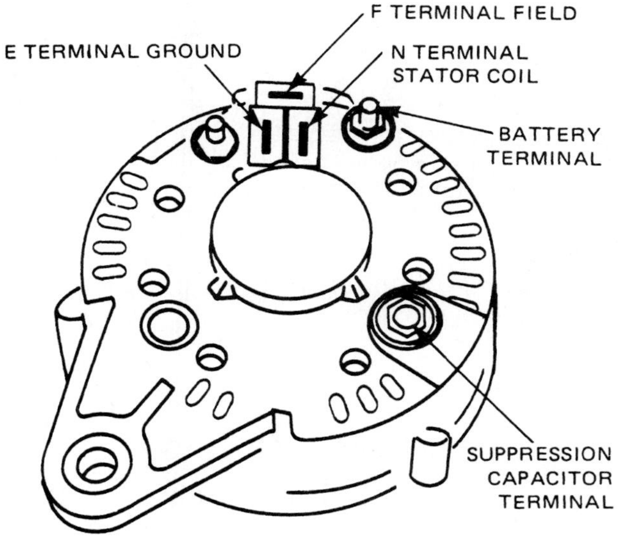

E TERMINAL GROUND

F TERMINAL FIELD

N TERMINAL STATOR COIL

BATTERY TERMINAL

SUPPRESSION CAPACITOR TERMINAL

SUPPRESSION CAPACITOR TERMINAL

BATTERY OUTPUT

N TERMINAL

F TERMINAL FIELD

E TERMINAL GROUND

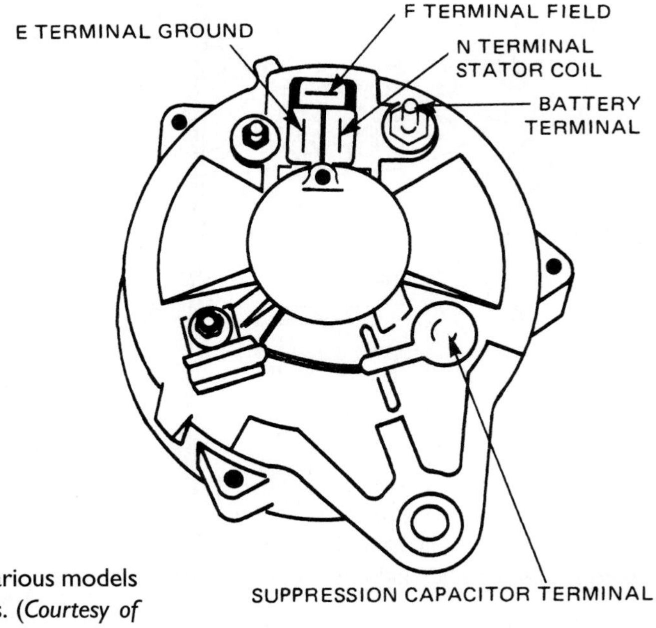

E TERMINAL GROUND

F TERMINAL FIELD

N TERMINAL STATOR COIL

BATTERY TERMINAL

SUPPRESSION CAPACITOR TERMINAL

FIGURE 11–57 Nippondenso (Denso) alternators. Used on various models and years of Toyota, Honda, and some Chrysler MMC products. (*Courtesy of Arrow Automotive Industries*)

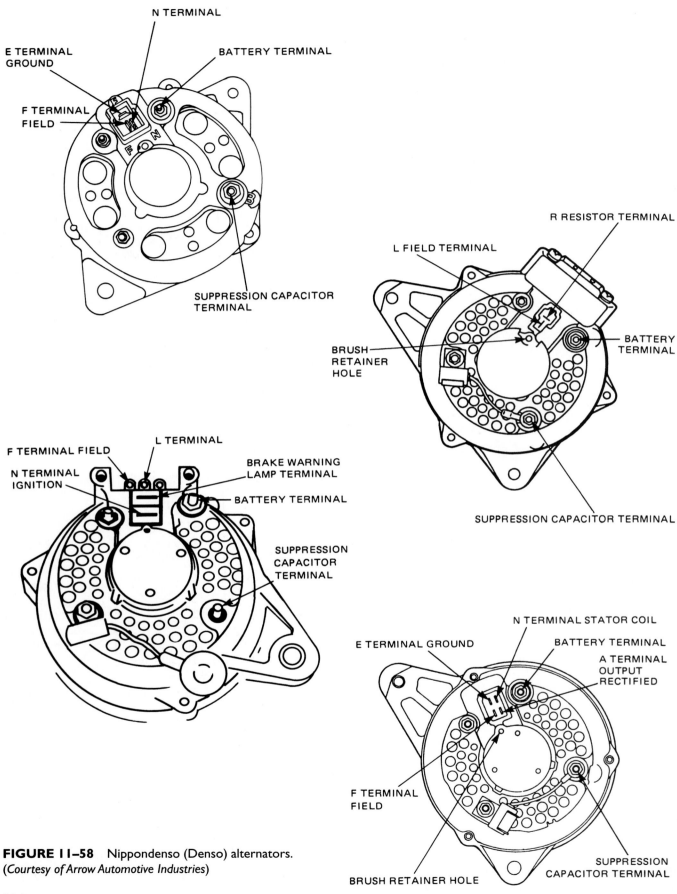

N TERMINAL

E TERMINAL
GROUND

BATTERY TERMINAL

F TERMINAL
FIELD

SUPPRESSION CAPACITOR
TERMINAL

R RESISTOR TERMINAL

L FIELD TERMINAL

BRUSH
RETAINER
HOLE

BATTERY
TERMINAL

SUPPRESSION CAPACITOR TERMINAL

F TERMINAL FIELD

L TERMINAL

N TERMINAL
IGNITION

BRAKE WARNING
LAMP TERMINAL

BATTERY TERMINAL

SUPPRESSION
CAPACITOR
TERMINAL

E TERMINAL GROUND

N TERMINAL STATOR COIL

BATTERY TERMINAL

A TERMINAL
OUTPUT
RECTIFIED

F TERMINAL
FIELD

BRUSH RETAINER HOLE

SUPPRESSION
CAPACITOR
TERMINAL

FIGURE 11–58 Nippondenso (Denso) alternators.
(*Courtesy of Arrow Automotive Industries*)

214

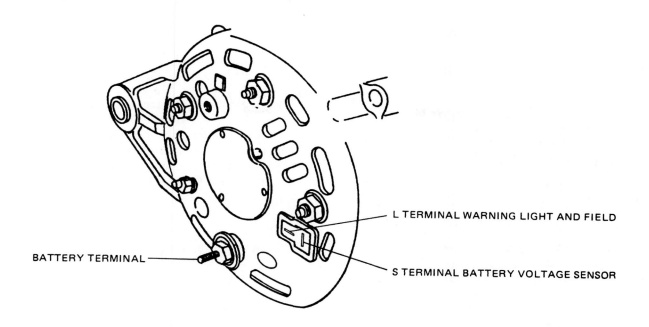

L TERMINAL WARNING LIGHT AND FIELD

BATTERY TERMINAL

S TERMINAL BATTERY VOLTAGE SENSOR

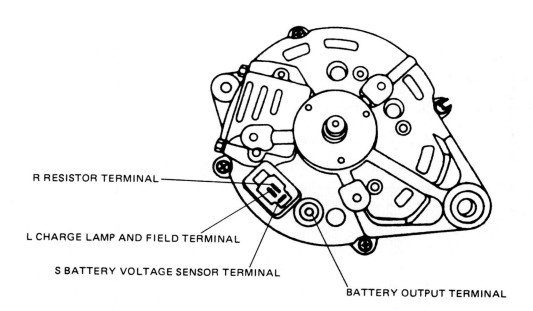

R RESISTOR TERMINAL

L CHARGE LAMP AND FIELD TERMINAL

S BATTERY VOLTAGE SENSOR TERMINAL

BATTERY OUTPUT TERMINAL

FIGURE 11–59 Nissan (Datsun) alternators. (*Courtesy of Arrow Automotive Industries*)

◀ TECH TIP ▶

THE WEAK, BUT GOOD ALTERNATOR

An 80-ampere alternator was tested at 2000 engine RPM and found to be producing only 69 amperes. The recommended specification for an alternator is that the output should be within 10% of the rated output. Ten percent of 80 amperes is 8 amperes; therefore, the minimum recommended output is 72 amperes (80 − 8 = 72). Because 69 amperes is less than 72 amperes, the alternator should be serviced (repaired or replaced). However, because the test result was so close to the specifications, it was decided that a "charging system requirement test" should be performed. This test determines the electrical load of the vehicle that may be required on a continuous basis. The test procedure is simple: Turn on everything electrical, except the horn or other short-term electrical accessories. Add 5 amperes to the reading and the result is the minimum current required of the alternator.

The electrical demand test indicated that only 49 amperes was needed. Add 5 amperes (49 + 5 = 54), and you see that a 54-ampere alternator is all that is needed. Because the original alternator is capable of 69 amperes, it is more than adequate for the vehicle.

SUMMARY

1. Charging system testing requires that the battery be at least 75% charged to be assured of accurate test results. The charge indicator light should be on with the ignition switch on, but should go out whenever the engine is running. Normal charging voltage (at 2000 engine RPM) is 13.5 to 15.0 volts.

2. If the charging system is not charging properly, the rear bearing of the alternator should be checked for magnetism. If the rear bearing is magnetized, the voltage regulator, brushes, and alternator rotor are functioning correctly. If the rear bearing is not magnetized, the voltage regulator, alternator brushes, or rotor is not functioning. Bypass the voltage regulator by supplying battery voltage to the field. If the rear bearing is now magnetized and the charging system output is normal, the voltage regulator is at fault.

3. To check for excessive resistance in the wiring between the alternator and the battery, a voltage-drop test should be performed.

4. Electricity is lazy, because it always travels the path of least resistance. Alternators are also lazy, because they do not produce their maximum-rated output unless it is required by circuit demands. Therefore, to test for maximum alternator output, the battery must be loaded to force the alternator to produce its maximum output.

◀ DIAGNOSTIC STORY ▶

THE 2-MINUTE ALTERNATOR REPAIR

A Chevrolet pickup truck was brought to a dealer for routine service. The owner stated that the battery required a jump-start after a weekend of sitting. Almost immediately, the technician who was assigned to service the truck found a slightly loose alternator belt. The belt felt tight (less than $1/2$ inch of deflection), yet the alternator cooling fan blade could be turned by hand. After retensioning the alternator drive belt, the technician tested the battery and charging system voltage using a small handheld digital multimeter. The battery voltage was 12.4 volts (about 75% charged), but the charging voltage was also 12.4 volts at 2000 RPM. Because normal charging voltage should be 13.5 to 15.0 volts, it was obvious that the charging system was not operating correctly.

The technician checked the dash and found that the "charge" light was not on even though the rear bearing was not magnetized, indicating that the voltage regulator was not working. Before removing the alternator for service, the technician checked the wiring connection on the alternator. When the two-lead regulator connector was removed, the connector was discovered to be rusty. After the contacts were cleaned, the charging system was restored to normal operation. The technician had learned that the simple things should always be checked first before tearing into a big (or expensive) repair.

◀ TECH TIP ▶

HELP!

A technician wanted help in determining what the alternator output should be on a Toyota truck. If the alternator is protected by a fuse, check the fuse rating as shown in figure 11–60. In this case, the fuse was listed as being 80 amperes. The 80% rule states that the maximum current in a circuit should not exceed 80% of the fuse rating. Eighty percent of 80 amperes is 64 amperes. The alternator output was measured to be 62 amperes, well within the normal range of within 10% of specifications (10% of 64 is 6.4 amperes).

FIGURE 11–60 The fusible link (or fuse) rating for the charging circuit should be greater than the alternator output by 20%. Therefore, the maximum alternator output should be 80% of the fuse rating or 64 amperes.

5. Each alternator should be marked across its case before disassembly to ensure proper clock position during reassembly. After disassembly, all alternator internal components should be tested using a con-

◀ DIAGNOSTIC STORY ▶

THE COLD WEATHER CHARGE LAMP PROBLEM

A customer brought his vehicle (Ford) to an independent service facility complaining that occasionally, whenever the temperatures dropped below 10° F (-12° C), his charge indicator lamp stayed on until he had driven for several minutes.

The customer left the vehicle overnight and the technician observed that, indeed, the charge lamp was on after starting the vehicle the next morning. The technician immediately got out of the vehicle, opened the hood, and checked to see if the rear bearing was magnetized—it was not. After a few minutes of operation, the charge lamp went out and the rear alternator bearing *was* magnetized. The technician then knew that the problem was sticking alternator brushes. The brushes had worn to less than one-half length, and the springs were not strong enough, when cold, to exert sufficient pressure on the rotor slip rings to conduct the current for the field (rotor). After the technician replaced the brushes and cleaned and checked all other alternator components, the problem never recurred.

tinuity light or an ohmmeter. The components that should be tested are the following:
  a. Stator
  b. Rotor
  c. Diodes
  d. Diode trio (if the alternator is so equipped)
  e. Bearings
  f. Brushes (should be more than $1/2$ inch in length)
6. Electronic voltage regulators can be tested either off the vehicle using a special tester or on the vehicle using the full-field bypass procedure.

REVIEW QUESTIONS

1. Describe how a small electronic voltage regulator can control the output of a typical 100-ampere alternator.

2. Describe how to test the voltage drop of the charging circuit.

3. Discuss how to measure the amperage output of an alternator.

4. Explain how testing can be used to determine whether a diode or stator is defective before removing the alternator from the vehicle.

MULTIPLE-CHOICE QUESTIONS

1. Technician A says that the diodes regulate the alternator output voltage. Technician B says that the field current can be computer controlled. Which technician is correct?
   a. A only
   b. B only
   c. Both a and b
   d. Neither a nor b

2. A magnetic field is created in the _____ in an alternator (AC generator).
   a. Stator
   b. Diodes
   c. Rotor
   d. Drive-end frame

3. The voltage regulator controls the current _____ .
   a. Through the alternator brushes
   b. Through the rotor
   c. Through the alternator field
   d. All of the above

4. Technician A says that two diodes are required for each stator winding lead. Technician B says that diodes change alternating current into direct current. Which technician is correct?
   a. A only
   b. B only
   c. Both a and b
   d. Neither a nor b

5. An acceptable charging circuit voltage on a 12-volt system is _____ .
   a. 13.5 to 15.0 volts
   b. 12.6 to 15.6 volts
   c. 12 to 14 volts
   d. 14.9 to 16.1 volts

6. Technician A says that by full-fielding the alternator, you are bypassing the voltage regulator. Technician B says that voltage regulators control the alternator output by controlling the field current through the rotor. Which technician is correct?
   a. A only
   b. B only
   c. Both a and b
   d. Neither a nor b

7. Technician A says that a voltage-drop test of the charging circuit should only be performed when current is flowing through the circuit. Technician B says to connect the leads of a voltmeter to the positive and negative terminals of the battery to measure the voltage drop of the charging system. Which technician is correct?
   a. A only
   b. B only
   c. Both a and b
   d. Neither a nor b

8. When an alternator rotor is checked, if an ohmmeter shows zero ohms between the slip rings and the rotor shaft, the rotor is _____ .
   a. Okay (normal)
   b. Defective (grounded)
   c. Defective (shorted)
   d. Okay (rotor windings are open)

9. An alternator diode is being tested using a digital multimeter set to the diode-check position. A good diode will read _____ if the leads are connected one way across the diode and _____ if the leads are reversed.
   a. 300; 300
   b. 0.575; 0.575
   c. OL; OL
   d. 0.651; OL

10. An alternator (AC generator) could test as producing lower than normal output, yet be okay, if _____ .
    a. The battery is weak or defective
    b. The engine speed is not high enough during testing
    c. The drive belt is loose or slipping
    d. All of the above

◀ Chapter 12 ▶

ELECTRONIC AND DISTRIBUTORLESS IGNITION OPERATION

OBJECTIVES

After studying chapter 12, the reader will be able to

1. List the parts of the ignition system.
2. Describe how the ignition system creates high-voltage sparks.
3. Discuss the purpose and function of pickup coils and crankshaft sensors.
4. Explain the purpose and function of the ignition module.

All spark ignition engines require a high-voltage spark at the spark plug to ignite the air-fuel mixture in the cylinders of the engine. It is the purpose and function of the ignition system to create and distribute the high-voltage spark.

IGNITION SYSTEM OPERATION

The ignition system includes components and wiring necessary to create and distribute a high voltage (up to 40,000 volts or more). All ignition systems apply voltage close to battery voltage to the positive side of the ignition coil and pulse the negative side to ground. Whenever the coil negative lead is grounded, the primary (low-voltage) circuit of the coil is complete and a magnetic field is created by the coil windings. When the

circuit is opened, the magnetic field collapses and induces a high-voltage spark from the secondary winding of the ignition coil. Early ignition systems used a mechanically opened set of contact points to make and break the electrical connection to ground. Electronic ignition uses a sensor such as a pickup coil or trigger to signal an electronic module that makes and breaks the primary connection of the ignition coil.

NOTE: *Distributor ignition* (DI) is the term specified by the Society of Automotive Engineers (SAE) for an ignition system that uses a distributor. *Electronic ignition* (EI) is the term specified by the Society of Automotive Engineers for an ignition system that does not use a distributor.

IGNITION COILS

The heart of any ignition system is the ignition coil. The coil creates a high-voltage spark by electromagnetic induction. Most ignition coils contain two separate but electrically connected windings of copper wire. Other coils are true transformers in which the primary and secondary windings are not electrically connected. See figure 12–1.

The center of an ignition coil contains a core of laminated soft iron (thin strips of soft iron). This core increases the magnetic strength of the coil. Surrounding the laminated core are approximately 20,000 turns of fine wire (approximately 42 gauge). These windings are

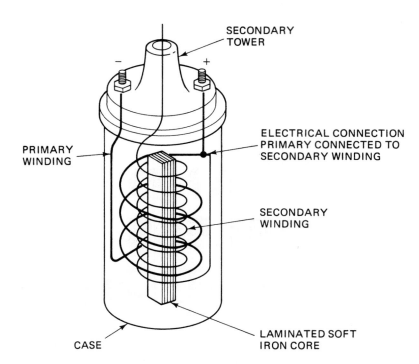

FIGURE 12–1   Internal construction of an oil-cooled ignition coil. Notice that the primary winding is electrically connected to the secondary winding. The polarity (positive or negative) of a coil is determined by the direction in which the coil is wound.

called the **secondary** coil windings. Surrounding the secondary windings are approximately 150 turns of heavy wire (approximately 21 gauge). These windings are called the **primary** coil windings. In many coils, these windings are surrounded with a thin metal shield and insulating paper and placed into a metal container. The metal container and shield help retain the magnetic field produced in the coil windings. The primary and secondary windings produce heat because of the electrical resistance in the turns of wire. Many coils contain oil to help cool the ignition coil. Other coil designs, such as those used on GM's HEI systems, use an air-cooled, epoxy-sealed **E coil.** It is called an E coil because the laminated soft-iron core is E-shaped, with the coil wire turns wrapped around the center "finger" of the E and the primary winding wrapped inside the secondary winding. See figure 12–2.

The primary windings of the coil extend through the case of the coil and are labeled as positive and negative. The positive terminal of the coil attaches to the ignition switch, which supplies current from the positive battery terminal. The negative terminal is attached to an electronic ignition module (igniter), which opens and closes the primary ignition circuit by opening or closing the ground return path of the circuit. With the ignition switch on, current should be available at *both* the positive terminal and the negative terminal of the coil if the primary windings of the coil have continuity. The labeling of positive (+) and negative (−) of the coil indicates that the positive terminal is *more* positive (closer to the

positive terminal of the battery) than the negative terminal of the coil. This is called the coil **polarity.** The polarity of the coil must be correct to ensure that electrons will flow from the hot center electrode of the spark plug. *The polarity of an ignition coil is determined by the direction of rotation of the coil windings.* The correct polarity is then indicated on the primary terminals of the coil. If the coil primary leads are reversed, the voltage required to fire the spark plugs is increased by 40%. The coil output voltage is directly proportional to the ratio of primary to secondary turns of wire used in the coil.

SELF-INDUCTION

Whenever current starts to flow into a coil, an opposing current is created in the windings of the coil. This opposing current generation is caused by self-induction and is called **inductive reactance.** Inductive reactance is similar to resistance because it opposes any increase in current flow in a coil. Therefore, whenever an ignition coil is first energized, there is a slight delay of approximately 0.01 seconds before the ignition coil reaches its maximum magnetic field strength. The point at which a coil's maximum magnetic field strength is reached is called **saturation.** Also see chapter 1 for details on self-induction.

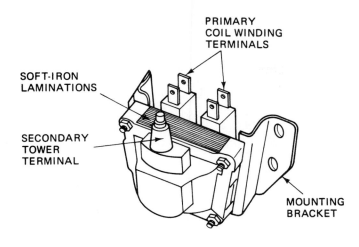

PRIMARY
COIL WINDING
TERMINALS

SOFT-IRON
LAMINATIONS

SECONDARY
TOWER
TERMINAL

MOUNTING
BRACKET

FIGURE 12–2   Typical air-cooled epoxy-filled E coil.

MUTUAL INDUCTION

In an ignition coil there are two windings, a primary and a secondary winding. Whenever there is a *change* in the magnetic field of one coil winding, there is a change in the other coil winding. Therefore, if the current is stopped from flowing (circuit is opened), the collapsing magnetic field cuts across the turns of the secondary winding and creates a high voltage in the secondary winding. The collapsing magnetic field also creates a voltage of up to 250 volts in the *primary* winding. See chapter 1 for details on mutual induction.

HOW IGNITION COILS CREATE 40,000 VOLTS

All ignition systems use electromagnetic induction to produce a high-voltage spark from the ignition coil. Electromagnetic induction means that a current can be created in a conductor (coil winding) by a moving magnetic field. The magnetic field in an ignition coil is produced by current flowing through the primary windings of the coil. The current for the primary winding is supplied through the ignition switch to the positive terminal of the ignition coil. The negative terminal is connected to the ground return through the use of movable mechanical ignition points or through an electronic ignition module.

If the primary circuit is completed, current (approximately 2 to 6 amperes) can flow through the primary coil windings. This creates a strong magnetic field inside the coil. When the primary coil winding ground return path connection is opened, the magnetic field *collapses* and induces a high-voltage (20,000- to 40,000-volt) low-amperage (20- to 80-milliampere) current in

the secondary coil windings. This high-voltage pulse flows through the coil wire (if the vehicle is so equipped), distributor cap, rotor, and spark plug wires to the spark plugs. For each spark that occurs, the coil must be charged with a magnetic field and then discharged. The ignition components that regulate the current in the coil primary winding by turning it on and off are known collectively as the **primary ignition circuit.** All of the components necessary to create and distribute the high voltage produced in the secondary windings of the coil are called the **secondary ignition circuit.** The components in each of these circuits include the following:

Primary Ignition Circuit

1. Battery
2. Ignition switch
3. Primary windings of the coil
4. Pickup coil (crank sensor)
5. Ignition module (igniter)

Secondary Ignition Circuit

1. Secondary windings of coil
2. Distributor cap and rotor (if the vehicle is so equipped)
3. Spark plug wires
4. Spark plugs

In vehicles that use a computer for ignition control, the computer does not operate the ignition coils directly, but instead controls when the ignition module should trigger the ignition coil(s) for optimum performance and fuel economy with lowest possible exhaust emissions. Many engines equipped with a distributor use a pickup coil to trigger the module.

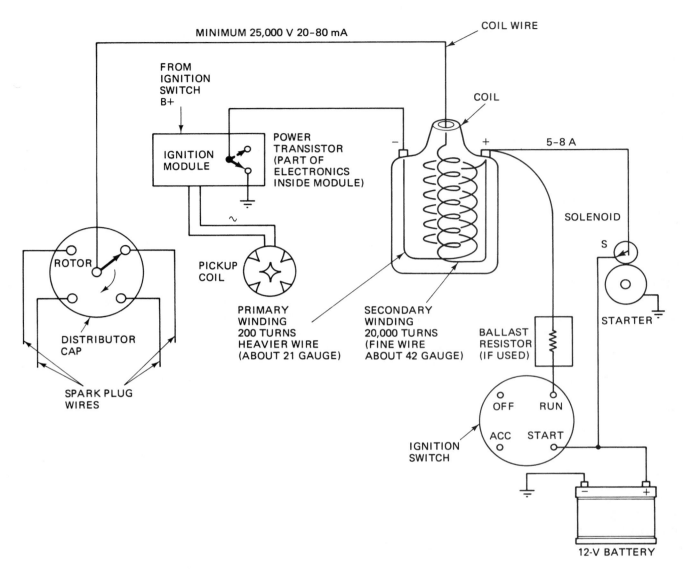

FIGURE 12–3 Typical primary and secondary electronic ignition using a ballast resistor and a distributor. To protect the ignition coil from overheating at lower engine speeds, many electronic ignitions do not use a ballast resistor, but use electronic circuits within the module.

The generic name for a pickup coil is a **pulse generator** because it creates a voltage pulse that is sent to the electronic ignition module.

ELECTRONIC IGNITION PRINCIPLES OF OPERATION

All inductive ignition systems use ignition coils to store electromagnetic energy. When the power to the coil is interrupted (opened), the stored energy in the coil discharges a high-voltage pulse from the secondary windings. This high-voltage, low-amperage electrical spark is conducted to the spark plug, and the electrical arc provides the ignition energy to ignite the air-fuel mixture.

With most electronic ignition systems, the positive side of the ignition coil is connected to full battery voltage through the ignition switch. The negative side of the coil is connected to the ignition module. It is the module that controls the current through the ignition coil (turns on and off the primary current). See figure 12–3.

The module must, itself, be triggered as to when to trigger the coil (turn on and off the coil primary current path). The trigger for the module is the pickup coil in the distributor or crankshaft sensor. To summarize:

1. The pickup coil or crankshaft sensor triggers the module.
2. The module triggers the ignition coil.
3. The ignition coil being turned on and off produces a high-voltage spark.

Since the early 1980s, most electronic ignition systems have also been controlled by the engine management computer. The computer controls ignition timing. Ignition timing is a matter of when the spark occurs in relation to the piston position. The computer receives a pulsing signal from the ignition module that corresponds to the engine speed (RPM) and piston position (through the pickup coil or crankshaft sensor). The computer calculates the best ignition timing based on information and values from all of its sensors and returns a pulse signal to the ignition module. This computer pulse is used by the module to trigger the ignition coil.

PULSE GENERATORS

A pulse generator consists of the following:

1. A permanent magnet (stationary part)
2. A pole piece (stationary part)
3. A reluctor (rotating part)

All three units occupy the area in the distributor below the rotor.

The component parts of a pulse generator differ among various manufacturers. Some of the terms commonly used are given in the following table.

Manufacturer	Stationary pickup coil	Rotating trigger wheel
Chrysler	Pickup coil	Reluctor
Ford	Stator	Armature
GM	Pole piece and magnetic pickup	Timer core

Surrounding the pickup coil is a magnetic field formed by the permanent magnet. When a conductor comes close to the magnetic lines of force, the **reluctance** (resistance to the magnetic lines of force) decreases. Therefore, the movable armature is often called a **reluctor** because it decreases the reluctance of the magnetic field surrounding the pickup coil. See figures 12–4 and 12–5.

As the armature "tooth" approaches the center of the stator, a strong magnetic field begins to build around the magnetic pickup, permitting the primary coil current to flow across the emitter-base circuit through the magnetic pickup to ground. This allows the ignition coil to build up a strong magnetic field. When the reluctor tooth passes the center of the magnetic pickup and starts away from it, it reverses the induced voltage and turns off the "base" of the switching transistor. This, in turn, switches off the emitter-collector circuit of the transistor and turns off the primary ignition coil current. The very rapid cutoff of primary current collapses the magnetic field in the ignition coil to produce the high secondary voltage required to fire the spark plug.

HALL-EFFECT SENSORS

The **Hall effect** was discovered by Edwin H. Hall (1855–1938) in 1879. He found that when a thin rectangular gold conductor, carrying a current, was crossed at right angles by a magnetic field, a difference of potential was produced at the edges of the gold conductor. Modern Hall-effect units use semiconductor material (usually silicon) instead of gold. See figure 12–6.

The Hall effect can be used as a very accurate electronic switch when a moving metallic shutter blocks the magnetic field from striking the semiconductor. Whenever the opening of the shutter allows the magnetic field to strike the sensor, a small voltage is produced and is sent to the electronic control unit. As the distributor rotates, a blocking shutter blocks the magnetic field and the current stops flowing from the sensor. The electronic control unit can be designed to either turn on or turn off the ignition coil primary current when the shutter blades (vanes) are blocking. See figure 12–7. Hall-effect ignition is used by many manufacturers, including Ford, GM, Chrysler, and many import brand vehicle manufacturers. The advantage of the Hall effect over the magnetic pulse generator is its accuracy. The Hall effect can easily trigger the ignition to within ±¼ degree of distributor rotation.

Not all Hall-effect sensors use a vane to shunt the magnetic lines of force. See figure 12–8 for examples of Hall-effect sensors that trigger off of notches or slots as used by Chrysler Corporation. A magnet is part of the sensor. As a notch or slot passes near the Hall-effect sensor, the strength of the magnetic field inside the sensor changes. The engine controller (computer) sends an 8-volt signal to the sensor. When a solid area is in line with the sensor, a low voltage (almost 0 volts) is sent to the controller. Then when a notched section of the camshaft or crankshaft passes by the sensor, a 5-volt signal is sent to the controller.

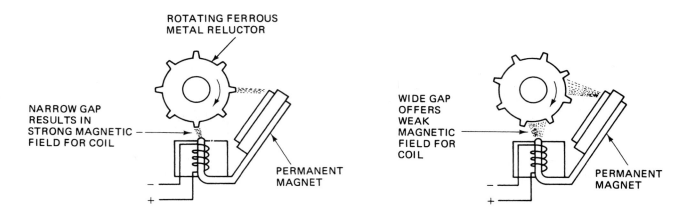

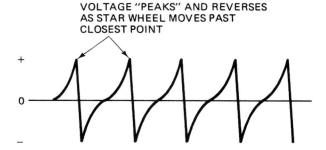

FIGURE 12–4   Operation of a typical pulse generator (pickup coil). At the bottom is a line drawing of a typical scope pattern of the output voltage of a pickup coil. The module receives this voltage from the pickup coil and opens the ground circuit to the ignition coil when the voltage starts down from its peak (just as the reluctor teeth start moving away from the pickup coil).

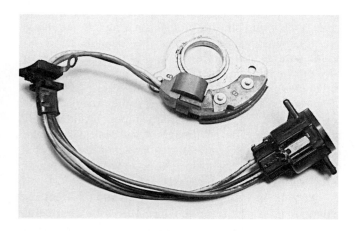

FIGURE 12–5   Typical pickup coil assembly from an older-style Ford electronic ignition.

GM HEI ELECTRONIC IGNITION OPERATION

High-energy ignition has been the standard-equipment ignition system on General Motors vehicles since the 1975 model year. Most V-6 and V-8 models use an igni-

tion coil inside the distributor cap. Some V-6, inline six-cylinder, and four-cylinder models use an externally mounted ignition coil. The operation of both styles is similar. The large-diameter distributor cap provides additional space between the spark plug connections to help prevent cross fire. Most HEI distributors also use 8-millimeter-diameter spark plug wires that use female connections to the distributor cap towers. HEI ignition coils must be replaced (if defective) with the exact replacement style. HEI coils differ and can be identified by the colors of the primary leads. The primary coil leads can be either white and red, or yellow and red. The correct color of lead coil must be used for replacement. The colors of the leads indicate the direction in which the coil is wound, and therefore its polarity.

DIRECT-FIRE IGNITION SYSTEMS

Direct-fire ignition is ignition without use of a distributor (also called distributorless, or simply EI). Direct-fire ignition was introduced in the mid-1980s and uses the on-board computer to fire the ignition coils. Direct-

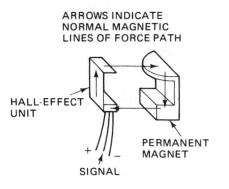

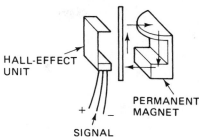

ARROWS INDICATE
NORMAL MAGNETIC
LINES OF FORCE PATH

HALL-EFFECT
UNIT

+   −
SIGNAL

PERMANENT
MAGNET

ARROWS INDICATE
HOW MAGNETIC LINES
OF FORCE ARE SHUNTED

HALL-EFFECT
UNIT

+   −
SIGNAL

PERMANENT
MAGNET

FIGURE 12–6 Hall-effect switches use metallic shutters to shunt magnetic lines of force away from a silicon chip and related circuits. All Hall-effect switches produce a square wave output for every accurate triggering.

FIGURE 12–7 Shutter blade of a rotor as it passes between the sensing silicon chip and the permanent magnet.

fire ignition systems were first used on some Saabs and some General Motors engines. Some four-cylinder engines use four coils, but usually a four-cylinder engine uses two ignition coils and a six-cylinder engine uses three ignition coils. Each coil is a true transformer in which the primary winding and secondary winding are not electrically connected. Each end of the secondary winding is connected to a cylinder exactly opposite the other in the firing order. See figure 12–9. This means that *both* spark plugs fire at the same time! When one cylinder (for example, #6) is on the compression stroke, the other cylinder (#3) is on the exhaust stroke. This spark that occurs on the exhaust stroke is called the **waste spark** because it does no useful work and is only used as a ground path for the secondary winding of the ignition cell. The voltage required to jump the spark plug gap on cylinder 3 (the exhaust stroke) is only 2 to 3 kilovolts

(kV) and provides the *ground circuit* for the secondary coil circuit. The remaining coil energy is used by the cylinder on the compression stroke. One spark plug of each pair fires straight polarity and the other cylinder fires reverse polarity. Spark plug life is not greatly affected by the reverse polarity. If there is only one defective spark plug wire or spark plug, two cylinders may be affected.

Direct-fire ignitions require a sensor (usually a crankshaft sensor) to trigger the coils at the correct time. The crankshaft sensor cannot be moved to adjust ignition timing. Ignition timing is not adjustable. The slight adjustment of the crankshaft sensor is designed to position the sensor exactly in the middle of the rotating metal disk for maximum clearance. Some engines do not use a camshaft position sensor, but use double Hall-effect crankshaft sensors. Again, ignition timing is not adjustable.

GM HALL-EFFECT SENSOR–TRIGGERED IGNITIONS

All Hall-effect sensor–triggered ignitions use a fourteen-pin module. Three types are used, depending on model year and exact engine application. All use ferrous metal (steel) vanes to shunt the magnetic lines of force from the Hall-effect sensor. The Hall-effect sensor produces a DC square wave of 6 to 8 volts.

Type I.   The type I ignition uses a single-piece coil pack manufactured by Magnavox. The spark plug wires connect to both sides of the coil pack. See figure 12–10. The module is triggered by a Hall-effect crankshaft sensor located behind the front crankshaft pulley. The camshaft position sensor is also used to

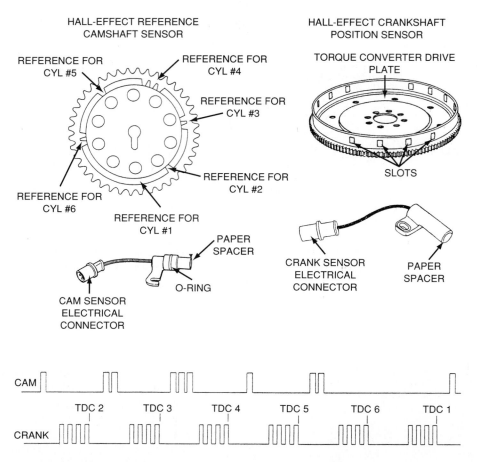

FIGURE 12–8 Some Hall-effect sensors look like magnetic sensors. This Hall-effect camshaft reference sensor and crankshaft position sensor have an electronic circuit built in that creates a 0- to 5-volt signal as shown at the bottom. These Hall-effect sensors have three wires: a power supply (8 volts) from the computer (controller); a signal (0 to 5 volts); and a signal ground.

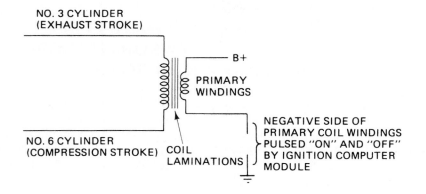

FIGURE 12–9 Ignition coils used in most distributorless (direct-fire) ignition systems are true transformers. There is no electrical connection between the primary and secondary windings.

FIGURE 12–10   General Motors type I ignition. Note that the coil is one piece. The module is under the coil pack. This unit is made by Magnavox.

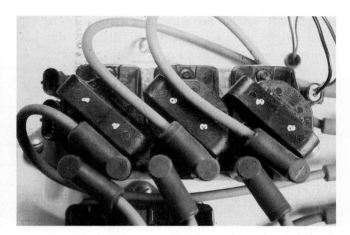

FIGURE 12–11   General Motors type II ignition made by Delco uses three individual replaceable coils.

give a camshaft (top dead center [TDC] #1 cylinder) pulse to the computer to trigger the start of the fuel-injection sequence. The camshaft sensor also physically replaces the distributor and drives the oil pump. Type I systems were called computer-controlled coil ignition (C^3I) systems.

Type II.   Type II ignitions are identified by individually constructed (and replaceable) ignition coils with all spark plug wires on one side of the coil. See figure 12–11. Type II coils are interchangeable and are manufactured by General Motors Delco Remy Division.

Type III.   Type III ignitions are similar to type I because the three coils are one unit. Type III uses a shorter version of the type I coil pack. Type III is commonly called the "fast start" system because the combination crankshaft sensor uses eighteen different shutter blades to give a more rapid indication to the computer of the engine position. See figure 12–12.

GM MAGNETIC SENSOR–TRIGGERED IGNITIONS

A magnetic sensor is an AC generator that produces a voltage whenever a metallic-toothed wheel is moved past the sensor. This type of sensor, used on many distributorless ignition systems as a crankshaft position sensor, is sensitive to vibrations and must be properly sealed.

The magnetic sensor also requires some internal signal modification (conditioning) to be useful to other electronic control (computer) circuits. The normal output of a magnetic sensor as a toothed (or notched) metal wheel passes near the sensor can be over 200 AC volts. The signal is sometimes converted, by an electronic circuit built into the sensor, from the sine wave output to a constant-amplitude square wave.

All magnetic sensor–triggered ignitions use an eleven-pin module. This style of ignition uses the individual coils manufactured by Delco Remy Division of General Motors Corporation. The engines using the magnetic sensor-triggered style of ignition include the four-cylinder (2.0 liter and 2.5 liter) and the 2.8-liter, 3.1-liter, and 3.4-liter V-6s. See figure 12–13. A variation of this system used on the QUAD 4 (2.3-liter) Oldsmobile-built four-cylinder is called integrated distributorless ignition (IDI), and also uses a magnetic sensor.

FORD ELECTRONIC IGNITION

Ford electronic ignition systems all function similarly, even though the name for the Ford electronic ignition system has changed many times since 1974.

1974–76	Ford solid-state ignition system
1977–78	Duraspark II—Larger distributor cap and 8-millimeter-diameter spark plug wires were major changes from earlier systems. (Duraspark I was used only in 1977–79 and only for California's V-8s.)

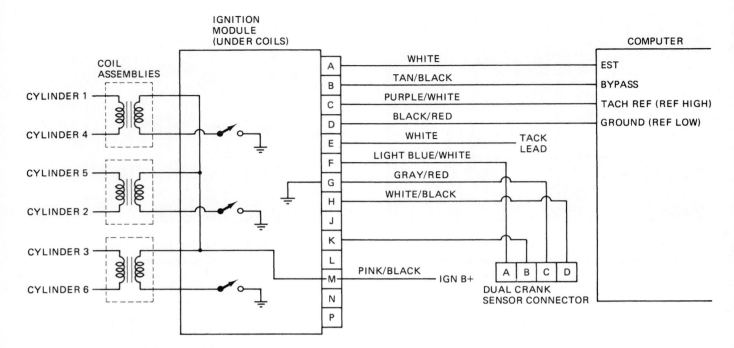

FIGURE 12–12 Typical wiring diagram of a V-6 distributorless (direct-fire) ignition system.

NOTE: The Duraspark II system can be modified to allow either altitude compensation or economy calibration. Modules designed for this "dual mode" modification are equipped with an added three-wire connector.

1978	Electronic engine control (EEC) I—Uses the Duraspark III ignition, which is basically the same as the Duraspark II except that some circuits have been eliminated because the EEC system performs their functions instead of the ignition module.
1979	EEC II—Is basically the same as the EEC I system except for some added components and changed circuits.
1980	EEC III—Changes were again mostly internal electronic circuits. EEC III uses the basic Duraspark III ignition system. See figure 12–14.
1982 and newer	EEC IV—Uses the computer engine control with DI and EI (called distributionless ignition system [DIS] and electronic distributionless ignition system [EDIS]).
1995 and newer	EEC V—Introduced and continues to use EDIS for spark control.

FORD THICK FILM–INTEGRATED IGNITION

The EEC IV system uses the **thick film–integrated** (TFI) ignition system. Thick film–integrated ignition systems were first used on the Escort and Lynx and similar models. This system uses a smaller control module attached to the distributor and uses an air-cooled epoxy E-style coil. Thick-film ignition means that all of the electronics are manufactured on small layers built up to form a thick film. See figure 12–15. Construction includes using pastes of different electrical resistances that are deposited on a thin, flat ceramic material by a process similar to silk-screen printing. These resistors are connected by tracks of palladium silver paste. Then the chips that form the capacitors, diodes, and integrated circuits are soldered directly to the palladium silver tracks. The thick-film manufacturing process is highly automated.

FORD MODULE IDENTIFICATION

Ford electronic ignition control units (modules) are identified by the color of the sealing block (grommet). Replacement modules should be the correct part number *and* have the same color of sealing block. The colors available include black, blue, brown, green, red, and white, in addition to sealing blocks with one yellow seal

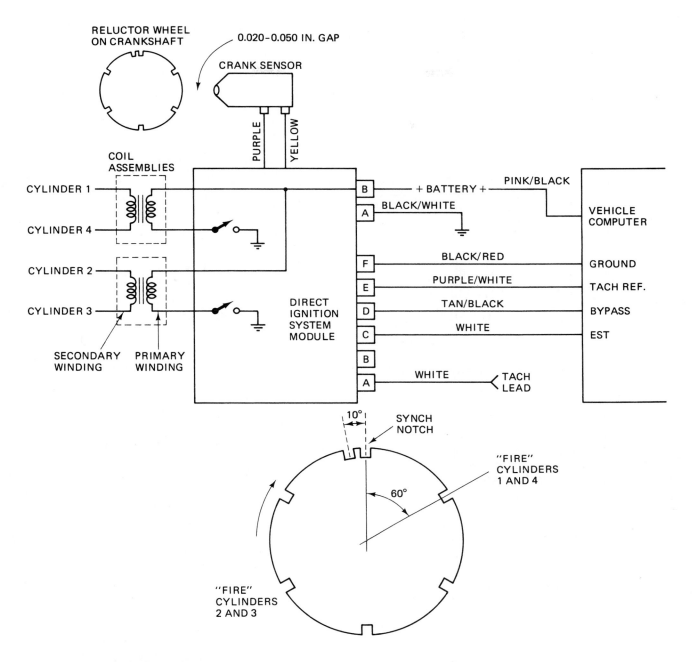

FIGURE 12–13 Wiring diagram of a typical four-cylinder direct-fire ignition system. Note that the computer receives signals from and sends signals to the ignition module, but the module is the unit that actually turns the primary coil circuit on and off.

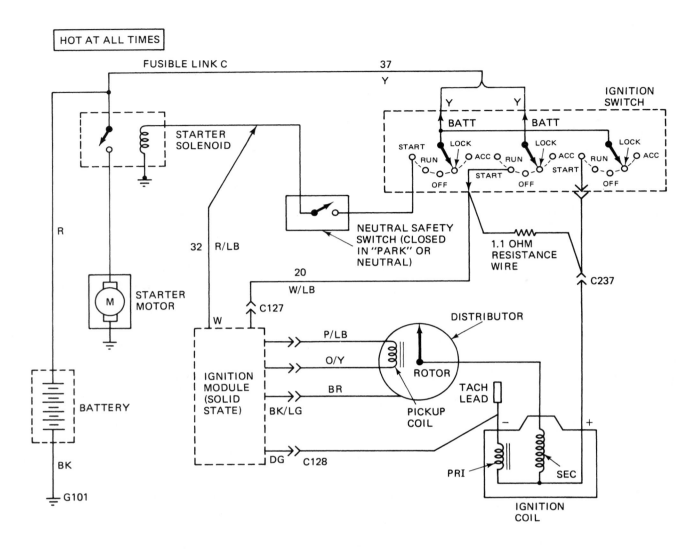

FIGURE 12–14 Wiring diagram of a typical Ford electronic ignition.

or two yellow seals. The module is simply an electronic switching circuit that turns the primary coil circuit on and off. The module can get hot during normal operation and is therefore mounted where normal airflow should keep the temperature from getting too high. Rustproofing materials or added under-the-hood accessories should be kept away from the ignition module.

OPERATION OF FORD ELECTRONIC IGNITION

Ford electronic ignition systems function in basically the same way regardless of year and name (Duraspark, EEC, etc.). Under the distributor cap and rotor is a magnetic pickup assembly. This assembly produces a small alternating electrical pulse (approximately 1.5 volts) whenever the distributor armature rotates past the pickup as-

sembly (stator). This low-voltage pulse is sent to the ignition module. The ignition module then switches (through transistors) off the primary ignition coil current. When the ignition coil primary current is stopped quickly, a high-voltage "spike" discharges from the coil secondary winding. Some Ford electronic ignition systems use a ballast resistor to help control the primary current through the ignition coil in the run mode (position); other Ford systems do not use a ballast resistor. The coil current is controlled in the module circuits by decreasing dwell (coil-charging time) depending on various factors determined by operating conditions.

FORD DIS AND EDIS

Ford's distributorless ignition typically uses a twelve-pin module mounted where it can be kept cool, yet still provide for relatively short wiring leads. The exact lo-

◀ **TECH TIP** ▶

IF IT'S SOFT—THROW IT AWAY

Ford uses a Hall-effect sensor in the distributor on most TFI module–equipped engines. The sensors were originally coated in a black plastic that would often become soft with age and break down electrically. The soft plastic sensor would also prevent proper connection to the TFI module as shown in figure 12–15. If a "no start" or rough engine operation occurs, always check the Hall-effect sensor and the connections to the module. The original Hall-effect units were black plastic and more prone to failure. Ozone formed by the high-voltage arcing in the distributor cap is very corrosive, and it chemically attacked the plastic. When this occurred, the plastic would become soft and pliable and similar to tar in feel and texture. If the sensor is soft like tar, replace the Hall-effect switch assembly. Later production units were changed to a more chemically stable white plastic material that is soft enough to get a fingernail into, yet is not sticky.

FIGURE 12–15 Thick film–integrated type of Ford electronic ignition. Note how the module plugs into the Hall-effect switch inside the distributor. Heat-conductive silicone grease should be used between the module and the distributor mounting pad to help keep the electronic circuits inside the module cool.

cation varies from engine to engine and model to model. A typical V-6 coil pack includes three coils and a four-pin connector. The coil pack is replaced as a unit, and individual coils are not replaceable even though the computer can set a separate trouble code for each of the three coils. The sixty-pin computer operates the ignition timing through modification of the Hall-effect crankshaft sensor signal. See figures 12–16 and 12–17.

CHRYSLER ELECTRONIC IGNITION

Chrysler was the first domestic manufacturer to produce electronic ignition as standard equipment. The Chrysler system consists of a pulse generator unit in the distributor (pickup coil and reluctor). Chrysler's name for its electronic ignition is **electronic ignition system** (EIS), and the control unit (module) is called the **electronic control unit** (ECU). The ECU used on 1971–79 models uses a five-pin connector, and 1980 and later models use a four-pin connector.

The pickup coil in the distributor (pulse generator) generates the signal to open and close the primary coil circuit. Some engines use two (dual) pickup coils. One pickup coil is called the **starting pickup** and provides slightly retarded ignition timing to aid in starting. The other pickup is called the **run pickup.**

CHRYSLER BALLAST RESISTOR

The five-pin ECU uses a dual-ballast resistor. The dual-ballast resistor uses a 0.5-ohm resistance to limit the voltage in the ignition primary circuit to help protect the ignition coil from overheating at low engine speeds. The *second* resistance, of 5-ohms, is used to limit the voltage to the ECU only. A single 0.5-ohm resistor is used on 1980 and later four-pin ECU ignitions to control coil primary voltage. Whenever a no-start or an intermittent spark occurs during cranking, the ballast resistor should be the first item checked on Chrysler vehicles. See figures 12–18 and 12–19 for an example of Chrysler electronic ignition as used on a V-6 engine.

COMPUTER-CONTROLLED IGNITION TIMING

Ignition timing is a matter of when the spark occurs in relation to piston position. Since the early 1980s, ignition timing has been controlled by the vehicle's computer system. Ignition timing still needs to be checked

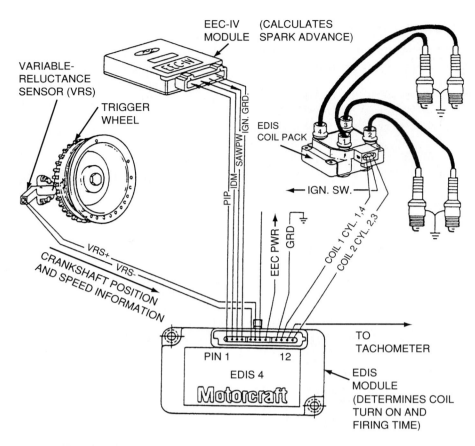

FIGURE 12–16 Typical Ford EDIS four-cylinder ignition system. The crankshaft sensor (called a variable-reluctance sensor—VRS) sends crankshaft position and speed information to the EDIS module. A modified signal is sent to the computer as a profile ignition pickup (PIP) signal. The PIP is used by the computer to calculate ignition timing, and the computer sends a signal back to the EDIS module as to when to fire the spark plug. This return signal is called the spark angle word (SAW) signal.

on engines using a distributor. The base timing position of the distributor is generally adjustable. The computer can only *add* timing, it *cannot* retard timing to lower than the base setting. Some computerized engine control test procedures (such as Ford's self-test) require the technician to check for a change in ignition timing during the test procedure.

As the engine wears, the opening and closing times of the valves are changed as a result of timing chain or gear wear (where applicable). This retarding effect also changes the base ignition timing. The computer adds (advances) the ignition timing based on programmed amounts relative to various sensor readings. If readings from sensors, such as engine load or coolant temperature sensors, are incorrect, the ignition timing is usually affected.

If a fault is detected in a computer-controlled circuit or sensor, the ignition timing is usually either fixed (set at one point by the computer) or defaults to a retarded mode of operation. This retarded mode of operation helps prevent engine damage due to excessively advanced ignition timing, yet provides enough advance to keep the engine running without overheating the catalytic converter. This backup or fail-safe mode usually results in greatly reduced fuel economy and performance.

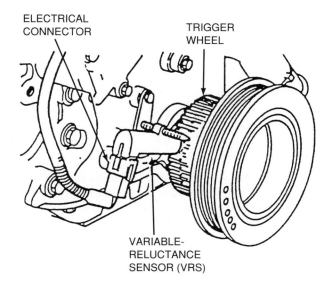

ELECTRICAL CONNECTOR

TRIGGER WHEEL

VARIABLE-RELUCTANCE SENSOR (VRS)

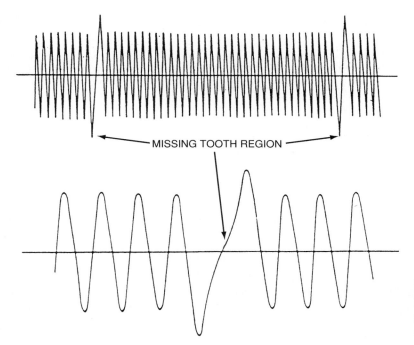

← MISSING TOOTH REGION →

FIGURE 12–17 The crankshaft sensor (VRS) identifies the exact position of the crankshaft by noting the location of the "missing tooth" portion of the signal.

SUMMARY

1. All inductive ignition systems supply battery voltage to the positive side of the ignition coil and pulse the negative side of the coil on and off to ground to create a high-voltage spark.
2. If an ignition system uses a distributor, it is called a DI system, meaning distributor ignition.
3. If an ignition system does not use a distributor, it is called simply an EI system, meaning electronic ignition.
4. Two types of sensors used to trigger ignition coils are magnetic and Hall effect.

REVIEW QUESTIONS

1. Explain how 12 volts from a battery can be changed to 40,000 volts for ignition.
2. Discuss how a Hall-effect sensor works.
3. Discuss how a magnetic sensor works.
4. Explain the concept of a wasted spark.

FIGURE 12–18 Ignition coil assembly is serviced (replaced) as an assembly. The computer controls the firing of the spark plugs. This Chrysler system does not use a separate ignition module.

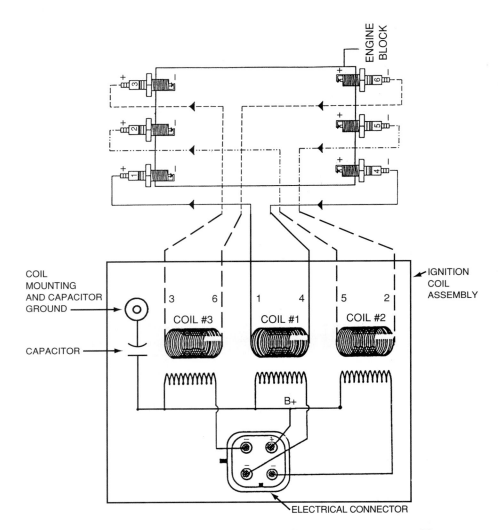

FIGURE 12–19 Wiring diagram of a V-6 Chrysler ignition system. The polarity of the spark is determined by the direction in which the coil is wound. The polarity does not matter because the energy and voltage of these systems are great enough that a reliable spark is always available.

MULTIPLE-CHOICE QUESTIONS

1. The pulse generator _____ .
   a. Fires the spark plug directly
   b. Signals the electronic control unit (module)
   c. Signals the computer that fires the spark plug directly
   d. Is used as a tachometer reference signal by the computer and does not have any other function

2. The primary (low-voltage) ignition system must be working correctly before any spark occurs from a coil. Which component is *not* in the primary ignition circuit?
   a. Spark plug wiring
   b. Ignition module (igniter)
   c. Pickup coil (pulse generator)
   d. Ignition switch

3. If the coil primary leads are reversed, _____ .
   a. No spark will occur out of the coil
   b. A spark will occur, but it will be weak
   c. The polarity is reversed so that the coil will produce its normal maximum-output voltage, but the voltage required to fire the spark plug is increased

4. Because of _____, an ignition coil cannot be fully charged (reach magnetic saturation) until after a delay of about 10 milliseconds.
   a. Voltage drop across the ignition switch and related wiring
   b. Resistance in the coil windings
   c. Inductive reactance
   d. Saturation

5. The ignition module has direct control over the firing of the coil(s) of an electronic ignition system. Which component(s) trigger (control) the module?
   a. Pickup coil
   b. Computer
   c. Crankshaft sensor
   d. All of the above

6. The pulse generator (pickup coil) or crankshaft sensor _____ .
   a. Signals (pulses) the ignition module that triggers (pulses) the ignition coil
   b. Signals (pulses) the negative side of the ignition coil
   c. Signals (pulses) the computer that triggers (pulses) the negative side of the ignition coil
   d. Both a and c

7. The module on a Ford TFI ignition system is _____ .
   a. Always located on the side of the distributor
   b. Located on the side of the distributor housing or remotely mounted elsewhere under the hood
   c. Usually located on the distributor, but can be bolted to the side of the computer
   d. Both b and c

8. Distributorless (direct-fire) ignition systems can be triggered by a _____ .
   a. Hall-effect sensor
   b. Magnetic sensor
   c. Spark sensor
   d. Either a or b

◀ Chapter 13 ▶

IGNITION SYSTEM PROBLEM DIAGNOSIS AND TESTING

OBJECTIVES

After studying chapter 13, the reader will be able to

1. Explain how to check for spark using a spark tester.
2. Describe how to test a pickup coil.
3. Discuss diagnosis of a no-start condition.
4. Explain how to test and inspect spark plug wires, distributor caps, rotors, and ignition coils.

The purpose of any ignition system is to produce high-voltage electrical pulses and distribute them to the spark plugs at the proper time. The spark occurring at the spark plugs ignites the air-fuel mixture inside the engine.

CHECKING FOR SPARK

In the event of a no-start condition, the first step should be to check for secondary voltage out of the ignition coil or to the spark plugs. If the engine is equipped with a separate ignition coil, remove the coil wire from the center of the distributor cap, install a **spark tester,** and crank the engine. See the tech tip Always Use a Spark Tester. A good coil and ignition system should produce a blue spark at the spark tester. See figures 13–1 through 13–3.

If the ignition system being tested does not have a separate ignition coil, disconnect any spark plug wire

from a spark plug and, while cranking the engine, test for spark available at the spark plug wire, again using a spark tester.

◀ TECH TIP ▶

ALWAYS USE A SPARK TESTER

A spark tester looks like a spark plug without a side electrode with a gap between the center electrode and the grounded shell. The tester commonly has an alligator clip attached to the shell so that it can be clamped on a good ground connection on the engine. A good ignition system should be able to cause a spark to jump this wide gap at atmospheric pressure. Without a spark tester, a technician might assume that the ignition system is okay because it can spark across a normal, grounded spark plug. The voltage required to fire a standard spark plug when it is out of the engine and not under pressure is about 3000 volts or less. An electronic ignition spark tester requires a minimum of 25,000 volts for the spark to jump the $^3/_4$-inch gap. Therefore, never assume that the ignition system is okay because it will fire a spark plug—always use a spark tester. *Always remember that an intermittent spark across a spark tester should be interpreted as a no-spark condition.*

FIGURE 13–1 Using a spark tester on an engine with direct-fire (distributorless) ignition. The spark tester is grounded to the rocker cover stud. This is the recommended type of spark tester, with the center electrode recessed down into the center insulator.

FIGURE 13–2 A style of spark tester *not* recommended for electronic ignition system problem diagnosis. Notice the extended center electrode design versus the design of the spark tester in figure 13–1.

FIGURE 13–3 The old method used to check for spark. Many manufacturers considered a spark that could jump ¼ inch from the coil wire to ground to be sufficient voltage. A spark tester is easier (and safer) to use because it provides a gap of a given distance, eliminating the need to attempt to hold a wire at a specified distance from ground.

NOTE: An intermittent spark should be considered a no-spark condition.

Typical causes of a no-spark (intermittent spark) condition include the following:

1. Weak ignition coil
2. Low or no voltage to the primary (positive) side of the coil
3. High-resistance or open coil wire or spark plug wire
4. Negative side of the coil not being pulsed by the ignition module
5. Defective pickup coil
6. Defective module

ELECTRONIC IGNITION OPERATION

All ignition systems function by completing and then opening the ground path for the primary ignition coil circuit. With an old point-type ignition system, this pulsing of the negative side of the coil was handled by the ignition points. In an electronic ignition, the turning on and off of the primary current through the coil is controlled by the electronic control module. The module is basically an electronic switch that completes or opens the primary coil circuit. Another unit, called a pickup coil, sends a low-voltage signal to the ignition module to trigger the module to turn the primary coil current on and off. A Hall-effect switch is often used to signal the ignition module instead of a pickup coil.

ELECTRONIC IGNITION TROUBLESHOOTING PROCEDURE

Whenever troubleshooting any electronic ignition system for no spark, follow these steps to help pinpoint the exact cause of the problem:

- *Step #1.* Turn the ignition on (engine off), and using either a voltmeter or a test light, test for battery voltage available at the positive terminal of the ignition coil. If voltage is not available, check for an open circuit at the ignition switch or wiring. Also check the condition of the ignition fuse (if used).

NOTE: Many Chrysler products use an **automatic shutdown** (ASD) relay to power the ignition coil. The ASD relay will not supply voltage to the coil unless the engine is cranking and the computer senses a crankshaft sensor signal. This little fact has fooled a lot of technicians.

- *Step #2.* Connect the voltmeter or test light to the negative side of the coil and crank the engine. The voltmeter should fluctuate or the test light should blink, indicating that the primary coil current is being turned on and off. If there is no pulsing of the negative side of the coil, the problem is a defective pickup, electronic control module, or wiring.

IGNITION COIL TESTING

If an ignition coil is suspected of being defective, a simple ohmmeter check can be performed to test the resistance of the primary and secondary winding inside the coil. For accurate resistance measurements, the wiring to the coil should be removed before testing.

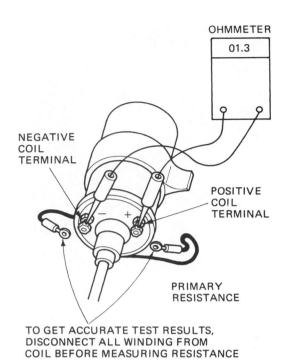

FIGURE 13–4 Testing the primary coil winding resistance using an ohmmeter.

FIGURE 13–5 Measuring the resistance of the primary winding of an ignition coil. The specification for this primary coil is "less than 1 ohm." The reading of 0.7 ohms, therefore, is okay.

FIGURE 13–6 An ohmmeter check on this coil indicated that the coil was okay. However, a visual inspection revealed that arcing had been occurring through the secondary tower to the primary terminals.

To test the primary coil winding resistance, follow these steps (figs. 13–4 through 13–6):

- *Step #1.* Set the meter to read low ohms.
- *Step #2.* Measure the resistance between the positive terminal and the negative terminal of the ignition coil. Most coils will give a reading between 1 and 3 ohms; however, some coils should indicate less than 1 ohm. Check the manufacturer's specifications for the exact resistance values.

To test the secondary coil winding resistance, follow these steps (figs. 13–7 and 13–8):

- *Step #1.* Set the meter to read kilo ohms (KΩ).
- *Step #2.* Measure the resistance between either primary terminal and the secondary coil tower. The normal resistance of most coils ranges between 6000 and 30,000 ohms. Check the manufacturer's specifications for the exact resistance values.

NOTE: Many ignition coils use a screw that is down inside the secondary tower of the ignition coil. If this screw is loose, an intermittent engine miss could occur. The secondary coil would also indicate high resistance if this screw was loose.

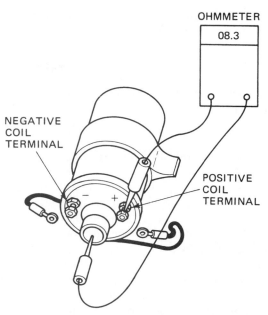

TO GET THE MOST ACCURATE TEST RESULTS, DISCONNECT ALL ELECTRICAL WIRING FROM COIL BEFORE MEASURING RESISTANCE

FIGURE 13–7 Testing the secondary coil winding with an ohmmeter. The secondary resistance specifications for most coils range from 6000 to 30,000 ohms.

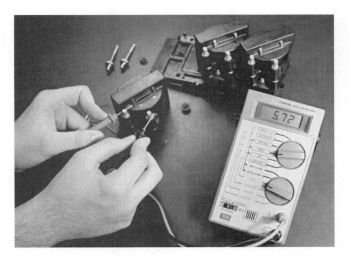

FIGURE 13–8 Testing the secondary winding of a GM DIS coil. The meter reads 5.72 KΩ (5720 ohms), and the specification calls for 5000 to 7000 ohms.

CONDENSER TESTING

Most electronic ignition systems use a condenser (capacitor), connected to the positive terminal of the coil, whose function is to control radio interference. Automotive condensers can be tested with a special condenser tester, which is usually built into electronic engine analyzers or which comes with some digital multimeters. Condensers can be tested for shorts using an ohmmeter. All condensers should measure infinity between the metal case and the wire terminal of the condenser. If an ohmmeter reading is obtained, the condenser is defective (shorted).

PICKUP COIL TESTING

The pickup coil, located under the distributor cap on many electronic ignition engines, can cause a no-spark condition if it is defective. The pickup coil must generate an AC voltage pulse to the ignition module so that the module can pulse the ignition coil.

A pickup coil contains a coil of wire, and the resistance of this coil should be within the range specified by the manufacturer. See figures 13–9 and 13–10. Some common specifications include the following:

Manufacturer	Pickup Coil Resistance
General Motors	500 to 1500 ohms (white and green leads)
Ford	400 to 1000 ohms (orange and purple leads)
Chrysler	150 to 900 ohms (orange and black leads)

If the pickup coil resistance is not within the specified range, replace the pickup coil assembly.

The pickup coil can also be tested for proper voltage output. During cranking, most pickup coils should produce a minimum of 0.25 volts AC. This can be tested with the distributor out of the vehicle by rotating the distributor drive gear with your hand.

IGNITION MODULE TESTING

Many equipment manufacturers offer electronic control module testers. Most of these testers simply send a voltage pulse (the same as a pickup coil pulse) to the module to determine whether or not the control module opens and closes the primary circuit. As a substitute for a module tester, the following procedure will work on most electronic ignition systems, except those equipped with Hall-effect sensors.

- *Step #1.* Turn the ignition on. Pull the secondary coil wire out of the center of the distributor cap and connect a spark tester to the coil wire. (If the system uses a coil inside the cap, re-

move any one spark plug wire and plug in a spark tester that is grounded.) Be certain that the distributor rotor is pointing toward the plug wire that is being connected to the spark tester.

- *Step #2.* Hold a 110-volt soldering gun as near to the distributor cap as possible. Turn the soldering gun on and observe the coil output. The soldering gun produces a moving magnetic field that is converted by the pickup coil windings into varying-voltage pulses. These pulses should be strong enough to trigger the module on and off, and a pulsing output should be observed from the coil. See figure 13–11.

FIGURE 13–9 Measuring the resistance of an HEI pickup coil using a digital multimeter set to the ohms position. The reading on the face of the meter is 0.796 KΩ or 796 ohms, right in the middle of the 500- to 1500-ohm specifications.

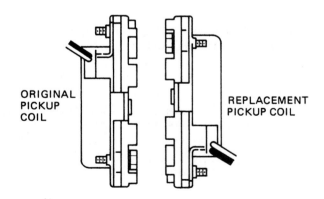

FIGURE 13–10 The original and the replacement GM pickup coils must *not* be attracted toward each other if held face to face. There are two different GM pickup coils that look identical except for the color-coded connector. The two pickup coils are wound in the opposite direction and therefore are of opposite polarity.

■ *Results* If the use of a soldering gun near the pickup coil does *not* produce a spark from the ignition coil, the problem is defective wiring or a defective control module. If the use of the soldering gun near the pickup coil does produce a spark from the ignition coil, the ignition system is functioning correctly. If this is the case but a problem still exists, check for possible intermittent problems such as poor electrical connections or grounds. See figure 13–12.

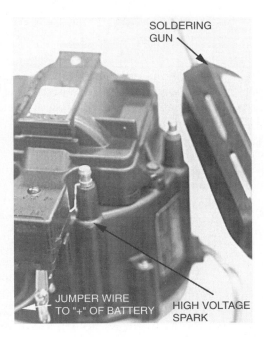

FIGURE 13–11 Testing an HEI distributor with a soldering gun. Jumper wires are attached from a battery to the "BAT" terminal of the HEI and ground. The soldering gun is turned on and held as close to the distributor as possible. The high-voltage spark indicates that everything in the system is functioning correctly.

GM (INTEGRAL COIL) HEI COIL IDENTIFICATION

A General Motors vehicle that uses an HEI system with the ignition coil in the distributor cap must have both the ignition coil and the pickup coil wound in the same direction. Always replace either by the following rule of thumb: A *yellow* connection or pickup coil uses an ignition coil with *yellow* and *red* leads. All other pickup coils use an ignition coil with *white* and *red* leads. See figure 13–13. If a vehicle does not have a proper match, refer to the following for a general list of what engines were built with which coil wire colors (colors of primary wires on coil).

Red and White

> Buick-built engines: all V-8s, 196–cu in V-6, 3.8-L (231–cu in) V-6, 3.0-L V-6, 4.1-L V-6

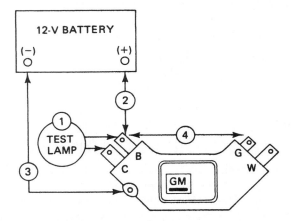

FIGURE 13–12 Hookup for testing a GM module using a test light and three jumper wires. If the module is okay the test light will go out when the fourth jumper wire is connected between terminals B and G. For a seven-pin module, use terminal P instead of G.

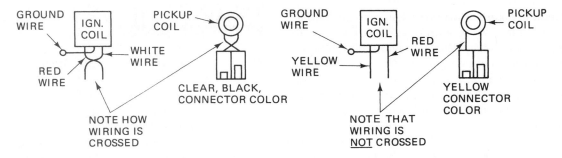

FIGURE 13–13 The ignition coil and the pickup coil must have the same polarity. If the incorrect ignition coil or pickup coil is used, the following symptoms may be experienced: a broken starter drive-end housing, backfiring, or surging at highway speeds.

Pontiac V-8s: 301 cu in (4.9 L), 350 cu in (5.7 L), 400 cu in 455 cu in

Olds-built V-8s: 260 cu in, 307 cu in (5.0 L), 350 cu in (5.7 L), 400 cu in, 403 cu in, 455 cu in (except Toronado V-8)

GMC and Chevrolet truck 292–cu in inline six-cylinder

1984 and newer Corvettes (5.7-L Chevrolet V-8) Cadillac 4.1-L V-8 (rear-wheel drive [RWD] only)

Red and Yellow

Chevrolet-built engines: 2.8-L V-6, 229–cu in (3.8-L) V-6, 267–cu in V-8, 305–cu in (5.0-L) V-8, 350–cu in (5.7-L) V-8, 4.3-L V-6, 250–cu in inline six-cylinder

All 151–cu in four-cylinder (2.5-L) engines

All AMC engines with HEI

All Jeep engines with HEI

Cadillac engine 500–cu in

Cadillac 425–cu in V-8

Cadillac 368–cu in V-8

Cadillac 4.1-L V-8, 4.5-L V-8 (front-wheel drive [FWD])

DISTRIBUTORLESS IGNITION TESTING

Direct (distributorless) ignition system problems are often difficult to detect and troubleshoot. Because the computer controls the fuel injection, the ignition timing, and the idle speed, a problem with either an ignition coil or a fuel injector may give the same symptoms to the driver—lower than normal power.

Ignition coils often fail because they are *shorted;* therefore, the output voltage may be weaker than normal. See the tech tip Bad Wire? Replace the Coil! This lower-output voltage may still be able to fire the spark plug(s) under all conditions except those in which required voltage exceeds available voltage. When this occurs, an engine misfire occurs. This misfire will usually occur when the engine is under load—a condition that requires an increase in spark plug firing voltage. Because the engine computer can quickly sense the misfire as excessive uncombined oxygen moving past the oxygen sensor, the problem may be compensated for by the computer, which will command a richer mixture. See chapters 15 through 18 for complete computer operation and testing procedures.

◄ **TECH TIP** ►

BAD WIRE? REPLACE THE COIL!

Whenever performing engine testing (such as a compression test), always *ground* the coil wire. Never allow the coil to discharge without a path to ground for the spark. High-energy electronic ignition systems can produce 40,000 volts or more of electrical pressure. If the spark cannot spark to ground, the coil energy can (and usually does) arc inside the coil itself, creating a low-resistance path to the primary windings or the steel laminations of the coil. See figure 13–14. This low-resistance path is called a "track" and could cause an engine miss under load even though all of the remaining component parts of the ignition system are functioning correctly. Often these tracks do *not* show up on any coil test, including most scopes. Because the track is a lower-resistance path to ground than normal, it requires that the ignition system be put under a load for it to be detected, and even then, the problem (engine missing) may be intermittent.

Therefore, whenever disabling an ignition system, follow one of the following procedures to prevent possible ignition coil damage:

1. Remove the power source wire from the ignition system to prevent any ignition operation.
2. On distributor-equipped engines, remove the secondary coil wire from the center of the distributor cap and connect a jumper wire between the disconnected coil wire and a good engine ground. (This ensures that the secondary coil energy will be safely grounded and prevents high-voltage coil damage.)

TESTING FOR POOR PERFORMANCE

Many diagnostic equipment manufacturers offer methods for testing distributorless ignition systems on an oscilloscope. If using this type of equipment, follow the manufacturer's recommended procedures and interpretation of their test results.

A simple method of testing distributorless (direct-fire) ignition systems with the engine off involves *removing* the spark plug wires (or connectors) from the spark plugs and installing short lengths (2 inches) of rubber vacuum hose in series.

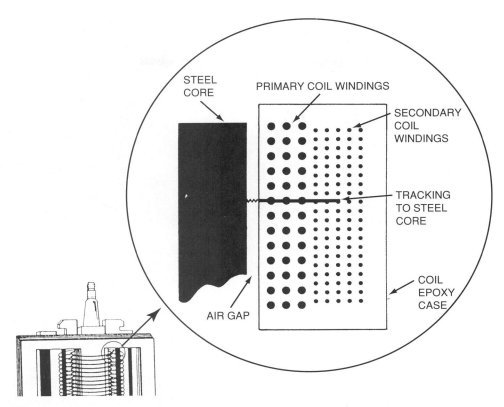

FIGURE 13–14 A track inside an ignition coil is not a short, but rather a low-resistance path or hole that has been burned through from the secondary wiring to the steel core.

NOTE: For best results, use rubber hose that is electrically conductive. Measure the vacuum hose with an ohmmeter. Suitable vacuum hose should give a reading of less than 10,000 ohms (10 KΩ) for a length of about 2 inches. See figures 13–15 through 13–17.

- *Step #1.* Start the engine and ground out each cylinder one at a time by touching the tip of a *grounded* test light to the rubber vacuum hose. Even though the computer will increase idle speed and increase fuel delivery to compensate for the grounded spark plug wire, a *change* in the operation of the engine should be noticed. If no change is observed or heard, the cylinder being grounded is obviously weak or defective. Check the spark plug wire or connector with an ohmmeter to be certain of continuity.
- *Step #2.* Check every cylinder by grounding out the cylinders one at a time. If one weak cylinder is found, check the other cylinder us-

◄ TECH TIP ►

MANY FUEL SYSTEM PROBLEMS ARE CAUSED BY THE IGNITION SYSTEM

An older technician once told a new apprentice that nine out of ten customer complaints about engine operation result from ignition system problems. Because a defective ignition system (spark plugs, plug wires, timing, etc.) often causes the engine to miss or act as if "the engine is not getting enough gas," many customers complain of "carburetor" (fuel system) problems. The older technician always carefully inspected the entire ignition system *before* checking any part of the fuel system.

ing the same ignition coil (except on Nissan engines that use an individual coil for each cylinder). If both cylinders are affected, the problem could be an open spark plug wire, defective spark plug, or defective ignition coil.

FIGURE 13–15   A length of vacuum hose being used for a coil wire. The vacuum hose is conductive because of the carbon content of the rubber in the hose. This hose measures only 1000 ohms and was 1 foot long. (This is lower resistance than most spark plug wires.) Notice the spark from the hose's surface to the tip of a grounded screwdriver.

■ *Step #3.* To help eliminate other possible problems to determine exactly what is wrong, switch the suspected ignition coil to another position (if possible).
  1. If the problem now affects the other cylinders, the ignition coil is defective and must be replaced.
  2. If the problem does not "change positions," the control module affecting the suspected coil or either cylinder's spark plug or spark plug wire could be defective.

TESTING FOR A NO-START CONDITION

A no-start condition (with normal engine cranking speed) can be the result of either no spark or no fuel delivery.

Computerized engine control systems use the ignition primary pulses as a signal to inject fuel (port or throttle body injection [TBI] style of fuel-injection system). If there is no pulse, then there is no squirt of fuel.

■ *Step #1.* Test the output signal from the crankshaft sensor. Most computerized engines with distributorless ignitions use a crankshaft position sensor. These sensors are either the Hall-effect type or the magnetic type. (See chapter 14 for procedures for scope testing these sensors.) The sensors must be able to produce a vi-

FIGURE 13–16   A distributorless ignition system (DIS) can be checked by unplugging *both* spark plug wires from one ignition coil and starting the engine. The spark should be able to jump the 1-inch (25 millimeters) distance between the terminals of the coil. No damage to the coil (or module) results because a spark occurs and does not find ground somewhere else.

FIGURE 13–17   Using a vacuum hose and a grounded test light to ground one cylinder at a time on a distributorless ignition system. This works on all types of ignition systems and provides a method for grounding out one cylinder at a time without fear of damaging any component.

able (either sine or digital) signal. A meter set on AC volts should read a voltage across the sensor leads when the engine is being cranked. If there is no AC voltage output, replace the sensor.

■ *Step #2.* If the sensor tests okay (step #1), check for a changing AC voltage signal at the ignition module.

NOTE: This step checks the wiring between the crankshaft position sensor and the ignition control module.

If there is no signal at the ignition module, replace or repair the defective wiring between the ignition module and the crankshaft position sensor.

■ *Step #3.* If the ignition control module is receiving a changing signal from the crankshaft position sensor, it must be capable of switching the power to the ignition coils on and off. Remove a coil or coil package, and with the ignition switched to on (run), check for voltage at the positive terminal of the coil(s).

NOTE: Several manufacturers program the current to the coils to be turned off within several seconds of the ignition being switched to "on" if no pulse is received by the computer. This circuit design helps prevent ignition coil damage in the event of a failure in the control circuit or driver error (keeping the ignition switch on [run] without operating the starter [start position]). Some Chrysler engines do not supply power to the positive side of the coil until a crank pulse is received by the computer.

If the module is not pulsing the negative side of the coil or not supplying battery voltage to the positive side of the coil, replace the ignition control module.

NOTE: Before replacing the ignition control module, be certain that it is properly grounded (where applicable) and that the module is receiving ignition power from the ignition circuit.

CAUTION: Most distributorless (direct-fire) ignition systems can produce 40,000 volts or more, with energy levels high enough to cause personal injury. Do not open the circuit of an electronic ignition secondary wire, because damage to the system (or to you) can occur.

IGNITION SYSTEM SERVICE

The term *tune-up* used to refer to the replacement of worn ignition parts but has now been redefined as diagnosis of engine performance and the replacement of parts found to be in need of replacement. Most "tune-up specifications" are now commonly called "performance specifications." Even though many electronic engine analyzers can help pinpoint suspected problem areas, close visual inspection of the distributor cap, rotor, spark plugs, and spark plug wires is still important.

NOTE: According to research conducted by General Motors, about one-fifth (20%) of all faults are detected during a *thorough visual inspection!*

DISTRIBUTOR CAP INSPECTION

Inspect a distributor cap for a worn or cracked center carbon insert, excessive side insert wear or corrosion, cracks, or carbon tracks, and check the towers for burning or corrosion by removing spark plug wires from the distributor cap one at a time. Remember, a defective distributor cap affects starting and engine performance, especially in high-moisture conditions. If a carbon track is detected, it is most likely the result of a high-resistance or open spark plug wire. Replacement of a distributor cap because of a carbon track without checking and replacing the defective spark plug wire(s) will often result in the new distributor cap failing in a short time. It is recommended that the distributor cap

◄ **TECH TIP** ►

THE HORIZONTAL IGNITION COIL PROBLEMS

Some Chrysler-made vehicles may stall whenever making a left turn. One cause is the horizontally mounted ignition coil. Whenever the vehicle is making a left turn, the oil inside the ignition coil is forced away from the secondary tower, and without oil at this location, an internal short is made available for the secondary voltage. Remounting the ignition coil so that the secondary tower points toward the front or rear of the vehicle often cures this hard-to-find problem.

FIGURE 13–18 Typical plastic cover over the distributor cap and portions of the spark plug wiring. This cover helps reduce dirt accumulation on the distributor cap and wiring. Dirt and moisture (especially morning dew) greatly increase the voltage necessary to fire the spark plugs.

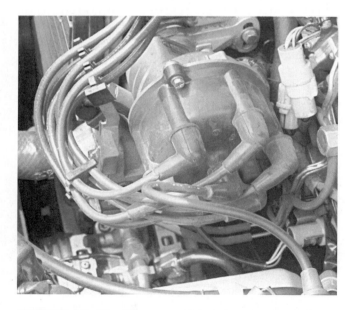

FIGURE 13–19 The same engine view as seen in figure 13–18 except with the dirt and moisture shield removed. Tests have indicated that moisture and dirt on the distributor cap and spark plug wires can increase the voltage required to fire the spark plugs by 5000 to 15,000 volts!

FIGURE 13–20 This distributor cap came off of a GM V-8 engine that was starting and running okay. The only problem seemed to be a "snapping" noise heard in the distributor.

and rotor be inspected every year and replaced if defective. The rotor should be replaced every time the spark plugs are replaced because all the ignition current flows through the rotor. Generally, distributor caps should only need replacement after every 3 or 4 years of normal service. See figures 13–18 through 13–23.

SPARK PLUG WIRE INSPECTION

Spark plug wires should be visually inspected for cuts or defective insulation and checked for resistance with an ohmmeter. Good spark plug wires should measure less than 10,000 ohms per foot of length. See figures 13–24 and 13–25. Faulty spark plug wire insulation can cause hard starting or no starting in damp weather conditions.

SILICONE GREASES

Silicone greases are not greases at all; even though they look like grease and feel like grease, they are not formulated like greases. Silicone grease is a dispersion of a silica thickening agent in a dimethyl silicone fluid. Although all silicone greases are water repellent and noncorrosive, certain properties can be emphasized for a particular application.

For example, when a slight amount of a metal oxide thickening agent is in the silicone fluid, the resulting product can act as a heat transfer agent. This type of silicone grease is used under electronic ignition modules (GM and Ford TFI) to transfer heat from the electronics. Other silicones are used for their electrical resistance

FIGURE 13–21 Good example of excessive aluminum oxide dusting of the side inserts of the HEI distributor cap. Also notice that the area around the center electrode is completely destroyed. The engine just would not start one day, although it had been running (barely) the day before.

FIGURE 13–23 Carbon track in a distributor cap. These faults are sometimes difficult to spot and can cause intermittent engine missing. The usual cause of a tracked distributor cap (or coil, if it is a distributorless ignition) is a defective (open) spark plug wire.

FIGURE 13–22 Distributor cap with broken center carbon insert that caused hard engine starting. (All testing failed to indicate this as a possible problem because the rotor gap voltage was still within specifications.)

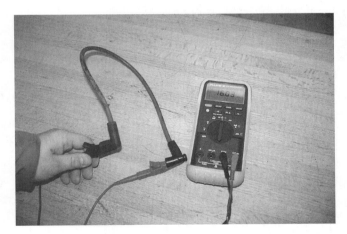

FIGURE 13–24 Measuring the resistance of a spark plug wire with a multimeter set to the ohms position. The reading of 16.03 KΩ (16,030 ohms) is okay because the wire is about 2 feet long. Maximum allowable resistance for a spark plug wire this long would be 20 KΩ (20,000 ohms).

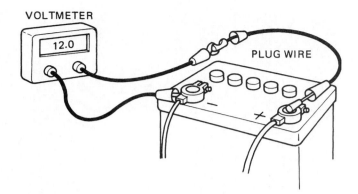

FIGURE 13–25 Besides being tested with an ohmmeter, spark plug wire condition can also be tested using a battery and a voltmeter. When a high-impedance digital meter is used, the voltmeter should indicate close to battery voltage when it is connected in series with a spark plug wire across (in parallel with) the battery terminals. If an analog (needle-type) meter is used, the wire is generally considered to be okay if the voltmeter reads 6 volts or higher.

(dielectric) value. The **dielectric strength** (resistance to electrical penetration) is about 500 volts per mil (0.001 inches).

Silicone grease can also be used on spark plug wire boots as a lubricant, a boot release, and a barrier against corrosion. Silicone dielectric grease is also used on some Ford distributor caps and rotors to reduce RFI emissions. Silicone grease has no melting point; it simply becomes a powder. Because silicone grease can be formulated for a variety of uses, do not use one product for all purposes. "General purpose" does not mean "all purpose." This is particularly important when using silicone grease for its heat transfer properties. Be certain that the grease used under ignition modules states on the tube or container that it is designed for this purpose.

SPARK PLUG SERVICE

Spark plugs should be inspected whenever an engine performance problem occurs and should be replaced regularly to ensure proper ignition system performance. With unleaded fuel and electronic ignition, some spark plugs have a service life of over 20,000 miles (32,000 kilometers). Platinum-tipped original equipment spark plugs have a typical service life of 100,000 miles (160,000 kilometers). Used spark plugs should *not* be cleaned and reused unless absolutely necessary. The labor required to remove and replace (R & R) spark plugs is the same whether the spark plugs are replaced or cleaned. Although cleaning spark plugs often restores proper engine operation, the service life of

◄ **TECH TIP** ►

A CLEAN ENGINE IS A HAPPY ENGINE

Many technicians clean every engine before a tune-up or other engine service. Steam cleaners can be used, but steam tends to remove paint from the engine. A hot water wash, often found at coin-operated washes, does an excellent job of removing grease, oil, and dirt, not only from the engine, but from all underhood components, including the battery. Some technicians keep the engine running while cleaning it with hot water. If the engine stalls, yet restarts after drying of the spark plug wires and distributor cap, faulty spark plug wire insulation and/or a faulty distributor cap is indicated.

CAUTION: Avoid direct water spray to the air cleaner inlet and alternator. Because water is thrown up on the engine components during normal driving on wet streets, no harm occurs from washing of these parts as long as direct water sprays are avoided. Some diesel engine manufacturers do not recommend engine cleaning, due to the close tolerances of the parts commonly found in the injection pump.

A clean engine will run cooler and is much easier to service. Oil leaks can also be easier to locate on a clean engine. Most customers are impressed to find a clean engine compartment—it is one of the few tune-up items that is visible to the average owner.

cleaned spark plugs is definitely shorter than that of new spark plugs. *Platinum-tipped spark plugs should not be regapped!* Using a gapping tool can break the platinum after it has been used in an engine.

Be certain that the engine is cool before removing spark plugs, especially on engines with aluminum cylinder heads. To help prevent dirt from getting down into the cylinder of an engine while removing a spark plug, use compressed air or a brush to remove dirt from around the spark plug prior to removal.

While removing spark plugs, place them in order so that they can be inspected to check for engine problems that might affect one or more cylinders. All of the spark plugs should be in the same condition, and the color of the center insulator should be light tan or gray. If all the spark plugs are black or dark, the engine should be

FIGURE 13–26   Spark plug removed from an engine after a 500-mile race. Note the clipped side (ground) electrode. The electrode design and narrow (0.025-inch) gap are used to ensure that a spark occurs during extremely high engine speed operation. The color and condition of the spark plug indicate that near-perfect combustion has been occurring.

FIGURE 13–27   Typical worn spark plug. Notice the rounded center electrode. The deposits indicate that there may be an oil usage problem.

checked for conditions that could cause an overly rich air-fuel mixture or possible oil burning. If only one or a few spark plugs are black, check those cylinders for proper firing (possible defective spark plug wire) or an engine condition affecting only those particular cylinders. See figures 13–26 through 13–30.

If all of the spark plugs are white, check for possible over-advanced ignition timing or a vacuum leak causing a lean air-fuel mixture. If only one or a few spark plugs are white, check for a vacuum leak affecting the fuel mixture only to those particular cylinders.

NOTE: The engine computer "senses" rich or lean air-fuel ratios by means of input from the oxygen sensor. If one cylinder is lean, the computer may make all other cylinders richer to compensate.

Inspect all spark plugs for wear by first checking the condition of the center electrode. As a spark plug wears, the center electrode becomes rounded. If the center electrode is rounded, higher ignition system voltage is required to fire the spark plug. When installing spark plugs, always use the correct tightening torque to ensure proper heat transfer from the spark plug shell to the cylinder head. See the following table.

FIGURE 13–28   New spark plug that was fouled by a too-rich air-fuel mixture. The engine from which this spark plug came had a defective (stuck partially open) injector on this one cylinder only.

| | Torque with torque wrench (in pound-feet) | | Torque without torque wrench (in turns) | |
Spark plug	Cast-iron head	Aluminum head	Cast-iron head	Aluminum head
Gasket				
14 mm	26–30	18–22	¼	¼
18 mm	32–38	28–34	¼	¼
Tapered seat				
14 mm	7–15	7–15	1/16 (snug)	1/16 (snug)
18 mm	15–20	15–20	1/16 (snug)	1/16 (snug)

NOTE: General Motors does *not* recommend the use of antiseize compound on the threads of spark plugs being installed in an aluminum cylinder head. The reason is the spark plug will be tightened too much. This excessive tightening torque places the threaded portion of the spark plug too far into the combustion chamber where carbon can accumulate and result in difficult-to-remove spark plugs. If antiseize compound is used on spark plug threads, reduce the tightening torque by 40%. Always follow the vehicle manufacturer's recommendations.

J-GAPPED SPARK PLUGS

A J-gapped spark plug is a plug whose side electrode is cut off so that the end is lined up with the centerline of the center electrode. See figure 13–32. A spark usually

jumps from a sharp edge. A new spark plug has sharp edges on the center electrode and requires less voltage to jump than does a worn, used spark plug whose center electrode has become rounded. Most new spark plugs, however, still fire to the flat surface of the side electrode. If the side electrode is filed or cut off, the spark will then occur between the sharp edges of the center

(a)

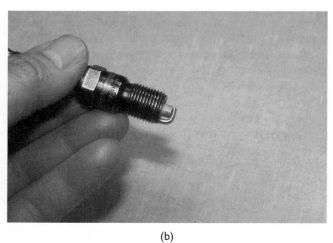

(b)

FIGURE 13–30   *(a)* Looks like a normal spark plug until you shake it. *(b)* The center porcelain has broken and now covers the center electrode. This is sometimes called a "click-click" spark plug because it clicks when you shake it.

FIGURE 13–29   Typical worn spark plug showing gasoline- or oil-additive deposits.

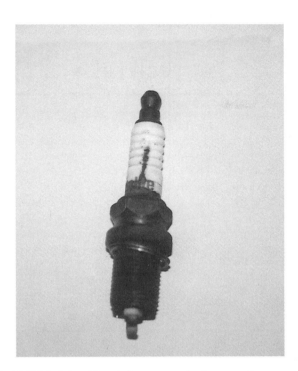

FIGURE 13–31 This defective spark plug was discovered using a megger test. A small crack in the porcelain caused the spark to jump from the wire directly to the metal shell of the plug.

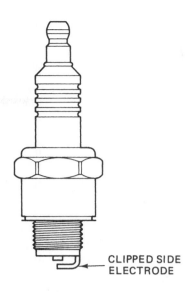

CLIPPED SIDE
ELECTRODE

FIGURE 13–32 Spark plug with a clipped (shortened) ground electrode. This type of plug gap design is often called a J gap because this style of electrode is commonly used on Champion spark plugs that use the letter *J* as a prefix letter, such as the lawn mower plug J-8.

◀ TECH TIP ▶

"MEGGER" TEST

An insulation resistance meter (sometimes called a **megger**) can be used to determine if spark plugs are fouled while they are still in the engine. A megger is an ohmmeter that has a scale of 10 megohms (10 million ohms) or higher.

To test spark plugs with an ohmmeter, set the ohmmeter scale to "10 MΩ" and connect one test lead to a good engine ground. Connect the other test lead to the center spark plug electrode with the spark plug still installed in the engine. The reading should be *more* than 10 megohms. If the resistance is less than 10 megohms, the spark plug is fouled or has poor insulation and should be inspected and cleaned or replaced. See figure 13–31.

NOTE: If this test indicates any resistance less than 10 megohms, the plug is definitely fouled. However, the plug could be fouled and that not be indicated by the test. So this test works as a positive test, but as with other electrical tests, it does not always prove that there is nothing wrong if a component passes the test.

◀ TECH TIP ▶

USE ORIGINAL EQUIPMENT MANUFACTURER SPARK PLUGS

A technician at an independent service center replaced the spark plugs in a Pontiac with new Champion brand spark plugs of the correct size, reach, and heat range. When the customer returned to pay his bill, he inquired as to the brand name of the replacement parts used for the tune-up. When told that Champion spark plugs were used, he stopped signing his name on the check he was writing. He said that he owned 1000 shares of General Motors stock and he owned two General Motors vehicles and he expected to have General Motors parts used in his General Motors vehicles. The service manager had the technician replace the spark plugs with AC brand spark plugs because this brand was used in the engine when the vehicle was new. Even though most spark plug manufacturers produce spark plugs that are correct for use in almost any engine, many customers prefer that original brand (original equipment manufacturer [OEM]) spark plugs be used in their engines.

◀ TECH TIP ▶

SPARK PLUG GAP AND A SMOOTH IDLE

A technician replaced the spark plugs in a Toyota with electronic fuel injection and electronic ignition. After the replacement of the spark plugs, along with the distributor cap and rotor, the engine had a slightly rough idle. Since the idle fuel mixture was not adjustable, the technician assumed that the cause of the rough idle was the ignition system. After carefully rechecking the ignition system to be certain that all spark plug wires were secured, he regapped the new spark plugs to the same wider gap as that of the old spark plugs he had removed. The idle was now perfect and the engine ran smoother. The specified spark plug gap was 0.040 inches (1.0 millimeters), with a maximum allowable gap of 0.055 inches (1.4 millimeters). A wider spark plug gap generally gives smoother idling and better fuel economy, whereas narrower-gapped spark plugs are used for racing and high-speed performance. While the factory-recommended spark plug gap should always be considered correct, a slight increase of about 0.005 to 0.010 inches (0.1 to 0.2 millimeters) may result in smoother engine operation and improved fuel economy. A decrease of about 0.005 to 0.010 inches (0.1 to 0.2 millimeters) may be required for combustion to occur at very high engine speeds.

◀ TECH TIP ▶

"4 MINUTES ON THE CLOCK"

During replacement, tapered-seat spark plugs should be tightened by the correct amount to ensure proper heat transfer and engine operation. The tightening torque specifications are 7 to 15 pound-feet (for spark plugs with a thread diameter of 14 millimeters) or one-sixteenth of a turn. Because many technicians do not use a torque wrench when installing spark plugs, simply remember that a tapered-seat spark plug should be tightened by about 4 minutes of rotation on a clock face (which is about one-sixteenth of a revolution).

factory with the shorter side electrode. AC calls this feature a "clipped" electrode design.

NOTE: Many premium platinum spark plugs use clipped (J-gapped) side electrodes with expensive platinum wire center electrodes, resulting in a long-lasting spark plug that delivers superior performance.

ORIGINAL EQUIPMENT SPARK PLUGS

It is useful at times to be able to tell if the spark plugs are originals from the factory or have been replaced. AC brand spark plugs, with which General Motors vehicles come equipped from the factory, usually have a painted dot (usually white, orange, or green) on the top of the spark plug terminal. If, for example, a GM vehicle came into your shop for service with 30,000 miles on the odometer, a technician could quickly determine if the spark plugs were original or had been replaced by removing a plug wire and looking for the dot on the terminal end of the spark plug. Some original Ford factory spark plugs also have a painted dot on the top terminal. This information can be used to help determine quickly what parts may be required for service.

PAIRED CYLINDERS

Whenever working on a distributorless ignition or replacing a distributor, it is nice to know what cylinders are paired or operate exactly opposite each other. For

electrode to the sharp edge of the side electrode. This reduces the voltage required to fire the spark plug and reduces the chance of misfire. The lower voltage requirement of a J-gapped spark plug is easily seen on a scope by the spark plug's shorter firing line height. Because the firing voltage is reduced, the spark plug gap can be increased by at least 0.005 inches to create a longer spark for better fuel economy and performance, while the spark plug still maintains the same (or a lower) firing voltage as a standard spark plug gapped at the original specifications. Why don't spark plug manufacturers J-gap all their spark plugs? Because the side electrode is welded to the shell of the spark plug, close tolerances would have to be used to locate the *exact* position of the end of the side electrode in the center of the center electrode. The useful life of a J-gap spark plug is also reduced slightly when it is operated over 200 hours compared to non–J-gapped spark plugs.

Why is it called J-gapped? Some Champion spark plugs with a *J* as part of the code number come from the

example, when one cylinder is at TDC on the compression stroke, another cylinder is at TDC on the exhaust stroke. But how can you determine which cylinder is opposite? Simply write down the firing order and determine the center point. Rewrite the right-hand numbers underneath the left-hand numbers. The top and bottom cylinder numbers represent paired cylinders.

For example: The Buick V-6 firing order is 165432. Split the firing order: 165, 432. Put the right-hand numbers under the left-hand numbers:

$\frac{165}{432}$. Cylinders paired are 1 and 4, 6 and 3, and 5 and 2.

QUICK AND EASY SECONDARY IGNITION TESTS

Most engine running problems are caused by defective or out-of-adjustment ignition components. Many ignition problems involve the high-voltage secondary ignition circuit.

- *Test #1.* If there is a crack in a distributor cap, coil, or spark plug, or a defective spark plug wire, a spark may be visible at night. Because the highest voltage is required during partial-throttle acceleration, the technician's assistant should accelerate the engine slightly with the gear selector in "drive" or second gear (if manual transmission) and the brake firmly applied. If *any* spark is visible, the location should be closely inspected and the defective parts replaced. A blue glow or "corona" around the shell of the spark plug is normal and *not* an indication of a defective spark plug.
- *Test #2.* For intermittent problems, use a spray bottle to apply a water mist to the spark plugs, distributor cap, and spark plug wires. With the engine running, the water may cause an arc through any weak insulating materials and cause the engine to miss or stall.

HINT: Adding a little *salt* or liquid *soap* to the water makes the water more conductive. This makes it easier to find those hard-to-diagnose intermittent ignition faults.

- *Test #3.* To determine if the rough engine operation is due to secondary ignition problems, connect a 6- to 12-volt test light to the negative side (sometimes labeled

tach) of the coil. Connect the other lead of the test light to the positive lead of the coil. With the engine running, the test light should be dim and steady in brightness. If there is high resistance in the secondary circuit (such as that caused by a defective spark plug wire), the test light will pulse brightly at times. If the test light varies noticeably, this indicates that the secondary voltage cannot find ground easily and is feeding back through the primary windings of the coil. This feedback causes the test light to become brighter.

IGNITION TIMING

Ignition timing should be checked and adjusted according to the manufacturer's specifications and procedures for best fuel economy and performance, and lowest exhaust emissions. Generally, for testing, engines must be at idle with computer engine controls put into "base" timing. Base timing is the timing of the spark before the computer advances the timing. To be assured of the proper ignition timing, follow, exactly, the timing procedure indicated on the underhood emission decal.

NOTE: Most older engines equipped with a vacuum advance must have the vacuum hose removed and plugged before they are checked for timing.

◄ TECH TIP ►

THE PINK SPARK PLUGS

A technician was performing a routine tune-up and discovered that the insulator color was not the normal tan or gray, but pink! After much discussion among the technicians, it was the general opinion that the color was due to either gasoline or oil additives. Because this color had not been observed on this customer's spark plugs before, they were all anxious to question the owner. The owner admitted that a new super premium unleaded gasoline had been used prior to the tune-up. Remember that other colors of spark plugs besides tan and gray could be "normal," depending on fuel- and/or oil-additive packages. A rust-colored insulator is also normally caused by a fuel additive.

If the ignition timing is too far *advanced*, the following symptoms may occur. (An example of advanced ignition timing is timing set at 12 degrees before top dead center (BTDC) instead of 8 degrees BTDC.)

1. Engine "ping" or spark knock may be heard, especially while driving up a hill or during acceleration.
2. Cranking (starting) may be slow and jerky, especially when the engine is warm.
3. The engine may overheat if the ignition timing is too far advanced.

If the ignition timing is too far *retarded*, the following symptoms may occur. (An example of retarded ignition timing is timing set at 4 degrees BTDC instead of 8 degrees BTDC.)

1. The engine may lack in power and performance.
2. The engine may require a long period of starter cranking before starting.
3. Poor fuel economy may result from retarded ignition timing.
4. The engine may overheat if the ignition timing is too far retarded.

PRETIMING CHECKS

Before the ignition timing is checked or adjusted, the following items should be checked to ensure accurate timing results:

◄ TECH TIP ►

THE "TURN THE KEY" TEST

If the ignition timing is correct, a warm engine should start immediately when the ignition key is turned to the start position. If the engine cranks a long time before starting, the ignition timing may be retarded. If the engine cranks slowly, the ignition timing may be too far advanced. However, if the engine starts immediately, the ignition timing, although it may not be exactly set according to specification, is usually adjusted fairly close to specifications. Whenever a starting problem is experienced, check the ignition timing first, before checking the fuel system or the cranking system for a possible problem. This procedure can be used to help diagnose a possible ignition timing problem quickly without tools or equipment.

1. The engine should be at normal operating temperature (the upper radiator hose should be hot and pressurized).
2. The engine should be at the correct timing RPM (check the specifications).
3. The vacuum hoses should be removed, and the hose from the vacuum advance unit on the distributor (if the vehicle is so equipped) should be plugged unless otherwise specified.
4. If the engine is computer equipped, check the timing procedure specified by the manufacturer. This may include disconnecting a "set timing" connector wire, grounding a diagnostic terminal, disconnecting a four-wire connector, or similar procedure.

NOTE: General Motors specifies ten different pretiming procedures depending on the engine, type of fuel system, and type of ignition system. For example, many four-cylinder engines use the *average* of the timing for cylinder #1 and cylinder #4! Always consult the emission decal under the hood for the *exact* procedure to follow.

TIMING LIGHT CONNECTIONS

For checking or adjusting ignition timing, make the timing light connections as follows:

1. Connect the timing light battery leads to the vehicle battery: the red to the positive terminal and the black to the negative terminal.
2. Connect the timing light high-tension lead to the #1 spark plug cable. See figure 13–33.

DETERMINING THE #1 CYLINDER

The following will help in determining the #1 cylinder:

1. Four- or six-cylinder engines: On all inline four- and six-cylinder engines, the #1 cylinder is the *most forward* cylinder.
2. V-6 or V-8 engines: Most V-type engines use the *left front* (driver's side) cylinder as the #1 cylinder, *except* for Ford engines and some Cadillacs, which use the right front (passenger's side) cylinder.
3. Sideways (transverse) engines: Most front wheel–drive vehicles with engines installed sideways use the cylinder to the *far right* (passenger's side) as the #1 cylinder (plug wire closest to the drive belt[s]).

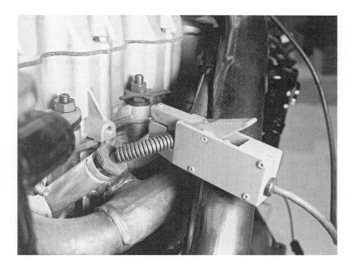

FIGURE 13–33 Inductive pickup for a timing light connected around cylinder #1 of a GM four-cylinder engine with a distributor. Even though the computer controls timing on most engines, the base (initial) timing can and should be checked and adjusted (if possible) as part of a thorough engine performance check.

Follow this *rule of thumb:* If the #1 cylinder is unknown for a given type of engine, it is the *most forward* cylinder as viewed from above (except in Pontiac V-8 engines). See figure 13–34 for typical #1 cylinder locations.

CHECKING OR ADJUSTING IGNITION TIMING

Follow these steps for checking or adjusting ignition timing:

1. Start the engine and adjust the speed to that specified for ignition timing.
2. With the timing light aimed at the stationary timing pointer, observe the position of the timing mark with the light flashing. Refer to the manufacturer's specifications on the underhood decal for the correct setting. See figure 13–35.

NOTE: If the timing mark appears ahead of the pointer, in relation to the direction of crankshaft rotation, the timing is advanced. If the timing mark appears behind the pointer, in relation to the direction of crankshaft rotation, the timing is retarded.

---

3. To adjust timing, loosen the distributor locking bolt or nut and turn the distributor housing until the timing mark is in correct alignment. Turn the distributor housing in the direction of rotor rotation to re-

tard the timing and against rotor rotation to advance the timing.
4. After adjusting the timing to specifications, carefully tighten the distributor locking bolt. It is sometimes necessary to readjust the timing after the initial setting because the distributor may rotate slightly when the hold-down bolt is tightened.

MAGNETIC TIMING

Since the late 1970s, many manufacturers have provided a receptacle for use with a magnetic ignition timing meter. Magnetic timing involves a magnetic pickup sensor that is inserted in a holder that is located close to TDC. The number of degrees by which the sensor is offset from true TDC (0 degrees) is called the **magnetic offset angle.** See figure 13–36.

The magnetic offset angle varies according to the manufacturer, and most are offset after TDC and are therefore negative. The following are typical magnetic offset angles.

GM	$-9.5°$
AMC	$-10°$
Chrysler	$-10°$
Ford*	
Mercedes	$-15°$
BMW	$-20°$
Renault	$-20°$
VW/Audi	$-20°$
Porsche	$-20°$
Volvo	$-20°$

*Magnetic timing is not recommended by Ford (offset angles vary according to engine plant, engine, and year). (Some typical Ford engine offset angles include 26°, 52°, 68°, 135°, 314°, and 334°.) Magnetic timing on Ford engines is designed to be used only on the assembly line during engine production.

Magnetic timing units (meters) are available through most auto supply stores. When the magnetic sensor is used, the harmonic balancer must be *clean* for best results. Magnetic timing is an excellent tool. It permits accurate ignition timing without the visual error (called **parallax**) that often results from using a timing light.

MECHANICAL TIMING ADVANCE

Older-model engines use mechanical advance weights to advance the ignition timing as engine speed increases. This mechanical advance provides additional engine power and performance. If the mechanical

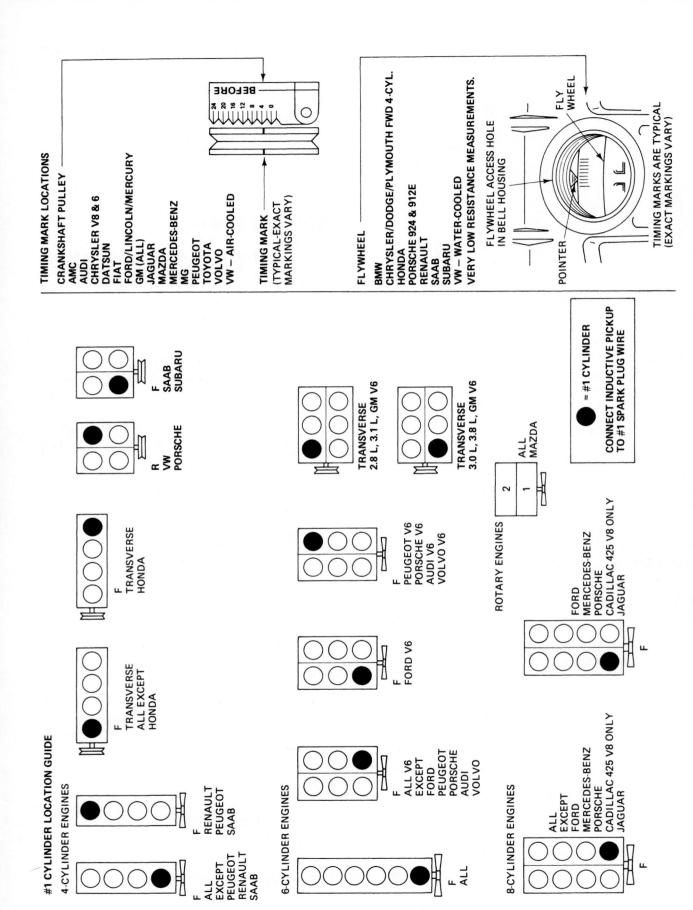

FIGURE 13-34 #1 cylinder and timing work location guide.

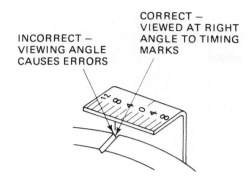

FIGURE 13–35 Parallax occurs when timing marks are viewed from an angle.

FIGURE 13–36 Magnetic timing receptacle offset from 0 degrees (TDC). A magnetic timing pickup probe senses the notch in the crankshaft pulley.

advance is not working, the driver most often complains of lack of power and performance. If the advance weights stick in the advanced position, the most frequent complaint is constant engine spark knock (ping). If the ignition timing is found to be advanced from specifications, always inspect the mechanical advance weights, because they could be stuck in an advanced position. With the engine not running and the distributor cap off, rotate the rotor and release it quickly. The rotor should "snap" back to its original location if the mechanical advance mechanism is operat-

◄ **DIAGNOSTIC STORY** ►

THE CASE OF THE RETARDED DISTRIBUTOR

An older-model Ford V-8 truck was towed into an independent service center because the engine had simply quit. After some preliminary checking, a technician moved all of the spark plug wires on the distributor cap one spot in the advanced direction—the engine started and ran. But because spark plug wires do not relocate themselves while a vehicle is running down the road, the technician decided to disassemble the front end of the engine. The technician decided that the timing chain must have slipped over the smaller crankshaft gear and retarded the valve and the ignition timing.

But the chain was perfect. After closer inspection, the problem was discovered. The distributor drive gear pin had sheared and allowed the distributor shaft to rotate. The ends of the sheared pin were still visible at both sides of the distributor gear. The engine ran perfectly after the sheared distributor drive gear pin was replaced and the engine was reassembled.

ing correctly. If the rotor does *not* snap quickly back, the distributor should be removed from the engine and disassembled. See figures 13–37 and 13–38.

VACUUM TIMING ADVANCE

On engines equipped with a vacuum advance unit, additional ignition timing is provided during partial-throttle operation for maximum fuel economy. Vacuum advance units are attached to the side of the distributor and move the breaker plate (pickup coil) to advance the timing during high-vacuum conditions. Vacuum advance has a major influence on fuel economy (up to 4 to 5 miles per gallon [mpg]) and only a slight effect on throttle response.

COMPUTERIZED TIMING ADVANCE

Engines equipped with computer-controlled fuel-handling devices usually use computer-controlled ignition timing. These computer-controlled systems (either

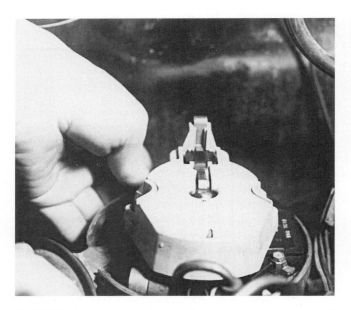

FIGURE 13–37   If an ignition distributor is to be removed from any engine, always mark the direction in which the rotor is pointing. Also mark the relative location of the distributor (or the direction in which the vacuum advance is pointing, if the vehicle is so equipped) before removing.

with or without a distributor) control the ignition timing based on inputs from various engine sensors. These sensors include

1. throttle position (TP)
2. manifold absolute pressure (MAP) (vacuum)
3. engine speed (RPM)
4. altitude (barometric pressure, also called BARO)
5. engine coolant temperature (ECT)
6. intake air temperature (IAT) (if the vehicle is so equipped)

The engine computer provides the optimum possible spark advance based on the values of all the different sensors. A failure in any one of the sensors may affect the total ignition timing advance.

If a problem develops in the computer or sensors, the ignition timing usually defaults to a more retarded advance than is normal. This reduced timing advance prevents possible engine damage. The computer (or other ignition control unit, such as the ignition module) provides enough spark advance to prevent overheating of the catalytic converter. The most noticeable symptom of having the computer default to base timing is reduced fuel economy. See the manufacturer's diagnostic procedures for pinpointing possible causes. See chapters 15 through 18, on computerized engine controls, for details.

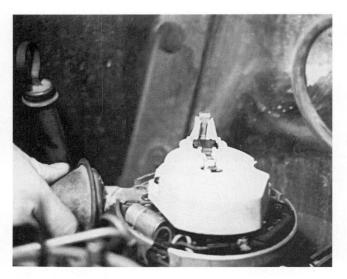

FIGURE 13–38   The key to being able to reinstall a distributor successfully is to make a second set of marks (two chalk marks in this photo) indicating the direction of the rotor when the distributor has just cleared the camshaft gear and stopped rotating. To reinstall, simply line the rotor up with the two marks, and the distributor should drop down and rotate until the rotor aligns with the original (one) mark.

IGNITION SYSTEM TROUBLESHOOTING GUIDE

The following list will assist technicians in troubleshooting ignition system problems.

Problem	*Possible Causes and/or Solutions*
1. No spark out of the coil	1. Possible open in the ignition switch circuit. Possible defective ignition module (if electronic ignition) coil. Possible defective pickup coil or Hall-effect switch (if electronic ignition). Possible shorted condenser.
2. Weak spark out of the coil	2. Possible high-resistance coil wire or spark plug wire. Possible poor ground between the distributor or module and the engine block.
3. Engine missing	3. Possible defective (open) spark plug wire. Possible worn or fouled spark plugs. Possible defective pickup coil. Possible defective module. Possible poor electrical connections at the pickup coil and/or module.

SUMMARY

1. Always use a spark tester that requires at least 25 kilovolts (KV) to fire whenever checking for spark.

2. Ignition coils usually test at about 1 ohm across the primary winding and from 6000 to 30,000 ohms across the secondary winding.

3. A typical magnetic pickup coil should measure approximately in the middle of its specification for resistance and be able to produce an AC voltage of at *least* 0.25 volts while the engine is cranking.

4. An open spark plug wire can damage the ignition coil.

5. A thorough visual inspection should be performed of all ignition components whenever diagnosing an engine performance problem.

6. Platinum spark plugs should not be regapped after use in an engine.

7. Always follow the manufacturer's recommended procedure exactly when checking or adjusting the ignition timing.

REVIEW QUESTIONS

1. Explain why a spark tester should be used to check for spark rather than using a standard spark plug.

2. Describe how to check an ignition coil using an ohmmeter.

3. Explain how to test a pickup coil for resistance and AC voltage output.

4. Discuss what harm can occur if the engine is cranked or run with an open (defective) spark plug wire.

5. Explain why platinum spark plugs should not be regapped after they are used in an engine.

6. Describe how to perform magnetic timing of an engine.

MULTIPLE-CHOICE QUESTIONS

1. Technician A says that a pickup coil (pulse generator) can be tested with an ohmmeter. Technician B says that ignition coils can be tested with an ohmmeter. Which technician is correct?
   a. A only
   b. B only
   c. Both a and b
   d. Neither a nor b

2. Technician A says that a defective spark plug wire can cause an engine miss. Technician B says that a defective pickup coil wire can cause an engine miss. Which technician is correct?
   a. A only
   b. B only
   c. Both a and b
   d. Neither a nor b

3. The _____ sends a pulse signal to an electronic ignition module.
   a. Ballast resistor
   b. Pickup coil
   c. Ignition coil
   d. Condenser

4. Typical primary coil resistance specifications usually range _____ .
   a. From 100 to 450 ohms
   b. From 500 to 1500 ohms
   c. From 1 to 3 ohms
   d. From 6000 to 30,000 ohms

5. Typical secondary coil resistance specifications usually range _____ .
   a. From 100 to 450 ohms
   b. From 500 to 1500 ohms
   c. From 1 to 3 ohms
   d. From 6000 to 30,000 ohms

6. Technician A says that an engine will not start and run without a pulse signal to the ignition module (igniter). Technician B says that one wire of any pickup coil must be grounded. Which technician is correct?
   a. A only
   b. B only
   c. Both a and b
   d. Neither a nor b

7. Technician A says that a GM HEI distributor rotor can burn through and cause an engine miss during acceleration. Technician B says that a defective pickup coil can cause an engine miss during acceleration. Which technician is correct?
   a. A only
   b. B only
   c. Both a and b
   d. Neither a nor b

8. The secondary ignition circuit can be tested using _____.
   a. An ohmmeter
   b. A test light
   c. An ammeter
   d. Both a and b

9. Electronic ignition modules can be tested using _____.
   a. Special electronic ignition module testers
   b. A soldering gun for some modules
   c. A test light and jumper wires for some modules
   d. All of the above

10. An ohmmeter reading of 1 ohm is an acceptable reading for a _____.
    a. Pickup coil
    b. Ignition coil
    c. Ignition module
    d. Spark plug wire

◀ Chapter 14 ▶

OSCILLOSCOPE TESTING

OBJECTIVES

After studying chapter 14, the reader will be able to

1. Explain a secondary ignition scope pattern.
2. Discuss how the slope of the spark line can indicate problems.
3. Describe how to test alternators using a scope.
4. Explain how to test sensors using a dual-trace scope.

An oscilloscope (usually called just a scope) is actually a high-impedance voltmeter that shows any change in voltage as a line on the scope.

SCOPE TESTING THE IGNITION SYSTEM

Any automotive scope will show an ignition system pattern. All ignition systems, whether electronic, Hall effect, or point type, must charge and discharge an ignition coil. With the engine off, most scopes will display a straight horizontal line. With the engine running, this horizontal (zero) line is changed to a pattern that will have sections both above and below the zero line. Sections of this pattern that are *above* the zero line indicate that the ignition coil is *discharging*. Sections of the scope pattern *below* the zero line indicate *charging* of the ignition coil. The height of the scope pattern indicates *voltage*. The length (from left to right) of the scope pattern indicates *time*. See figure 14–1.

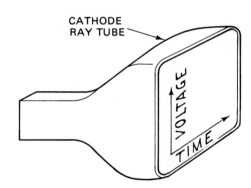

FIGURE 14–1 An automotive oscilloscope (scope) is of the same construction as a cathode ray tube (CRT) or television screen. An automotive oscilloscope is a visual voltmeter. The higher up a trace (line) on the scope, the higher the voltage. The scope illustrates time from left to right. The longer the horizontal line, the longer the amount of time.

CONNECTING THE SCOPE LEADS

All scopes must be connected at four points to function correctly (fig. 14–2):

1. Connection to the coil wire. This connection or inductive pickup around the coil wire (or on the distributor cap for HEI systems) signals—to the electronics of the scope—the intensity and polarity of the discharging and charging of the coil. This connection primarily determines the scope pattern.

261

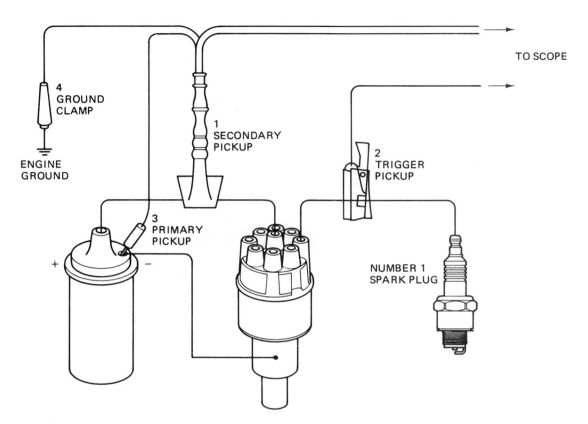

FIGURE 14–2   Typical engine analyzer hookup that includes a scope display. (*1*) Coil wire on top of the distributor cap if integral type of coil; (*2*) number 1 spark plug connection; (*3*) negative side of the ignition coil; (*4*) ground (negative) connection of the battery.

2. Connection to the #1 spark plug wire. The connection or inductive pickup around the #1 spark plug wire signals the scope to start the sequence of coil discharge patterns so that the patterns will be displayed correctly on the screen. The #1 spark plug connection is commonly used to operate the timing light and tachometer units of the scope (if it is so equipped).

3. Connection to the negative side of the coil. The connection on the negative side of the coil triggers the dwell meter. The connection to the negative side of the coil also allows the ignition system to ground out a single cylinder at a time to check the power balance of the engine.

4. Connection to ground. This last connection must be to a clean metal connection on the engine block or to a noninsulated engine bracket to ensure a proper ground connection for power balance testing and accurate dwell meter readings.

HOW TO READ A SCOPE PATTERN

Automotive oscilloscopes provide controls that permit viewing of a pattern for either the primary ignition circuit or the secondary ignition circuit. Many technicians view just the secondary pattern because the primary ignition pattern is reflected in the secondary pattern. Each section of a scope pattern has a name. The name of the scope pattern section also describes the section of the ignition operation.

FIRING LINE

The leftmost vertical (upward) line is called the **firing line.** The height of the firing line should be between 5000 and 15,000 volts (5 and 15 kV) with not more than a 3-kV difference between the highest and the lowest cylinder's firing line. See figure 14–3.

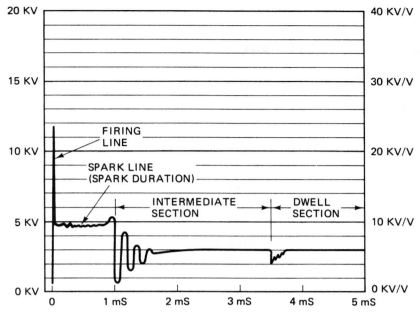

FIGURE 14–3 Typical secondary ignition oscilloscope pattern.

The height of the firing line indicates the *voltage* required to fire the spark plug. It requires a high voltage to make the air inside the cylinder electrically conductive (to ionize the air). A higher than normal height (or height higher than that of other cylinders) can be caused by one or more of the following:

1. A spark plug gapped too wide
2. A lean fuel mixture
3. A defective spark plug wire

If the firing lines are higher than normal for *all* cylinders, then possible causes include one or more of the following:

1. A worn distributor cap and/or rotor (if the vehicle is so equipped)
2. Excessive wearing of all spark plugs
3. A defective coil wire (the high voltage could still jump across the open section of the wire to fire the spark plugs)

See Examples of Firing Line Problems later in this chapter for further information on firing line analysis.

SPARK LINE

The **spark line** is a short horizontal line connected to the firing line. The height of the spark line represents the voltage required to maintain the spark across the spark plug after the spark has started. The height of the spark line should be one-fourth of the height of the firing line (between 1.5 and 2.5 kilovolts). The length (from left to right) of the line represents the length of time for which the spark lasts (duration). The duration of the spark should be from 1 to 2 milliseconds (ms). The spark stops at the end (right side) of the spark line as shown in figure 14–4.

INTERMEDIATE OSCILLATIONS

After the spark has stopped, there is still some remaining energy left in the coil.

This remaining energy dissipates in the coil windings and the entire secondary circuit. The oscillations are also called the "ringing" of the coil as it is pulsed.

The secondary pattern amplifies any voltage variation occurring in the primary circuit because of the turns ratio between the primary and secondary windings of the ignition coil.

A correctly operating ignition system should display five or more "bumps" (oscillations) (three or more for a GM HEI system).

TRANSISTOR-ON POINT

After the intermediate oscillations, the coil is empty (not charged), as indicated by the scope pattern being on the zero line for a short period. When the transistor

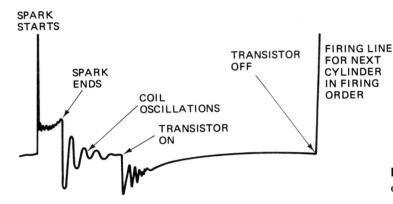

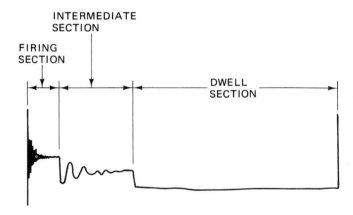

FIGURE 14–4 Drawing showing what is occurring electrically at each part of the scope pattern.

turns on an electronic system, the coil is being charged. Note that the charging of the coil occurs slowly (coil charging oscillations) because of the inductive reactance of the coil as shown in figure 14–4.

DWELL SECTION

Dwell is the time that the current is charging the coil from the transistor-on point to the transistor-off point. At the end of the dwell section is the beginning of the next firing line. This point is called transistor off and indicates that the primary current of the coil is stopped, resulting in a high-voltage spark out of the coil.

PRIMARY PATTERN

The scope pattern of the primary ignition circuit shown in figure 14–5 is similar to the secondary because the secondary pattern reflects the operation of the primary circuit.

SCOPE PATTERN ANALYSIS

To get accurate problem-solving results using a scope, it is best to have the engine at normal operating temperature. Extremely cold or overheated engines may be operating incorrectly as a result of the temperature rather than a mechanical problem. The engine is warm when the upper radiator hose is hot and pressurized or when the cooling fans have cycled at least twice.

PATTERN SELECTION

The basic pattern illustrated in figure 14–4 is not seen in its totality on a scope. Ignition oscilloscopes use three

FIGURE 14–5 Typical primary pattern.

positions to view certain sections of the basic pattern more closely. These three positions are as follows:

1. *Superimposed.* This position is used to look at differences in patterns between cylinders in all areas except the firing line. There are no firing lines illustrated in superimposed positions. See figure 14–6.
2. *Raster (stacked).* The #1 cylinder is at the bottom on most scopes. Use the raster position to look at the spark line length and transistor-on point. The raster (stacked) pattern shows all areas of the scope pattern except the firing lines. See figure 14–7.
3. *Display (parade).* Display (parade) is the only position in which firing lines are visible. The firing line section for the #1 cylinder is on the far right side of the screen, with the remaining portions of the pattern on the left side. This selection is used to compare the height of firing lines among all cylinders. See figure 14–8.

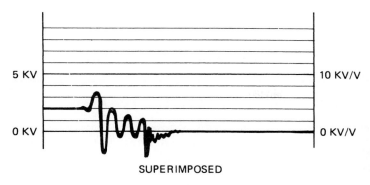

SUPERIMPOSED

FIGURE 14–6 Typical secondary ignition pattern. Note the lack of firing lines on superimposed pattern.

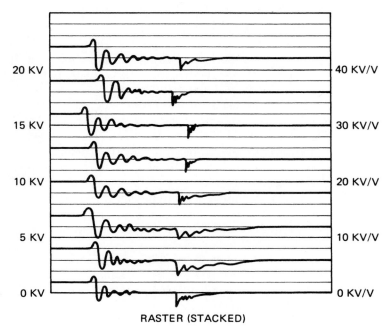

RASTER (STACKED)

FIGURE 14–7 Raster is the best scope position to use to view the spark lines of all the cylinders to check for differences. Most scopes display the #1 cylinder at the bottom. The other cylinders are positioned by firing order above #1.

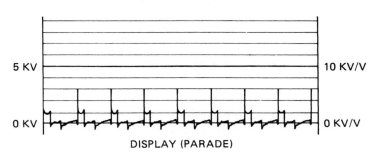

DISPLAY (PARADE)

FIGURE 14–8 Display is the only position to view the firing lines of all cylinders. The #1 cylinder is displayed on the left (except for its firing line, which is shown on the right). The cylinders are displayed from left to right by firing order.

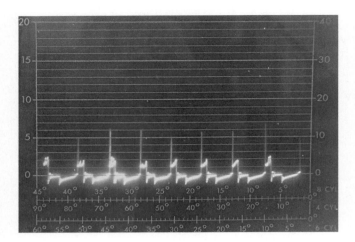

FIGURE 14–9 Typical eight-cylinder display (parade) pattern. Notice that the firing line for the #1 cylinder is at the far right of the screen. Also notice the differences in firing line heights and lengths and slopes of the spark lines.

READING THE SCOPE ON DISPLAY (PARADE)

Start the engine and operate at approximately 1000 RPM to ensure a smooth and accurate scope pattern. Firing lines are visible only on the display (parade) position. The firing lines should all be 5 to 15 kilovolts in height and be within 3 kilovolts of each other. If one or more cylinders have high firing lines, this could indicate a defective (open) spark plug wire, a spark plug gapped too far, or a lean fuel mixture affecting just those cylinders.

A lean mixture (not enough fuel) requires a higher voltage to ignite because there are not as many droplets of fuel in the cylinder for the spark to use as "stepping stones" for the voltage to jump across. Therefore, a lean mixture is less conductive than a rich mixture.

EXAMPLES OF FIRING LINE PROBLEMS

If the height of the two firing lines that are side by side is less than that of the rest of the firing lines, the distributor cap is defective (carbon tracked between the two inserts) or the spark plug wires are crossed. The firing lines are low because the spark is being sent to a cylinder *not* under the high pressure of the compression stroke. It requires a lower voltage (lower firing line) to fire a spark plug under low compression. If the

◀ **DIAGNOSTIC STORY** ▶

A TECHNICIAN'S TOUGHIE

A vehicle ran poorly, yet its scope patterns were "perfect." Remembering that the scope indicates only that a spark has occurred (not necessarily inside the engine), the technician grounded one spark plug wire at a time using a vacuum hose and a test light. Every time a plug wire was grounded, the engine ran worse, until the last cylinder was checked. When the last spark plug wire was grounded, the engine ran the same. The technician checked the spark plug wire with an ohmmeter; it tested within specifications (less than 10,000 ohms per foot of length). The technician also removed and inspected the spark plug. The spark plug looked normal. The spark plug was reinstalled and the engine tested again. The test had the same results as before–the engine seemed to be running on seven cylinders, yet the scope pattern was perfect.

The technician then replaced the spark plug for the affected cylinder. The engine ran correctly. Very close examination of the spark plug showed a thin crack between the wire terminal and the shell of the plug. Why didn't the cracked plug show on the scope? The scope simply indicated that a spark had occurred. The scope cannot distinguish between a spark inside and outside the engine. In this case, the voltage required to travel through the spark plug crack to ground was about the same as the voltage required to jump the spark plug electrodes inside the engine. The spark that occurred across the cracked spark plug may, however, have been visible at night with the engine running.

firing lines are high, then lower, then high, then lower (like a roller coaster), the fuel mixture (usually the idle mixture) is unequal, with the high firing lines representing a lean fuel mixture. See figure 14–9.

A high firing line that also extends below the zero line is an indication of a defective (open) spark plug wire. If the firing line is high, yet the firing line does *not* drop below the zero line, the high-voltage spike has found a path to ground. This path to ground could be through a carbon track in the distributor cap or rotor or be caused by poor insulation on a plug wire.

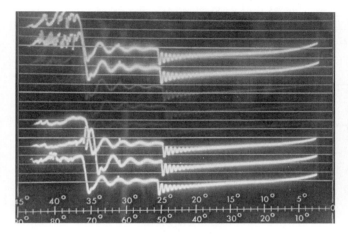

FIGURE 14–10 This six-cylinder engine was operating on only five cylinders because the pickup coil had an intermittent open in the wiring to the module.

READING THE SPARK LINES (RASTER [STACKED] OR SUPERIMPOSED)

Spark lines can easily be seen on either superimposed or raster (stacked) position. On the raster (stacked) position, each individual spark line can be viewed. See figure 14–10.

The spark lines should be level and one-fourth as high as the firing lines (1.5 to 2.5 kilovolts). The *length* of the spark line is the critical factor for determining proper operation of the engine because it represents the spark duration time. There is only a limited amount of energy in an ignition coil. If most of the energy is used to ionize the air gaps of the rotor and the spark plug, there may be not enough energy remaining to create a spark of a duration long enough to completely burn the air-fuel mixture. Many scopes are equipped with a **millisecond (ms) sweep.** This means that the scope will sweep only that portion of the pattern that can be shown during a 5- or 25-millisecond setting. The following are guidelines for spark line length:

0.8 milliseconds—too short

1.5 milliseconds—average

2.5 milliseconds—too long

If the spark line is too short, possible causes include the following:

1. Spark plug(s) gapped too widely
2. Rotor tip to distributor cap insert distance gapped too widely (worn cap or rotor)

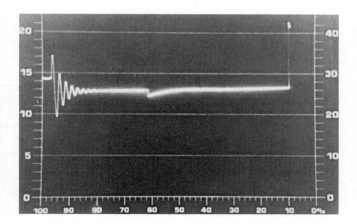

FIGURE 14–11 Notice that the length of the spark line is about 4% for this four-cylinder engine. The pattern length control should be adjusted before reading the spark line length to make certain that the pattern is full length on the screen.

3. High-resistance spark plug wire
4. Air-fuel mixture too lean (vacuum leak, broken valve spring, etc.)

If the spark line is too long, possible causes include the following:

1. Fouled spark plug(s)
2. Spark plug(s) gapped too closely
3. Shorted spark plug or spark plug wire

Many scopes do not have a millisecond scale. Some scopes are labeled in degrees and/or percentage (%) of dwell. See figure 14–11. The following chart can be used to determine acceptable spark line length.

Normal Spark Line Length (at 700 to 1200 RPM)

Number of cylinders	Milliseconds	Percentage (%) of dwell scale	Degrees (°)
4	1.0–1.5	3–6	3–5
6	1.0–1.5	4–9	2–5
8	1.0–1.5	6–13	3–6

SPARK LINE SLOPE

Downward-sloping spark lines indicate that the voltage required to maintain the spark duration is decreasing during the firing of the spark plug. This downward slope

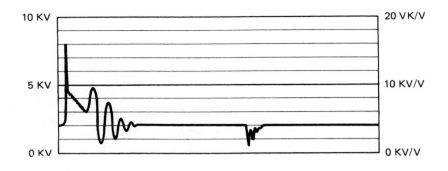

FIGURE 14–12 A downward-sloping spark line usually indicates high secondary ignition system resistance or an excessively rich air-fuel mixture.

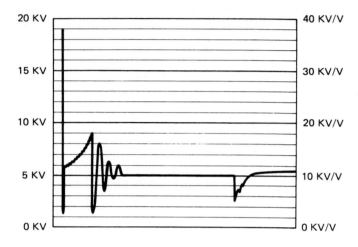

FIGURE 14–13 An upward-sloping spark line usually indicates a mechanical engine problem or a lean air-fuel mixture.

usually indicates that the spark energy is finding ground through spark plug deposits (the plug is fouled) or other ignition problems. See figure 14–12.

An *upward*-sloping spark line usually indicates a mechanical engine problem. A defective piston ring or valve would tend to seal better in the increasing pressures of combustion. As the spark plug fires, the effective increase in pressures increases the voltage required to maintain the spark, and the height of the spark line rises during the duration of the spark. See figure 14–13.

An upward-sloping spark line can also indicate a lean air-fuel mixture. Typical causes include

1. Clogged injector(s)
2. Vacuum leak
3. Sticking intake valve

READING THE INTERMEDIATE SECTION

The intermediate section should have five or *more* oscillations (bumps) for a correctly operating ignition system (three or more for a GM HEI system). Because there are approximately 250 volts in the primary igni-

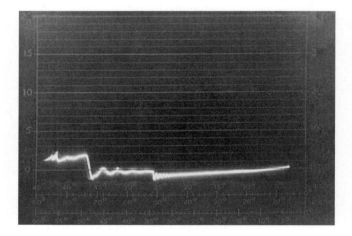

FIGURE 14–14 Lack of oscillations in the intermediate section usually indicates a defective ignition coil or loose (or corroded) coil terminal connections.

tion circuit when the spark stops flowing across the spark plugs, this voltage is reduced by about 75 volts per oscillation. Additional resistances in the primary circuit would decrease the number of oscillations. If there are fewer than five oscillations, possible problems include the following (fig. 14–14):

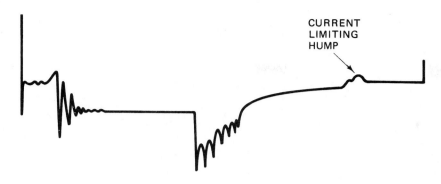

CURRENT
LIMITING
HUMP

FIGURE 14–15 Many electronic ignition systems show a current-limiting hump on the scope pattern. This hump is caused by the circuitry inside of the module, which limits the primary current to as high a level as is possible (for maximum combustion efficiency) while still protecting the ignition coil and module from excessive current.

1. Shorted ignition coil
2. Leaky condenser (if point-type ignition)
3. Loose or high-resistance primary connections on the ignition coil or primary ignition wiring

ELECTRONIC IGNITION AND THE DWELL SECTION

Electronic ignitions also use a dwell period to charge the coil. Dwell is not adjustable with electronic ignition, but it does change with increasing RPM with many electronic ignition systems. This change in dwell with RPM should be considered normal.

Many electronic ignition systems also produce a "hump" in the dwell section, which reflects a current-limiting circuit in the control module. These current-limiting humps may have slightly different shapes depending on the exact module used. For example, the humps produced by various GM HEI modules differ slightly. See figure 14–15.

DWELL VARIATION (ELECTRONIC IGNITION)

A worn distributor gear, worn camshaft gear, or other distributor problem may cause engine performance problems because the signal created in the distributor will be affected by the inaccurate distributor operation.

However, many electronic ignitions vary the dwell electronically in the module to maintain acceptable current flow levels through the ignition coil and module without the use of a ballast resistor.

Different electronic ignition systems use one of three different designs. The dwell change characteristic and the types of electronic ignition systems that use each design are as follows:

1. Dwell remains *constant* as the engine speed is increased. Types of ignition systems include
   Chrysler Hall effect with EIS
   Ford solid-state ignition
   Ford Duraspark II
   Ford EEC I
   Ford EEC II
2. Dwell *decreases* as the engine speed is increased. Types of ignition systems include
   Chrysler electronic ignition system (EIS)
   Chrysler electronic lean burn (ELB)
   Chrysler electronic spark control (ESC)
3. Dwell *increases* as the engine speed is increased. Types of ignition systems include
   All GM HEI systems
   Ford Duraspark I
   Ford EEC III
   Ford TFI
   AMC-Prestolite breakerless inductive discharge (BID)
   Chrysler Hall effect with ESC

NOTE: Distributorless ignition systems also vary dwell time electronically within the engine computer or ignition module.

COIL TESTING

With the scope connected and the engine running, observe the scope pattern in the superimposed mode. If the pattern is upside down, the primary wires on the coil may be reversed, causing the coil polarity to be reversed.

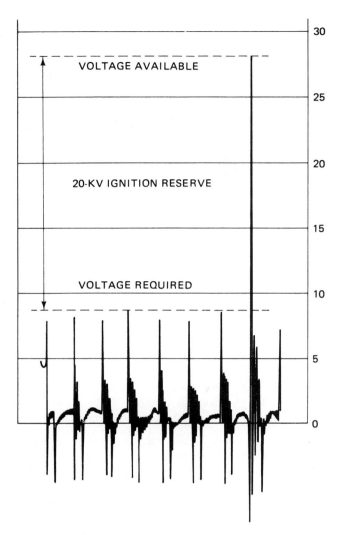

FIGURE 14–16 The highest voltage that a coil can produce occurs if a secondary spark plug wire is held away from the spark plug. This method is generally *not* recommended because the high voltage resulting from this action can cause damage to the ignition coil (or to the person removing the plug wire).

NOTE: Check the scope hookup and controls before deciding that the coil polarity is reversed.

The reversed polarity greatly increases the voltage required to fire the spark plugs and often causes the engine to miss on acceleration.

To test the output of a coil, it must be "forced" to produce its maximum-output voltage. This is done by disconnecting any spark plug wire (except #1) and holding the spark plug wire away from ground. With the engine running and the scope pattern selector on display (parade) and the high-voltage scale, observe the height of the firing line for the cylinder with the disconnected plug wire. See figure 14–16. The minimum acceptable coil output voltage is as follows:

Point-type ignition: 20,000 volts (20 kilovolts) *minimum*

Electronic ignition: 25,000 volts (25 kilovolts) *minimum*

Distributorless ignition: 30,000 volts (30 kilovolts) *minimum*

Replace the coil if the output voltage is low. See figure 14–17.

NOTE: Check the distributor cap and rotor before replacing the ignition coil. A worn or defective distributor cap or rotor could cause the coil test to indicate output of too low a voltage.

CAUTION: Some manufacturers do not recommend coil testing by checking for maximum open-circuit voltage, especially on computer-equipped engines. Most coils can be accurately tested by observing the spark line duration. If the coil is producing normal spark line duration and the spark plugs are not fouled, the coil is usable. If the ignition coil is still suspected of being defective, remove the coil from the engine and test it separately on the scope following the test equipment manufacturer's recommended procedures.

ACCELERATION CHECK

With the scope selector set on the display (parade) position, rapidly accelerate the engine (gear selector in park or neutral with the parking brake on). The results should be interpreted as follows:

1. All the firing lines should rise evenly (not to exceed 75% of maximum coil output) for properly operating spark plugs.
2. If the firing lines on one or more cylinders *fail to rise*, this indicates fouled spark plugs.

ROTOR GAP VOLTAGE

The rotor gap voltage test measures the voltage required to jump the gap (0.030 to 0.050 inches [0.8 to 1.3 millimeters]) between the rotor and the inserts

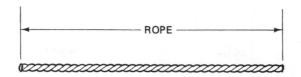

LENGTH OF ROPE REPRESENTS AMOUNT
OF ENERGY STORED IN IGNITION COIL

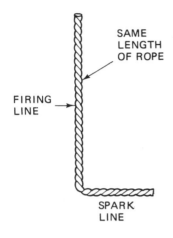

SAME
LENGTH
OF ROPE

FIRING
LINE

SPARK
LINE

SAME LENGTH OF ROPE (ENERGY).
IF HIGH VOLTAGE IS REQUIRED TO
IONIZE SPARK PLUG CAP, LESS
ENERGY IS AVAILABLE FOR SPARK
DURATION. (A LEAN CYLINDER IS
AN EXAMPLE OF WHERE HIGHER
VOLTAGE IS REQUIRED TO FIRE
WITH A SHORTER-THAN-NORMAL
DURATION.)

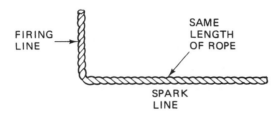

FIRING
LINE

SAME
LENGTH
OF ROPE

SPARK
LINE

IF LOW VOLTAGE IS REQUIRED TO FIRE
THE SPARK PLUG (LOW FIRING LINE),
MORE OF THE COIL'S ENERGY IS
AVAILABLE TO PROVIDE A LONG-
DURATION SPARK LINE. (A FOULED
SPARK PLUG IS AN EXAMPLE OF LOW
VOLTAGE TO FIRE, WITH A LONGER-
THAN-NORMAL DURATION.)

FIGURE 14–17   The relationship between the height of the firing line and length of the spark line can be illustrated using a rope. Because energy cannot be destroyed, the stored energy in an ignition coil must dissipate totally regardless of engine operating conditions.

(segments) of the distributor cap. Select the display (parade) scope pattern and remove a spark plug wire using a jumper wire to provide a good ground connection. Start the engine and observe the height of the firing line for the cylinder being tested. Because the spark plug wire is connected directly to ground, the firing line height on the scope will indicate the voltage required to jump the air gap between the rotor and the distributor cap insert. The normal rotor gap voltage is 3 to 7 kilovolts, and the voltage should not exceed 8 kilovolts. If the rotor gap voltage indicated is near or above 8 kilovolts, inspect and replace the distributor cap and/or rotor as required. See figure 14–18.

POWER BALANCE TEST

The power balance test is used to determine if all cylinders are producing power equally. Each cylinder should have the same effect on engine speed. The power balance test grounds out the primary ignition circuit for only one cylinder at a time. If the cylinder is grounded out and no spark is sent to that cylinder, the idle speed should drop.

Most scopes have buttons, dials, or an automatic cylinder-canceling section for carrying out this test. With the engine at idle and the scope pattern selection on display (parade), cancel one cylinder at a time and note the engine RPM. The engine RPM should decrease

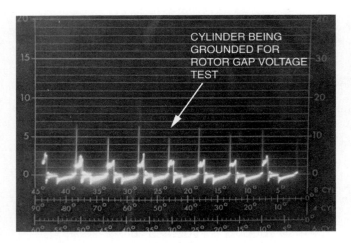

FIGURE 14–18 The voltage required to arc between the tip of the rotor and the distributor insert is 5 kilovolts in this example.

equally for each cylinder. The amount of RPM drop is *not* important. All cylinders should, however, be within 50 RPM of each other. If the engine RPM does not drop enough (or drop at all), the cylinder is not "working." If the RPM *increases* whenever a cylinder is canceled, this could indicate:

1. Crossed spark plug wires
2. Defective (cracked) distributor cap
3. Spark occurring too early in the cylinder, possibly caused by stray electrical impulses to the module from a spark plug wire, alternator, or other sources

If the power balance test indicates a "dead" or "weak" cylinder, further tests, including a compression test, should be performed to determine the exact cause.

POWER BALANCING A COMPUTER-EQUIPPED ENGINE

Whenever a balance test is being performed, a computer-equipped engine will automatically increase idle speed or otherwise compensate for the dead (canceled) cylinder. To prevent the computer controls from compensating for a canceled cylinder, disconnect the coolant sensor, oxygen sensor, and/or idle speed control device. With the sensor(s) disconnected, the computer will not be able to compensate when a cylinder is canceled. After testing, the sensors should be reconnected and the computer fault code(s) erased.

FIGURE 14–19 Normal alternator scope pattern. This AC ripple is on top of a DC voltage line. The ripple should be less than $1/2$ volt high.

FIGURE 14–20 Alternator pattern indicating a shorted diode.

FIGURE 14–21 Alternator pattern indicating an open diode.

NOTE: Check the vehicle service manual for the exact method to prevent possible computer or safety procedure errors.

SCOPE TESTING ALTERNATORS

Defective diodes and open or shorted stators can be detected on a scope. Connect the scope leads as usual, *except* for the coil negative connection, which attaches to the alternator output ("Bat") terminal. With the pattern selection set to raster (stacked), start the engine and run to approximately 1000 RPM (slightly higher than normal idle speed). The scope should show an even ripple pattern reflecting the slight alternating up-and-down level of the alternator output voltage.

If the alternator is controlled by an electronic voltage regulator, the rapid on-and-off cycling of the field current can create vertical spikes evenly throughout the pattern. These spikes are normal. If the ripple pattern is *jagged* or *uneven*, a defective diode (open or shorted) or a defective stator is indicated. See figures 14–19 through 14–21. If the alternator scope pattern does not show even ripples, the alternator should be disassembled and all internal components tested. See chapter 11 for alternator test procedures.

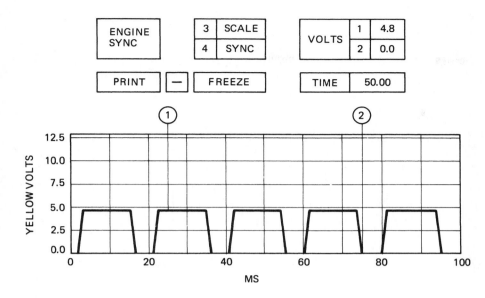

| ENGINE SYNC | | 3 | SCALE | VOLTS | 1 | 4.8 |
| | | 4 | SYNC | | 2 | 0.0 |

| PRINT | — | FREEZE | | TIME | 50.00 |

FIGURE 14–22 Engine analyzer printout of a digitized scope pattern of a Hall-effect crankshaft sensor.

OTHER SCOPE TESTS

Many scopes are also capable of the following:

1. Testing electronic ignition pickup coil pulses
2. Testing fuel-injection operating pulses
3. Coil testing (off the vehicle)
4. Condenser testing (off the vehicle)

See the scope manufacturer's instructions for exact hookups, procedures, and precautions. Figure 14–22 shows an engine analyzer printout of a digitized scope pattern of a Hall-effect crankshaft sensor.

DUAL-TRACE BENCH SCOPES

Bench or lab-type oscilloscopes (scopes) are another useful diagnostic tool. The term *bench scope* refers to the fact that its relatively small size permits it to be used on a "bench" rather than being on wheels (or an overhead track) as is a large automotive analyzer.

A dual-trace scope allows the technician to view two related electrical events at the same time. See figure 14–23. For example, a technician could probe and look at the output signal from the crankshaft sensor and the camshaft sensor at the same time. The relationship between the two patterns could help diagnose the cause of intermittent or minor electrical interference problems.

Sequential fuel-injection and distributorless (direct-fire) ignition systems must also be timed

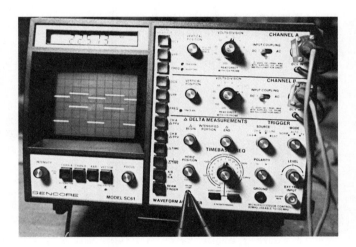

FIGURE 14–23 Typical dual-trace bench scope. Notice the LCD frequency counter readout above the scope. This feature is useful for diagnosis of Ford MAP sensor or mass airflow (MAF) sensor outputs. (Some digital multitesters also include a frequency scale.)

(or be phased) with sensors if the engine is to perform correctly. A dual-trace scope can help test these systems.

The AC portion of the alternator output can best be seen on a bench scope. Usually the AC voltage is on top of the DC voltage. The AC portion may be only about 0.2 volt ripples over the DC voltage. With a bench scope, the DC voltage can be blocked to permit showing of only the AC portion of the pattern.

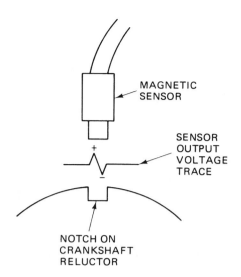

FIGURE 14–24 Typical scope pattern from a magnetic crankshaft sensor. Some magnetic sensors incorporate electronic circuits that convert the output signal to a square wave before it leaves the sensor.

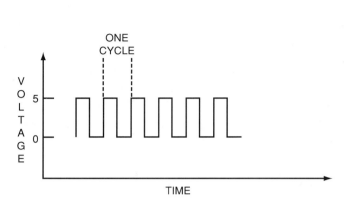

FIGURE 14–25 One cycle is the time it requires for a voltage pulse to complete one event. Frequency is the measure of how often each cycle repeats in a second.

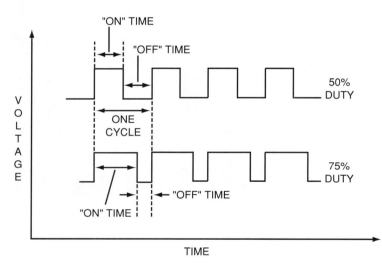

FIGURE 14–26 Both the top and bottom pattern have the same frequency; however, the amount of on time varies. Duty cycle is the percentage of the time during a cycle that the signal is turned on.

NOTE: The DC portion of the alternator output is blocked internally in the scope by use of a capacitor. A capacitor (condenser) blocks DC, but passes AC voltages.

Most bench scopes (whether single or dual trace) can show waveforms from which frequency measurements can be obtained. See figure 14–24. Some bench scopes even incorporate a frequency counter that gives a digital display of the frequency. This type of frequency measurement is especially helpful when testing computer sensors that produce a variable frequency (instead of voltage), such as Ford MAP sensors and many mass airflow sensors. See chapter 16 for further computer sensor information.

FREQUENCY

Frequency is the measure of how often a voltage pulse repeats, or how many cycles per second or **hertz** (Hz). One cycle is the time it takes to complete one event. See figure 14–25.

A good example of the use of frequency is a crankshaft sensor. As the engine rotates, the crankshaft sensor produces voltage pulses similar to those shown in figure 14–25. The engine computer simply counts the pulses to calculate engine speed.

Frequency can be determined using a scope or a digital multimeter that has frequency measurement capability. This allows a quick and easy method for checking crankshaft, vehicle speed, and wheel speed sensors.

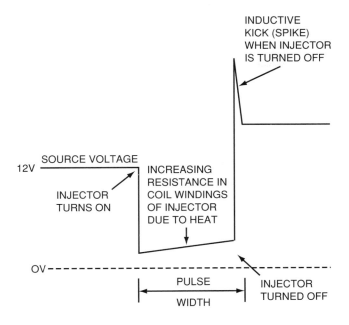

INDUCTIVE KICK (SPIKE) WHEN INJECTOR IS TURNED OFF

SOURCE VOLTAGE

12V

INJECTOR TURNS ON

INCREASING RESISTANCE IN COIL WINDINGS OF INJECTOR DUE TO HEAT

0V

PULSE WIDTH

INJECTOR TURNED OFF

FIGURE 14–27   Typical injector waveform as viewed on a scope.

DUTY CYCLE

Frequency by itself does not describe everything that may be occurring. For example, a voltage signal may have a constant frequency, but may vary in the amount of time for which the voltage is high (on). See figure 14–26.

PULSE WIDTH

The pulse duration of a fuel injector is usually expressed as **pulse width.** Pulse width represents the amount of time the injector is turned on, as shown in figure 14–27.

The injector-on time determines the amount of fuel delivered to the engine. Most fuel injectors are turned on by completing the injector circuit to ground. With battery voltage on one side of the injector and low voltage (almost zero) on the other side, the injector coil is energized and the pintle inside the injector opens to allow pressurized fuel to squirt into the intake manifold.

SUMMARY

1. All oscilloscopes are high-impedance voltmeters that display voltage variations on a screen.
2. A secondary ignition scope pattern includes a firing line, spark line, intermediate oscillations, and transistor-on and transistor-off points.
3. The slope of the spark line can indicate incorrect air-fuel ratio or other engine problems.
4. Alternators can be tested for defective diodes using a scope.

REVIEW QUESTIONS

1. List the sections of a secondary ignition scope pattern.
2. Explain what the slope of the spark line can indicate about the engine.
3. Explain how to perform a rotor gap voltage test.
4. Describe how to perform a scope analysis of an alternator.

MULTIPLE-CHOICE QUESTIONS

1. The height of firing lines can be observed on _____ .
   a. Display (parade) position only
   b. Raster (stacked) position only
   c. Superimposed position only
   d. All settings

2. The length of the spark line should be _____ .
   a. 5 to 15 kilovolts
   b. 1.0 to 1.5 milliseconds
   c. 5 or more bumps
   d. 1.5 to 2.0 milliseconds

3. Too short a spark line on all cylinders could indicate _____ .
   a. A worn distributor cap and/or rotor
   b. An open coil wire (if the vehicle is so equipped)
   c. Too lean a fuel mixture
   d. All of the above

4. A high firing line without a downward spike below the zero line indicates _____ .
   a. A defective spark plug wire with good insulation
   b. A defective spark plug wire with poor insulation
   c. A weak ignition coil
   d. A rich fuel mixture in the affected cylinder

5. The roller coaster height pattern of the firing lines usually indicates _____ .

   a. A mechanical engine problem
   b. A distributor cap or rotor problem
   c. A fuel mixture problem
   d. A spark plug wire problem

6. Some electronic ignition systems show _____ .
   a. No firing lines on the scope
   b. A current-limiting hump
   c. No transistor-on point
   d. No transistor-off point

7. To test the rotor gap voltage _____ .
   a. A spark plug wire must be removed
   b. A spark plug wire must be grounded
   c. The rotor must be removed from the engine
   d. The engine must not be running

8. Dwell on a scope pattern is read at _____ .
   a. The transistor on point
   b. The transistor off point
   c. The coil section
   d. The spark line section

9. Technician A says that the dwell on the scope should increase as the engine speed is increased on some engines. Technician B says that all firing lines should be within 3 kilovolts of each other. Which technician is correct?
   a. A only
   b. B only
   c. Both a and b
   d. Neither a nor b

10. Technician A says that if one cylinder drops in RPM much more than the remaining cylinders during a power balance test, the cylinder is weak. Technician B says that rotor gap voltage must be tested with a spark plug wire grounded. Which technician is correct?
    a. A only
    b. B only
    c. Both a and b
    d. Neither a nor b

◀ Chapter 15 ▶

COMPUTER PRINCIPLES

OBJECTIVES

After studying chapter 15, the reader will be able to

1. Describe how a computer works.
2. List the inputs of a vehicle computer.
3. List the outputs of a vehicle computer.
4. Explain how closed-loop fuel handling is accomplished.

Computers have revolutionized the automobile industry. Vehicles built before 1981 are often called "BC" (before computers). A thorough understanding of vehicle computers is essential for proper diagnosis and troubleshooting.

COMPUTER OPERATION

Input signals from various sensors are converted to digital (on-and-off) signals that the computer can understand and use. Based on the values of the various sensors, the computer can turn on and off various output devices to control the operation of the engine's systems. This control of engine systems is usually referred to as the **engine management system**. The Society of Automotive Engineers' recommended name for all vehicle computers is the **powertrain control module** (PCM). The computer controls engine operation plus the transmission operation. All outputs are called **actuators** and operate at the control of the computer.

THE PURPOSE OF THE COMPUTER ENGINE MANAGEMENT SYSTEM

The purpose of the computer engine management system is to maintain proper air-fuel mixture close to 14.7 parts of air to 1 part of fuel. This exact ratio of 14.7:1 is called the **stoichiometric ratio**. The term *stoichiometric ratio* means that *all* of the fuel is completely burned by *all* of the oxygen in the air when the ratio between air and fuel is 14.7:1.

To achieve this ratio, computerized engine control systems use an **oxygen sensor,** which is abbreviated as **O2S**. The "2" indicates that one oxygen molecule has two atoms of oxygen, and the "S" is an abbreviation for sensor. See chapter 16 for details on the oxygen and other sensors.

Whenever an engine computer problem is diagnosed, the following must be considered:

1. The engine itself must be mechanically sound to be assured of proper sensor operation and consequential computer operation.
2. All non-computer-controlled systems should be checked before checking or replacing computer sensors or actuators.
3. If trouble codes exist, follow the exact manufacturer's recommended troubleshooting procedures.

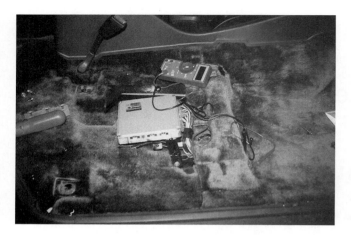

FIGURE 15–1 Vehicle computers can be located almost anywhere where there is room. This computer is located under the passenger seat. Other vehicles may locate the computer under the passenger floor, behind a kick panel, or under the hood.

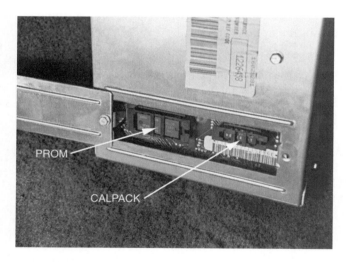

FIGURE 15–2 Many General Motors vehicles use replacement PROMs that determine the parameters of the engine management computer. The calibration package (Calpack) is used as a backup circuit for the fuel-injection system. New computers use a combination chip that incorporates the functions of both (called a memory calibration [memcal] chip).

NOTE: Most vehicle manufacturers' troubleshooting procedures include instructions to the technician to check various non-computer-controlled aspects of the engine, including checking for possible vacuum leaks, defective spark plug wires, and other items that might prevent the proper operation of the engine.

◄ **TECH TIP** ►

GARBAGE IN EQUALS GARBAGE OUT

"Garbage in = Garbage out" is an old computer saying. Any computer processes input signals and gives output (control) information based on input data. If the engine coolant temperature sensor is defective, the computer will still process the incorrect temperature and provide a richer or leaner air-fuel mixture based on the incorrect temperature sensor reading.

A loose or corroded ground wire(s) for the computer's logic can cause the computer to flash false codes and provide incorrect output control signals. (See chapter 3 for additional information on the importance of sound logic lows [grounds].)

The computer uses a **microprocessor** to process all of the signals from the input sensors and to process appropriate output signals to all of the actuators. The microprocessor is a nonreplaceable chip in the computer. This microprocessor is the "brain" of the computer and is also called the **central processing unit** (CPU). See figure 15–1 for a typical vehicle computer location. The microprocessor cannot do all of the processing by itself—it requires the following:

1. Temporary memory locations for calculating information
2. Instructional guidelines for each particular vehicle (this information is usually burned into a separate chip called a **programmable read-only memory** [PROM])
3. A clock crystal that oscillates at a certain frequency to keep all communication between the various parts of the computer on the same time sequence (fig. 15–2)

NOTE: On some vehicles the PROM is the only technician-serviceable part of the automotive computer. Some PROMs are actually EEPROMs, and their instructional information can be changed using specialized reprogramming equipment available at the dealership.

The purpose of the reprogrammable capability of the service PROM is to permit updated changes into vehicles already in service without having to stock replacement PROMs.

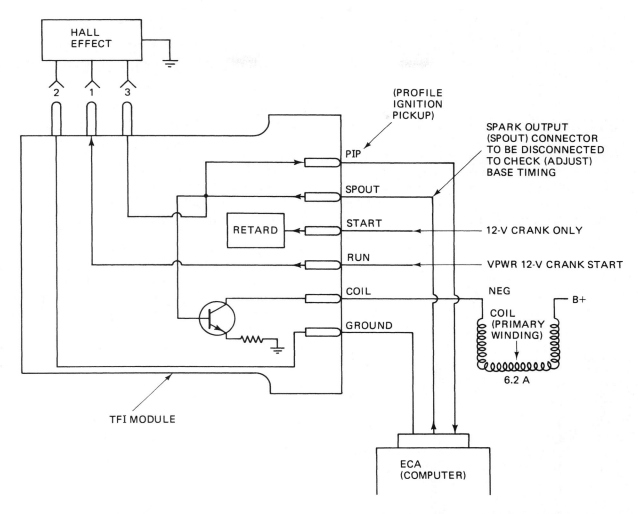

FIGURE 15–3 Wiring diagram of a typical Ford TFI ignition system. The Ford computer processes the input signals directly from the Hall-effect sensor and delivers a modified signal back to the module. The TFI module does the actual pulsing of the ignition coil.

"HOT ROD" PROMS

The performance of many vehicles can be improved by replacing the factory PROM with a high-performance PROM or chip. Often these hot rod chips advance the ignition timing, requiring the driver to use higher-octane fuel than might normally be required. Some computers have to be sent to the aftermarket company for modification because the factory PROM is part of the computer itself and not in a separate replaceable chip. The aftermarket chip modifications usually change the operation of the engine at higher speeds and loads than may be encountered in an exhaust emission inspection. Therefore, most vehicles equipped with a high-performance PROM will usually be able to pass a state or local exhaust emission test.

INPUTS

Inputs to an automotive computer include both analog (variable) and digital (on-and-off signal) voltages from various sensors. These input sensors include the following:

1. Engine coolant temperature (ECT) sensor
2. Throttle position (TP) sensor
3. Oxygen sensor (O2S)
4. Manifold absolute pressure (MAP) (engine load) sensor
5. Intake air temperature sensor (IAT)
6. Barometric pressure (BARO or altitude) sensor
7. Vehicle speed (VS) sensor
8. Engine speed (RPM) sensor—see figure 15–3

The input signals from the sensors are analyzed by the CPU, and the necessary actuators (control units) are operated by the output circuits of the computer to achieve optimum engine operation. See figures 15–4 and 15–5.

OUTPUTS

Computer outputs are always digital ("on" or "off"), yet these on and off times can be changed to provide a varying output. The computer can pulse a fuel injector on for a relatively long time or a relatively short time. The amount of time the injector is on (opened) is called the **duty cycle** or **pulse width**. See figure 15–6.

Typical outputs that are computer controlled include the following:

1. Ignition timing
2. Fuel-injection on time
3. EGR valve(s) control
4. Air pump valve control
5. Fuel pump operation (fuel-injected engines)
6. Torque converter clutch operation
7. Cooling fan operation
8. Canister purge

See figures 15–7 and 15–8.

PULL-UP AND PULL-DOWN RESISTORS

Computer circuits frequently use variable-resistance sensors for input information. These sensors are frequently resistors whose resistances vary with temperature. Typical examples of this type of sensor are coolant temperature sensors and intake air temperature sensors. Most of these sensors are negative coefficient thermistors in which the resistance of the sensor decreases as the temperature increases. The computer senses this change, not by the voltage of the returning signal, but rather by the voltage level after the resistor inside the computer. See figure 15–9.

If external resistance is high, signal voltage will be low.

If external resistance is low, signal voltage will be higher.

The explanation for this is as follows: If both resistances were the same, the voltage drop across each would be the

◄ TECH TIP ►

COMPUTERS DO NOT LIKE THREE THINGS

Computers are sensitive electronic devices that can be damaged if subjected to

1. High voltage—especially static electricity
2. High current (amperes)—current through a computer circuit is usually limited to 1 ampere or less
3. High heat—electronic devices work best when isolated from extreme heat

There is another item that may be of interest. While troubleshooting a computer-related problem, this author found the vehicle computer full of water due to a leaky windshield. So add another item to the list—computers can't swim!

same—2.5 volts each. Remember as mentioned in chapter 2, the voltage drop across a resistor is in proportion to the value of the resistor. Because both resistances are the same, each resistor would cause the voltage to drop 2.5 volts to equal the 5.0-volt source voltage. If the resistance of the sensor were zero (shorted to ground, for example), the entire voltage drop would occur across the resistor inside the computer. Therefore, the voltage after the resistor would be zero. As the resistance of the external sensor increases, the voltage level after the resistor in the computer increases. The computer monitors this voltage and translates this voltage into data usable by the computer.

If a two-wire sensor is used, the same process normally occurs. The second wire is the ground return path that is completed inside the computer. This internal grounding of the sensor circuit helps prevent radio-frequency interference from affecting the voltage levels. Many two-wire sensor leads are twisted to help prevent RFI, because two parallel wires usually make a good antenna.

The terms *pull-up* and *pull-down* refer to the effect a resistor has on voltage.

Pull-up resistor—If the resistance value increases the signal voltage, the resistor is usually referred to as a pull-up resistor.

Pull-down resistor—If the resistance value decreases the signal voltage, the resistor is usually referred to as a pull-down resistor.

The exact terminology depends upon the application and where in the circuit the voltage is being monitored.

OIL LEVEL/
TEMPERATURE
SENSOR

FIGURE 15–4 Oil level and oil temperature are also inputs to some computers. The computer has taken over the job of turning on dash warning lights, which were once controlled by pressure sending units.

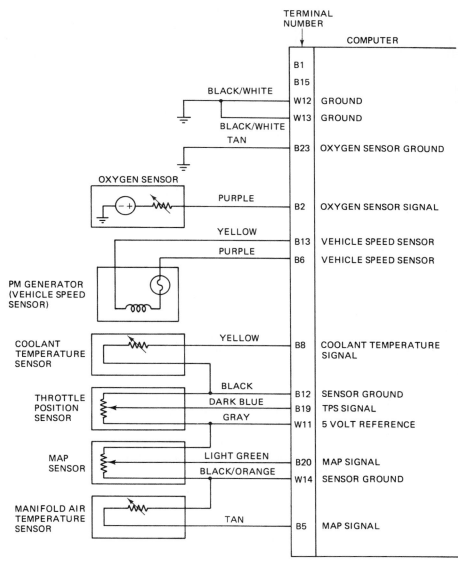

TERMINAL NUMBER

COMPUTER

B1		
B15		
W12	GROUND	BLACK/WHITE
W13	GROUND	BLACK/WHITE
B23	OXYGEN SENSOR GROUND	TAN
B2	OXYGEN SENSOR SIGNAL	PURPLE
B13	VEHICLE SPEED SENSOR	YELLOW
B6	VEHICLE SPEED SENSOR	PURPLE
B8	COOLANT TEMPERATURE SIGNAL	YELLOW
B12	SENSOR GROUND	BLACK
B19	TPS SIGNAL	DARK BLUE
W11	5 VOLT REFERENCE	GRAY
B20	MAP SIGNAL	LIGHT GREEN
W14	SENSOR GROUND	BLACK/ORANGE
B5	MAP SIGNAL	TAN

OXYGEN SENSOR

PM GENERATOR
(VEHICLE SPEED
SENSOR)

COOLANT
TEMPERATURE
SENSOR

THROTTLE
POSITION
SENSOR

MAP
SENSOR

MANIFOLD AIR
TEMPERATURE
SENSOR

FIGURE 15–5 Typical computer inputs for a General Motors vehicle. Notice that 5-volt reference voltage and sensor grounds are often shared among several sensors. A problem with one sensor could cause a trouble code to be stored for a fault in a shared sensor circuit.

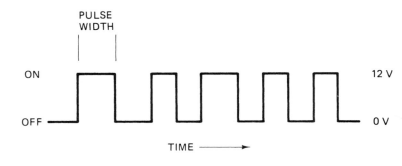

FIGURE 15–6 The amount of on time of a unit is called the pulse width time (usually measured in milliseconds [1/1000 of a second]). *Duty cycle* is a related term. If a unit is kept on 60% of the time, then its duty cycle is 60%.

BINARY NUMBERS

Digital computers use a binary form of communication and calculation. The word *binary* means two—either on or off (of voltage) in the language of the computer. Each high (1) or low (0) signal is called a **bit.** A single bit cannot be used by a computer because it does not represent enough information. But a series of eight (or sixteen or thirty-two, etc.) can be grouped together to form a **byte** or a **word** or words. A byte is eight bits. Early computers could only handle eight-bits at a time and were referred to as eight-bit machines. Newer and faster microprocessors were developed that could process information sixteen bits at a time. Now sixteen bits are used as a unit called a word. Faster microprocessors can process thirty-two or sixty-four bits at a time.

Even the newest, fastest microprocessor does not process all of the string of bits at one time. The microprocessor usually processes four bits (called a nibble) at a time.

Early automotive microprocessors could only handle several hundred thousand calculations per second, whereas newer, faster units can process millions of bits of information per second. Each bit represents a special number to a computer based on its location in the string of eight. The bit on the far right represents the number 1. The bits toward the left represent a doubling of the numbers until the number 128 is reached. See figure 15–10.

These eight bits can be used to represent the number 0 to the computer if all bits are turned off (low). If all bits are turned on (high), the number represented is 255. All numbers, therefore, between 0 and 255 (256 different numbers, counting the zero) can be represented by the various combinations of bits being on. These binary numbers (and their corresponding nibbles) are used by the computer microprocessor in its calculations.

A technician often sees these binary numbers as readings of various functions on a diagnostic scan tool or engine analyzer. The number 128 is the midpoint be-

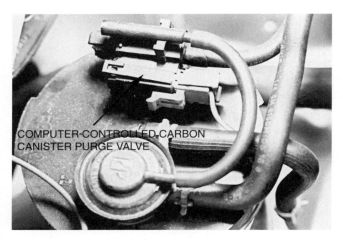

FIGURE 15–7 Computer-controlled carbon canister purge valve.

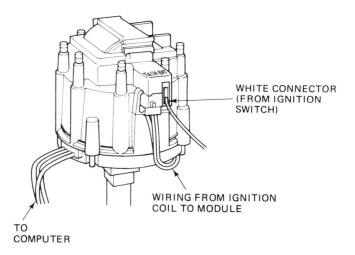

FIGURE 15–8 The on-board computer controls the ignition of this HEI distributor through the four wires illustrated. To disable an HEI ignition, remove the ignition wire that feeds battery voltage from the ignition switch to the ignition coil.

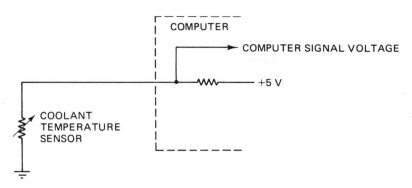

FIGURE 15–9   As the resistance of a sensor changes, the voltage drop across a resistor inside the computer changes. The resulting voltage level after the resistor represents the computer input signal.

8-BIT BINARY NUMBERS DEPENDING ON WHICH BITS ARE ON (HIGH) INDICATES WHAT NUMBER (FROM ZERO – NONE "ON" TO 255 – ALL "ON")

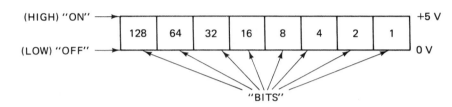

FIGURE 15–10   Binary numbers are numbers from 0 to 255 and depend on whether a bit is on or off in a numbered location.

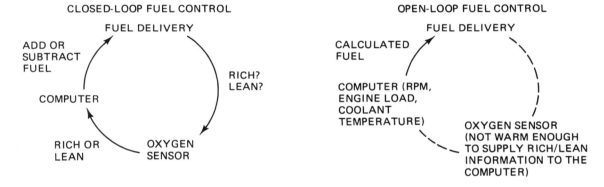

FIGURE 15–11   Open-loop operation occurs when the engine is cold or when the oxygen sensor is not warm enough to supply a usable (varying) voltage signal. Once all other factors have been met and the oxygen sensor is functional, the computer determines fuel delivery in a closed-loop mode.

tween 0 and 255 and usually represents the midpoint and normal reading for the function being selected.

See chapter 16 for further details on scan tool testing.

OPEN- AND CLOSED-LOOP OPERATION

Computer systems do not start controlling all aspects of the fuel and ignition immediately upon startup of a cold engine. The oxygen (O2S) sensor must be above 600° F (315° C) before it can supply useful exhaust oxygen content information to the computer. Therefore, the PROM supplies values for fuel mixture and ignition timing when the engine is cold. When the engine is operating with these preset values, the engine operation is called **open loop**. It can be easily remembered by the term *open circuit*, meaning that no current flows. In open-loop operation, the system is not closed, meaning that the oxygen sensor does not signal the computer regarding the oxygen content of the exhaust. When the oxygen sensor starts to produce usable signals, the computer is capable of going into **closed-loop** operation. See figure 15–11.

STATIC ELECTRICITY PRECAUTIONS

Whenever working on or near a computer, the technician should wear a grounding wrist strap to prevent a possible electrostatic discharge from damaging the computer circuits.

For example, a person sliding across cloth upholstery or walking on carpet can discharge up to 35,000 volts on a dry day and up to 2000 volts on a damp day. A person walking on a vinyl floor can discharge up to 12,000 volts on a dry day and up to 400 volts on a damp day. A person handling a styrofoam cup or handling plastic or cellophane tape can discharge up to 5000 volts. Static electricity is often called **electrostatic discharge** or ESD.

When dealing with static electricity, if you can

feel it—it is 3000 volts or more

see it—it is 10,000 volts or more

hear it—it is 20,000 volts or more

According to General Motors, electronic components can be damaged by ESD levels as low as 30 volts. But we cannot feel ESD until it is about 3000 volts. To prevent damage, follow these simple steps:

- *Step #1.* Do not take the electronic component out of its protective packaging until you are ready to install it.
- *Step #2.* Ground yourself often to any metal such as a seat track to drain away any static charge.
- *Step #3.* Never touch terminals of any electronic device.

RADIO-FREQUENCY INTERFERENCE

Radio-frequency interference (RFI) can cause harm to computer circuits. Often RFI can cause false trouble codes or intermittent poor engine operation. The usual cause of damaging RFI is a poor connection or defective component in the secondary ignition circuit.

SUMMARY

1. Vehicle computers control various engine functions, plus automatic transmission operation.
2. The microprocessor is the actual central processing unit (CPU), whereas the PROM provides the instructional guidelines to the CPU.
3. Inputs to a computer can be digital (on or off) or variable.
4. Outputs from the computer are digital on and off, but the time on can vary.

REVIEW QUESTIONS

1. List five vehicle computer inputs.
2. List five vehicle computer outputs.
3. Explain how a computer "knows" the temperature of an engine by simply sensing the voltage inside the computer.
4. Describe what is meant by closed-loop fuel control.

MULTIPLE-CHOICE QUESTIONS

1. Most automotive computer systems control_____ .
   a. Fuel delivery
   b. Air delivery
   c. Ignition timing
   d. A and c only
   e. All of the above

2. The "brain" of a computer is called_____ .
   a. RAM
   b. PROM
   c. Microprocessor
   d. EPROM

3. The only technician-serviceable part of some computers is the_____ .
   a. PROM
   b. EPROM
   c. EEPROM
   d. CPU

4. An automotive computer can be called_____ .
   a. PCM
   b. ECA
   c. CPU
   d. Any of the above, depending on vehicle manufacturer

5. Stoichiometric means_____ .
   a. HC and CO being converted
   b. Exactly 14.7:1 air-fuel ratio
   c. A three-way catalytic converter
   d. CPU-controlled EGR system

6. Which is *not* a typical computer input?
   a. Engine RPM
   b. Coolant temperature
   c. Exhaust gas hydrocarbon content
   d. Exhaust gas oxygen content

7. Which is *not* a typical computer output?
   a. Coolant thermostat
   b. Ignition timing control
   c. Fuel-injection control
   d. Exhaust gas recirculation (where applicable)

8. A bit is_____ .
   a. One-fourth of a byte
   b. An "on" or "off" voltage signal (level)
   c. The same as a nibble
   d. The same as a word

◄ Chapter 16 ►

COMPUTER SENSORS—OPERATION AND TESTING

OBJECTIVES

After studying chapter 16, the reader will be able to

1. Discuss the operation of and testing procedure for an engine coolant temperature sensor.
2. Explain how to test an exhaust gas oxygen sensor.
3. Describe how to test a throttle position sensor.
4. Explain the operation of a mass airflow sensor.

The correct operation of computerized engines depends on accurate and dependable sensors. Proper testing of sensors is an important part of computer problem diagnosis and troubleshooting.

ENGINE COOLANT TEMPERATURE SENSORS

Computer-equipped vehicles use an **engine coolant temperature** (ECT) sensor. See figure 16–1.

When the engine is cold, the fuel mixture must be richer to prevent stalling and engine stumble. When the engine is warm, the fuel mixture can be leaner to provide maximum fuel economy with the lowest possible exhaust emissions. The ignition timing can also be tailored to engine (coolant) temperature. A hot engine cannot have the spark timing as far advanced as can a

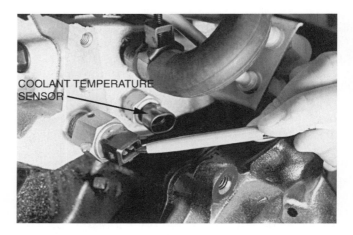

FIGURE 16–1 Typical General Motors engine coolant temperature sensor (ECT). Most coolant temperature sensors are located near or on the thermostat housing to best sense engine temperature. The pen is pointing to a thermotime switch used in some fuel-injection systems to control the operation of the cold-start injector. The cold-start injector is not computer controlled.

cold engine. Most coolant sensors have very high resistance when the coolant is cold and low resistance when the coolant is hot. This is referred to as having a **negative temperature coefficient** (NTC), which is opposite to the situation with most other electrical components. Therefore, if the coolant sensor has a poor

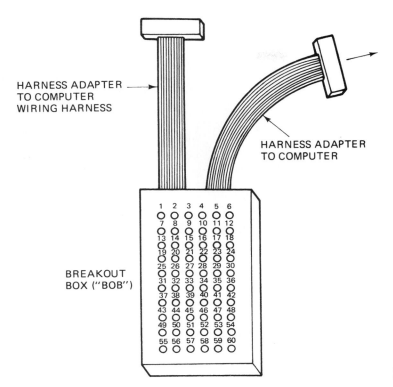

HARNESS ADAPTER
TO COMPUTER
WIRING HARNESS

HARNESS ADAPTER
TO COMPUTER

BREAKOUT
BOX ("BOB")

FIGURE 16–2   Typical breakout box.

connection (high resistance) at the wiring connector, the computer will supply a richer than normal fuel mixture based on the resistance of the coolant sensor. Therefore, poor fuel economy and a possible "rich" code can be caused by a defective sensor or high resistance in the sensor wiring. If the sensor were shorted or defective and had too low a resistance, a leaner than normal fuel mixture would be supplied to the engine. A too-lean fuel mixture can cause driveability problems and a possible "lean" computer code.

TESTING THE ENGINE COOLANT TEMPERATURE SENSOR

Three different types of test instruments can be used to check the coolant temperature sensor:

1. A digital ohmmeter to measure the resistance of the sensor or a digital voltmeter to measure the sensor voltage.
2. A scan tool or a specific tool recommended by the vehicle manufacturer.
3. A breakout box that is connected, in series, between the computer and the wiring harness connector(s). A typical breakout box includes test points at which the engine coolant temperature

sensor values can be measured with a high-impedance meter. See figure 16–2.

Use jumper wires, a scan tool, or a breakout box to gain electrical access to the wiring of the coolant temperature sensor. Typical resistance values include the following:

−40° F	(−40° C)	100,000 ohms
70° F	(21° C)	about 3000 ohms
200° F	(94° C)	about 200 ohms

If resistance values match with the appropriate coolant temperature and there is still a coolant sensor trouble code, the problem is generally in the wiring between the sensor and the computer. Always consult the manufacturer's recommended procedures for checking this wiring. If the resistance values do not match, the sensor may need to be replaced.

Normal operating temperature varies with vehicle make and model. Some vehicles are equipped with a thermostat with an opening temperature of 180° F (82° C), whereas other vehicles use a thermostat that is 195° F (90°C) or higher. Before replacing the ECT sensor, be sure that the engine is operating at the temperature specified by the manufacturer. Most manufacturers recommend checking the ECT sensor after the cooling fan has cycled twice, indicating a fully warmed engine.

◀ **DIAGNOSTIC STORY** ▶

THE COLD-START, STALL PROBLEM

A dealer technician had several new vehicles that stalled after a cold start, but ran perfectly at all other times. The technician had already installed the third-generation PROM (third updated PROM for this particular vehicle and engine). Because it was a fuel-injected engine, the coolant sensor was the most important sensor, especially for starting and running before the system went into closed-loop operation. The technician had already replaced the coolant sensor once, but this time decided to check all of the coolant sensors in the parts department for resistance. Most coolant sensors should measure about 3000 ohms at room temperature (70° F, 21° C).

The parts department had about fifteen coolant sensors in stock, and the resistance varied by about 200 ohms. The technician selected the *highest*-resistance coolant sensor and installed it in the problem vehicle. The problem of stalling after a cold start was solved.

The higher-resistance coolant sensor solved the problem because the computer added just a little more fuel based on the coolant temperature sensor value. The repair was legal because a stock replacement part was used, but as with any part, slight differences do occur.

NOTE: Many manufacturers install a pull-up resistor inside the computer to change the voltage drop across the ECT sensor. This is done to expand the scale of the ECT sensor and to make the sensor more sensitive. Therefore, if measuring *voltage* at the ECT sensor, check with the service manual for the proper voltage for each temperature.

PRESSURE SENSORS

Various pressure sensors are used by various engine manufacturers to determine engine intake (inlet) manifold pressure (vacuum) and/or atmospheric pressure. See figure 16–3. When engine vacuum is high, manifold pressure is low. Therefore, the engine computer can detect engine load by sensing the voltage output from a pressure sensor. See figure 16-4. Most pressure sensors have a 5-volt input supplied by the engine computer.

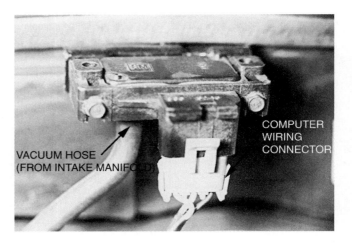

FIGURE 16–3 Typical MAP sensor. The vacuum hose must run directly to a manifold vacuum source.

The pressure sensor sends back to the computer a voltage proportional to the amount of pressure detected. A vacuum hose to the pressure sensor that is defective or pinched closed commonly causes hesitation on acceleration and other driveability problems. Some sensors send a high voltage (almost 5 volts) to the computer when the engine vacuum is high. Typically, a vacuum sensor (such as a MAP sensor) has a low voltage (usually less than 1 volt) when the engine vacuum is high. Some engines use a barometric pressure (baro) sensor to signal to the computer a change in altitude.

TESTING THE PRESSURE SENSOR

Pressure sensors (such as MAP, vacuum [VAC], or baro sensors) generally operate on 5 volts from the computer and return a signal (voltage or frequency) based on the pressure (vacuum) applied to the sensor.

Three different types of test instruments can be used to test a pressure sensor:

1. A digital voltmeter with three test leads connected in series between the sensor and the wiring harness connector.
2. A scan tool or a specific tool recommended by the vehicle manufacturer.
3. A breakout box that is connected in series between the computer and the wiring harness connection(s). A typical breakout box includes test points at which pressure sensor values can be measured with a digital voltmeter (or frequency counter, if a frequency-type MAP sensor is being tested).

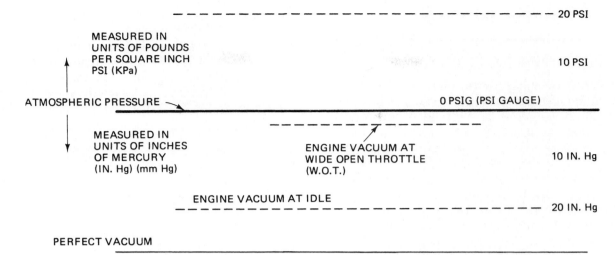

FIGURE 16–4 As an engine is accelerated under a load, the engine vacuum drops. This drop in vacuum is actually an increase in absolute pressure in the intake manifold. A MAP sensor senses all pressures greater than that of a perfect vacuum.

NOTE: Always check service literature for the exact testing procedures and specifications for the vehicle being tested.

Use jumper wires, a scan tool, or a breakout box to gain electrical access to the wiring to the pressure sensor. Most pressure sensors use three wires:

1. A 5-volt wire from the computer
2. A variable-signal wire back to the computer
3. A ground or reference low wire

The procedure for testing the sensor is as follows:

1. Turn the ignition on (engine off).
2. Measure the voltage (or frequency) of the sensor output.
3. Using a hand-operated vacuum pump (or other variable vacuum source), apply vacuum to the sensor.

A good pressure sensor should change voltage (or frequency) in relation to the applied vacuum. If the signal does not change or the values are out of range according to the manufacturer's specifications, the sensor must be replaced.

If a MAP or VAC sensor is being tested, make certain that the vacuum hose and hose fittings are sound and making a good, tight connection to a manifold vacuum source on the engine.

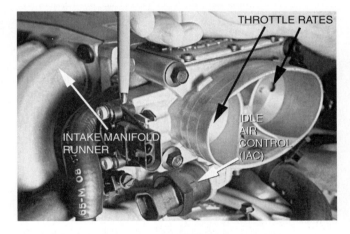

FIGURE 16–5 Typical TP sensor. This throttle position sensor is adjustable. The TP sensor setting has a major effect on the operation of the engine.

THROTTLE POSITION SENSORS

Most computer-equipped engines use a throttle position sensor to signal to the computer the position of the throttle. See figure 16–5. A typical sensor has three wires: one wire is a 5-volt feed wire from the computer, another is a ground wire, and the third wire is the voltage feed wire back to the computer. As the throttle is opened, the voltage to the computer changes. The computer senses this change in throttle position and changes the fuel mixture and ignition timing. The actual

◀ **TECH TIP** ▶

CHECK THE HOSE

A defective vacuum hose to a MAP sensor can cause a variety of driveability problems including poor fuel economy, hesitation, stalling, and rough idle. A small air leak (vacuum leak) around the hose can cause these symptoms and often set a trouble code in the vehicle computer. Whenever working on a vehicle that uses a MAP sensor, make certain that the vacuum hose travels consistently *downward* on its route from the sensor to the source of manifold vacuum. Inspect the hose, especially if another technician has previously replaced the factory-original hose. It should not be so long that it sags down at any point. Condensed fuel and/or moisture can become trapped in this low spot in the hose and cause all types of driveability problems and MAP sensor codes.

change in fuel mixture and ignition timing is also partly determined by the other sensors, such as the manifold pressure (engine vacuum), engine RPM, coolant temperature, and oxygen sensors. Some throttle position sensors are adjustable and should be set according to the *exact* engine manufacturer's specifications. A defective or misadjusted throttle position sensor can cause hesitation on acceleration and other driveability problems. On some vehicles equipped with an automatic transmission, the throttle position sensor also affects the application of the torque converter clutch.

The **throttle position** (TP) sensor used on fuel-injected vehicles acts as an "electronic accelerator pump." If the TP sensor is unplugged or defective, the engine may still operate satisfactorily, but hesitate upon acceleration as though the carburetor were in need of a new accelerator pump.

TESTING THE THROTTLE POSITION SENSOR

Three different types of test instruments can be used to check a TP sensor:

1. A digital voltmeter with three test leads connected in series between the sensor and the wiring harness connector.

2. A scan tool or a specific tool recommended by the vehicle manufacturer.
3. A breakout box that is connected in series between the computer and the wiring harness connector(s). A typical breakout box includes test points at which TP voltages can be measured with a digital voltmeter.

NOTE: The procedure that follows is the usual method used by many manufacturers. Always refer to service literature for the exact recommended procedure and specifications for the vehicle being tested.

Use jumper wires, a scan tool, or a breakout box to gain electrical access to the wiring to the TP sensor. Most sensors use three wires:

1. A 5-volt wire from the computer
2. A variable-signal wire back to the computer
3. A ground or reference low wire

The procedure for testing the sensor is as follows:

1. Turn the ignition switch on (engine off).
2. Measure the voltage between the signal wire and ground (reference low) wire. The voltage should be about 0.5 volts.

NOTE: Consult the service literature for exact wire colors or locations.

---

3. With the engine still *not running* (but with the ignition still on), slowly increase the throttle opening. The voltage signal from the TP sensor should also increase. Look for any "dead spots" or open circuit readings as the throttle is increased to the wide-open position.

HINT: If TP sensor specifications are not available, use the fact that the TP sensor voltage at idle should be about 10% of the voltage at the **wide-open throttle** (WOT) position. Therefore, if the WOT voltage is 4.50 volts, then TP sensor voltage at idle should be about 0.450 volts.

---

4. With the voltmeter (or scan tool) still connected, slowly return the throttle down to the idle position. The voltage from the TP sensor should also decrease evenly on the return to idle.

The TP sensor voltage at idle should be within the acceptable range as specified by the manufacturer. Some throttle position sensors can be adjusted by loosening their retaining screws and moving the sensor in relation to the throttle opening. This movement changes the output voltage of the sensor.

All TP sensors should also provide a smooth transition voltage reading from idle to WOT and back to idle. Replace the TP sensor if erratic voltage readings are obtained or if the correct setting at idle cannot be obtained.

Testing the TP Sensor Using the Min-Max Method

Many times, a break in the TP sensor happens too rapidly to be detected by a digital voltmeter. The typical "capture rate" of a digital meter is 200 ms or 5 times per second. Often the problem occurs in just a thousandth of a second. Use a digital meter (such as a Fluke 87) set to min-max and 1 ms. Then slowly open the throttle to the wide open position. The meter will record all readings that last 1/1000 second or longer. With the touch of a button, the low reading and the high reading will be displayed. If there is a gap to 0 volts or an open (infinity or OL), the meter will display it.

Scope Testing the Sensor

Using a scope is the best method for testing any sensor because a scope can show problems that even a fast meter cannot detect. Simply connect the leads to the signal wire and ground of the sensor and operate the TP sensor.

NOTE: Be certain to use the ground of the sensor and not the ground of the vehicle. If a strange reading (higher than normal) is found, connect the scope leads to the sensor ground and vehicle ground—there should *not* be a difference in voltage if everything is okay. A smooth line that moves up and down on the scope screen indicates a properly operating sensor.

EXHAUST GAS OXYGEN SENSORS

Most automotive computer systems use a sensor in the exhaust system to measure the oxygen content of the exhaust. These sensors are called oxygen (O2S) sensors. See figures 16–6 and 16–7. If the exhaust contains

FIGURE 16–6   Typical zirconia oxygen sensor.

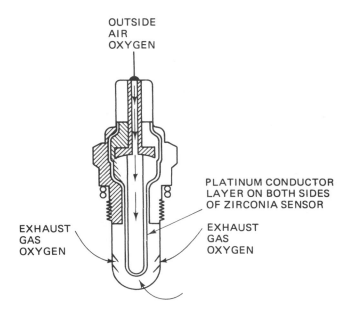

FIGURE 16–7   A cross-sectional view of a typical zirconia oxygen sensor.

very little oxygen (O_2), the computer assumes that the intake charge is rich (too much fuel) and reduces fuel delivery. On the other hand, when the oxygen level is high, the computer reduces fuel delivery. See chapter 18 for diagnosis procedures.

TESTING THE OXYGEN SENSOR

Most oxygen sensors are constructed of **zirconia** (zirconium oxide), and therefore produce a voltage (like a small battery) when in the *absence* of oxygen, when the sensor is hot (over 600° F [315° C]). The output voltage

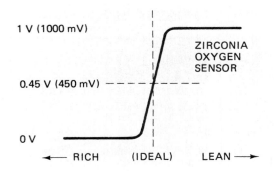

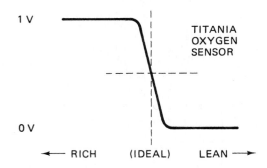

FIGURE 16–8 Titania and zirconia are two types of oxygen sensors, and their operating characteristics are opposite.

of a typical oxygen sensor varies depending on the oxygen content of the exhaust gases passing the sensor.

Typical oxygen sensor values are as follows:

Rich exhaust—oxygen sensor voltage above 800 millivolts

Lean exhaust—oxygen sensor voltage below 200 millivolts

Other oxygen sensors are constructed of the metallic element **titania** (titanium dioxide). Titania changes in resistance whenever exposed to varying percentage amounts of oxygen. The engine computer can monitor the resistance of a titania oxygen sensor for fuel management instead of monitoring voltage changes, as with a zirconia oxygen sensor. The changing resistance of a titania oxygen sensor changes the voltage of the oxygen sensor circuit. The voltage change is opposite to that of a zirconia oxygen sensor. (See figure 16–8 for a diagram of operation of the two types of oxygen sensors.)

Test Procedure Using a Scan Tool

A good oxygen sensor should be able to sense the oxygen content and change voltage outputs rapidly. How fast an oxygen sensor switches from high (above

450 millivolts) to low (below 350 millivolts) is measured in oxygen sensor **cross counts.** A cross count is the number of times an oxygen sensor changes voltage from high to low (from low to high voltage is not counted) in 1 second (or 1.25 seconds depending on scan tool and computer speed).

NOTE: On a carbureted engine at 2000 engine RPM, 1 to 3 cross counts is normal. On a fuel-injected engine at 2000 engine RPM, 8 to 10 cross counts is normal. The higher the number of cross counts, the better.

Oxygen sensor cross counts can only be determined using a scan tool or other suitable tester that reads computer data.

In both cases (carbureted and fuel-injected engine), the higher the number of cross counts, the better. If the cross counts are low (or zero), the oxygen sensor may be contaminated, or the fuel delivery system is delivering a constant rich or lean air-fuel mixture.

Test Procedure without a Scan Tool

The oxygen sensor can be checked for proper operation using a digital high-impedance voltmeter.

1. With the engine off, unplug the oxygen sensor at the terminal.
2. Install a jumper wire (or wires, if it is an electrically heated oxygen sensor).

NOTE: The jumper wire permits access to the electrical connection between the sensor and the computer while still allowing the correct operation of the system. A breakout box can also be used, rather than a jumper wire.

---

3. Start the engine and allow it to reach closed-loop operation.
4. In closed-loop operation, the oxygen sensor voltage should be constantly changing as the fuel mixture is being controlled.

The results should be interpreted as follows:

1. If the oxygen sensor fails to respond, and its voltage remains at about 450 millivolts, the sensor may be defective and require replacement. Before replacing the oxygen sensor, check the manufacturer's recommended procedures.

2. If the oxygen sensor reads high all the time (above 550 millivolts), the fuel system could be supplying too rich a fuel mixture or the oxygen sensor may be contaminated.

3. If the oxygen sensor voltage remains low (below 350 millivolts), the fuel system could be supplying too lean a fuel mixture. Check for a vacuum leak or partially clogged fuel injector(s). Before replacing the oxygen sensor, check the manufacturer's recommended procedures.

Testing the Sensor Using the Min-Max Method

A digital meter set on DC volts can be used to record the minimum and maximum voltage with the engine running. A good oxygen sensor should be able to produce a value of less than 300 millivolts and a maximum voltage above 800 millivolts. Replace any oxygen sensor that fails to go above 700 millivolts or lower than 300 millivolts.

Scope Testing the Sensor

A scope can also be used to test an oxygen sensor. Connect the scope to the signal wire and ground for the sensor (if it is so equipped). With the engine operating in closed loop, the voltage signal of the sensor should be constantly changing.

OXYGEN SENSOR INSPECTION

Whenever an oxygen sensor is replaced, the old sensor should be carefully inspected to help determine the cause of the failure. This is an important step because if the cause of the failure is not discovered, it could lead to another sensor failure.

Inspection may reveal the following:

1. *Black sooty deposits.* This type of deposit usually indicates a rich air-fuel mixture.

2. *Whitish chalky deposits.* This type of deposit is characteristic of silica contamination. Usual causes for this type of sensor failure include silica deposits in the fuel or a technician's having used the wrong type of silicone sealant during the servicing of the engine.

3. *White sandy or gritty deposits.* A white sandy-textured deposit is characteristic of antifreeze (ethylene glycol) contamination. A defective cylinder head or intake manifold gasket could be the cause, or a cracked cylinder head or engine block.

◀ **DIAGNOSTIC STORY** ▶

HOW COULD USING SILICONE SEALER ON A ROCKER COVER GASKET AFFECT THE OXYGEN SENSOR?

The wrong type of silicone room-temperature vulcanization (RTV) sealer on a rocker cover gasket gives off fumes during the curing process. These fumes enter the crankcase area by way of the oil drain-back holes in the cylinder head, as well as through pushrod openings and other passages in the engine. During engine operation, these fumes are drawn into the intake manifold through the (PCV) positive crankcase ventilation system and are burned in the engine. The harmful silica then exits through the exhaust system, where the contamination affects the oxygen sensor.

Antifreeze may also cause the oxygen sensor to become green as a result of the dye used in antifreeze.

4. *Dark brown deposits.* Dark brown deposits on the oxygen sensor are an indication of excessive oil consumption. Possible causes include a defective positive crankcase ventilation (PCV) system or a mechanical engine problem such as defective valve stem seals or piston rings.

INTAKE AIR TEMPERATURE SENSORS

Many fuel-injected engines use a temperature sensor to measure the temperature of the air entering the engine. This sensor is called an **intake air temperature** (IAT) sensor.

This sensor may be located anywhere in the air inlet section of the engine, such as in the air cleaner housing, built into the mass airflow sensor, or in the intake manifold. Even though most of these systems also use a coolant temperature sensor, the computer is better able to fine-tune the best air-fuel ratio and ignition timing if the temperature (and therefore, the relative density) of the intake air is known.

Cold Air Temperature

1. Requires a richer air-fuel mixture

2. Permits more advanced ignition timing for optimum performance and fuel economy

◄ TECH TIP ►

IF IT'S GREEN, IT'S A SIGNAL WIRE

Ford-built vehicles usually use a green wire as the signal wire back to the computer from sensors. It may not be a solid green, but if there is green somewhere on the wire, then it is the signal wire. The other wires are the power and ground wires to the sensor.

Warm Air Temperature

1. Requires a leaner air-fuel mixture
2. Requires less spark advance for best performance without harmful detonation (ping)

NOTE: Before 1993, the intake air temperature (IAT) sensor was assigned many names by different manufacturers, including the following:

Air temperature sensor (ATS)
Air charge temperature (ACT)
Manifold air temperature (MAT)

VEHICLE SPEED SENSORS

Most computerized vehicles use a vehicle speed sensor. This sensor is used (in combination with other sensors) to control one or more of the following:

1. Electric cooling fan
2. Torque converter clutch (lockup torque converter)
3. Fuel and spark optimization for fuel economy during cruise conditions
4. Speed (cruise) control system

WHEEL SPEED SENSORS

Vehicles equipped with a computerized antilock brake system (ABS) are equipped with **wheel speed sensors** (WSS) (usually at each wheel). Most wheel speed sensors are magnetic-type sensors that produce an alternating voltage and frequency proportional to wheel rotational speed.

Wheel speed sensor input is used by the central computer (or ABS controller computer) to control hydraulic and electronic outputs that control wheel spin

for braking and acceleration (traction) purposes. Wheel speed sensors are also an input of reactive (active) suspension systems.

AIRFLOW SENSORS

Fuel-injection computer systems require a method for measuring the amount of air the engine is breathing in, to be able to match the correct fuel delivery. There are two basic methods used:

1. Speed density method
2. Airflow method

The speed density method does *not* require an air quantity sensor, but rather, calculates the amount of fuel required by the engine. The computer uses information from sensors to calculate the needed amount of fuel.

1. *MAP sensor*—The value of the intake (inlet) manifold pressure (vacuum) is a direct indication of engine load.
2. *TP sensor*—The position of the throttle plate and its rate of change is used as part of the equation to calculate the proper amount of fuel to inject.
3. *Temperature sensors*—Both engine coolant temperature (ECT) and intake air temperature (IAT) are used to calculate the density of the air and the need of the engine for fuel. A cold engine (low coolant temperature) requires a richer air-fuel mixture than a warm engine.

The airflow method actually measures the amount of air as part of the computer input information necessary for accurate fuel delivery control. There are three basic types of airflow sensors used on port-injected engines: the air vane sensor, the hot film sensor, and the hot wire sensor.

Air Vane Sensor. This sensor uses a movable vane that translates the amount of movement of the vane into the amount of air being drawn into the engine.

Hot Film Sensor. This type of sensor uses a temperature-sensing resistor (thermistor) to measure the temperature of the incoming air. Through the electronics within the sensor, a conductive film is kept at a temperature 70° C above the temperature of the incoming air. Because the amount *and* density of the air both tend to contribute to the cooling effect as the air passes through the sensor, this type of sensor can actually produce an output based on the mass of the airflow. The

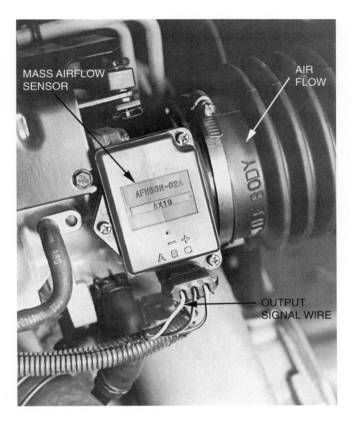

FIGURE 16–9 Typical hot wire mass airflow sensor. This style of sensor samples only 2% of the air flowing into the engine. The computer computes the correct amount of fuel based on this small sample.

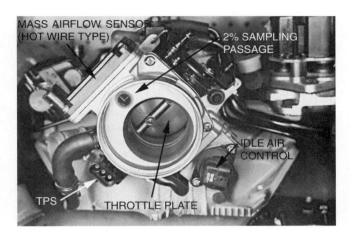

FIGURE 16–10 Same sensor as shown in figure 16–9, except from another view, with the air inlet hose removed.

◀ **TECH TIP** ▶

THE TAP TEST

The tap test is a genuine diagnostic test for a mass airflow sensor. With the engine operating, simply tap on the sensor located in the air inlet before the throttle valve. Do not hit the sensor with a heavy object; just tap on the sensor with your fingers. If the engine stalls, hesitates, or changes its operation when the MAF sensor is being tapped, the MAF sensor (or its electrical connections) is defective and must be replaced (or serviced).

The tap test is also a useful test to perform on engine computers (powertrain control modules). With the engine running lightly, tap on the side of the computer with the four fingers of your open hand. If the engine stumbles or stalls, replace the computer.

CAUTION: Do not use your fist or any tool that can damage the component being tested.

output of this type of sensor is usually a frequency based on the amount of air entering the sensor. The more air that enters the sensor, the more the hot film is cooled. The electronics inside the sensor, therefore, increase the current flow through the hot film to maintain the 70° C temperature differential between the air temperature and the temperature of the hot film. This change in current flow is converted to a frequency output that the computer can use as a measurement of airflow. Most of these types of sensors are referred to as mass airflow sensors, because unlike the air vane sensor, the MAF sensor takes into account relative humidity, altitude, and temperature of the air. See figures 16–9 and 16–10. The denser the air, the greater the cooling effect on the hot film sensor and the greater the amount of fuel required for proper combustion.

Hot Wire Sensor. This type of sensor is similar to the hot film type but uses a hot wire to sense the mass airflow instead of the hot film. Like the hot film sensor, the hot wire sensor uses a temperature-sensing resistor (thermistor) to measure the temperature of the air en-

tering the sensor. The electronic circuitry within the sensor keeps the temperature of the wire at 70° C above the temperature of the incoming air. Hot wire sensors also use a burn-off circuit to keep the wire clean.

The burn-off circuit is usually computer controlled and involves passing a high current through the hot wire for about ½ second when the engine is shut off to "burn off" any accumulated dirt. If the burn-off circuit does not work, the accumulated dirt on the hot wire can change air measurement and dramatically affect the operation of the engine.

HINT: This burn-off circuit can be easily checked by placing a mirror at the air inlet to the airflow sensor and having an assistant turn off the engine. If all of the conditions for burn off have occurred (closed-loop operation, etc.), the wire in the center of the sensor should glow red hot for about ½ second. If this burn off does not occur, check the manufacturer's service information for the exact troubleshooting procedure.

OTHER COMPUTER OUTPUTS

The typical automotive computer is capable of processing over 100,000 commands per second. (Some systems are capable of over 1,000,000 commands per second.) Many computers control other functions in addition to those indicated previously. These additional functions include the following:

1. *Electric engine cooling fan operation.* The computer "knows" the coolant temperature, idle speed, and vehicle speed, and turns the electric cooling fan on or off as required. If the electric fan is off, less current is required from the alternator, and therefore, the engine can achieve better fuel economy.

2. *Torque converter clutch operation.* The torque converter clutch (lockup converter) reduces the slippage losses of a normal torque converter. The computer uses the inputs from the throttle position sensor, engine vacuum (vacuum, MAP, or baro) sensor, and vehicle speed sensor to calculate the correct application time for the clutch.

3. *EGR valve operation.* Exhaust gas recirculation is critical for maintaining the proper internal engine fuel-burning rate to maintain lowest oxides of nitrogen (NO_x) emissions and to prevent harmful engine detonation (ping). EGR valves are vacuum operated, and the computer can (on some models) control the vacuum going to the EGR valve. The computer-controlled EGR includes a solenoid switch to switch the vacuum on and off. Because of this on-and-off signal from the computer, this type of EGR control is often called **pulse-width modulated** (PWM) (controlled).

Some computer systems also control air-conditioner clutch operation, electric fuel pump operation, blower motor speed, and heater, defroster, and air-

FIGURE 16–11 Typical knock sensor. Knock sensor locations vary, depending on engine, year, and application.

conditioning airflow "doors," plus many other functions not related to engine performance.

KNOCK SENSORS

A knock sensor is a piezoelectric sensor that transforms the engine detonation vibrations directly into an electrical signal that is sent to the computer. The knock control permits the maximum timing advance for best fuel economy and performance, yet retards automatically to prevent damaging detonation. With this detonation control, the ignition timing will be automatically retarded if lower-octane fuel is used. See figure 16–11.

AIR MANAGEMENT

Many computer-equipped engines use an **air injection reaction** (AIR) pump as part of the emission control system. This pump provides the air necessary for the oxidizing catalytic converter. The computer controls the airflow from the pump by switching on and off various solenoid valves. When the engine is cold, the air pump output is directed to the exhaust manifold to help provide enough oxygen to convert HC (unburned gasoline) and CO (carbon monoxide) to H_2O (water) and CO_2 (carbon dioxide). When the engine becomes warm, the computer operates the air valves so as to direct the air pump output to the catalytic converter.

Whenever the vacuum rapidly increases above the normal idle level, as during rapid deceleration, the computer diverts the air pump output to the air cleaner assembly to silence the air. Diverting the air to the air cleaner prevents exhaust backfire during deceleration.

IDLE SPEED CONTROL

Most computer-equipped engines include some type of engine **idle speed control** (ISC). Carburetor-equipped engines often use an idle speed control stepper motor operated by the computer. A stepper motor is a type of permanent-magnet motor that can be controlled precisely using the electronics of the computer. If the engine speed sensor detects a drop in engine speed (such as can happen when the steering wheel is turned if the vehicle is equipped with power steering), the ISC increases the throttle opening to maintain the proper idle speed.

On an engine equipped with fuel injection (TBI or port injection), the idle speed is controlled by increasing or decreasing the amount of air bypassing the throttle plate. Again, an electronic stepper motor is used to maintain the correct idle speed. This control is often called the **idle air control** (IAC).

Many computer-controlled throttle linkage units use manifold vacuum with a computer-controlled solenoid valve to control the idle speed. This type of arrangement is often called a **throttle kicker solenoid.**

IGNITION TIMING CONTROL

Most engine computers control the ignition timing. Conventional vacuum and mechanical advance mechanisms cannot accurately maintain the *exact* ignition timing that is possible with computer control. The computer controls the timing by controlling the ignition module primary ignition circuit turn-off time. The computer uses the various input signals, compares the results with the program (PROM), and changes the ignition instantly if that is needed to maintain the most ideal spark timing. The spark timing changes according to the following factors:

1. *Low engine temperature.* Timing can be advanced.
2. *High engine temperature.* Timing should be retarded.
3. *High altitude.* Timing can be advanced.
4. *High engine load* (low vacuum). Timing should be retarded.
5. *Light engine load* (high vacuum). Timing can be advanced.

The computer can calculate the correct ignition timing considering all of the various input factors. Some computer systems are capable of retarding the ignition timing (up to 30 degrees) if detonation is detected by a knock sensor.

COMPUTER-OPERATED UNITS

The engine computer takes the input information from the various sensors and compares it against the program (instructions in ROM). Based on the inputs, the computer controls various units to keep the engine operating within the standards established in the computer memory (PROM). See figure 16–12. Most computers control the following units (computer outputs):

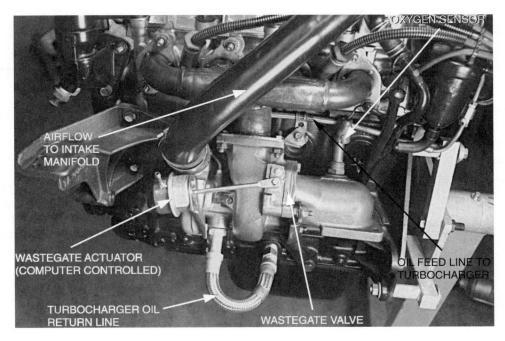

FIGURE 16–12 Typical turbocharger installation. The wastegate is computer controlled based on input signals from RPM, coolant temperature, MAP, and other sensors.

◀ TECH TIP ▶

USE THE MAP AS A VACUUM GAUGE

A MAP sensor measures the pressure inside the intake manifold compared to absolute zero (perfect vacuum). For example, an idling engine that has 20 inches mercury of vacuum has a lower pressure inside the intake manifold than when the engine is under a load and the vacuum is at 10 inches mercury. A decrease in engine vacuum results in an increase in manifold pressure. A normal engine should produce between 17 and 21 inches of mercury at idle. Comparing the vacuum reading with the voltage reading output of the MAP sensor will indicate a reading between 1.62 and 0.88 volts. Therefore, a DVOM or scope (instead of a vacuum gauge) can be used to measure engine vacuum.

NOTE: This chart was developed by testing a MAP sensor at a location about 600 feet above sea level. For best results, a chart based on your altitude should be made by applying a known vacuum (from a vacuum source) and reading the voltage of a known good MAP sensor. Vacuum usually drops about 1 inch per 1000 feet of altitude.

Vacuum (in. Hg)	Volts	Vacuum (in. Hg)	Volts	Vacuum (in. Hg)	Volts
0	4.80	9	3.10	18	1.42
1	4.52	10	2.94	19	1.20
2	4.46	11	2.76	20	1.10
3	4.26	12	2.54	21	0.88
4	4.06	13	2.36	22	0.66
5	3.88	14	2.20	23	0.44
6	3.66	15	2.00	24	0.22
7	3.50	16	1.80	25	0.06
8	3.30	17	1.62	26	0.02

1. Mixture control (carburetor solenoid or fuel injectors)
2. Idle speed control
3. Ignition timing control
4. Air management (air pump)

Related functions may include electric cooling fan operation, air-conditioner clutch operation, torque converter clutch operation, and EGR valve operation, plus other functions that depend on exact application.

MIXTURE CONTROL

The computer provides the ground for a 12-volt circuit to a solenoid or fuel-injector coil. The amount of fuel can be controlled by grounding or ungrounding the cir-

cuit for the mixture control (MC) solenoid. A typical mixture control solenoid opens and closes the fuel solenoid circuit 10 times per second. The computer determines the length of time for which the fuel solenoid is delivering fuel. The solenoid may be turned on and off 10 times per second, but the "on time" can vary.

The on time is determined by the computer to deliver the exact amount of fuel necessary for the engine speed, throttle position, engine load, and oxygen content of the exhaust. The on time may be called **duty cycle** or **pulse width.**

SUMMARY

1. As the temperature of the engine coolant increases, the resistance of the ECT sensor decreases.

2. A throttle position sensor can best be checked with a voltmeter set on min-max or with a scope.

3. An oxygen sensor should switch from high to low rapidly on a fuel-injected engine operating in closed loop.

4. A mass airflow sensor actually measures the density and amount of air flowing into the engine. This results in very accurate engine control.

5. A knock sensor detects engine-damaging detonation and signals the computer to retard the ignition timing.

REVIEW QUESTIONS

1. Explain how to test an engine coolant temperature sensor.

2. Describe how best to test a MAP sensor.

3. Describe how a zirconia oxygen sensor works and how best to determine if it is operating correctly.

4. Explain how a hot film MAF sensor works.

MULTIPLE-CHOICE QUESTIONS

1. The sensor that most determines fuel delivery when a fuel-injected engine is first started is the _____ .
   a. Oxygen sensor
   b. Engine coolant temperature sensor
   c. MAP sensor
   d. Baro sensor

2. The sensor that must be warmed up and functioning before the engine management computer will go "closed loop" is the _____ .
   a. Oxygen sensor
   b. Engine coolant temperature sensor
   c. MAP sensor
   d. Baro sensor

3. As the load on an engine increases, the manifold vacuum decreases and the manifold absolute pressure _____ .
   a. Increases
   b. Decreases
   c. Changes with barometric pressure only (altitude or weather)
   d. Remains constant (absolute)

4. Which sensor is generally considered to be the electronic accelerator pump of a fuel-injected engine?
   a. The oxygen sensor
   b. The engine coolant temperature sensor
   c. The manifold absolute pressure sensor
   d. The throttle position sensor

5. The voltage output of a zirconia oxygen sensor when the exhaust stream is lean (excess oxygen) is _____ .
   a. Relatively high (close to 1 volt)
   b. About in the middle of the voltage range
   c. Relatively low (close to zero volts)
   d. Either a or b, depending on atmospheric pressure

6. A fuel-injection system that does not use a sensor to measure the amount (or mass) of air entering the engine is usually called _____ type of system.
   a. An air vane–controlled
   b. A speed density
   c. A mass airflow
   d. A hot wire

7. The standardized name for the sensor that measures the temperature of the air being drawn into the engine is called _____ .
   a. An intake air temperature sensor (IAT)
   b. An air temperature sensor (ATS)
   c. An air charge temperature (ACT) sensor
   d. A manifold air temperature (MAT) sensor

8. Which type of sensor uses a burn-off circuit?
   a. An oxygen sensor
   b. A hot wire mass airflow sensor
   c. A hot film mass airflow sensor
   d. A vane-type airflow sensor

9. Typical TP sensor voltage at idle is about _____ .
   a. 2.50 to 2.80 volts
   b. 0.5 volts or 10% of WOT TP sensor voltage
   c. 1.5 to 2.8 volts
   d. 13.5 to 15.0 volts

10. Which of the following describe acceptable oxygen sensor cross counts?
    a. 128 to 136
    b. A minimum of 8 at 2000 RPM
    c. The higher the number, the better
    d. Both b and c

◀ Chapter 17 ▶

COMPUTERIZED CARBURETION AND FUEL INJECTION

OBJECTIVES

After studying chapter 17, the reader will be able to

1. List the six circuits of a carburetor.
2. Explain how a throttle body fuel-injection system operates.
3. Describe how a port fuel-injection system works.
4. List the typical fuel pump pressures for the various fuel-injection systems.

Engine management computers use engine sensors to determine the air-fuel mixture that the engine needs for best performance with the lowest level of exhaust emissions. It is the carburetor or fuel-injection system that mixes the air and fuel and delivers the mixture to the engine.

COMPUTERIZED CARBURETORS

Computerized carburetors are standard carburetors that have been modified for computer-controlled operation of one or more sections or "circuits" of their operation. All carburetors are pressure differential devices. The difference between the air pressure of the atmo-

sphere and the low pressure (vacuum) on the intake manifold causes air to flow. Most automotive-type gasoline carburetors use six different, but related, circuits.

Float Circuit

The float circuit uses a float that floats in a bowl of gasoline (float bowl). The float is mechanically connected to a needle valve used to control the level of the fuel in the float bowl. This level is critical for the proper operation of the carburetor because it is this level that determines the fuel pressure levels inside of the carburetor.

1. A higher than normal float level causes a richer than normal fuel delivery.
2. A lower than normal float level causes a leaner than normal fuel delivery.
3. If a float becomes saturated with fuel and becomes heavier than normal, the fuel is raised to a level that is higher than normal, which results in a richer than normal fuel delivery. See figure 17–1.

NOTE: Some computerized carburetor systems use a solenoid valve for the atmospheric vent on top of the float bowl to help control fuel delivery. Most computerized carburetors, however, do *not* control the operation of the float circuit.

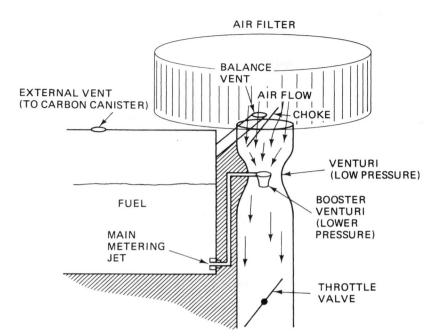

AIR FILTER

BALANCE VENT

AIR FLOW

CHOKE

EXTERNAL VENT (TO CARBON CANISTER)

VENTURI (LOW PRESSURE)

FUEL

BOOSTER VENTURI (LOWER PRESSURE)

MAIN METERING JET

THROTTLE VALVE

FIGURE 17–1 Cross-sectional view of a typical carburetor showing the relationship between float bowl venting and the air-fuel ratio.

Idle and Low-Speed Circuit

The idle and low-speed circuit of a carburetor is usually controlled by the computer. Some sources separate the operation of the idle and low-speed circuit into two separate circuits. Therefore, these sources indicate that a typical carburetor uses seven (instead of six) circuits. Because the operations of these two circuits are closely related, they are combined here for ease of discussion. Fuel delivery at idle must be richer to provide acceptable idle quality because the throttle is closed and the airflow through the carburetor is reduced.

The fuel from the float bowl is drawn through the main jet in the bottom of the bowl and through small drilled passages to be discharged below the throttle plate(s). To help atomize the fuel (make fuel droplets as small as possible to aid in the combustion process), small air passages called **air bleeds** are provided to premix air with the fuel before it leaves the **idle discharge port** below the throttle plate.

As the throttle is opened, additional passages are exposed to engine vacuum, which draws additional air-fuel mixture through the passages. This additional fuel delivery is commonly called the low-speed circuit. The slots or holes through which this additional fuel flows are called **transfer ports** or **transition ports**.

Main Metering Circuit

Once the throttle plate (valve) opens to a point past the transfer ports, enough air flows through the venturi to

cause a pressure drop that in turn causes fuel to be drawn from the float bowl and be discharged into the center of the venturi. This fuel flow is controlled by the size of the main jet in the bottom of the float bowl. See figure 17–2.

Tapered metering rods are often used to control the amount of fuel flow out of the float bowl going through the main jets.

Many computerized carburetors use solenoids (mixture control solenoids) to control the metering rods. When the solenoid is energized by the computer, the metering rods are forced down, restricting the amount of fuel that can flow out of the float bowl and into the venturi and eventually into the engine. When the mixture control solenoid is shut off by the computer, the spring-loaded metering rod lifts up allowing more fuel to flow. The computer typically pulses the mixture control solenoid 10 times per second. However, in the case of General Motors computer-controlled carburetors, the duty cycle can be varied from 10% to 90% (see the tech tip What Does Duty Cycle Mean?).

Power Circuit

The power circuit involves those passages and components that provide additional fuel for high-load (low-engine vacuum) conditions. The power circuit is *not* computer controlled. The computer controls only the idle and low speed plus the main metering circuits.

For an engine to produce more power, it must consume more fuel, and the power circuit is designed to

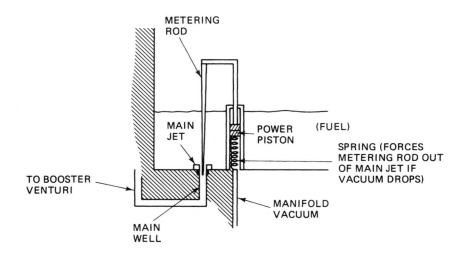

FIGURE 17–2 Cross-sectional view of a typical carburetor illustrating how the metering rods can control the air-fuel mixture.

◀ **TECH TIP** ▶

NOW THAT'S LEAN!

A carburetor, whether or not computer controlled, can provide a varying air-fuel mixture to the engine. With the choke on, a carburetor provides about an 8:1 (relatively rich) air-fuel ratio. Under highway cruise conditions, a typical carburetor can supply a mixture as lean as 18:1.

In a fuel-injected engine, the fuel delivery is completely controlled by the computer. During starting of a cold engine, the computer can command a mixture as rich as 1.5:1 at –40°F (–40°C). During periods of deceleration, the computer can actually shut off all fuel delivery, and that's about as lean as it gets!

	Rich Mixture	*Lean Mixture*
Carburetor	8:1	18:1
Fuel injection	1.5:1	No fuel at all

Remember, a carburetor, whether it is computer controlled or not, still provides a limited range of air-fuel ratios; whereas a fuel-injection system can vary the fuel delivery from a very rich mixture to no fuel at all.

This wide range of fuel delivery capability is the reason why the engine coolant temperature sensor is so critical on a fuel-injected engine. Even a slight miscalibration of engine temperature makes a drastic change in the operation of the engine.

◀ **TECH TIP** ▶

WHAT DOES DUTY CYCLE MEAN?

Duty cycle is a term commonly used when describing the operation of computer-controlled output devices. The term *duty cycle* refers to the amount (percentage) of time for which a unit is turned on. If the solenoid (or any other device) is turned on 70% of the time and kept off 30% of the time, the duty cycle is 70%.

provide this additional fuel, yet shut off or become inoperative under light-load conditions to conserve fuel. There are two basic types of power enrichment circuits—power valve and metering rod.

Power Valve

A power valve carburetor (such as most Holley brand and older Ford carburetors) uses vacuum to keep the valve closed. During acceleration, the load on the engine decreases engine manifold vacuum, and the spring, which is part of the power valve, opens the valve. Because the valve is located in the float bowl, additional fuel, beyond that provided by the main jets, flows into the main well and out through the booster venturi discharge ports.

Whether a power valve is "on" or "off" depends on the calibrations of the closing spring. Engine vacuum acts on the rubber diaphragm of the power valve and works against the force of the closing spring. Therefore, when vacuum is high (i.e., light engine load), the power valve is kept closed. When engine vacuum decreases (i.e., heavier engine load), the power valve spring opens the valve and allows additional fuel to flow from the carburetor.

Some replacement power valves (such as those designed for use in Holley carburetors) are stamped with the opening vacuum level. (High numbers indicate valves that open sooner, at higher vacuum settings than those marked with lower numbers.)

For example: An opening vacuum setting of 10.5 means that the power valve opens whenever manifold vacuum is below 10.5 inches Hg. This valve provides more fuel sooner for more power with reduced fuel economy. An opening vacuum setting of 6.5 means that the valve will open when manifold vacuum is below 6.5 inches Hg. This valve remains closed until the engine vacuum drops below this point, providing improved fuel economy.

NOTE: Power valves are often called **economy valves** or **economizer valves** because they remain closed much of the time for best fuel economy and only open when necessary for additional power.

Metering Rods

A carburetor that uses metering rods for fuel control typically provides the best fuel economy because the tapered metering rod is gradually lifted (pushed) out of the main jet(s) proportionally to the decrease in engine manifold vacuum. This method of fuel control provides the optimum arrangement because fuel control is directly related to engine load.

1. As engine load increases, manifold vacuum decreases and the metering rod is lifted out of the main jet.
2. As engine load decreases, manifold vacuum increases and the metering rod is drawn down into the main jet, restricting the amount of fuel that can be drawn out of the discharge nozzle.

Computerized engine control systems use a vacuum (VAC) or manifold absolute pressure (MAP) sensor(s) to provide input to the computer for engine load calculations. Along with oxygen sensor readings, this input enables the computer to control fuel delivery through a carburetor.

◄ **TECH TIP** ►

NO SPARK, NO SQUIRT

Most electronic fuel-injection computer systems use the distributor (or crank sensor) pulse as the trigger for when to inject (squirt) fuel from the injectors (nozzles). If this signal were not present, no fuel would be injected. Because this pulse is also necessary to trigger the module to create a spark from the coil, it can be said that no spark could also mean no squirt.

Therefore, if the cause of a no-start condition is observed to be a lack of fuel being injected, *do not* start testing or replacing fuel system components until the ignition system is checked for proper operation. See figure 17–3.

Accelerator Pump Circuit

Whenever the accelerator is depressed, additional air can quickly be drawn into the engine through the throttle plates. However, because fuel weighs more than air, there is a slight delay period between the opening of the throttle and the delivery of additional fuel. The accelerator pump circuit is designed to provide a short shot of fuel only when the accelerator is first depressed to provide the fuel needed to prevent the hesitation that would otherwise occur during this delay.

The accelerator pump circuit consists of an inlet and outlet check valve and a rubber diaphragm or cup to pressurize the fuel whenever the accelerator pedal is depressed. The fuel is discharged through an outlet nozzle(s) toward or near the booster venturi of the carburetor. The accelerator pump circuit is *not* controlled by the computer on vehicles equipped with a carburetor and a computer.

Choke Circuit

All engines require a richer air-fuel mixture to start. On carburetor-equipped engines, this is usually provided by a choke system that restricts the airflow through the carburetor during starting and cold engine operation. This choke plate restriction causes a low-pressure area to be developed beneath the choke plate and in the discharge nozzle area. This lower pressure draws additional fuel from the main jet and provides the richer mixture necessary for proper cold engine operation.

INJECTOR NOZZLE

INJECTOR WIRING
HARNESS CONNECTOR

FIGURE 17–3 Older-style General Motors throttle body injection unit. A special light called a **noid** (short for *solenoid*) light can be installed in the wiring connector and the engine cranked. If the light flashes, the computer is receiving an ignition (RPM) pulse and is capable of pulsing the injector nozzle.

Even though some thermostatic choke springs are electrically heated, the choke circuit is *not* computer controlled.

ELECTRONIC FUEL INJECTION

Electronic fuel-injection systems use the computer to control the operation of fuel injectors and other functions based on information sent to the computer from the various sensors. Most electronic fuel-injection systems share the following:

1. Electric fuel pump (usually located inside the fuel tank)
2. Fuel pump relay (usually controlled by the computer)
3. Fuel pressure regulator (mechanically operated using a spring-loaded rubber diaphragm to maintain proper fuel pressure
4. Fuel-injector nozzle or nozzles

There are two basic types of electronic fuel-injection systems—a throttle body unit and a port injection type.

Throttle Body Unit

The throttle body type of fuel injection uses one or two injectors (nozzles) to spray atomized fuel into a throttle body that is similar to the base of a carburetor. The air and fuel mix together in the throttle body unit and flow as a mixture down the intake manifold to the intake valves.

Most throttle body electronic fuel-injection units operate at a relatively low fuel pump pressure of about 10 psi (9 to 13 psi). Some TBI units, however, operate at higher pressures of 30 to 40 psi. These are often called **high-pressure TBI** systems.

A typical TBI system uses a throttle position sensor and an idle control valve. The TP is an input to the computer, and the idle control is an output from the computer. The throttle body injection unit costs less to manufacture, because it only uses one or two injectors (nozzles), whereas port injection systems require an injector for every cylinder, plus the additional computer capabilities to control all of the injectors.

NOTE: Some port injection systems used on engines with four or more valves per cylinder may use two injectors per cylinder. One injector is used all of the time, and the second injector is operated by the computer whenever high–engine

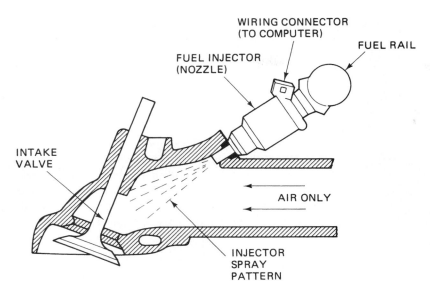

WIRING CONNECTOR
(TO COMPUTER)

FUEL RAIL

FUEL INJECTOR
(NOZZLE)

INTAKE
VALVE

AIR ONLY

INJECTOR
SPRAY
PATTERN

FIGURE 17–4 A typical port injection system squirts fuel into the low pressure (vacuum) of the intake manifold, near (about 3 inches [70 to 100 millimeters]) from the intake valve.

speed and high-load conditions are detected by the computer. Typically, the second injector is injecting fuel into the high-speed intake ports of the manifold. This system permits good low-speed power and throttle response, with superior high–engine speed power.

A typical TBI unit provides an improvement in driveability and fuel economy over that provided by a mechanical (or electronically controlled) carburetor. Unlike a port injection system, many TBI units require that heated air be used along with a heated intake manifold system to help vaporize the fuel that is squirted into the incoming air inside the throttle body unit.

PORT FUEL INJECTION

Port injection systems used on gasoline-powered engines inject a fine mist of fuel into the *intake manifold*. The pressure in the intake manifold is below atmospheric pressure on a running engine, and the manifold is, therefore, a vacuum. See figure 17–4.

Diesel engines, however, inject fuel directly into the high pressure of the combustion chamber. This direct injection of fuel into the combustion chamber requires very high injector discharge pressures. If, for example, a diesel injector were operated in the atmosphere, the fuel spray could penetrate the skin of a person near the discharging injector.

Gasoline fuel injectors operate at a much lower regulated pressure of approximately 35 to 45 psi (240 to 310 kPa).

The major advantage of using port injection instead of the more simple throttle body injection is that the intake manifolds on port-injected engines only contain air, not a mixture of air and fuel. This allows the engine design engineer the opportunity to design long, "tuned" intake manifold runners that help the engine produce increased torque at low engine speeds. See figures 17–5 and 17–6.

This type of tuned intake manifold runner is only possible with a port injection fuel delivery system. If fuel and air were mixed together in the intake manifold, the gasoline droplets would "fall out" of the mixture during travel from the throttle to the engine intake valve. In a port injection fuel delivery system, only air is in the intake manifold, and the fuel is injected into this low-pressure portion of the intake tract near the intake valve. See figures 17–7 and 17–8.

WHAT THE COMPUTER CONTROLS

Most electronic fuel-injection systems use the computer to control the following aspects of their operation:

1. Pulsing the fuel injectors on and off. The longer they are held open, the greater the amount of fuel that is injected into the cylinder.
2. Operating the fuel pump relay circuit. The computer usually controls the operation of the electric fuel pump located inside (or near) the fuel tank. The computer uses signals from the ignition switch and RPM signals from the ignition to energize the fuel pump relay circuit.

FIGURE 17–5 High-performance V-6 port-injected engine that has four valves per cylinder. Notice that each intake valve has its own intake runner and how the intake runner length varies. This permits the engine to develop a high-torque output over a wide range of engine speeds.

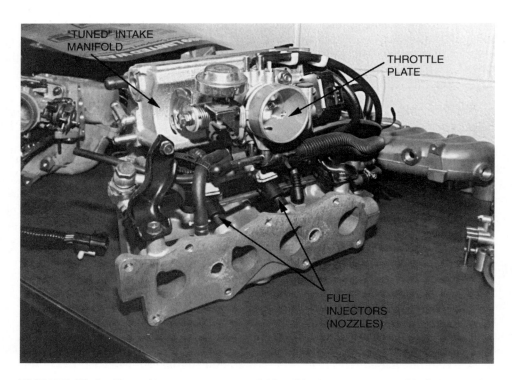

FIGURE 17–6 Typical port injection manifold and fuel-injection assembly from an inline four-cylinder engine. Notice the tuned intake manifold and the location of the fuel injectors (nozzles) in relation to the opening to the cylinder head.

NOTE: This is a safety feature, because if the engine stalls and the tachometer (engine speed) signal is lost, the computer will shut off (de-energize) the fuel pump relay and stop the fuel pump.

3. Controlling the ignition timing and other functions that are shared by other computer-controlled engine management systems.

Computer-controlled fuel-injection systems are basically reliable systems if the proper service proce-

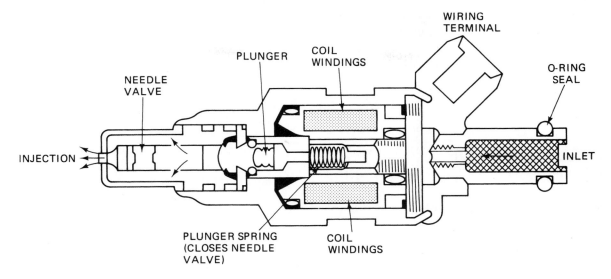

FIGURE 17–7 Cross-section of a typical port fuel-injection nozzle assembly. These injectors are serviced as an assembly only; no part replacement or service is possible except for replacement of external O-ring seals.

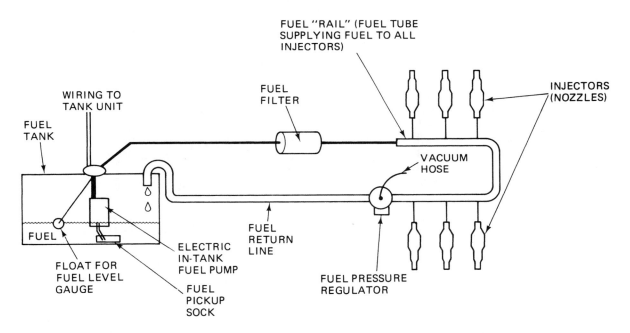

FIGURE 17–8 Typical port fuel-injection system, indicating the location of various components. Notice that the fuel pressure regulator is located on the fuel *return* side of the system. The computer does *not* control fuel pressure, but does control the operation of the electric fuel pump (on most systems) and the pulsing on and off of the injectors.

dures are followed. It is important to keep in mind that fuel-injection systems use the gasoline flowing through the injectors to lubricate and cool the injector electrical windings and pintel valves.

1. Avoid operating the vehicle on a near-empty tank of fuel. The water or dirt that settles near the bottom of

the fuel tank can be drawn through the fuel system and cause damage to the pump and injector nozzles.

2. Replace the fuel filter regularly.

3. Replace the air filter regularly.

4. Service or replace the positive crankcase ventilation valve regularly.

5. Carbon buildup on the back side of port injection fuel systems seems to be a common problem. Besides cleaning the throttle body regularly (see chapter 18 for details), keeping the oil changed and servicing the PCV valve and air filter regularly seem to reduce the problem. See figures 17–9 and 17–10.

NORMAL MODES OF OPERATION

Automotive computer systems are programmed to operate under several different starting and driving conditions. These various conditions are called modes of operation and include:

Starting Mode
The first mode of operation is the starting mode. The computer and PROM provide for starting enrichment based on a signal from the engine coolant temperature sensor, which sends to the computer a true indication of the engine temperature. The air-fuel mixture supplied can vary from 1.5:1 at –40°F (–40°C) to 14.7:1 at 212°F (100°C).

Clear Flood
If the engine floods (too much fuel) when attempting to start the engine, depressing the accelerator beyond 80% throttle signals the computer to switch modes. If the RPM is less than 400 and the accelerator pedal is 80 to 100% depressed (as determined by the TP sensor), the air-fuel ratio delivered is 20:1 to help clear a flooded engine.

NOTE: Some port-injected engines supply *no fuel* at all if the engine is cranking and the throttle is more than 80% open.

Open Loop
After the engine starts, it runs according to a predetermined program set in the computer memory until the O_2 (oxygen) sensor becomes warm enough to start producing usable data for the computer.

Closed Loop
Whenever the O_2 sensor starts to provide usable oxygen content information from the exhaust to the computer, and if the engine coolant temperature sensor indicates above 150°F (66°C), the computer switches to closed-loop operation. In closed loop, ig-

◄ TECH TIP ►

THE ELECTRIC FUEL PUMP CLUE

The on-board computer controls the operation of the electric fuel pump, fuel-injection pulses, and ignition timing. With a distributorless ignition system, it is difficult at times to know what part in the system is not operating if there is no spark from any of the ignition coils. A fast and easy method for determining if the crankshaft sensor is operating is to observe the operation of the electric fuel pump.

With most electronic fuel-injection systems, the computer will operate the electric fuel pump only for a short time (usually about 2 seconds) unless a crank pulse is received by the computer.

Most manufacturers provide a fuel pump test lead with which the technician can monitor the electrical operation of the pump. On most vehicles, if voltage is maintained to the pump during engine cranking for longer than 2 seconds, then the crankshaft sensor is working. If the pump only runs for 2 seconds, then turns off during cranking of the engine, then the crankshaft sensor, wiring, or the computer may be defective.

NOTE: Another way of testing is to use a scan tool or breakout box. If an RPM signal is processed and displayed by the computer, then the crank sensor is functioning. See chapter 18 for diagnostic test procedures.

---

nition timing is optimized for maximum gas mileage and performance. Torque converter clutch and other systems are also engaged to ensure lowest emissions and maximum gas mileage.

Acceleration Mode
Whenever operating in closed loop and the accelerator is depressed, the computer provides greater fuel flow for the power necessary for maximum acceleration. The torque converter clutch is also released and other factors are changed for power, not economy.

Deceleration Mode
When deceleration occurs, the computer reduces the amount of fuel that would normally be supplied.

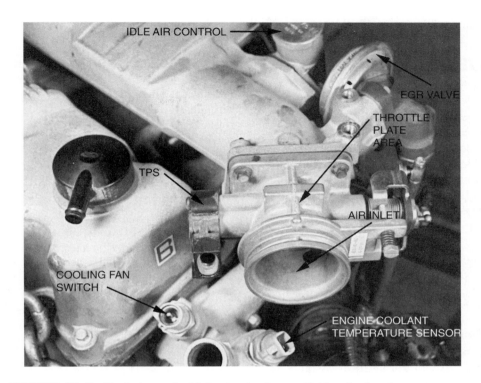

FIGURE 17–9 Typical port fuel-injection intake manifold and related components.

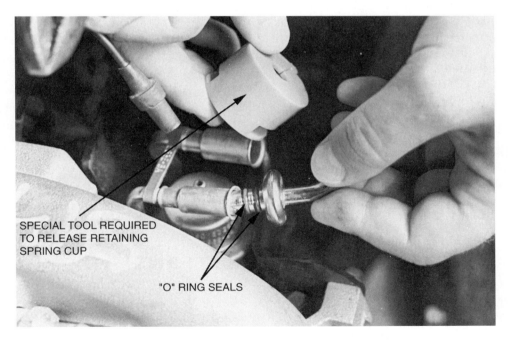

FIGURE 17–10 Special tools are often necessary to service the high-pressure port-injected fuel systems. This photo shows the special tool necessary for removing the fuel line junction used on many Ford vehicles.

TYPICAL FUEL PUMP PRESSURES

Most carburetors use fuel from an engine-driven mechanical fuel pump that delivers fuel at a pressure varying from a low of 3 psi to a high of about 8 psi (21 to 55 kPa). Most fuel-injection systems operate at either a low pressure of about 10 psi or a high pressure of between 35 and 45 psi. In both types of systems, maximum fuel pump pressure is about double the normal operating pressure.

	Normal Operating Pressure (psi)	Maximum Pump Pressure (psi)
Low-pressure TBI units	9–13	18–20
High-pressure TBI units	25–35	50–70
Port fuel-injection systems	35–45	70–90

The maximum fuel pump pressure is about double normal operating pressure to ensure that a continuous flow of cool fuel is being supplied to the injector(s) to help prevent vapor from forming in the fuel system. Although vapor or foaming in a fuel system can greatly affect engine operation, the cooling and lubricating flow of the fuel must be maintained for the durability of injector nozzles.

INJECTOR CLOGGING

Since the mid-1980s, most gasoline refiners have added detergents to gasoline. The original reason for adding detergents was to clean fuel-injection nozzles and keep them clean. The injector nozzles become partially clogged as a result of heat and short-trip driving that allow the olefins (a classification of organic compound) in the gasoline to accumulate and form deposits on the critical surfaces of the injector nozzle. The added detergents did help dissolve the deposits and keep injectors clean, but they also tend to create deposits on the intake valves in the engine. For this reason, additional fuel-injector cleaner may hurt instead of help a driveability problem.

CAUTION: The use of fuel-injector cleaner may damage the electrical windings of the fuel injector. Gasoline flows over the copper coil windings of an injector to help keep it cool. If a strong solvent is used in the fuel, the varnish insulation on the coil may be damaged. As a result, the coil windings may short against each other, lowering the resistance of the injector.

Throttle body injection units seldom become clogged because the nozzle(s) are far enough away from engine heat that the deposits do not seem to form.

SUMMARY

1. A typical carburetor (computer controlled or not) contains six different circuits: the float, idle and low-speed, main metering, power, accelerator pump, and choke circuits.
2. The computer only controls the idle and low-speed circuit and the main metering circuit.
3. A typical throttle body fuel injector uses a computer-controlled injector solenoid to spray fuel into the throttle body unit above the throttle plates.
4. A typical port fuel-injection system uses an individual fuel injector for each cylinder and squirts fuel directly into the intake manifold about 3 inches (80 millimeters) from the intake valve.

REVIEW QUESTIONS

1. List the circuits of a carburetor that are controlled by the engine computer.
2. Describe the difference between a throttle body and a port fuel-injection system.
3. List the modes of operation of a typical fuel-injected engine.
4. Explain why some vehicle manufacturers warn about using fuel injector cleaner.

MULTIPLE-CHOICE QUESTIONS

1. The computer controls which circuit(s) on a computer-controlled carburetor?
   a. Float and accelerator pump circuits
   b. Idle and main metering circuits
   c. Choke and accelerator pump circuits
   d. Power and float circuits

2. The range of air-fuel ratios that a typical carburetor and fuel-injection system can deliver to an engine is as follows: _____.
   a. 1.5:1 to 20:1
   b. 8:1 to 14.7:1
   c. 11:1 to 15:1
   d. 12:1 to 16:1

3. Throttle body fuel-injection systems deliver fuel _____.
   a. Directly into the cylinder
   b. In the intake manifold, near the intake valve
   c. Above the throttle plate of the throttle body unit
   d. Below the throttle plate of the throttle body unit

4. Port fuel-injection systems deliver fuel_____ .
   a. Directly into the cylinder
   b. In the intake manifold, near the intake valve
   c. Above the throttle plate of the throttle body unit
   d. Below the throttle plate of the throttle body unit

5. Port fuel-injection systems use long-length intake manifold runners _____ .
   a. To direct the fuel smoothly into the cylinder
   b. To ram the fuel into the cylinder with air pressure in the intake manifold
   c. To build pressure for the fuel injectors (nozzles)
   d. To aid in the engine "tuning" for maximum torque production

6. In a typical port fuel-injection system, the computer does *not* control_____ .
   a. The fuel pump relay
   b. The fuel injector (nozzle) "on time"
   c. Fuel pressure regulation
   d. Both a and c

7. In a typical port-injection system, the fuel pressure is regulated_____ .
   a. By a regulator located on the fuel return side of the fuel rail
   b. By a regulator located on the pressure side of the fuel rail
   c. By the computer by pulsing the regulator on and off.
   d. Either b or c

8. The back side of the throttle plate of many port-injected engines becomes covered in carbon deposits because _____ .
   a. Many systems route exhaust gases near this area as part of the EGR system
   b. Many systems route crankcase fumes near this area as part of the PCV system
   c. Both a and b
   d. None of the above

9. Typical fuel-injection *operating* fuel pressure is_____.
   a. 4 to 8 psi for TBI units
   b. 9 to 13 psi for most port fuel-injection systems
   c. 9 to 13 for most TBI units
   d. 80 to 90 psi for most port fuel-injection systems

10. Clogged port fuel injectors are most likely to occur during _____ .
    a. High-speed highway driving
    b. Short-trip driving
    c. A combination of mostly highway driving with some city driving
    d. Both a and c

DIAGNOSIS AND TROUBLESHOOTING OF COMPUTER SYSTEMS

OBJECTIVES

After studying chapter 18, the reader will be able to

1. List the precautions that should be taken when working on computerized engine control systems.
2. Explain the troubleshooting procedures to follow if a diagnostic trouble code has been set.
3. Explain the troubleshooting procedures to follow if no diagnostic trouble codes have been set.
4. Discuss the operation of a vehicle equipped with the second generation of on-board diagnostics (OBD II).

It is important that all automotive service technicians know how to diagnose and troubleshoot engine computer systems.

COMPUTER PRECAUTIONS

All automotive computers are sensitive to high voltage and high temperatures. There are several service-related activities that should *never* be attempted on *any* computer-equipped vehicle without special precautions being taken.

1. *Never* disconnect *any* 12-volt operating unit while the ignition switch is on (engine running or not run-

ning). Because of the self-induction of any coil, when an electrical unit is disconnected, a spike or transient of extremely high voltage is created (over 7000 volts is possible), which can severely damage the computer and/or sensors. Following is a partial list of units that should *never* be disconnected while the engine is running or when the ignition switch is on:

a. Either battery cable
b. Mixture control solenoid
c. Idle speed control unit (stepper motor)
d. Electronic fuel injector
e. Air management solenoid (air pump solenoid)
f. Ignition module wiring
g. The PROM from the computer
h. Any computer wiring
i. Blower motor wiring connections
j. Air-conditioning clutch wiring

2. *Never* jump-start another vehicle or receive a jump-start from another vehicle unless the jumper cables are connected and disconnected with the ignition switch off.

3. Do not mount radio speakers near the computer. The speaker magnets can damage the circuits and components inside the computer.

4. Do not use an electric arc welder on the vehicle body without first disconnecting (unplugging) the

computer. Use care when performing body repairs near the computer or sensors.

5. Be certain to ground yourself by touching the vehicle body before removing or installing a PROM. Static electricity can damage computer circuits.

6. Repair windshield leaks as soon as possible to prevent moisture damage to kick panel–mounted computers.

7. Never use an analog (needle-type) ohmmeter on any computer sensor unless that is specified in the test procedure. A high-impedance meter is required to prevent the voltage from the test meter from damaging sensors and computer circuits.

8. Do not use a test light while troubleshooting any computer-connected electrical unit. To prevent possible computer or sensor damage, always use a digital high-impedance meter during testing unless otherwise instructed.

9. Be certain never to touch the terminals of any computer. Static electricity can easily damage electronic components and circuits.

TYPICAL NONCOMPUTER PROBLEMS

If the driver has noticed a "check engine," "power loss," or "power limited" light—called the **malfunction indicator lamp** (MIL)—proceed through the troubleshooting sequences specified by the manufacturer. If the engine running complaint has *not* triggered a system warning lamp, proceed with basic engine troubleshooting as if the engine were not computer equipped. Typical noncomputer problems and possible causes include the following:

Rough Idle (Possible Stalling)

1. Idle speed too low
2. Idle mixture incorrect or unequal (vacuum leak)
3. Timing retarded
4. Clogged PCV valve or hoses
5. Defective spark plug wire
6. Worn or cracked spark plug
7. Cracked or defective purge valve for the charcoal canister system
8. Defective power valve in the carburetor (if the vehicle is so equipped)
9. EGR valve stuck open

Missing on Acceleration

1. Defective spark plug wire

2. Cracked or defective distributor cap
3. Defective distributor rotor
4. Crossed spark plug wires
5. Shorted or cracked ignition coil
6. Loose primary coil lead connection
7. Clogged fuel filter
8. Weak fuel pump
9. Cracked or softened fuel lines

Poor Fuel Economy

1. Retarded ignition timing
2. Clogged exhaust system
3. Defective vacuum advance unit on the distributor
4. Vacuum leak around the carburetor or intake manifold, or a defective vacuum hose
5. Defective choke (closed all the time)
6. Defective power valve in the carburetor (if the vehicle is so equipped)
7. Clogged air filter
8. Defective thermostatic air cleaner, permitting warm air to enter the engine all the time
9. EGR valve stuck open
10. Defective cooling system thermostat

Pings on Acceleration

1. Ignition timing too far advanced
2. Too low a grade of fuel
3. Vacuum leak near the carburetor or intake manifold, or a defective vacuum hose
4. EGR valve not opening correctly
5. Clogged heat riser, allowing exhaust heat under the carburetor all the time
6. Defective thermostatic air cleaner, allowing warm air to enter the engine all the time

TROUBLESHOOTING COMPUTERIZED ENGINES

Computer-controlled fuel-injection systems use all sensors (O2S, TP, MAP, etc.) to determine the best fuel delivery amounts and ignition timing under all operating conditions. But what happens when a sensor fails to operate correctly? The computer has logic circuits that will detect if a sensor value is out of range in relation to the rest of the sensors. For example, say that the engine has been running for an hour and the ECT sensor has become unplugged, and the computer now gets a reading indicating that the coolant temperature is $-40°$ F

◀ DIAGNOSTIC STORY ▶

"CHECK ENGINE" LIGHT ON, BUT NO CODES

A GM vehicle came to an independent service facility because the amber-colored "check engine" light (malfunction indicator lamp or MIL) remained on all the time that the engine was running. This usually indicates a hard failure (a failure that is definite, that is not intermittent, and that affects the ability of the computer to properly operate the engine).

No trouble codes were found, and no code 12 either, which would indicate a possible computer (electronic control module [ECM]) problem. After several hours of troubleshooting for loose or defective computer terminals, another technician came along and found that the three-ampere fuse for the ECM was blown. After replacement of the fuse, the computer (and the MIL) returned to normal operation.

The customer later admitted that he may have been guilty of blowing the fuse when he had attempted to install his own sound system into the existing wiring and fuses.

(−40° C). The logic circuits within the microprocessor ignore the obviously incorrect temperature reading and do three things:

1. Substitute a replacement value for the defective coolant temperature
2. Store a trouble code and display a trouble light to tell the driver that the computer has detected a problem (fig. 18–1)
3. Turn on the cooling fan to ensure that the engine does not overheat

SCAN TOOL TESTING

Many technicians simply start scrolling through scan tool data looking for something out of range. When diagnosing a problem using a scan tool, follow these steps to quickly narrow down the possibilities.

NOTE: Even though a scan tool is a wonderful and powerful diagnostic tool, do not forget to start all diagnostics with a *thorough visual inspection*! Simple items such as defective vacuum hoses, corroded connectors, and loose wires can often be compensated for by the engine computer, covering up the real problem.

- *Step #1.* Check for any stored diagnostic trouble codes (DTCs). Follow the vehicle manufacturer's recommended procedures. If no DTC is set, go to step #2.

- *Step #2.* Before starting the engine, use the scan tool to determine the engine coolant temperature and intake air temperature readings. Both should be the same because both the air temperature and the coolant temperature should be at the ambient (surrounding) air temperature. If the two temperatures do not match, the sensor (or wiring) giving the reading that varies most from the ambient air temperature is at fault. If both temperatures agree, start and run the engine, still observing both sensors. The coolant temperature reading should increase up to normal operating temperature, and the intake air temperature reading should only increase by a slight amount. After observing coolant and intake air temperature values, scan all other data to see if they are within the normal operating range of values.

- *Step #3.* Check the idle air control position (IAC). The position should be close to the center of the acceptable range. For example, for a General Motors fuel-injected engine, the range may be 5 to 50 counts. The preferred range is 16 to 20 counts.

  1. *If the IAC position is too low,* this indicates that the computer is commanding less air or a lower idle speed. The most common reason for this is a vacuum leak caused by a defective vacuum hose, PCV valve, or gasket.
  2. *If the IAC position is too high,* this reading indicates a partially clogged throttle plate or a misadjusted throttle linkage. If the idle speed is also too high, the computer is commanding a higher than normal idle, usually to compensate for low battery voltage or an engine that is running too hot. (See figure 18–1)

- *Step #4.* The fourth step is to check the oxygen sensor(s) (O2S) for proper operation and to see if the vehicle computer can control the air-fuel mixture. Operate the engine at about 2000 RPM and observe the oxygen sensor voltage. Check the O2S for range (minimum

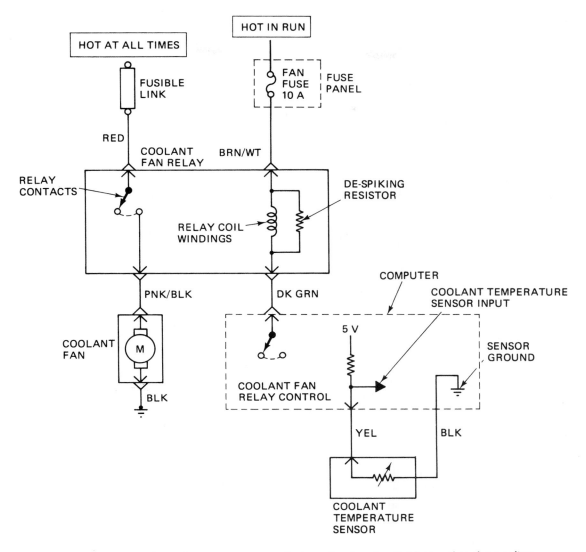

FIGURE 18–1 Typical computer-controlled cooling fan circuit. Notice that the cooling fan motor is controlled by the computer based on coolant temperature sensor data. If a fault is detected in the coolant temperature sensor circuit, the computer activates the cooling (radiator) fan and keeps it operating for as long as the ignition is on as a safety precaution.

of 200 millivolts and a maximum of 800 millivolts), as well as cross counts. Does it change rapidly? O2S voltage should fluctuate up and down rapidly.

1. Temporarily disconnect a vacuum hose. The voltage should decrease slightly, then return to normal as the computer adds fuel to compensate for the air leak.
2. Slowly add propane to the air intake and observe the O2S. The O2S voltage should read high for a short time until the computer de-

creases the amount of fuel delivered to the engine to compensate for the added propane.

These two tests confirm that the O2S can signal the computer and that the computer is capable of controlling fuel delivery.

- *Step #5.* Look at long-term fuel trim (LTFT). It should be zero, indicating that the computer is neither adding nor subtracting fuel. If the LTFT exceeds 20%, on either the positive or the negative side, a possible fuel or engine problem is indicated.

◀ DIAGNOSTIC STORY ▶

THE EASY SOLUTION TO A DIFFICULT PROBLEM

The owner of a Cadillac equipped with two-nozzle throttle body fuel injection came into a service facility complaining that the engine would miss and cut out at speeds above 40 miles per hour. The technician assigned to the repair replaced many parts that could have contributed to the problem including

1. Distributor cap and rotors
2. Spark plugs
3. Spark plug wires
4. Fuel filter
5. Air filter
6. Ignition module

The replacement of each part did improve the operation of the engine slightly, but the problem still existed. The engine itself was determined to be in sound mechanical condition. A timing light was connected to the engine coil wire and the trigger taped in the "on" position. The timing light was then taped to the windshield so that the driver could see if the engine missing would cause the timing light to blink intermittently, indicating an ignition problem. The hood was carefully closed so that it did not disturb the timing light wiring. The vehicle was driven until it started missing. The timing light did not indicate an ignition problem.

Next, the technician connected separate LED test lights to each of the fuel-injector wiring connectors. The long leads were taped to the windshield and the vehicle was again test driven.

NOTE: If only one of the two fuel injectors had stopped functioning, the engine would only be getting fuel to every other cylinder and the engine would miss and cut out, especially at higher engine speeds. Some port-injected engines use two different injector circuits, each with its own fuse.

The LED test lights confirmed that both injectors were being pulsed by the computer all the time.

The next day, the technician added 10 gallons of gasoline to the tank because the "low fuel" lamp had come on during the last test drive. After the fuel was added, the engine started to operate better and better. Finally, after about 5 miles of driving, the engine ran perfectly normally.

The customer later told the service manager that he had always kept the fuel level low and had never added more than a few dollars of gas at a time. Obviously, condensed moisture had accumulated in the bottom of the fuel tank and was being drawn through the fuel system. Because water does not burn, the engine would miss and run poorly. After the fuel tank was drained and cleaned, the vehicle was returned to the customer. The customer thanked the service manager for having finally found that "computer" and "fuel-injection" problem that no one else could find!

FIGURE 18–2 Typical General Motors ALCL connector. The ALCL is also called an assembly line diagnostic link (ALDL). When terminals A and B are electrically connected, the computer starts flashing the amber "check engine" light to indicate any stored trouble codes.

GM PROBLEM DIAGNOSIS AND SERVICE

Since 1981, many computer systems have had built-in on-board diagnosis capability. By checking the trouble codes, the technician can determine where the problem is located in most cases.

The GM system uses a "check engine" or "check engine soon" MIL to notify the driver of possible system failure. If the MIL is on, the computer is *not* working. The engine is running in the backup or "limp in" mode of limited spark advance and rich fuel mixture.

Under the dash (on most GM vehicles) is a **diagnostic link connector** (DLC) called an **assembly line communications link** (ALCL). The terminals are lettered. The top right-side terminals are labeled A and B, and when they are connected (with a wire spade connector, paper clip, or other suitable tool), they will cause the "check engine" lamp to begin flashing a code when the ignition switch is on (engine not running). See figure 18–2. Each code flashes three times, then all codes repeat in numerical sequence.

NOTE: Trouble codes can vary according to year, make, model, and engine. Always consult the service literature or service manual for the exact vehicle being serviced.

RETRIEVING GM DIAGNOSTIC TROUBLE CODES

The following are GM diagnostic trouble code numbers and their meaning:

13	O_2 sensor circuit
14	ECT—high temperature
15	ECT—low temperature
16	Low voltage
17	Camshaft sensor circuit
21	TP sensor (voltage high)
22	TP sensor (voltage low)
23	IAT sensor (low temperature)
24	VSS
25	IAT sensor (high temperature)
26	QUAD—driver module circuit (MIL and gauges)
27	QUAD—driver module circuit (EVAP SOL and TCC)
28	Transmission range (TR) pressure switch assembly (4L80-E); or QUAD—driver module circuit (A/C clutch relays)
29	QUAD—driver module circuit for 4T60

◀ **TECH TIP** ▶

THE "UNPLUG IT" TEST

If a sensor is supplying *incorrect* data to the computer, the computer may use this data and respond with incorrect fuel delivery or ignition timing. The result is a poorly operating engine, possibly with no trouble codes stored in the computer. A common example involves the MAF sensor used on many General Motors vehicles. If the MAF sensor is unplugged and the engine runs better (or starts, whereas it would not start before the sensor was unplugged), then the problem is a defective MAF sensor. As long as the sensor is supplying data within the parameters (guidelines) of the computer, the data will be processed. But if the suspected unit is unplugged, no data is received from the sensor and the computer substitutes a replacement value based on values of other related sensors. For example, the throttle position sensor and/or MAP sensor may back up a defective (or unplugged) MAF sensor.

Therefore, if the engine does not start, but then starts if the MAF sensor is unplugged, the MAF sensor is defective.

33	MAP sensor circuit (low vacuum)
34	MAP sensor circuit (high vacuum)
35	IAC—idle speed error
36	24 X signal circuit error (3.4 SFI)
37	Brake switch stuck on
38	Brake switch stuck off
39	TCC stuck off
42	Ignition control circuit error
43	Knock sensor (KS) circuit
44	O_2—lean exhaust
45	O_2—rich exhaust
51	EPROM error
52	High system voltage
53	Battery over voltage
54	Low voltage to fuel pump
55	Power enrichment too lean
58	Transmission fluid temperature (high temperature)
59	Transmission fluid temperature (low temperature)
65	Fuel injector (low current)

66	A/C refrigerant pressure sensor circuit (low); or 3–2 shift control
67	TCC solenoid circuit fault
68	Transmission slipping
69	TCC stuck on
70	A/C refrigerant pressure sensor circuit (high)
72	Loss of transmission output speed signal
73	Transmission pressure control solenoid circuit
74	Transmission input speed (TIS) sensor circuit
75	Digital EGR #1 error; or system voltage low
76	Digital EGR #2 error
77	Digital EGR #3 error
79	VSS (high) or transmission fluid over temperature
80	VSS (low)
81	Brake switch error; or 2–3 shift solenoid circuit
82	Ignition control 3 X signal error; or 1–2 shift solenoid circuit
83	TCC PWM solenoid circuit fault
85	PROM error/or transmission ratio error
86	Transmission low ratio error
87	A/D error; or transmission high ratio error; or EEPROM error

GM SYSTEM PERFORMANCE CHECK

After the trouble codes have been corrected (or if no trouble codes are indicated), the operation of the computer can be checked. Checking the operation of the computer is called the system performance check.

A carburetor-equipped General Motors vehicle that is equipped with a computer is checked with a dwell meter. The dwell meter is connected to a separate test lead under the hood, identified by a blue wire with a green open connector. The dwell meter indicates the amount of time that the solenoid is energized. This on time is called the **duty cycle**. When the M/C (mixture control) solenoid is energized, the metering rods inside the carburetor are forced downward and the carburetor delivers its leanest mixture. When the solenoid is deenergized (no current), a spring(s) raise the metering rods and the carburetor can supply its richest mixture. The dwell meter is usually set on the six-cylinder scale regardless of the number of cylinders. If the solenoid were always energized (metering rods down—lean), the dwell meter would read 60 degrees. If the solenoid were not energized at all (metering rods up—rich), the dwell meter would read 0 degrees. Because the M/C solenoid is *always* cycled 10 times a second, it cannot be on or off for more than 90% of the time. Therefore, the highest dwell meter reading possible is 54 degrees (90% of 60 degrees).

A high dwell meter reading indicates that a rich mixture is present in the engine and the computer is attempting to compensate by keeping the metering rods down (high dwell). *A low dwell meter reading indicates that a lean mixture is present* and the computer is attempting to compensate by leaving the metering rods up (no current—low dwell—to the M/C solenoid).

A properly running engine (in closed loop) should idle with a dwell reading that is close to 30 degrees (25 to 35 degrees) and that is varying slightly to the left and right. With the engine set at *exactly* 3000 RPM, the dwell meter should indicate a value between 10 and 50 degrees (preferably between 35 and 45 degrees). When the engine is still in open loop (not warm enough to go into closed loop), the computer is sending a *fixed* dwell value to the M/C solenoid. The value of the dwell reading is not adjustable or changeable and is based on the temperature of the engine as determined by the coolant sensor. Once the engine reaches normal operating temperature and goes into closed loop, the dwell (fuel mixture control) reading will be between 10 and 50 degrees (2 to 4 degrees is the normal dwell meter swing range). The dwell does vary because the computer is reacting to oxygen sensor information and making the necessary changes. The actual dwell swing should be read from the average of the dwell meter readings.

HINT: For best performance, the larger the engine, the higher the dwell reading should be at 3000 RPM. For example, a four-cylinder engine will perform satisfactorily at a dwell reading of 35 degrees. A larger V-6 runs best around 40 degrees, and a V-8 delivers its best performance near 45 degrees. A dwell reading above 30 degrees means that the fuel mixture being delivered to the engine is slightly rich and the computer is attempting to make the mixture leaner. This situation provides improved throttle response over that of a lean mixture being driven rich.

The dwell of the M/C solenoid is changed by adjusting the rich stop and lean stop screws inside the carburetor. The dwell at idle can be changed by the adjustment of the idle air bleed and/or idle mixture screws. These adjustments require special gauging tools, and the values should be set to factory-specified limits.

GM FUEL-INJECTION PROBLEM DIAGNOSIS

Whether the engine is in closed loop or open loop, a rich or lean condition can easily be determined by connecting terminals A and B in the DLC (ALCL) and starting the engine. Check the operation of the "check engine" lamp.

With the engine running and the diagnostic terminal B grounded (DLC terminals A connected to B), the "check engine" lamp should be off when the exhaust is lean and on when it is rich. The procedure is called the **field service mode.**

1. *Open loop.* "Check engine" lamp flashes at a rapid rate of 2 times per second.
2. *Closed loop.* "Check engine" lamp flashes at a slower rate of 1 time per second.
3. *Lean exhaust.* "Check engine" lamp is out all or most of the time.
4. *Rich exhaust.* "Check engine" lamp is on all or most of the time.

GM IGNITION TIMING

General Motors uses more than eight different methods and test procedures for testing the ignition timing, depending on the engine, engine equipment, and body style. Most methods involve disconnecting the computer from the ignition distributor. This usually involves disconnecting the four-way conductor at the junction a few inches from the distributor. Other engines require that the computer be in diagnostics mode (A and B terminals together at the DLC) or use the average timing methods. Consult the under-the-hood emission decal for the *exact* procedure before attempting to set ignition timing.

FORD PROBLEM DIAGNOSIS AND SERVICE

A **microprocessor control unit** (MCU) is used on selected Ford cars and trucks, whereas the **electronic engine control** (EEC) system is used on all other models. Both the MCU and the EEC systems have built-in diagnostic codes.

RETRIEVING FORD DIAGNOSTIC CODES

The best tool to use during troubleshooting of a Ford vehicle is a **self-test automatic readout** (STAR) **tester.** If a STAR tester is not available, a needle (analog) type of voltmeter can be used for MCU and EEC IV systems. Connect a jumper lead and an analog voltmeter as illustrated in figure 18–3. The test connector is usually located under the hood on the driver's side (except on EEC III systems). See figures 18–4 and 18–5.

Key On–Engine Off Test. With the ignition key on (engine off), watch the voltmeter pulses, which should appear within 5 to 30 seconds. (Ignore any initial surge of voltage when the ignition is turned on.)

The computer will send a two-digit code that will cause the voltmeter to pulse or move from left to right. For example, if the voltmeter needle pulses 2 times, then pauses for 2 seconds, and then pulses 3 times, the code is 23. There is normally a 4-second pause between codes.

After all of the codes have been reported, the computer will pause for about 6 to 9 seconds, then cause the voltmeter needle to pulse once, and then pause for another 6 to 9 seconds. This is the normal separation between current trouble codes and continuous memory codes (for intermittent problems). Code 11 is the normal pass code, which means that no fault has been stored in memory. Therefore, normal operation of the diagnostic procedure using a voltmeter should indicate the following if no codes are set: one pulse (2-second pause), one pulse (6- to 9-second pause), one pulse (6- to 9-second pause), one pulse (2-second pause), and finally, one pulse. These last two pulses are separated by a 2-second internal represent a code 11, which is the code used between current and intermittent trouble codes.

Engine Running Test. Start the engine and raise the speed to 2500 to 3000 RPM within 20 seconds of starting. Hold a steady high engine speed until the initial pulses appear (2 pulses for a four-cylinder engine, 3 pulses for a six-cylinder, and 4 pulses for an eight-cylinder). Continue to hold a high engine speed until the code pulses begin (10 to 14 seconds). See figure 18–6 for the EEC codes. If any trouble codes appear, you must use the factory "pinpoint tests" to trace the problem.

IGNITION TIMING

Some Ford engines can be timed and others cannot be timed. If the vehicle is equipped with a knock sensor or three-connector module, disconnect the knock sensor and set the timing as usual. Also see chapter 13. For other ignition system types, check the emission decal under the hood or the service manual for the exact procedures recommended.

◀ TECH TIP ▶

PUT A WIRE IN THE ATTIC AND A LIGHT IN THE BASEMENT!

Retrieving diagnostic trouble codes from a Ford using low-cost test equipment is easier when you remember the following:

"Put a wire in the attic and a light in the basement."

After warming the engine to operating temperature, perform these simple steps:

- *Step #1.* Locate the diagnostic link connector (DLC) under the hood. Connect a jumper wire from the single-wire pigtail called the **self-test input** to terminal #2 at the top (attic) of the connector.
- *Step #2.* To read diagnostic trouble codes, connect a standard 12-volt test light (*not* a self-powered continuity light) to the *positive* battery terminal and the lower (basement) terminal (#4) of the DLC. See figure 18–3.

Turn the ignition to on (engine off). The diagnostic trouble codes will be displayed by means of the light flashes of the test light.

CHRYSLER PROBLEM DIAGNOSIS AND SERVICE

Trouble code information is displayed only for major problems. The computer checks a number of functions when the engine starts and monitors other functions while the engine is running. Codes of intermittent faults are stored in memory for approximately fifty start-ups. If the fault does not reoccur within the fifty start-ups, the computer is programmed to erase the code from memory. If the fault reoccurs, the fault code is again retained in memory (but retained for 100 engine starts if the same code is set again).

RETRIEVING CHRYSLER DIAGNOSTIC TROUBLE CODES

To put the computer into the self-diagnostic mode, the ignition switch must be turned on and off twice within a 5-second period. The computer will flash a series of fault codes in a manner similar to the GM system. Early models of Chrysler products used a light-emitting diode (LED) located on the side of the logic module located

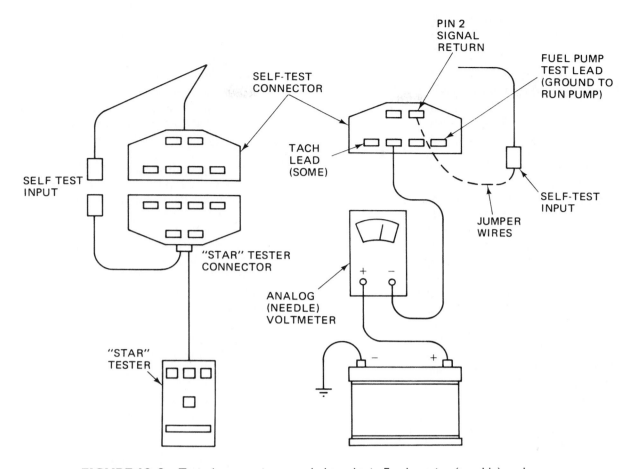

FIGURE 18–3 Typical connections needed to obtain Ford service (trouble) codes.

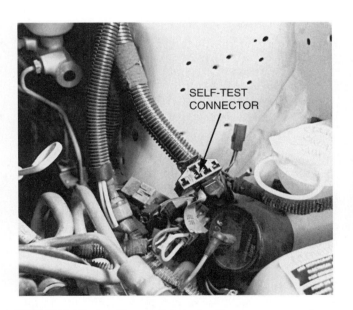

FIGURE 18–4 Photo of typical self-test connector location. The exact location of this connector varies with model and year of manufacture.

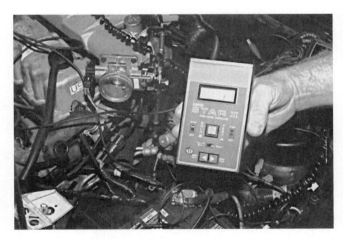

FIGURE 18–5 STARII Ford scan tool.

Code

11	Pass
12	RPM not within self-test upper rpm limit band
13	RPM not within self-test lower rpm limit band
13	D.C. motor did not move (2.3/2.5/1.0L CFI)
13	D.C. motor does not follow dashpot (2.3/2.5/1.0L CFI)
14	PIP circuit fault
15	ROM test failed
16	RPM too low to perform fuel test
18	Loss of tach input to processor—SPOUT circuit grounded
19	Failure in EEC reference voltage
21	Indicates ECT out of self-test range
22	Indicates MAP/BP out of self-test range
23	Indicates TP out of self-test range
24	Indicates ACT out of self-test range
25	Knock not sensed during dynamic response test
29	Insufficient input from V.S.S.
31	EPT/EVP below minimum voltage
32	EVP voltage out of static limit
32	EGR valve not seated (PFE)
33	EGR valve not opening
34	Insufficient EGR flow (1.9L, 2.3L T/C EFI/2.3L, 3.8L CFI)
34	EVP voltage above static limit (SONIC)
34	Defective EPT sensor (PFE)
34	Exhaust pressure high/defective EPT sensor
35	EPT/EVP circuit above maximum voltage
41	EGO sensor circuit indicates system lean—no EGO switch detected
42	EGO sensor circuit indicates system rich—no EGO switch detected
43	EGO lean at W.O.I.
44	Thermactor air system inoperative (cylinders 1–4 dual EGO)
45	Thermactor air upstream during self-test
46	Thermactor air not bypassed during self-test
51	−40° indicated ECT sensor circuit open
52	PSPS circuit open
52	PSPS did not change states
53	TPS circuit above maximum voltage
54	−40°F indicated ACT—sensor circuit open
55	Key power circuit low
57	NPS circuit failed open
61	254°F indicated ECT—circuit grounded
63	TPS circuit below minimum voltage
64	254° indicated ACT—circuit grounded
67	NPS circuit failed closed—A/C on during self-test
67	NDS circuit open—A/C on during self-test
72	Insufficient MAP change during dynamic response test
73	Insufficient TP change during dynamic response test
74	BOO switch circuit open
75	BOO switch circuit closed—ECA input open
77	Operator error (dynamic response/cylinder balance test)
78	Power interrupt detected
81	AM2 circuit failure (OCC test)
82	AM1 circuit failure (OCC test)
84	EVR circuit failure (OCC test)
85	CANP circuit failure (OCC test)
87	Fuel pump test failed (OCC test)
89	CCO circuit failure (OCC test)
91	EGO sensor input indicates system lean (cylinders 5–8)
92	EGO sensor input indicates system rich (cylinders 5–8)
94	Thermactor air system inoperative (cylinders 5–8, dual EGO)
98	Hard fault present, **FMEM MODE**
99	Idle not learned, ignore codes 12 and 13

FIGURE 18–6 Typical Ford service codes.

behind the kick panel and behind a plastic plug. Newer Chrysler products flash the "power loss" or "power limited" lamp on the dash. A typical location of the diagnostic connector is shown in figure 18–7. See figure 18–8 for typical Chrysler diagnostic trouble codes.

NOTE: Unlike other manufacturers, most Chrysler vehicles equipped with OBD II can still display two-digit flash codes by cycling the ignition key as previously performed on older vehicles.

CHRYSLER M/C SOLENOID TEST

Chrysler uses a voltmeter instead of a dwell meter to read the duty cycle of the carburetor mixture control solenoid. Because the computer controls the ground side of the M/C solenoid, the voltmeter reads 0 volts for a lean command (rich mixture) and 16 volts for a rich command (lean mixture).

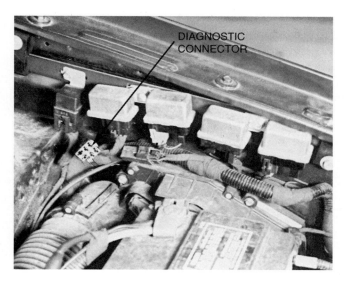

FIGURE 18–7 Typical location of Chrysler diagnostic connector.

CHRYSLER IGNITION TIMING

Chrysler computer-controlled ignition timing can be checked using a procedure to set the computer in a backup mode. A backup mode (also called the limp-home mode) involves a special circuit within the computer that controls the operation of the engine in the event of a system or component failure. In the backup mode, the timing is set to the base timing value. To get the computer into the backup mode, unplug the coolant temperature sensor and then reconnect it with the engine running. The computer then sends a fixed timing signal to the ignition system. Make certain that the "power loss" or "power limited" lamp has come on and that the engine speed (RPM) is within the specifications indicated on the under-the-hood emission decal. Check and adjust the timing as necessary. On some Chrysler models, the ignition timing is checked by removing the vacuum hose from the control unit, usually located near the driver's side headlight (under the hood).

HONDA PROBLEM DIAGNOSIS

The ECM is found in different locations depending on exact model and year. Most computers are located under the driver's or passenger's seat or under the passenger's floor panel. The diagnostic trouble codes are read

Code	
11	Distributor reference circuit
12	Battery feed to logic module recently lost
13	MAP sensor circuit (vacuum)
14	MAP sensor circuit (electrical)
15	Vehicle speed sensor
16	Loss of battery voltage
21	Oxygen sensor circuit
22	Coolant temperature circuit
23	Charge temperature circuit (turbo)
24	Throttle position circuit
25	Automatic idle speed circuit
26	Fuel (peak injection current not reached)
27	Fuel (no current in diagnostic transistor)
31	Purge solenoid
32	Powerloss lamp circuit
33	A/C wide-open throttle circuit
34	EGR solenoid circuit
34	Spare driver circuit
35	Fan relay circuit
36	Spare driver circuit
37	Shift indicator circuit (manual)
41	Charging system
42	Auto shutdown relay circuit
43	Ignition and fuel control interface
44	Logic module
44	Battery temperature out of range
45	Overboost (turbo)
46	Battery voltage high
47	Battery voltage low
51	Oxygen feedback system
51	Closed-loop latched lean
52	Closed-loop latched rich
52 and 53	Logic module
53	ROM bit sum fault
54	Distributor signal circuit
55	End of test sequence
88	Start of test sequence

FIGURE 18–8 Chrysler trouble codes. To access the stored codes, turn the ignition on, off, on, off, then on within 5 seconds, and the "power loss" or "power limited" light will flash any codes.

by simply turning the ignition on (engine off) and counting the flashes of the LED. Early models used LEDs that could be viewed without having to remove a cover. See figure 18–9 for an example of a typical one-LED display and figure 18–10 for a four-LED display.

The DLC for 1991 and newer Honda models requires that a jumper wire be used to connect it as shown

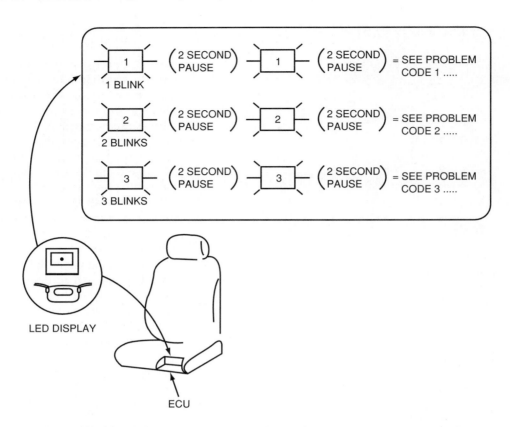

FIGURE 18–9 Early Hondas used one LED inside the computer to flash diagnostic trouble codes. The LED would flash whenever the ignition was turned on (engine off).

in figure 18–11, then the amber MIL on the dash labeled "check engine" must be watched for trouble codes.

NOTE: Abbreviations and terms used in this chapter for particular vehicles and years may not agree with today's standardized terms.

RETRIEVING HONDA DIAGNOSTIC TROUBLE CODES FOR CARBURETED ENGINES

The following are Honda DTCs for carbureted engines

Code 1	Oxygen content
Code 2	Vehicle speed pulsar
Code 3	Manifold absolute pressure (MAP)
Code 4	Vacuum switch signal
Code 5	Manifold absolute pressure (MAP)
Code 6	Coolant temperature
Code 7	Coolant switch signal (MT) or shift position switch signal (AT) (1990–91 engines only)
Code 8	Ignition coil signal
Code 9	No. 1 cylinder position sensor
Code 10	Intake air temperature sensor (IAT sensor)
Code 12	Exhaust gas recirculation (EGR) system
Code 13	Barometric pressure sensor (BARO sensor)
Code 14	Idle air control (IAC valve) or faulty ECM
Code 15	Ignition output signal
Code 16	Fuel injector
Code 17	Vehicle speed sensor (VSS)
Code 19	A/T lockup control solenoid valve
Code 20	Electric load detector (ELD)
Code 21	V-TEC control solenoid
Code 22	V-TEC pressure switch
Code 23	Knock sensor
Code 30	A/T FI signal A
Code 31	A/T FI signal B
Code 41	Heated oxygen sensor heater
Code 43	Fuel supply system
Code 48	Heated oxygen sensor

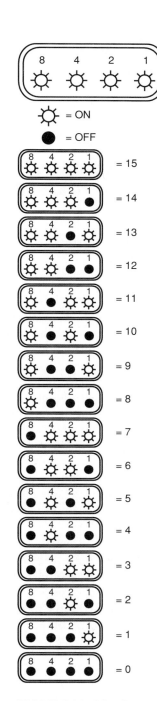

1. • EACH LED HAS A NUMERIC VALUE.
   –THE <u>LEFT</u> LED HAS A VALUE OF **8**.
   –THE NEXT LED IN LINE HAS A VALUE OF **4**.
   –THE NEXT LED IN LINE HAS A VALUE OF **2**.
   –THE <u>RIGHT</u> LED HAS A VALUE OF **1**.

2. • ADD VALUES OF THE LIGHTED LEDS TO GET THE TROUBLE CODE. (OFF LEDS HAVE A VALUE OF ZERO.)

EXAMPLE OF CODE ZERO:

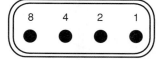

NO LEDS ARE LIT, INDICATING A CODE ZERO ("0").

EXAMPLE OF CODE 2:

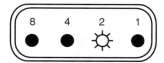

LED 2 IS LIT, INDICATING A CODE 2.

EXAMPLE OF CODE 10:

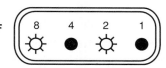

LEDS 8 AND 2 ARE LIT, INDICATING A CODE 10.
(8 + 2 = 10).

3. • TROUBLE CODES FROM ZERO (NO LEDS LIT) THROUGH 15 (ALL LEDS LIT) ARE USED.

4. • WHEN MORE THAN ONE CODE IS STORED:
   –EACH TROUBLE CODE IS PRESENTED ONCE.
   –THERE IS A **2-SECOND PAUSE** BETWEEN CODES.

FIGURE 18–10   Some older Hondas use four LEDs to display diagnostic trouble codes.

RETRIEVING HONDA DIAGNOSTIC TROUBLE CODES FOR FUEL-INJECTED ENGINES

The following are Honda DTCs for fuel-injected engines:

Code 0   Electronic control module (ECM)
Code 1   Heated oxygen sensor
Code 2   Oxygen content or electronic control module (ECM)
Code 3   Manifold absolute pressure (MAP)
Code 4   Crankshaft position sensor or faulty ECU
Code 5   Manifold absolute pressure (MAP)
Code 6   Engine coolant temperature (ECT)
Code 7   Throttle position sensor (TP sensor)
Code 8   Top dead center sensor (TDC sensor)

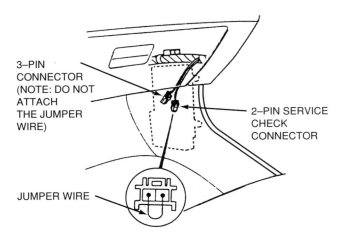

3–PIN CONNECTOR (NOTE: DO NOT ATTACH THE JUMPER WIRE)

2–PIN SERVICE CHECK CONNECTOR

JUMPER WIRE

FIGURE 18–11 1991 and newer Hondas (and Acuras) require that a jumper wire be used to connect the terminals of the under-dash diagnostic link connector.

Code 9	No. 1 cylinder position sensor
Code 10	Intake air temperature sensor (IAT sensor)
Code 11	Electronic control module (ECM)
Code 12	Exhaust gas recirculation (EGR) system
Code 13	Barometric pressure sensor (BARO sensor)
Code 14	Idle air control (IAC valve)
Code 15	Ignition output signal
Code 16	Fuel injector
Code 17	Vehicle speed sensor (VSS)
Code 19	A/T lockup control solenoid valve
Code 20	Electric load detector (ELD)
Code 21	V-TEC control solenoid
Code 22	V-TEC pressure switch
Code 23	Knock sensor
Code 30	A/T FI signal A
Code 31	A/T FI signal B
Code 41	Heated oxygen sensor heater
Code 43	Fuel supply system
Code 48	Heated oxygen sensor

CLEARING HONDA DIAGNOSTIC TROUBLE CODES

Diagnostic trouble codes can be erased by disconnecting the negative battery terminal. This method will erase the DTC, but it will also cause the clock and radio station setting to be erased. Be prepared to reprogram these to the original settings.

TOYOTA PROBLEM DIAGNOSIS

Toyota vehicles use the "check engine" MIL to display diagnostic trouble codes. See figure 18–12 for connections necessary to retrieve Toyota diagnostic trouble codes.

RETRIEVING TOYOTA DIAGNOSTIC TROUBLE CODES

The following are Toyota DTCs:

1983–84 Engines

Code 1	Normal operation
Code 2	Open or shorted airflow meter circuit; or defective airflow meter or electronic control unit
Code 3	Open or shorted airflow meter circuit; or defective airflow meter or electronic control unit (ECU)
Code 4	Open water thermosensor (THW) circuit; or defective water thermosensor (THW) or electronic control unit (ECU)
Code 5	Open or shorted oxygen sensor circuit (lean or rich indication); or defective oxygen sensor or electronic control unit (ECU)
Code 6	No ignition signal—defective ignition system circuit, integrated ignition assembly (IIA), or electronic control unit (ECU)
Code 7	Defective throttle position (TP) sensor circuit or electronic control unit (ECU)

1985–87 Engines

NOTE: The 1985 2.0-L engines use 1984 codes.

Code 1	Normal operation
Code 2	Open or shorted airflow meter circuit; or defective airflow meter or electronic control unit (ECU)
Code 3	No signal from the igniter 4 times in succession—defective igniter or main relay circuit, igniter, or electronic control unit (ECU)

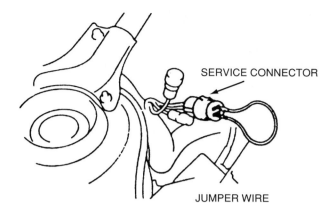

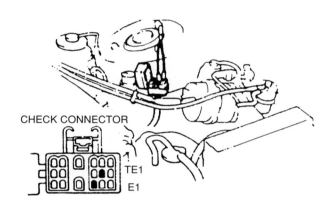

FIGURE 18–12 Toyotas require that a jumper wire be used to connect two terminals of a diagnostic link connector under the hood to retrieve diagnostic trouble codes. Terminal E is chassis ground.

Code 4   Open water thermosensor (THW) circuit; or defective water thermosensor (THW) or electronic control unit (ECU)

Code 5   Open or shorted oxygen sensor circuit (lean or rich indication); or defective oxygen sensor or electronic control unit (ECU)

Code 6   No engine (NE) revolution sensor signal to electronic control unit (ECU) or engine revolution value of over 1000 RPM in spite of lack of signal to ECU—defective igniter circuit, igniter distributor, or electronic control unit (ECU)

Code 7   Open or shorted throttle position (TP) sensor circuit; or defective throttle position (TP) sensor or electronic control unit (ECU)

Code 8   Open or shorted intake air thermosensor circuit; or defective intake air thermosensor or electronic control unit (ECU)

Code 10   No starter switch signal to electronic control unit (ECU) with vehicle speed at 0 and engine speed over 800 RPM—defective speed sensor circuit, main relay circuit, igniter switch to starter circuit, igniter switch, or electronic control unit (ECU)

Code 11   Short circuit in check connector terminal T with the air-conditioning switch on or throttle switch (IDL) point off—defective air-conditioner switch, throttle position sensor circuit, throttle position sensor, or electronic control unit

Code 12   Knock control sensor signal—defective knock control sensor circuit, knock control sensor, or electronic control unit

Code 13   Knock CPU faulty

1988–93 Engines

Constant blinking indicates no faults detected

Code 11   Momentary interruption in power supply to the ECU (up to 1991)

Code 12   Engine revolution signal to ECU—missing within several seconds after the engine is cranked

Code 13   RPM signal to ECU—missing when engine speed is above 1000 RPM

Code 14   Igniter signal to ECU—missing 4 to 11 times in succession

Code 16   ECT control signal

Code 21   Main oxygen sensor signal—voltage output does not exceed a set value on the lean and rich sides continuously for a certain period of time; or open or short sensor heater circuit

Code 22   Water temperature sensor circuit—open or short for 500 milliseconds or more

Code 23   Intake air temperature signal

Code 24   Intake air temperature sensor circuit—open or short for 500 milliseconds or more

Code 25   Air-fuel ratio lean malfunction—oxygen sensor output is less than 0.45 volts for at least 90 seconds when oxygen sensor is warmed up (engine racing at 2000 RPM); or air-fuel ratio feedback compensation or adaptive control—feedback value continues at upper (lean) limit or is not renewed for a certain period of time (California only)

Code 26   Air-fuel ratio rich malfunction; or air-fuel ratio feedback compensation or adaptive control—feedback value continues at lower (rich) limit or is not renewed for a certain period of time (California only)

Code 27   Sub-oxygen sensor signal—detection of sensor or signal deterioration or open or short sensor heater circuit (California only)

Code 28   #2 oxygen sensor signal or heater signal

Code 31   Airflow meter circuit—open or shorted when idle contacts are closed

Code 31   Vacuum or MAP sensor signal—open or short circuit

Code 32   Airflow meter circuit—circuit open or shorted when idling

Code 34   Turbocharging pressure signal—excessive pressure

Code 35   Altitude compensation sensor signal—open or short

Code 35   Turbocharging pressure sensor signal—open or short

Code 36   Turbocharging pressure sensor signal—open or short detected for 0.5 seconds or more

Code 41   Throttle position sensor circuit—open or short

Code 42   Vehicle speed sensor circuit

Code 43   No starter switch signal to ECU until engine speed reaches 800 RPM when cranking

Code 51   A/C signal on, throttle switch contact off, or shift position in R, D, 2, or 1 range (with check terminals T and E1 connected)

Code 52   Knock sensor signal circuit—open or short

Code 53   Knock control signal in ECU—ECU knock control faulty

Code 71   EGR system malfunction—EGR gas temperature signal is below water temperature sensor signal or below intake air temperature sensor signal plus

86° F (30° C), after driving for 240 seconds in EGR operation range (California only)

Code 72   Fuel cut solenoid signal circuit open (up to 1991)

Code 81   Throttle control module (TCM) communication

Code 83   Throttle control module (TCM) communication

Code 84   Throttle control module (TCM) communication

Code 85   Throttle control module (TCM) communication

CLEARING TOYOTA DIAGNOSTIC TROUBLE CODES

Stored codes will remain in memory until cleared. To clear codes, turn the ignition to off, then remove the proper fuse. (Most fuel-injected engines use the electronic fuel-injection [EFI] fuse to clear codes.)

If the battery is disconnected, be prepared to reset all radio stations and the clock before returning the vehicle to the customer.

After clearing codes, test drive the vehicle and retrieve codes after the test drive. If the same or a different code is now displayed, continue the repair procedures.

OBD II

OBD II stands for *on-board diagnostics, second generation.* OBD I took effect in 1988 and required that the driver be notified by a malfunction indicator light that a computer-related failure had occurred. The Clean Air Act of 1990 directed the Environmental Protection Agency (EPA) to develop new regulations for on-board diagnostics. Starting with the 1996 model year, all vehicles sold in the United States must use the same type of 16-pin **data link connector** (DLC) and must monitor emission-related components. See figure 18–13.

RETRIEVING OBD II CODES— 16 PIN

A scan tool is *required* to retrieve diagnostic trouble codes (DTC) from an OBD II vehicle. Every OBD II scan tool will be able to read all generic (SAE) DTCs from any vehicle. See figures 18–14 and 18–15 for examples of the codes and code definitions.

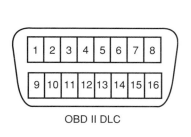

PIN
NO.   ASSIGNMENTS

1.   MANUFACTURER'S DISCRETION
2.   BUS + LINE, SAE J1850
3.   MANUFACTURER'S DISCRETION
4.   CHASSIS GROUND
5.   SIGNAL GROUND
6.   MANUFACTURER'S DISCRETION
7.   K LINE, ISO 9141
8.   MANUFACTURER'S DISCRETION
9.   MANUFACTURER'S DISCRETION
10. BUS–LINE, SAE J1850
11. MANUFACTURER'S DISCRETION
12. MANUFACTURER'S DISCRETION
13. MANUFACTURER'S DISCRETION
14. MANUFACTURER'S DISCRETION
15. L LINE, ISO 9141
16. VEHICLE BATTERY POSITIVE
     (4 A MAX)

OBD II DLC

FIGURE 18–13 Sixteen-pin OBD II DLC with terminals identified. Scan tools use the power (#16) pin and ground (#4) pin for power so that a separate cigarette lighter plug is not necessary on OBD II vehicles.

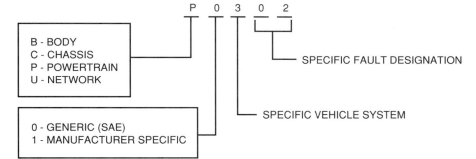

EXAMPLE: PO302 = CYLINDER #2 MISFIRE DETECTED

FIGURE 18–14 OBD II diagnostic trouble code identification format.

OBD II ACTIVE TESTS

The vehicle computer must run tests on the various emission-related components and turn on the malfunction indicator lamp (MIL). OBD II is an *active* computer analysis system because it actually tests the operation of the oxygen sensors, exhaust gas recirculation system, and so forth whenever conditions permit. It is the purpose and function of the powertrain control module (PCM) to monitor these components and perform these active tests.

For example, the PCM may open the EGR valve momentarily to check its operation while the vehicle is decelerating. A change in the manifold absolute pressure (MAP) sensor signal will indicate to the computer that the exhaust gas is, in fact, being introduced into the engine. Because these tests are active and certain conditions must be present before these tests can be run, the computer uses its internal diagnostic program to keep track of all of the various conditions and to schedule active tests so that they will not interfere with each other.

OBD II DRIVE CYCLE

The vehicle must be driven under a variety of operating conditions for all active tests to be performed. A **trip** is defined as an engine-operating drive cycle that contains all of the necessary conditions for a particular test to be performed. For example, for the EGR test to be performed, the engine has to be at normal operating temperature and decelerating for a minimum amount of time. Some tests are performed when the engine is cold, whereas others require that the vehicle be cruising at a steady highway speed.

TYPES OF DIAGNOSTIC TROUBLE CODES

Not all OBD II DTCs are of the same importance for exhaust emissions. Each type of DTC has different requirements for it to set, and the computer will only turn on the MIL for emissions-related DTCs.

DTC	Definitions
PO102	Mass Air Flow (MAF) sensor circuit low input
PO103	Mass Air Flow (MAF) sensor circuit high input
PO112	Intake Air Temperature (IAT) sensor circuit low input
PO113	Intake Air Temperature (IAT) sensor circuit high input
PO117	Engine Coolant Temperature (ECT) sensor circuit low input
PO118	Engine Coolant Temperature (ECT) sensor circuit high input
PO122	Throttle Position (TP) sensor circuit low input
PO123	Throttle Position (TP) sensor circuit high input
PO125	Insufficient Coolant Temperature to enter closed-loop fuel control
PO132	Upstream Heated Oxygen sensor (HO2S 11) circuit high voltage (Bank #1)
PO135	Heated Oxygen sensor heater (HTR 11) circuit malfunction
PO138	Downstream Heated Oxygen sensor (HO2S 12) circuit high voltage (Bank #1)
PO140	Heated Oxygen sensor (HO2S 12) circuit no activity detected (Bank #1)
PO141	Heated Oxygen sensor heater (HTR 12) circuit malfunction
PO152	Upstream Heated Oxygen sensor (HO2S 21) circuit high voltage (Bank #2)
PO155	Heated Oxygen sensor heater (HTR 21) circuit malfunction
PO158	Downstream Heated Oxygen sensor (HO2S 22) circuit high voltage (Bank #2)
PO160	Heated Oxygen sensor (HO2S 22) circuit no activity detected (Bank #2)
PO161	Heated Oxygen sensor heater (HTR 22) circuit malfunction
PO171	System (adaptive fuel) too lean (Bank #1)
PO172	System (adaptive fuel) too rich (Bank #1)
PO174	System (adaptive fuel) too lean (Bank #2)
PO175	System (adaptive fuel) too rich (Bank #2)
PO300	Random Misfire detected
PO301	Cylinder #1 Misfire detected
PO302	Cylinder #2 Misfire detected
PO303	Cylinder #3 Misfire detected
PO304	Cylinder #4 Misfire detected
PO305	Cylinder #5 Misfire detected
PO306	Cylinder #6 Misfire detected
PO307	Cylinder #7 Misfire detected
PO308	Cylinder #8 Misfire detected
PO320	Ignition Engine Speed input circuit malfunction
PO340	Camshaft Position (CMP) sensor circuit malfunction
PO402	Exhaust Gas Recirculation (EGR) flow excess detected (valve open at idle)
PO420	Catalyst system efficiency below threshold (Bank #1)
PO430	Catalyst system efficiency below threshold (Bank #2)
PO443	Evaporative emission control system Canister Purge Control Valve (CANP) circuit malfunction
PO500	Vehicle Speed Sensor (VSS) malfunction
PO505	Idle Air Control (IAC) system malfunction
PO605	Powertrain Control Module (PCM)—Read Only Memory (ROM) test error
PO703	Brake On/Off switch input malfunction
PO707	Manual Lever Position (MLP) sensor circuit low input
PO708	Manual Lever Position (MLP) sensor circuit high input

FIGURE 18-15 Generic OBD II powertrain DTCs.

1. **Type A codes.** A type A DTC is emission related and will cause the MIL to be turned on on the *first trip* if the computer has detected a problem. Engine misfire or a very rich or lean air-fuel ratio, for example, would cause a type A DTC. These codes alert the driver to an emission problem that may cause damage to the catalytic converter.

2. **Type B codes.** A type B code will be stored and the MIL will be turned on during the *second consecutive trip*, alerting the driver to the fact that a diagnostic test was performed and failed.

NOTE: Type A and B codes are emission-related codes that will cause the lighting of the malfunction indicator lamp, usually labeled "check engine" or "service engine soon."

3. **Type C and D codes.** Type C and D codes are for use with non-emission-related diagnostic tests; they will cause the lighting of a "service" lamp (if the vehicle is so equipped).

OBD II FREEZE-FRAME

To assist the service technician, OBD II requires the computer to take a "snapshot" or freeze-frame of all data at the instant an emission-related DTC is set. A scan tool is required to retrieve this data.

NOTE: Although OBD II requires that just one freeze-frame of data be stored, the instant an emission-related DTC is set, vehicle manufacturers usually provide expanded data about the DTC beyond that required. However, to retrieve this enhanced data usually requires the use of the vehicle-specific scan tool.

CLEARING OBD II DIAGNOSTIC TROUBLE CODES

A DTC should not be cleared from the vehicle computer memory unless the fault has been corrected and the technician is so directed by the diagnostic procedure. If the problem that caused the DTC to be set has been corrected, the computer will automatically clear the DTC after forty consecutive warm-up cycles with no further faults detected (misfire and excessively rich or lean

condition codes require eighty warm-up cycles). The codes can also be erased by using a scan tool or by disconnecting the battery for 30 seconds or longer.

NOTE: Most vehicle manufacturers recommend using a scan tool to erase DTCs rather than disconnecting the battery. All learned parameters are lost, as well as the memory for the radio and seats, if the battery is disconnected.

INJECTOR BALANCE TEST

Each port fuel injector must deliver an equal amount of fuel, or the engine will idle roughly or perform poorly. Testing injectors for equal fuel delivery can involve one of two methods.

Electrical Balance Test

The electrical balance test involves measuring the injector coil winding resistance. For best engine operation, all injectors should have the same electrical resistance. To measure the resistance, carefully release the locking feature of the connector and remove the connector from the injector.

NOTE: Some engines require specific procedures to gain access to the injectors. Always follow the manufacturer's recommended procedures.

With an ohmmeter, measure the resistance across the injector terminals. The results should be within 0.3 to 0.4 ohms of each other (the resistance of the lowest-resistance injector subtracted from that of the highest-resistance injector). If any injector measures close to or over 1.0 ohm different from the others, it must be replaced after making certain that the terminals of the injector are electrically sound. A variation in resistance of injectors can be summarized as follows:

Resistance Too High

1. Lower current flow
2. Slower-opening injector
3. Delivers a leaner fuel mixture

Resistance Too Low

1. Higher current flow
2. Faster-opening injector
3. Delivers a richer fuel mixture

Pressure Balance Test

The pressure balance test involves using an electrical timing device to pulse the fuel injectors on for a given amount of time (usually 500 milliseconds) and observing the drop in pressure that accompanies the pulse. If the *fuel flow* through each injector is equal, the drop in pressure in the system will be equal. Most manufacturers recommend that the pressures be within about $1\frac{1}{2}$ psi (10 kPa) of each other for satisfactory engine performance.

This test method not only tests the electrical functioning of the injector (for definite time and current pulse), but also tests for mechanical defects that could affect fuel flow amounts.

SUMMARY

1. Care should be taken not to induce high voltage or current around any computer or computer-controlled circuit or sensor.
2. A thorough visual inspection is the first step in the diagnosis and troubleshooting of any engine performance problem or electrical malfunction.
3. If the MIL is on, retrieve the DTC and follow the manufacturer's recommended procedure to find the root cause of the problem.
4. All DTCs should be cleared after the repair.
5. OBD II vehicles use a sixteen-pin DLC and common DTCs.

REVIEW QUESTIONS

1. List five precautions that should be taken whenever working with vehicle computers.

2. Explain the procedure to follow when diagnosing a vehicle without any stored DTCs using a scan tool.

3. Discuss what the PCM does during a drive cycle to test emission-related components.

4. Explain the difference between a type A and a type B OBD II DTC.

MULTIPLE-CHOICE QUESTIONS

1. Whenever working on a computer-equipped vehicle, be certain _____ .
   a. To connect positive to positive and negative to negative if jump-starting
   b. Never to disconnect electrical components when the ignition switch is on
   c. To always use high-impedance meters when measuring voltage of a computer circuit
   d. All of the above

2. Technician A says that any and all performance or driveability problems will set a computer diagnostic trouble code. Technician B says that a loose connection or loose ground wire can cause some computers to turn on the MIL or store false trouble codes. Which technician is correct?
   a. A only
   b. B only
   c. Both a and b
   d. Neither a nor b

3. Technician A says that poor fuel economy could be due to a non-computer-controlled system. Technician B says that the engine thermostat is computer controlled on most engines equipped with a computer. Which technician is correct?

   a. A only
   b. B only
   c. Both a and b
   d. Neither a nor b

4. Technician A says that the production of engine vacuum is controlled by the computer on most engines equipped with a computer. Technician B says that the "check engine" or "service engine soon" light flashes diagnostic trouble codes on GM engines if the ignition is on (engine off) and terminals A and B are electrically connected at the DLC (ALCL). Which technician is correct?
   a. A only
   b. B only
   c. Both a and b
   d. Neither a nor b

5. For a computer-controlled engine to go into closed-loop operation, _____ .
   a. The oxygen sensor must be supplying a usable, changing voltage
   b. The coolant temperature sensor must be at a predetermined level
   c. The computer must have all other factors correct
   d. All of the above

6. Technician A says that diagnostic trouble codes are determined by unplugging the diagnostic link on GM cars and trucks. Technician B says that diagnostic trouble codes on most Chrysler vehicles are accessed by applying 20 inches Hg of vacuum to the MAP sensor and reading flashes of the "power loss" light. Which technician is correct?

   a. A only
   b. B only
   c. Both a and b
   d. Neither a nor b

7. In the "field service mode" a GM fuel-injected vehicle will flash the "check engine" (or "service engine soon") lamp.

   a. Rapidly if in closed loop
   b. Slowly if in closed loop
   c. Only if trouble codes are stored
   d. Only if the engine and ignition switch are off

8. Technician A says that a STAR tester is *required* to retrieve stored trouble codes from a Ford EEC IV system. Technician B says that the computer controls the operation of the cooling (radiator) fan on many vehicles. Which technician is correct?

   a. A only
   b. B only
   c. Both a and b
   d. Neither a nor b

9. A freeze-frame is generated on an OBD II vehicle _____ .

   a. Whenever a type C or D DTC is set
   b. Whenever a type A or B DTC is set
   c. Every other "trip"
   d. Whenever the PCM detects a problem with the O2S

10. An ignition misfire or fuel mix problem is an example of what type of DTC?

    a. A
    b. B
    c. C
    d. D

SAMPLE ASE CERTIFICATION TEST

1. Copper wiring resistance _____ as the temperature increases.
   a. Increases
   b. Decreases

2. A voltage spike is created whenever any component containing a coil is shut off.
   a. True
   b. False

3. A corroded light socket could most likely cause _____.
   a. A fuse to blow in the circuit
   b. The light to be dim as a result of reduced current flow
   c. A feedback to occur to another circuit
   d. Damage to occur to the bulb as a result of decreased voltage

4. A fuse keeps blowing. Technician A says that a test light can be used in place of the fuse to help find the problem. Technician B says that a circuit breaker can be used in the place of the fuse. Which technician is correct?
   a. A only
   b. B only
   c. Both a and b
   d. Neither a nor b

5. Technician A says that a low or zero reading on an ohmmeter indicates continuity. Technician B says that a meter reading indicating infinity means no continuity. Which technician is correct?
   a. A only
   b. B only
   c. Both a and b
   d. Neither a nor b

6. What makes a meter a high-impedance tester?
   a. The effective resistance of the meter circuit
   b. The amount of current the meter can safely carry
   c. The maximum voltage that can be measured
   d. The maximum resistance that can be measured

7. An alternator is _not_ charging and the rear alternator bearing is _not_ magnetized. Technician A says that the voltage regulator could be defective. Technician B says that the alternator brushes may be defective. Which technician is correct?
   a. A only
   b. B only
   c. Both a and b
   d. Neither a nor b

8. The wire at the output terminal of an alternator connects to _____ .
   a. The ignition switch input terminal
   b. The starter at the S terminal
   c. The battery positive terminal
   d. The fuse panel

9. When the parking lamps are on and the turn signal is flashing, the side marker lamp alternates flashes with the turn signal. The reason for this is that _____ .
   a. There are opposing voltages at the marker light filament
   b. The marker lamp ground path goes through the turn signal lamp
   c. The marker lamp feed comes from the parking lamp circuit
   d. All of the above

10. The headlamp on the right side is dim and yellow when turned on. The left headlamp is bright and normal in color. Which statement is *false?*
    a. The left side has more current.
    b. The left side is normal.
    c. The right side has more resistance.
    d. The right side has a bad sealed beam.

11. A meter reads OL. This means that the component or circuit being measured _____ .
    a. Is open
    b. Is shorted
    c. Is grounded
    d. Has low resistance

12. A starter motor is drawing too many amperes (current). Technician A says that this could be due to low battery voltage. Technician B says that it could be due to a defective starter motor. Which technician is correct?
    a. A only
    b. B only
    c. Both a and b
    d. Neither a nor b

13. All of the following could be a cause of excessive starter ampere draw *except* _____ .
    a. A misadjusted starter pinion gear
    b. A loose starter housing
    c. Armature wires separated from the commutator
    d. A bent armature

14. The starter motor armature has been rubbing on the pole shoes. The probable cause is _____ .
    a. A bent starter shaft
    b. A worn commutator on the armature
    c. Worn starter bushing(s)
    d. Both a and c

15. Technician A says that a radio without an antenna will operate on FM, but not AM. Technician B says that a "pop" in the radio speakers could be caused by a defective (open) air-conditioning clutch diode. Which technician is correct?
    a. A only
    b. B only
    c. Both a and b
    d. Neither a nor b

16. Technician A says that either a defective circuit breaker or a defective ground connection can cause *all* power windows to fail to operate. Technician B says that if one *direction* wire is disconnected, the window will operate in one direction only (up *or* down). Which technician is correct?
    a. A only
    b. B only
    c. Both a and b
    d. Neither a nor b

17. A starter cranks for a while, then whines. Technician A says that the starter solenoid may be bad. Technician B says that the starter drive may be bad. Which technician is correct?
    a. A only
    b. B only
    c. Both a and b
    d. Neither a nor b

18. A poor ground on an electromagnetic (GM-type) fuel gauge will _____ .
    a. Result in a *higher* than normal reading
    b. Result in a *lower* than normal reading
    c. Result in no change because the fuel gauge is above ground
    d. Cause the oil pressure gauge to read *lower* and the fuel gauge to read *higher* than normal

19. All airbag wiring is _____ .
    a. Red
    b. Orange
    c. Yellow
    d. Blue

20. A blower motor stopped working on all speeds. A technician tested the motor by touching a jumper wire from the battery positive terminal to the motor power terminal, and the motor did run. Technician A says that the motor should be checked using a fused jumper lead to test for excessive current draw. Technician B says that the resistor pack and/or relay is likely to be defective. Which technician is correct?
    a. A only
    b. B only
    c. Both a and b
    d. Neither a nor b

21. The correct hookup procedure for a voltage-drop test of the cranking circuit is as follows: _____ .
    a. Disconnect the negative cable, and connect the voltmeter between the battery post and the disconnected cable end
    b. Set the voltmeter on low scale, connect the red lead to the most positive terminal and the black lead to the most negative part of the component being tested, and crank the engine
    c. Connect the red lead to the positive and the black lead to the negative post of the battery, and crank the engine
    d. Disconnect the positive battery cable, connect the voltmeter between the cable end and ground, and crank the engine

22. A technician is checking the charging system for low output. A voltage drop of 1.67 volts is found between the alternator output terminal and the battery positive terminal. Technician A says that a corroded connector could be the cause. Technician B says that a defective rectifier diode could be the cause. Which technician is correct?
    a. A only
    b. B only
    c. Both a and b
    d. Neither a nor b

23. An ohmmeter on the 30K scale reads 1.93 on a digital face. How many ohms of resistance is being measured?
    a. 193
    b. 19,300
    c. 1930
    d. 19.30

24. In a parallel 12-volt circuit with three bulbs (each 10 ohms in resistance), which statement below would be correct if one of the bulbs burned out (had an open)?
    a. The total resistance would be the same.
    b. The total resistance would be lower.
    c. The current would increase in the circuit.
    d. The current would decrease in the circuit.

25. Technician A says that high resistance in the cables or connections can cause rapid clicking of the solenoid. Technician B says that a battery must be 75% charged for accurate testing of the starting and charging systems. Which technician is correct?
    a. A only
    b. B only
    c. Both a and b
    d. Neither a nor b

26. On a negative ground battery system, _____ .
    a. Disconnect the ground cable first and reconnect the positive cable first
    b. Disconnect the ground cable first and reconnect the positive cable last
    c. Disconnect the positive cable first and reconnect the ground cable first
    d. Disconnect the positive cable first and reconnect the ground cable last

27. A starter motor is drawing too many amperes (current) and the starter motor is not working. Technician A says that this could be due to low battery voltage. Technician B says that it could be due to a defective (grounded) starter motor. Which technician is correct?
    a. A only
    b. B only
    c. Both a and b
    d. Neither a nor b

28. On a single-headlight system, the right-side high beam does not work. The probable cause is _____ .
    a. A bad dimmer switch
    b. A bad headlight
    c. A bad headlight ground
    d. A discharged battery

29. Fusible links are used in electrical circuits _____ .
    a. To take the place of fuses
    b. To "short to ground" if the voltage reaches a predetermined point
    c. To take the place of circuit breakers
    d. To prevent a fire hazard, and to back up multiple fuses in a circuit

30. A driver turns the ignition switch to "start" and nothing happens (the dome light remains bright). Technician A says that dirty battery connections or a defective or discharged battery could be the cause. Technician B says that an *open* control circuit such as a defective neutral safety switch could be the cause. Which technician is correct?
    a. A only
    b. B only
    c. Both a and b
    d. Neither a nor b

31. Normal battery drain (parasitic drain) on a vehicle with many computer and electronic circuits is _____ .
    a. 20 to 30 milliamperes
    b. 2 to 3 amperes
    c. 150 to 300 milliamperes
    d. 0.3 to 0.4 amperes

32. Whenever jump-starting, _____ .
    a. The last connection should be the positive post of the dead battery
    b. The last connection should be the engine block of the dead vehicle
    c. The alternator must be disconnected on both vehicles
    d. The bumpers should touch to provide a good ground between the vehicles

33. Technician A says that a voltage-drop test of the charging circuit should only be performed when current is flowing through the circuit. Technician B says to connect the lead of a voltmeter to the positive and negative terminals of the battery to measure the volt-

age drop of the charging system. Which technician is correct?

a. A only

b. B only

c. Both a and b

d. Neither a nor b

34. A charge light is on, but dim. The most likely cause is _____ .

a. A defective rectifier bridge

b. A defective diode trio

c. A defective rotor

d. Worn brushes

35. An electric motor is drawing more current (amperes) than specified. Technician A says that a corroded connector at the motor could be the cause. Technician B says that a corroded ground connection could be the cause. Which technician is correct?

a. A only

b. B only

c. Both a and b

d. Neither a nor b

36. An OBD II DLC has _____ .

a. 8 pins

b. 12 pins

c. 14 pins

d. 16 pins

37. A power cord connected to the cigarette lighter is required to power an OBD II scan tool.

a. True

b. False

38. A pickup coil is being measured with a digital multimeter set to the kilo-ohm position. The specification for the resistance is 500 to 1500 ohms. The digital face reads 0.826. Technician A says that the coil is okay. Technician B says that the resistance is below specifications. Which technician is correct?

a. A only

b. B only

c. Both a and b

d. Neither a nor b

39. Technician A says that to check for spark by connecting a spark tester to the end of a spark plug wire. Technician B says that a regular spark plug should be connected to the end of a spark plug wire to check for spark. Which technician is correct?

a. A only

b. B only

c. Both a and b

d. Neither a nor b

40. Engine ping during acceleration can be caused if the ignition time is _____ .

a. Advanced

b. Retarded

41. A defective (open) spark plug wire was found in an engine that was missing during acceleration. Technician A says that the distributor and rotor should also be replaced because the defective wire could have caused a carbon track. Technician B says that the ignition coil should be replaced because the bad wire could have caused the coil to become tracked internally. Which technician is correct?

a. A only

b. B only

c. Both a and b

d. Neither a nor b

42. Technician A says that all spark plugs should be gapped before being installed in the engine. Technician B says that platinum spark plugs should *not* be regapped after having been used in an engine. Which technician is correct?

a. A only

b. B only

c. Both a and b

d. Neither a nor b

43. The vacuum hose to a MAP sensor became disconnected. Technician A says that the lack of vacuum to the sensor will cause the computer to provide a rich mixture to the engine. Technician B says that the computer will supply a lean mixture to the engine. Which technician is correct?

a. A only

b. B only

c. Both a and b

d. Neither a nor b

44. The connector to the throttle position (TP) sensor became disconnected. Technician A says that the engine will not idle correctly unless reconnected. Technician B says that the engine may hesitate on acceleration. Which technician is correct?

a. A only

b. B only

c. Both a and b

d. Neither a nor b

45. An oxygen sensor (O2S) is being tested. Technician A says that the O2S voltage should fluctuate from above 700 millivolts to below 300 millivolts. Technician B says the O2S has to be above 600° F (315° C) before testing can begin. Which technician is correct?

a. A only

b. B only

c. Both a and b

d. Neither a nor b

46. An oxygen sensor in a fuel-injected engine is slow to re-act to changes in air-fuel mixture. Technician A says that cleaning the O2S could help restore proper operation. Technician B says the cross count rate may be below specifications. Which technician is correct?

    a. A only
    b. B only
    c. Both a and b
    d. Neither a nor b

47. Ignition timing on an engine equipped with computer-control distributor ignition (DI) is being discussed. Technician A says that the computer can only advance the timing. Technician B says that the signal from the knock sensor (KS) can cause the timing to retard. Which technician is correct?

    a. A only
    b. B only
    c. Both a and b
    d. Neither a nor b

48. Two technicians are discussing jump-starting a com-puter-equipped vehicle with another computer-equipped vehicle. Technician A says that the ignition of both vehi-cles should be in the off position while making the jumper cable connections. Technician B says that the computer-equipped vehicles should not be jump-started. Which technician is correct?

    a. A only
    b. B only
    c. Both a and b
    d. Neither a nor b

49. Technician A says that OBD II generic codes are the same for all OBD II vehicles. Technician B says that the DLC is located under the hood on all OBD II vehicles. Which technician is correct?

    a. A only
    b. B only
    c. Both a and b
    d. Neither a nor b

50. Two technicians are discussing an OBD II diagnostic trouble code (DTC) P0301. Technician A says that this is a generic code. Technician B says that the code is a man-ufacturer's specific code. Which technician is correct?

    a. A only
    b. B only
    c. Both a and b
    d. Neither a nor b

GLOSSARY

AIR Air injection reaction. A type of emission control system.

Air management system The system of solenoids and valves that controls the output of the air pump to the catalytic converter, air cleaner housing, or exhaust manifold.

ALCL Assembly line communications link.

ALDL Assembly line diagnostic link.

Alnico A permanent-magnet alloy of *al*uminum, *ni*ckel, and *co*balt.

Alternator An electric generator that produces alternating current.

AM Amplitude modulation.

Ammeter An electrical test instrument used to measure amperes (unit of measurement for the amount of current flow). An ammeter is connected in series with the circuit being tested.

Ampere The unit of measurement for the amount of current flow. Named for André Ampère (1775–1836).

Ampere-turns The unit of measurement for electrical magnetic field strength.

Analog A type of dash instrument that indicates values by use of the movement of a needle or similar device. An analog signal is continuous and variable.

Anode The positive electrode; the electrode toward which electrons flow.

ANSI American National Standards Institute.

Antenna trimmer A method used to calibrate the antenna for an AM radio.

Antimony A metal added to non-maintenance-free or hybrid battery grids to add strength.

Armature The rotating unit inside a DC generator or starter, consisting of a series of coils of insulating wire wound around a laminated iron core.

ATC After top center.

ATDC After top dead center.

Atom The smallest unit of matter that still retains its separate unique characteristics.

AWG American wire gauge. A system used for describing wire size.

Backlight The rear window of a vehicle.

Bakelite A brand name of the Union Carbide Company for phenolformaldehyde resin plastic.

Ballast resistor A variable resistor used to control the primary ignition current through the ignition coil. At lower engine speed, the temperature of the ballast resistor is high and its resistance is high. When engine RPM level is high, the ballast resistance is low, permitting maximum current through the ignition coil.

Baro sensor A sensor used to measure barometric pressure.

Base The section of a transistor that controls the current flow through the transistor.

Battery A chemical device that produces a voltage created by two dissimilar metals submerged in an electrolyte.

Bendix drive An inertia-type starter engagement mechanism not used on vehicles since the early 1960s.

Bias In electrical terms, the voltage applied to a device or component to establish the reference point for operation.

Blower motor An electric motor and squirrel cage type of fan that moves air inside the vehicle for heating, cooling, and defrosting.

Brush A copper or carbon conductor used to transfer electrical current from or to a revolving electrical part such as that used in an electric motor or generator.

BTDC Before top dead center.

CAFE Corporate average fuel economy.

Calcium A metallic chemical element added to the grids of a maintenance-free battery to add strength.

Candlepower The unit of measurement for the

amount of light produced by a bulb.

Capacitance Electrical term used to describe how much charge can be stored in a capacitor (condenser) for a given voltage potential difference. Capacitance is measured in farads or smaller increments of farads, such as microfarads.

Capacitor A condenser; an electrical unit that can pass alternating current, yet block direct current. Used in electrical circuits to control fluctuations in voltage.

Carbon pile An electrical test instrument used to provide an electrical load for testing batteries and the charging circuit.

Catalytic converter An emission control device located in the exhaust system that changes HC and CO into harmless H_2O and CO_2. If it is a three-way catalyst, NO_X is also separated into harmless hydrogen (N) and oxygen (O).

Cathode The negative electrode.

CCC Computer command control. The name of the General Motors computer engine control system.

Cell A group of negative and positive plates capable of producing 2.1 volts. Each cell contains one more negative plate than positive plate.

CEMF Counter electromotive force.

Centrifugal advance A spark advance mechanism that uses centrifugal force (outward force increasing with rotational speed) to increase timing advance in proportion to engine speed.

Charging circuit Electrical components and connections necessary to keep a battery fully charged. Components include the alternator, voltage regulator, battery, and interconnecting wires.

Chassis ground In electrical terms, the desirable return circuit path. Ground can also be undesirable and provide a shortcut path for a defective electrical circuit.

Circuit The path that electrons travel from a power source, through a resistance, and back to the power source.

Circuit breaker A mechanical unit that opens an electrical circuit in the event of excessive flow.

CO Carbon monoxide.

Cold cranking amperes (CCA) The rating of a battery's ability to provide battery voltage during cold weather operation. CCA is the number of amperes that a battery can supply at $0°$ F ($-18°$ C) for 30 seconds and still maintain a voltage of 1.2 volts per cell (7.2 volts for a 12-volt battery).

Collector One terminal of a transistor.

Commutator The copper segments of the armature of a starter or DC generator. The revolving segments of the commutator collect the current from or distribute it to the brushes.

Composite headlight A type of headlight that uses a separate replaceable bulb.

Compound wound A type of electric motor in which some field coils are wired in series and some field coils are wired in parallel with the armature.

Conductor A material that conducts electricity and heat. A metal that contains fewer than four electrons in its atom's outer shell.

Conventional theory The theory that states that electricity flows from positive to negative.

Coulomb Term used to describe 6.28×10^{18} (6.28 billion billion) electrons.

Courtesy light General term used to describe all interior lights.

Cranking circuit Electrical components and connections required to crank the engine to start. Includes starter motor, starter solenoid or relay, battery, neutral safety switch, ignition control switch, and connecting wires and cables.

CRT Cathode ray tube.

Cunife A magnetic alloy made from copper (Cu), nickel (Ni), and iron (Fe).

Current Electron flow through an electrical circuit, measured in amperes.

Current limiter One section of a voltage regulator for a DC generator charging system. The current limiter section opens the field current circuit whenever generator amperage output exceeds safe limits to protect the generator from overheating damage.

Cutout relay One section of a voltage regulator for a DC generator charging system. The cutout relay section prevents battery current from flowing through the DC generator toward ground whenever generator voltage is lower than battery voltage.

Darlington pair Two transistors electrically connected to form an amplifier. This arrangement permits a very small current flow to control a large current flow. Named for Sidney Darlington, a physicist at Bell Laboratories from 1929 to 1971.

Deep cycling The full discharge and then the full recharge of a battery.

Delta wound A type of stator in which all three coils are connected in a triangle shape. Named for the triangle-shaped Greek capital letter.

Digital A method of display that uses numbers instead of a needle or similar device.

Dimmer switch   An electrical switch used to direct the current to either bright or dim headlight filaments.

Diode   An electrical one-way check valve made by combining a P-type material and an N-type material.

Diode trio   Three diodes grouped together with one output used to put out the charge indicator lamp and provide current for the field from the stator windings on many alternators.

Direct current   Electric current that flows in one direction.

Distributor   Electromechanical unit used to help create and distribute the high voltage necessary for spark ignition.

Doping   The adding of impurities to pure silicon or germanium to form either P or N semiconductor materials.

DPDT switch   Double-pole, double-throw switch.

Dwell   The number of degrees of distributor cam rotation for which the points are closed.

Earth ground   The most grounded ground. A ground is commonly used as a return current path for an electrical circuit.

EEPROM   Electronically erasable programmable read-only memory.

EFI   Electronic fuel injection.

EGR   Exhaust gas recirculation. An EGR device is an emission control device for reducing NO_X (oxides of nitrogen).

Electricity   The movement of free electrons from one atom to another.

Electrolyte   Any substance that, in solution, is separated into ions and is made capable of conducting an electric current. The acid solution of a lead-acid battery.

Electromagnetic gauges   A type of dash instrument gauge that uses small electromagnetic coils for the needle movement of the gauge.

Electromagnetic induction   The generation of a current in a conductor that is moved through a magnetic field. Discovered in 1831 by Michael Faraday.

Electromagnetism   A magnetic field created by current flow through a conductor.

Electromotive force   The force (pressure) that can move electrons through a conductor.

Electron   A negatively charged particle; 1/1800 of the mass of a proton.

Electron theory   The theory that states that electric-ity flows from negative to positive.

Electronic circuit breaker   See PTC.

Electronic ignition   General term used to describe any of various types of ignition systems that use electronic components instead of mechanical components, such as contact points.

Element   Any substance that cannot be separated into different substances.

EMF   Electromotive force.

Emitter   One terminal of a transistor. The arrow used on a symbol for a transistor is on the emitter, and the arrow points toward the negative section of the transistor.

EPROM   Erasable programmable read-only memory.

ESC   Electronic spark control. The computer system is equipped with a knock sensor that can retard spark advance if necessary to eliminate spark knock.

EST   Electronic spark timing. The computer controls spark timing advance.

Farad   A unit of capacitance named for Michael Faraday (1791–1867), an English physicist. A farad is the capacity to store 1 coulomb of electrons at 1 volt of potential difference.

Feedback   The reverse flow of electrical current through a circuit or electrical unit that should not normally be operating. This feedback current (reverse-bias current flow) is most often caused by a poor ground connection for the same normally operating circuit.

Fiber optics   The transmission of light through special plastic that keeps the light rays parallel even if the plastic is tied in a knot.

Field coils   Coils or wire wound around metal pole shoes to form the electromagnetic field inside an electric motor.

Filament   The light-producing wire inside a light bulb.

FM   Frequency modulation.

Forward bias   Current flow in the normal direction.

Full-fielding   Supplying full battery voltage to the magnetic field of a generator as part of the troubleshooting procedure for the charging system.

Fuse   An electrical safety unit constructed of a fine tin conductor that will melt and open the electrical circuit if excessive current flows through the fuse.

Fusible link   A type of fuse that will melt and open the protected circuit in the event of a short circuit, which could cause excessive current flow through the fusible link. Most fusible links are actually wires four gauge sizes smaller than the wire of the circuit being protected.

Gassing The release of hydrogen and oxygen gas from the plates of a battery during charging or discharging.

Gauge Wire size as assigned by the American wire gauge system. The smaller the gauge number, the larger the wire.

Gauss A unit of magnetic induction or magnetic intensity named for Carl Friedrich Gauss (1777–1855), a German mathematician.

Generator A device that converts mechanical energy into electrical energy.

Grid The lead-alloy framework (support) for the active materials of an automotive battery.

Ground The lowest possible voltage potential in a circuit. In electrical terms, a ground is the desirable return circuit path. Ground can also be undesirable and provide a shortcut path for a defective electrical circuit.

Growler Electrical tester designed to test starter and DC generator armatures.

Hall-effect sensor A type of electromagnetic sensor used in electronic ignition and other systems. Named for Edwin H. Hall (1855–1938), who discovered the Hall effect in 1879.

Hash An unclear or messy section of a scope pattern.

Hazard flashers Emergency warning flashers; lights at all four corners of the vehicle that flash on and off.

HC Hydrocarbons (unburned fuel). When combined with NO_X and sunlight, they form smog.

Heat sink Usually, a metallic finned unit used to keep electronic components cool.

HEI High-energy ignition. General Motors' name for their electronic ignition.

Hold-in winding One of two electromagnetic windings inside a solenoid; used to hold the movable core in the solenoid.

Hole theory A theory that states that as an electron flows from negative to positive, it leaves behind a hole. According to the hole theory, the hole will move from positive to negative.

Horsepower A unit of power; 33,000 foot-pounds per minute. One horsepower equals 746 watts.

Hybrid Something (such as a battery) made from two or more different elements.

Hydrometer An instrument used to measure the specific gravity of a liquid. A battery hydrometer is calibrated to read the expected specific gravity of battery electrolyte.

IAC Idle air control.

Ignition circuit Electrical components and connections that produce and distribute high-voltage electricity to ignite the air-fuel mixture inside the engine.

Ignition coil An electrical device consisting of two separate coils of wire: a primary and a secondary winding. The purpose of an ignition coil is to produce a high-voltage (20,000- to 40,000-volt), low-amperage (about 80-milliampere) current necessary for spark ignition.

Ignition timing Determining the exact point of ignition in relation to piston position.

ILC Idle load control.

Inductive reactance An opposing current created in a conductor whenever there is a charging current flow in the conductor.

Insulator A material that does not readily conduct electricity and heat. A nonmetal material that contains more than four electrons in its atom's outer shell.

Ion An atom with an excess or deficiency of electrons forming either a negatively or a positively charged particle.

ISC Idle speed control.

IVR Instrument voltage regulator. An IVR is used to maintain constant voltage to thermoelectric gauges to maintain accuracy.

Joule A unit of electrical energy. One joule equals 1 watt times 1 second ($1 V \times 1 A \times 1 s$).

Jumper cables Heavy-gauge (4 to 00) electrical cables with large clamps, used to connect a vehicle that has a discharged battery to a vehicle that has a good battery.

Kilo A prefix meaning 1000. Abbreviated K.

Knock sensor A sensor that can detect engine spark knock.

LCD Liquid crystal display.

Lead peroxide The material of the positive plate of an automotive-style battery. The chemical symbol is $PbSO_4$.

Lead sulfate The material into which both battery plates turn when the battery is discharged. The chemical symbol for lead sulfate is $PbSO_4$.

LED Light-emitting diode.

Lumbar Pertaining to the lower section of the back.

Magnequench A magnetic alloy made from neodymium, iron, and boron.

Magnetic timing A method of measuring ignition that uses a magnetic pickup tool to sense the location of a magnet on the harmonic balancer.

Manifold vacuum Low pressure (vacuum) measured

at the intake manifold of a running engine (normally between 17 and 21 inches Hg at idle).

M/C solenoid   Mixture control solenoid.

MAP   Manifold absolute pressure.

Meniscus   The puckering or curvature of a liquid in a tube. A battery is properly filled with water when the electrolyte first becomes puckered.

Module   A group of electronic components functioning as a component of a larger system.

Mutual induction   The generation of an electric current as the result of a changing magnetic field of an adjacent coil.

Neutron   A neutrally charged particle; one of the basic particles of the nucleus of an atom.

NO$_X$ Oxides of nitrogen. When combined with HC and sunlight, they form smog.

NTC   Negative temperature coefficient. Usually used in references to a temperature sensor (coolant or air temperature). As the temperature increases, the resistance of the sensor decreases.

N-type material   Silicon or germanium doped with phosphorus, arsenic, or antimony.

Nucleus   The central part of an atom, which has a positive charge and contains almost all of the mass of the atom.

NVRAM   Nonvolatile random access memory.

Ohm   The unit of electrical resistance. Named for Georg Simon Ohm (1787–1854).

Ohmmeter   An electrical test instrument used to measure ohms (unit of electrical resistance). An ohmmeter uses an internal battery for power and must never be used when current is flowing through a circuit or component.

Ohm's law   An electrical law that states that it requires 1 volt to push 1 ampere through 1 ohm of resistance.

Omega   The last letter of the Greek alphabet, and a symbol for ohm, the unit of electrical resistance.

Open circuit   Any circuit that is not complete and in which no current flows.

Oscilloscope   A visual display of electrical waves on a fluorescent screen or cathode ray tube.

Partitions   Separations between the cells of a battery. Partitions are made of the same material as that of the outside case of the battery.

Pasting   The process of applying active battery materials to the grid framework of each plate.

PCV   Positive crankcase ventilation.

Permalloy   A permanent-magnet alloy of nickel and iron.

Permeability   The measure of a material's ability to conduct magnetic lines of force.

Photoelectric principle   The principle by which electricity is created when light strikes certain sensitive materials, such as selenium or cesium.

Piezoelectric principle   The principle by which certain crystals become electrically charged when pressure is applied.

Pinion gear   A small gear on the end of the starter drive that rotates the engine flywheel ring gear for starting.

PM motor   A permanent-magnet electric motor.

Polarity   The condition of being positive or negative in relation to a magnetic pole.

Porous lead   Lead with many small holes in its surface; used in battery negative plates. The chemical symbol for lead is Pb.

Ported vacuum   Low pressure (vacuum) measured above the throttle plates. As the throttle plates open, the vacuum increases until it has the same value as the manifold vacuum.

Power side   The wires leading from the power source (battery) to the resistance (load) of a circuit.

PROM   Programmable read-only memory.

Proton   A positively charged particle; one of the basic particles of the nucleus of an atom.

PTC   Positive temperature coefficient. Usually used in reference to a conductor or electronic circuit breaker. As the temperature increases, the electrical resistance also increases.

P-type material   Silicon or germanium doped with boron or indium.

Pull-in winding   One of two electromagnetic windings inside a solenoid; used to move a movable core.

Pulse generator   An electromagnetic unit that generates a voltage signal used to trigger the ignition control module that controls (turns on and off) the primary ignition current of an electronic ignition system.

Pulse width   The amount of "on time" of an electronic fuel injector.

Radial grid   A lead-alloy framework for the active materials of a battery that has radial support spokes to add strength and to improve battery efficiency.

Radio choke   A small coil of wire installed in the power lead leading to a pulsing unit such as an IVR to prevent radio interference.

RAM   Random access memory.

Rectifier   An electronic device that converts alternating current into direct current.

Rectifier bridge   A group of six diodes, three positive and three negative, commonly used in alternators.

Relay   An electromagnetic switch that uses a movable arm.

Reluctance   The resistance to the movement of magnetic lines of force.

Reserve capacity   The number of minutes for which a battery can produce 25 amperes and still maintain a battery voltage of 1.75 volts per cell (10.5 volts for a 12-volt battery).

Residual magnetism   Magnetism remaining after the magnetizing force is removed.

Resistance   The opposition to current flow.

Reverse bias   Current flow in the opposite direction from normal.

Rheostat   An adjustable two-wire variable resistor.

Rise time   The time, measured in microseconds, needed for the output of a coil to rise from 10% to 90% of maximum output.

ROM   Read-only memory.

RPM   Revolutions per minute.

RTV   Room-temperature vulcanization.

Saturation   The point of maximum magnetic field strength of a coil.

Sediment chamber   A space below the cell plates of some batteries to permit the accumulation of sediment deposits flaking from the battery plates. Use of a sediment chamber keeps the sediment from shorting the battery plates.

Self-induction   The generation of an electric current in the wires of a coil when the current is first connected or disconnected.

Semiconductor   A material that is neither a conductor nor an insulator; it has exactly four electrons in the atom's outer shell.

Separators   In a battery, nonconducting, porous, thin materials used to separate positive and negative plates.

Series wound   In a starter motor, a type of arrangement in which the field coils and the armature are wired in series. All of the current flows through the field coils, through the hot brushes, through the armature, and then to the ground through the ground brushes.

Servo unit   A vacuum-operated unit that attaches to the throttle linkage to move the throttle on a cruise control system.

Shelf life   The length of time for which something can remain on a storage shelf and not have its performance level reduced from that of a newly manufactured product.

Short circuit   A circuit in which current flows, but in which it bypasses some or all of the resistance in the circuit. A short to voltage that results in a copper-to-copper connection.

Short to ground   A short circuit in which the current bypasses some or all of the resistance of the circuit and flows to ground. Because ground is usually steel in automotive electricity, a short to ground (being grounded) is a copper-to-steel connection.

Shunt   A device used to divert or bypass part of the current from the main circuit.

Smog   The term used to describe a combination of *smoke* and *fog*. Formed by NO_X and HC with sunlight.

Solenoid   An electromagnetic switch that uses a movable core.

Specific gravity   The ratio of the weight of a given volume of a liquid to the weight of an equal volume of water.

Sponge lead   Lead with many small holes used to make the surface porous or spongelike for use in battery negative plates also called porous lead. The chemical symbol for lead is Pb.

Starter drive   A term used to describe the starter motor drive pinion gear with overrunning clutch.

State of charge   The degree to which a battery is charged. A fully charged battery would have a state of charge of 100%.

Stator   Three interconnected windings inside an alternator. A rotating rotor provides a moving magnetic field and induces a current in the windings of the stator.

Stepper motor   A motor that provides a specified amount of rotation.

Stoichiometric   Term used to describe an air-fuel ratio of exactly 14.7:1.

Stroboscopic light   A very bright pulsing light triggered by the firing of one spark plug. Used to check and adjust ignition timing.

Tach   Abbreviation for *tachometer;* an instrument or gauge used to measure RPM.

TBI   Throttle body injection.

TDC   Top dead center.

Telltale light   Dash warning light.

TFI   Thick film integration; the name of the Ford type of electronic ignition system.

Thermistor A resistor that changes resistance with temperature. A positive coefficient thermistor has increased resistance with an increase in temperature. A negative coefficient thermistor has increased resistance with a decrease in temperature.

Thermoelectric meter A type of dash instrument that uses heat created by current flow through the gauge to deflect the indicator needle.

Thermoelectric principle The principle by which current flow is created when the connection of two dissimilar metal is heated.

Throttle kicker A device used on some computer engine control systems to increase engine speed (RPM) under certain operating conditions, such as when the air-conditioning system is on.

Torque A twisting force that may or may not result in motion.

Trade number The number stamped on an automotive light bulb. All bulbs of the same trade number have the same candlepower and wattage, regardless of the manufacturer of the bulb.

Transducer An electrical and mechanical speed-sensing and control unit used on speed control systems.

Transistor A semiconductor device that can operate as an amplifier or an electrical switch.

VAC Vacuum sensor.

Vacuum Pressure below atmospheric level, measured in units of inches of mercury (inches Hg).

Vacuum advance A spark advance unit that advances the ignition timing in relation to engine vacuum.

Vacuum kicker A computer-controlled throttle device used to increase idle RPM under certain operating conditions, such as when the air-conditioning system is operating.

Volt The unit of measurement of electrical pressure; named for Alessandro Volta (1745–1827).

Voltage regulator An electronic or mechanical unit that controls the output voltage of an electrical generator or alternator by controlling the field current of the generator or alternator.

Voltmeter An electrical test instrument used to measure volts (unit of measure for electrical pressure). A voltmeter is connected in parallel with the unit or circuit being tested.

VTF Vacuum tube fluorescent.

Watt An electrical unit of power. Watts equals current (amperes) times voltage (1 horsepower equals 746 watts). Named after James Watt (1736–1819), a Scottish inventor.

WOT Wide-open throttle.

Wye wound A type of stator in which all three coils are connected to a common center connection. Called wye because the connections look like the letter Y.

Zener diode A specially constructed (heavily doped) diode designed to operate with a reverse-bias current after a certain voltage has been reached. Named for Clarence Melvin Zener.

ANSWERS TO EVEN-NUMBERED MULTIPLE-CHOICE QUESTIONS

CHAPTER 1

2. b 4. b 6. b 8. b

CHAPTER 2

2. a 4. a 6. a 8. a

CHAPTER 3

2. d 4. c 6. d 8. c 10. d

CHAPTER 4

2. c 4. d 6. d 8. a 10. a

CHAPTER 5

2. c 4. b 6. c 8. b 10. d

CHAPTER 6

2. c 4. c 6. d 8. a

CHAPTER 7

2. a 4. d 6. c 8. a

CHAPTER 8

2. a 4. a 6. d 8. d 10. b

CHAPTER 9

2. d 4. b 6. c 8. d 10. b

CHAPTER 10

2. b 4. a 6. d 8. a

CHAPTER 11

2. c 4. c 6. c 8. b 10. d

CHAPTER 12

2. a 4. c 6. d 8. d

CHAPTER 13

2. c 4. c 6. d 8. a 10. c

CHAPTER 14

2. d 4. a 6. b 8. a 10. b

CHAPTER 15

2. c 4. d 6. c 8. b

CHAPTER 16

2. a 4. d 6. b 8. b 10. d

CHAPTER 17

2. a   **4.** b   **6.** c   **8.** c   **10.** b

CHAPTER 18

2. b   **4.** b   **6.** d   **8.** b   **10.** a

INDEX